READING THE NATION IN ENGLISH LITERATURE

This volume contains primary materials and introductory essays on the historical, critical, and theoretical study of "national literature," focusing on the years 1550–1850 and the impact of ideas of nationhood from this period on contemporary literature and culture.

The book is helpfully divided into three comprehensive parts. Part I contains a selection of primary materials from various English-speaking nations, written between the early modern and the early Victorian eras. These include political essays, poetry, religious writing, and literary theory by major authors and thinkers ranging from Edmund Spenser, Anne Bradstreet and David Hume to Adam Kidd and Peter Du Ponceau. Parts II and III contain critical essays by leading scholars in the field: Part II introduces and contextualizes the primary material and Part III brings the discussion up-to-date by exploring its impact on contemporary issues such as canon-formation and globalization.

The volume is prefaced by an extensive introduction to and overview of recent studies in nationalism, the history and debates of nationalism through major literary periods, and discussion of why the question of nationhood is important.

Reading the Nation in English Literature is a comprehensive resource, offering coherent, accessible readings on the ideologies, discourses, and practices of nationhood.

Contributors: Terence N. Bowers, Andrea Cabajsky, Sarah M. Corse, Andrew Escobedo, Andrew Hadfield, Deborah L. Madsen, Elizabeth Sauer, Imre Szeman, Julia M. Wright.

Elizabeth Sauer is Professor of Early Modern Literature at Brock University.

Julia M. Wright is Canada Research Chair in European Studies at Dalhousie University.

READING THE NATION IN ENGLISH LITERATURE: A CRITICAL READER

edited by
Elizabeth Sauer and Julia M. Wright

First edition published 2010 by Routledge
2 Park Square, Milton Park, Abingdon, OX14 4RN

Simultaneously published in the USA and Canada
by Routledge
270 Madison Ave, New York, NY 10016

Routledge is an imprint of the Taylor & Francis Group, an informa business

Typeset in Garamond and Helvetica Neue by
The Running Head Limited, Cambridge, www.therunninghead.com
Printed and bound in Great Britain by
CPI Antony Rowe, Chippenham, Wiltshire

British Library Cataloguing in Publication Data
A catalogue record for this book is available from the British Library

Library of Congress Cataloging in Publication Data
Reading the nation in English literature : a critical reader / edited by Elizabeth Sauer and Julia M. Wright.—1st ed.
p. cm.
Includes bibliographical references and index.
1. Nationalism—Literary collections. 2. English literature.
3. Nationalism in literature. 4. Nationalism and literature—English-speaking countries. I. Sauer, Elizabeth, 1964– II. Wright, Julia M.
PR1111.N29R43 2009
820.9'3581—dc22
2009004938

ISBN10: 0–415–44523–X (hbk)
ISBN10: 0–415–44524–8 (pbk)
ISBN10: 0–203–87303–3 (ebk)

ISBN13: 978–0–415–44523–8 (hbk)
ISBN13: 978–0–415–44524–5 (pbk)
ISBN13: 978–0–203–87303–8 (ebk)

CONTENTS

Notes on contributors ix

Acknowledgments xi

Introduction by Elizabeth Sauer and Julia M. Wright 1

PART I WRITING THE NATION, c. 1550–1850 **21**

1 From *The Complaynt of Scotland* (1549?) 23

2 From John Foxe, *Actes and Monuments* (1563) 26

3 From Edmund Spenser, *A View of the State of Ireland* (1596) 30

4 From Richard Hakluyt, *The Principal Navigations, Voyages, Traffiques and Discoveries of the English Nation* (1599); *The Third and Last Volume* (1600) 37

5 From The King James Bible (1611) 44

6 John Lilburne, William Walwyn, Thomas Prince, Richard Overton, *An Agreement of the Free People of England* (1649) 52

7 Anne Bradstreet, "A Dialogue between Old *England* and New, concerning their present troubles. Anno 1642" (1650) 62

8 From John Milton, *A Defence of the People of England* (1651, 1692) 71

9 From Daniel Defoe, *The Original Power of the Collective Body of the People of England, Examined and Asserted* (1702) 78

10 From Jonathan Swift, *A Letter to the Whole People of Ireland* (1724) 83

11 From David Hume, "Of National Characters" (1748) 87

12 From Henry Home, *Sketches of the History of Man* (1774) 92
13 From Thomas Cary, *Abram's Plains: A Poem* (1789) 99
14 Anna Letitia Barbauld, "To a Great Nation" (1793) 103
15 From William Drennan, *Letter to the Right Honorable William Pitt* (1799) 104
16 "Of a National Character in Literature" (1818) 108
17 From Lady Sydney Morgan, "Absenteeism.—No. III" (1825) 112
18 Adam Kidd, "Preface" and "Cathleen" from *The Huron Chief, and Other Poems* (1830) 114
19 From Peter Du Ponceau, *A Discourse on the Necessity and the Means of Making our National Literature Independent of that of Great Britain* (1834) 118
20 "National Character," *The Nation* (1843) 122
21 From Giuseppe Mazzini, "Europe: Its Condition and Prospects" (1852) 125

PART II READING THE NATION, c. 1550–1850 **133**

1 The Nation in the Renaissance
Andrew Hadfield 135

2 The Peculiar Status of Early Modern England
Elizabeth Sauer 144

3 Nationhood in the Age of Enlightenment
Terence N. Bowers 155

4 Nationalist Discourses in the British Isles, 1780–1850
Julia M. Wright 164

5 From Colony to Republic: Building the American Nation
Deborah L. Madsen 175

6 Occupation, Assimilation, Partnership: Canadian Literature in English and French, 1769–1899
Andrea Cabajsky 186

PART III MODERN PERSPECTIVES **201**

7 No Early-Modern Nations? Revising Modern Theories of Nationalism
Andrew Escobedo 203

8 Nationalism and Canon-Formation
Sarah M. Corse 211

9 Nationalism and Globalization
Imre Szeman 220

PART IV BIBLIOGRAPHY FOR PARTS II AND III **229**

Bibliography 231

Index 245

CONTRIBUTORS

Terence N. Bowers, Professor of English at the College of Charleston, has published a number of articles on eighteenth- and nineteenth-century literature. He is currently working on an essay titled "Reading the Earth in Conrad's *Heart of Darkness*."

Andrea Cabajsky is Assistant Professor of Comparative Canadian Literature at the Université de Moncton. She is co-editor of *National Plots: Historical Fiction and Changing Ideas of Canada* (Wilfrid Laurier University Press, forthcoming 2009) and holds an FESR/Heritage Canada Standard Research Grant for 2007–2009.

Sarah M. Corse is Associate Professor of Sociology at the University of Virginia. She is the author of *Nationalism and Literature: The Politics of Culture in Canada and the United States* (Cambridge University Press, 1997) and is currently working on a book about art and domestic interiors.

Andrew Escobedo, Associate Professor of English at Ohio University, is the author of *Nationalism and Historical Loss in Renaissance England: Foxe, Dee, Spenser, Milton* (Cornell University Press, 2004). He is currently working on a manuscript about personification as an expression of Renaissance ideas about the will.

Andrew Hadfield is Professor of English at Sussex University. His publications include *Shakespeare and Republicanism* (Cambridge University Press, 2005) and *Literature, Politics and National Identity: Reformation to Renaissance* (Cambridge University Press, 1994). He is co-editor of *The Oxford History of the Irish Book, Vol. III: The Irish Book in English, 1550–1800* (Oxford University Press, 2006) and the recipient of the 2006 Sixteenth-Century Society Conference Roland H. Bainton Prize for Literature.

Deborah L. Madsen is Professor of American Studies at the University of Geneva. Her monographs include *Allegory in America: From Puritanism to Postmodernism* (Palgrave, 1996) and *American Exceptionalism* (University Press Mississippi, 1998). She has also edited twelve books, including

Native Authenticity: Transatlantic Approaches to Native American Literature (SUNY Press, forthcoming), and co-edited *Diasporic Histories: Archives of Chinese Transnationalism* (Hong Kong University Press, 2009).

Elizabeth Sauer is Professor of English at Brock University, Canada. She has authored two books, including *"Paper-Contestations" and Textual Communities in England* (University of Toronto Press, 2005), and edited ten volumes, including *Milton and Toleration* with Sharon Achinstein (Oxford University Press, 2007) and *Reading Early Modern Women* with Helen Ostovich (Routledge, 2004). She is the recipient of awards from the Milton Society of America, Choice, the Society for the Study of Early Modern Women, and the Canada Council for the Arts (Killam Research Fellowship).

Imre Szeman is Canada Research Chair in Cultural Studies at the University of Alberta. He is author of *Zones of Instability: Literature, Postcolonialism and the Nation* (Johns Hopkins University Press, 2003) and co-author of *Popular Culture: A User's Guide* (Nelson 2004, 2009).

Julia M. Wright is Canada Research Chair in European Studies at Dalhousie University and has published two monographs: *Ireland, India, and Nationalism in Nineteenth-century Literature* (Cambridge University Press, 2007) and the award-winning *Blake, Nationalism, and the Politics of Alienation* (Ohio University Press, 2003). She has edited Sydney Owenson's *The Missionary: An Indian Tale* (Broadview, 2002) and *Irish Literature, 1750–1900: An Anthology* (Blackwell, 2008), and co-edited a number of volumes, including (with Jason Haslam) *Captivating Subjects: Writing Confinement, Citizenship and Nationhood in the Nineteenth Century* (University of Toronto Press, 2005). She also co-edits the new Ashgate Series in Nineteenth-Century Transatlantic Studies, and is currently editing *A Companion to Irish Literature* for Blackwell.

ACKNOWLEDGMENTS

This project began in the very collegial surrounding of an informal Canadian research network on nationalism, and we would like to thank all of the members of that group for the nurturing climate in which this project first took root, especially Judith Thompson, Peter Sabor, Robert Lapp, Angela Esterhammer, Lisa Vargo, and Cindy Holder. As this grew from an idea into a book, we benefitted enormously from the expertise, generosity, and promptness of our contributors, from the incisive reports of the reviewers of the manuscript, and from the astute advice of our editor at Routledge, Polly Dodson.

For invaluable support of our research nationally and internationally, we gratefully acknowledge the Social Sciences Humanities Research Council of Canada. We extend sincerest thanks as well to our research assistants, Meagan Timney, Christopher Stampone, and Jeremy DeVito, for their precise and diligent editorial work, and to Carol Merriam for her Latin translations. Additionally, Julia Wright would like to thank the Canada Research Chairs Program for its generous funding of her work, her colleagues at Dalhousie for their steady good humour and lively conversation, and Jason Haslam, as always, for everything. Particularly influential for Elizabeth Sauer has been the scholarship on nationalism and literature by such early modernists as Paul Stevens, Claire McEachern, Richard Helgerson, Andrew Hadfield, Andrew Escobedo, and John Kerrigan, and the intellectual community of her colleagues and students in the Humanities at Brock University.

This book is dedicated to Professor Balachandra Rajan, transnationalist, revered mentor, and honored scholar, whose educated imagination and intellectual rigor imbued the art of criticism with an enduring significance. His many students benefitted not only from his broad knowledge and critical acumen but also from his generosity as a scholar and his profound commitment to academic enquiry.

ACKNOWLEDGEMENTS

INTRODUCTION

Elizabeth Sauer and Julia M. Wright

> If it be a high point of wisdom in every private man, much more is it in a Nation to know it self.
>
> John Milton, *The History of Britain* (1670)

> I hope I shall be able to prove to you that the advancement of our literature absolutely requires that we should cease to look up so exclusively as we have hitherto done to the literature of Great Britain, as the model of our own, and that a more intimate acquaintance with that of other countries will . . . enlarge our ideas.
>
> Peter Du Ponceau, *A Discourse on the Necessity and the Means of Making Our National Literature Independent of that of Great Britain* (1834)

Reading the Nation in English Literature is a resource of primary materials and introductory essays on the historical, critical, and theoretical studies of the ideologies, discourses, and practices of nationhood in the English-speaking Western world from 1550–1850. The flexible design of this *Reader* is intended to strike a balance between primary and secondary material, and the international and comparative perspective to show that ideas of nationhood are both varied and relational in literatures in English. As Sarah M. Corse notes in her chapter, "'Reading the nation' is more than a metaphor: it is a reference to the ways that national literatures may literally read a nation into being" (p. 215). National identity in the British Isles is neither natural nor self-produced but rather was fashioned in relation to the nations of the Atlantic archipelago (England, Ireland, Scotland, Wales), as well as through ideological and materialist associations with continental and transatlantic nations—and vice versa, as our epigraph from Du Ponceau attests. By showing how various early forms of nationhood were written and the multiple ways in which they can be read, we also suggest that the early modern through to the Romantic invites a rethinking of the modernist position on questions of nation and nationalism.

This Introduction begins with an overview of recent nationalism studies in literary and historical scholarship, with an emphasis on key concepts, points of debate, and concerns particularly significant in literary studies, before turning to the use of literature to pursue and contest ideas of nationhood under the headings of major transnational literary periods: the Renaissance, the Enlightenment, and the Romantic Era. Then, in conjunction with the idea that the writing of English literature and the writing of the nation are complementary, intersecting practices, we turn to the idea of a national literature as a representation of national identity, a vehicle of national education, and a measure of national merit, as well as a key subject in the discipline of literature.

Key terms and debates

National identity has emerged as a considerable research and pedagogical interest across various disciplines ever since the publication of influential studies by leading nationalism scholars such as Benedict Anderson, Ernest Gellner, E. J. Hobsbawm, and Anthony D. Smith in the late 1970s and early 1980s. Questions of nationhood are of increasing importance in literary studies from 1550–1850, and recent years have seen the publication of major volumes by such scholars as Richard Helgerson, Andrew Hadfield, Claire McEachern, Willy Maley, Andrew Escobedo, Patrick Schwyzer, Udo J. Hebel, David Loewenstein and Paul Stevens, John Kerrigan, Juan E. DeCastro, David Avrom Bell, and Julia M. Wright.[1] This scholarly interest has led not only to courses that deal extensively with these issues, but also to key changes in the way that we teach "national literatures" in the classroom. The rise of "transatlantic literature," "world literature," and other transnational literatures demonstrates the degree to which "national literature" is widely recognized as a construct rather than an inevitable organizing structure.

What is a "nation" and what role does literary history play in producing ideas of the nation? In his discussion here of Edmund Spenser, Andrew Hadfield reveals how poetry in particular offers a critical space for the production of counter-factual narratives that "represent the real truth of the nation and inspire the reader to help shape its future" (p. 140). By the late eighteenth century, poetry was not only a vehicle for debate about the nation but also itself a measure of the nation's status—great nations must have great poetry, and bad poetry was read as a sign of cultural and civic backwardness or decline. The literary evidence for and representations of the early nation are rich, endlessly suggestive, and inevitably transform the way modern manifestations of the nation are imagined and understood, a subject that Andrew Escobedo explores in his contribution to this volume. While social sciences and postcolonial studies of nationalism have concentrated on the post-1780 period, this volume works within literary studies' growing interest in a larger trajectory that takes into account the development of the modern state, national iconography, and the role of territorial conflicts in ideas of nationhood beginning with the early age of European imperial expansion in the Renaissance. The anthologized materials and essays here on the period 1550–1850 thus not only extend and complicate the genealogy of national discourse but also pursue a wide range of literary forms in which it is expressed.

"Nation" is a common concept in everyday discourse, widely understood to refer to a people with a shared history, culture, and language who have an emotional attachment to a particular territory; nationalism is generally tied to the belief that this people and territory should be governed by an autonomous state, and in the value of the nation. But these ideas were widely contested in our period of study. Take, for instance, the emphasis on territory in this standard definition, a position influentially supported by the eighteenth-century thinker J. G. von Herder: "Their own mode of representing things is the more deeply imprinted in every nation, because it is adapted to themselves, is suitable to their own earth and sky . . ."[2] Edmund Burke, however, famously declared in 1796, "Nation is a moral essence, not a geographic arrangement."[3] In 1862, discussing Giuseppe Mazzini, excerpted below, Lord Acton asserted, "exile is the nursery of nationality."[4] Nationalism scholars have also widely debated the specifics of the term. Anderson, famous for coining the phrase "imagined communities" to grasp the production of the nation through culture, has followed Acton to argue that it is through diaspora that territorial attachments become significant to nationalism, while Joep Leerssen has recently entered the debate to take the position that nationalism is fundamentally oppositional via "commonplaces and stereotypes of how we identify, view and characterize others as opposed to ourselves."[5] Some scholars associate modern nationalism's emergence with the Industrial Revolution (Gellner) and others with the political revolutions of the late eighteenth century (Hobsbawm, Anderson), while Anthony D. Smith argued in 1976 for nationalism as the philosophical product of the interweaving of Enlightenment and Romantic precepts but three decades later argued for "the antiquity of nations."[6] The mechanics of how an idea of a nation becomes a popular and deeply held belief also remain shadowy. Smith strenuously rejects "social constructionism" as an approach which views nationalism as a "top-down" phenomenon in which an elite imposes its views on the masses through cultural work. Smith echoes Hobsbawm's earlier critique of Gellner in arguing for the consideration of both elite and populist perspectives, but Smith invokes vague concepts such as "love . . . and duty" instead of imagination or hegemony to describe that populist perspective.[7] The emotional dimension of nationalism remains difficult to theorize and explain, and yet, whether the nation is a "moral essence" or a relationship to territory, nationalism consistently solicits strong emotional attachments and responses—most strikingly when it spurs national subjects to risk their lives on the battlefield.

History and literary history likewise have a way of resisting the containment of definitions and etymologies, and this is certainly the case for the term "nationhood": "the state or fact of being a nation; national independence or autonomy; national, ethnic, or cultural identity" (OED). The OED's first example of the term's usage is taken from a mid-nineteenth-century Irish ballad (though it appears earlier in the century), Thomas Davis' "The West's Asleep": "That chainless wave and lovely land / Freedom and Nationhood demand."[8] While democratic forms of the nation-state have come to be associated with "nationhood," particularly in its sense of "national independence," earlier forms of government were also tied to the principle of national identity and political independence, as evidenced in the numerous examples of imagined, written nations found in English literatures back as far as the medieval period. A nascent nationhood found expression in the thirteenth and fourteenth centuries. The Scottish Declaration of Arbroath (1320) defended national sovereignty in terms of an "uninterrupted succession of 113 kings, all of our own native and royal stock" and in relation to English efforts to restrain Scottish liberties: "It is liberty alone that we fight and contend for . . . to live at peace in that narrow spot of Scotland beyond which we have no habitation."[9] Welsh fabulist, Geoffrey of Monmouth, composed *Historia regum Britanniae* (c. 1136) long before the literary culture of Geoffrey Chaucer's era helped bring English national consciousness to the fore, and in relation to that recurring element of nationhood, a common language. Though not printed until the early modern era (1508), Monmouth's popular chronicle of British kings not only shaped the historical imagination about England and Wales through to the seventeenth century but also became a major resource for English authors. The Renaissance works indebted to Monmouth range from Spenser's allegorical Arthurian romance, the *Faerie Queene* (1590; 1596), both celebrating and admonishing Queen Elizabeth I, to Milton's *History of Britain, That Part especially now call'd England* (begun 1649; pub. 1670), which opens with a statement about the elusive origins of nations in histories and fables, and serves as a contemporary comment on the betrayal of such cherished values as civility, valour, and liberty associated with Milton's *true* nation.

While a familiar term, "the nation" has a palimpsestic etymological, cultural, and political history and multiple manifestations. "Nation" as "nacioun" enters English usage by way of the French term "nation" originating from the Latin *natio* (*nat- 'born,'* from the verb *nasci*).[10] Increasingly the term would become used in reference to a people's sovereign status.[11] Historians and theorists of the nation have been helpfully clarifying the meanings of such related concepts as ethnicity, empire, public sphere, kingdom, commonwealth, nation-state, community, and patriotism.[12] As Leerssen notes, "*Ethnicity*" in nationalism studies and related fields "means nothing more or less than the collective acceptance of a shared self-image," and it can work aslant or with national identity.[13] While ethnic nationalism tacitly ties membership in the nation to the accident of birth, requiring at least "myths of common origins and descent for that population,"[14] liberal or civic nationalism, rooted in the legitimization of the state through popular political participation of the sort imagined by John Locke, allows membership in the nation to be a choice.[15] "Empire" refers to a territorial and legal formation held together by structures of differentiation and containment, and, more directly in the case of England, to the domination of a nation over more than one geographical area.[16] A nation-state is a sovereign state whose subjects are in possession of the state, a concept that is conventionally associated with a post-Lockean era when the concept of the people as collectively sovereign (in distinction to a sovereign monarch) demanded more democratic formulations of the state. And, as the public sphere emerged as a major site of political debate in the eighteenth century, the nation became further constituted in relation to the popular instead of the elite, a crucial innovation strongly related to the modern, post-1780 nationalism on which the social sciences focus: "We the People," begins the American Constitution, adopted in 1787, enshrining the concept of the nation-state as an expression of popular will and sovereignty.[17] As Julia M. Wright asserts in this volume, nationalism could be evoked in support of or in opposition to the present direction of the government, in large measure because of the difference between "nation" and "nation-state."

Diverse nationalisms are represented and analyzed across the various periods featured in this volume. Romantic nationalism is grounded in affection for the land and rurality in general—folk culture, the original national language, and the local (in distinction to the cosmopolitan or global). Diasporic nationalism, conversely, flows beyond the nation's borders, allowing a cohesive nationalist community in an international space. The proliferation of "nation" and its cognates in literary criticism and in nationalism studies more broadly speaks to the complications concealed in simple definitions, complications generated by different experiences and ideas of the nation and of the subject's ties to the nation. Exploring this complexity, our *Reader* strives to keep the notion of nation sufficiently inclusive: it is a public space—geographical and conceptual—in which competing views about nationhood are evidenced; it is a corporate identity based on crown, church, or land;[18] it is a guarantor of liberty and the subject of criticism and commendation; it is a collectivity that can ask for individual sacrifice and define the subject; and most importantly for this volume, it is a discursive, literary construction that is debated across diverse high culture and popular culture genres, from histories to poems, novels, anthologies, maps, travel literatures, translations, philosophical writings, scriptures, and foundational narratives. This range of genres also speaks to a wide range of subject matter, reflected in the primary materials provided here, as the legitimacy and power of the nation was explored in a variety of arenas and frames of reference, from emotional and religious ties (Foxe) to economic supremacy (Hakluyt) and autonomy (for instance, Swift), to constitutional, civic and political rights (Milton; Lilburne et al.), to the strength of the people through struggle (Home), to territorial claims ("National Character"), language (*The complaynt of Scotland*; Spenser; the King James Bible), and literature itself (Du Ponceau).

Through this collection of materials and critical essays we aim to show in particular the power of imaginative literature in the conception and formation of early nationhood. *The Construction of Nationhood*, Adrian Hastings' reply to Hobsbawm's *Nations and Nationalism since 1780*, which focuses on the modernity of the concept of nationalism, presents a compelling case for a pre-early modern nation, though Smith suggests that, along with its strengths, the study overemphasizes "vernacular literature" and the Christian world.[19] At the same time, like other literary scholars, Hastings argues that the experience of English nationhood matures in the early modern era.[20] England became an empire in 1533 through the Act in Restraint of Appeals, empire referring in the sixteenth century to a "sovereign territorial state which was completely independent of the pope and all foreign princes."[21] An English–Scottish allegiance would emerge through Protestantism—the chief mobilizing force in the history of the nation—and through conflict with France. The "Auld Alliance" between Scotland and France was severed with the withdrawal of French troops from Scotland in 1560. At the end of the century, William Shakespeare's *Henry V* (1598–1599) rehearses an English victory over France in terms of the Elizabethan subjugation of Ireland. Shakespeare's canonized and frequently anthologized works in general, and his history plays in particular, present abundant evidence on early literary conceptions of a national British identity.[22] Among other monumental representations of nationhood in the Tudor Age are histories and travel literatures, including Raphael Holinshed's *Chronicles of England, Scotland, and Ireland* (1577, 1587), which characterizes the early peoples of the British Isles while curiously omitting "Britain" in the title; William Camden's *Britannia* (1586), designed as a history of Roman Britain; and Richard Hakluyt's *The Principal Navigations, Voyages, Traffiques and Discoveries of the English Nation (*1599, 1600), excerpted in this *Reader*.

The relationship between England and Britain remained tenuous throughout the period represented in this *Reader*, despite the ongoing practice of using these terms interchangeably in the modern as in the pre-modern eras. Historians have for several decades been instrumental in pointing out that the four realms—comprising England, Scotland, Ireland, Wales—were never smoothly consolidated despite various efforts to that effect. In light of the pioneering work of J. G. A. Pocock on the "problem of Britain,"[23] and in conjunction with the debates and analyses it provoked, we acknowledge differences in English writing that problematize the status of the nation from its origins. Sixteenth-century writers asserted what Hadfield called "an English hegemony within Britain, colonising the imagined space as English."[24] Literary critics have productively entered the conversation with historians on the "British problem."[25] Attentive to the multifarious nature of the represented

British identity, we feature a broad genealogy of writings from the British Isles. The anthologizing of materials from *The Complaynt of Scotland* and *The Nation* as well as works by such writers as Defoe, Drennan, and Du Ponceau is designed to remind our readers that the writing of nation is relational. English identity remained interconnected ideologically, culturally, and politically to Ireland, Scotland, and Wales throughout the early modern era to the present day, and vice versa. In the sixteenth century, Ireland and Wales did not represent themselves as nations, though "they did indeed have identities with an imperial British state thrust upon them,"[26] and in this *Reader*, Spenser's *A View of the Present State of Ireland* offers one particularly disturbing piece of literary evidence thereof.

Early Modern

Beginning this *Reader* around 1550 allows us to call attention to an important dimension of English nationhood in the era of the Reformation—the wedding of the nation-state to an official church, and the problems of citizenship for Catholics, Jews, dissenters, and other non-Anglicans until religious tests for full political participation were gradually eliminated in the nineteenth century. Moreover, both Anderson and Gellner suggest that the Reformation was instrumental in the emergence of nationalism.[27] Elizabeth I herself had cultivated a relation between monarchy and the nation through the established church, whose status was affirmed by the incredibly popular *Actes and Monuments* (1563) excerpted in this *Reader*, as well as by Richard Hooker's *Laws of Ecclesiastical Polity (*1593) and the *Book of Common Prayer*, the official service book of the Church of England first issued in 1549. At the same time, parliamentary legislature secured allegiance to the monarchy in the universities. The result thereof was a heightened consciousness of students' roles as "national subjects," as education integrated the individual into the nation.[28]

The 1603 accession to the English throne of the Scoto-English James VI, who became James I in the "Union of the Crowns," launched a Stuart myth of a national British state—a myth given legislative form a century later through the Act of Union (1707) which brought Scotland, England, and Wales under the control of a single parliament and crown. (Ireland would maintain its own legislature until the 1800 Act of Union, focusing much of its struggle for nationhood on first the autonomy of that legislature and then its reinstatement after 1800.) The Britain of the Jacobean era is celebrated in Stuart poet Michael Drayton's chorographical poem *Poly-Olbion* (1612), in which Albion is draped in a map that serves also as a historical chronicle featuring the legendary Brutus (descendant of Aeneas and founder of the Roman Republic), Julius Caesar, Hengist the Saxon, and the Norman, William the Conqueror, from whose progeny sprung the nation. John Speed in his *Theatre of the Empire of Great Britaine* (1611), dedicated to James as "Uniter of the British Empire," seizes the opportunity to explore imaginatively the origins and reaches of the now supreme "Eden of Europe" as he defines Britain through geographic and historical coordinates.[29] National identity and the forms of nationhood were intimately bound up with kingship, but national allegiances also increasingly generated discontent with the Crown. King James scoffed at objectors to monarchical government who believed that "every man is borne to carry such a natural zeal and duty to his commonwealth as to his mother," and that "good citizens will be forced, for the natural zeal and duty they owe to their own native country, to put their hand to work for freeing their commonwealth" from tyrannous kings. As James strove to reinforce the identification of the nation with the form and body of the king, he also exposed the tensions between loyalty to the country and obedience to kingship.[30] Having long dominated political discourse, the metaphor of the body politic would give way to the abstract concept of nationhood resistant to specific institutional identities and compatible with or overriding "ties of class, region, and religion."[31] The rise of printing and correspondingly of literacy rates, the Civil Wars, the 1647 Putney Debates which laid the foundation for the Levellers' *Agreement of the Free People of England* (1649), the proliferation of religious dissent, the 1649 regicide of Charles I, the Cromwellian republican experiment, and the foreign policies and imperialist agendas of the Protectorate multiplied the ways in which nationhood was imagined, managed, and written across various genres.

The self-consciousness that distinguishes emergent nations like England became associated with the institution of a Christian liberty-granting polity, a concept staunchly supported by the Humanist and Protestant Englishman, Milton. In his *Pro Populo Anglicano Defensio* (1651) / *Defence of the People of England* (1692), *true* liberty and nationhood are synonymous with and embodied in those people who most fully display civic virtues. The year 1651 also saw the publication of *Leviathan*, composed by Thomas Hobbes, early modern England's most important political theorist who defended absolute sovereignty based on social contract by which both royal authority and popular rights alike were rendered irrelevant. In the Restoration era, when the nation again embraced monarchy, the scale of toleration shifted further to the right. *Indulgence and Toleration Considered* (1667) by the conservative nonconformist John Owen concludes with a statement about state-legislated toleration as conducive to national harmony and prosperity: "There is no Nation under Heaven, wherein such an INDULGENCE or TOLERATION as is desired [in England], would be more Welcome, Useful, Acceptable, or more subservient to Tranquility, Trade, Wealth and Peace" and that those nations who practice tolerance will earn even greater esteem.[32] Such positions were hardly popular, and in the midst of the crises over toleration, the nonconformist minded envisaged a disembodied nation in contradistinction to the settled nation-state.[33]

On the international stage, Richard Hakluyt's *Principal Navigations* (1599, 1600) had promoted imperialism as national destiny and as a means for the

Protestant nation to prevent Catholic Spain's own imperialist ambitions from being realized, notably in the New World. Spain's dominance may have been temporarily checked in Europe through the 1588 defeat of its Armada in Elizabethan England, and the fracturing of its empire by the end of the Thirty Years' War; yet Spain maintained a stronghold in the English imagination as a papist nation and imperial competitor on the European stage and across the Atlantic. To understand the nature of early modern nationhood, one must turn, however, not only to England's relations with its continental neighbors but also to its colonial outposts, for which England's nationhood functioned as a paradigm or antithesis. England's transatlantic expansion found expression both in the colonization as well as in the settling of many thousands of religiously persecuted peoples, who envisioned the new nation as one that would permit liberty of conscience. Emigrés imported biblical paradigms for the new nation that included the now famous image of "a Citty upon a Hill," to which John Winthrop refers upon approaching the promised land, the Puritan New World.[34] The Canadian encounter would see the transplantation of French and then British history and culture across the Atlantic into a contested space in which military conflict was followed by (yet ongoing) debates about unified Canadian national identity. The eighteenth- and nineteenth-century literatures that registered and contested the colonial, cultural formulations of French and British Canada are the subject of Andrea Cabajsky's chapter in this *Reader*.

The Enlightenment

Setting aside analogy for precedent, and tradition for reason, the Enlightenment made possible the querying of the established social order in European culture through the premise that the individual is both unique and capable of intellectual and emotional development. The Enlightenment was a transnational philosophical movement that helped solidify modern views on science, education, and individual rights, but it was also complicated by a pervasive contradiction: on the one hand, an emphasis on the universality of the human condition, and on the other the often tacit and sometimes explicit exclusion of women, non-Europeans, and the lower classes from that universality. The Enlightenment is also tied to the "rise of the novel" through its attention to individual character and proto-realism in plot and other elements,[35] but apart from some notable exceptions—Aphra Behn's *Oroonoko* (1688), for instance—it remained a reflection of the expansion of literacy to middle-class men and well-to-do women rather than a comprehensive exploration of the varieties of human experience in eighteenth-century Europe and its colonies. The novel and Enlightenment philosophy, then, make claims of universality but define that universality through a small sector of the population. Nationalism, emerging in its modern, populist form during the same era, both follows and elaborates on this contradiction: it claims to include all in the idea of the nation but generally defines itself in relation to particular interests or sectors of society; it espouses the principle of national freedom, but demands certain beliefs and behaviors from its members. As Terence N. Bowers details in his chapter in this volume, print culture and official bureaucracies were alike mobilized to resolve this contradiction by extending the reach of the nation, one fostering wider "bottom-up" participation in national culture and knowledge and the other "top-down" control.

Ideas of nationality in the eighteenth century were predicated on the slippage between "nation" and "race"—used as synonyms until the late nineteenth century—as deterministic categories. Hence the roots of nationalism in European intellectual history lie largely in formulations of "national character," part of a larger national iconography (traced here by Bowers) and nascent scientific racism,[36] theorizations which sidestep Locke and the Enlightenment premise of universality in order to rationalize age-old stereotypes, as well as distill a plurality of individuals into a people who share a "character" or "spirit" and hence can be imagined to have a uniform "will." The key debate, however, addressed the mechanism by which such uniformity was created. On the one hand, continental European writers such as Montesquieu and Herder argued for the impact of climate on identity, rendering national character in part biologically determined. In Scotland, David Hume dismissed such biological factors to argue for the impact of a shared culture and history, contending that members of nations share general tendencies because of "all circumstances which are fitted to work on the mind as motives or reasons, and which render a peculiar set of manners habitual to us" (p. 87). Because national continuities are cultural rather than biological, moreover, Hume argues against confusing a general national character with the character of all individuals in the nation. It is a short step from Hume's interest in the cultural transmission of values and practices to the idea of a national literature, a step that was facilitated by the Enlightenment's emphasis on education as the basis of individual identity. As modern theorists of nationalism such as Smith have suggested, education was a building block of modern nationalism:

> Education here stands for more than mere enlightenment. It is a process of self-development, of drawing out of oneself hidden and suppressed potentialities, until full self-realisation has been attained. Such education is closely linked to the elevation of culture as the source of politics. Both neo-classicism and Romanticism turn to morality and culture, in a word, to Nature, against external artifice and political rules.[37]

Gellner takes a bleaker view of education, noting that in practice it is often the state-sponsored circulation of "high culture" that serves the interests of a centralized, industrialized state: "nationalism is *not* the awakening of an old, latent, dormant force, though that is how it does indeed present itself. It is in reality the consequence of a new form of social organization, based on deeply internalized, education-dependent high cultures, each protected by its own state"—because "a modern industrial state can only function with a mobile, literate, culturally standardized, interchangeable population."[38] Instead of achieving self-development through education, Gellner's individual is hoodwinked into a kind of conformity that facilitates the operation of the modern nation-state. (Excerpts here from writers such as Swift and Defoe register the interweaving of economic and national concern even before the Industrial Revolution.) Enlightenment universality thus becomes national uniformity, eliding the uniqueness of the individual in order to maintain the principle of a national identity. At the same time, the distinction between Herder and Hume would found an ongoing tension in discussions of national culture between Romantic organicism and Enlightenment teleology (as Smith has traced[39]): is national culture the natural expression of a core identity, or is it subject to intellectual and civil improvement?

Romanticism

While the Enlightenment framed national identity and literature through narratives of progress and education, the Romantic period (roughly 1785–1850) returned to the essentialisms that shadowed the Enlightenment but to valorize them as "natural" rather than simply inevitable. Notions of the nation as organism emerged to grasp both national harmony and a shared agenda as effects of nature, whether through a return to the "physical causes" of environment that Hume disputed or the mystification of simple analogy in which being "like" an organism makes the nation function as one. Though posited as a "natural" ground, the nation was highly contested in its details as writers debated whether the nation was conservative Protestant or tolerant, rural or industrial, liberty-loving or imperial—even British or English.[40] Despite state censorship, the proliferation of plays criticizing as well as sanctioning British state policy speaks to the space of the theaters as part of the Habermasian public sphere. From R. B. Sheridan's *The Critic* (1779), responding to the American war, to Mariana Starke's pro-imperial plays around 1790, to the popular early nineteenth-century panoramas that celebrated military victories, the nation was staged as a spectacle that elicited strong responses from its audiences.[41] The expansion of popular print culture is heralded by such nationalism scholars as Anderson as instrumental in the development of national identity, but its value as a tool to propagate ideas of the nation also made popular culture a nationalist concern and hence suggested a need to police it. William Wordsworth's lament in the 1802 Preface to the *Lyrical Ballads* about "sickly and stupid German Tragedies" corrupting the popular taste both reinforces the importance of theater to the public sphere and contributes to his larger argument for the national authenticity of rural folk—to be natural, the English must be insular.[42] Such claims draw their philosophical support from a branch of nationalism inflected by concepts of the primitive. Writers from Friedrich Schiller to Wordsworth asserted that rural peoples and children were the strongest link to a national origin in which the natural still held sway: as Schiller wrote of rural and ancient peoples, "They are what we *were*; they are what we *should become again*. We were natural like them."[43]

Linking popular sovereignty and popular culture to the nation's political rights and cultural identity through the unchallengeable ground of "nature" was an easy maneuver for the English who had a comparatively uncomplicated relationship between the polity and the state, but this belies the ongoing emphasis on education. Anthologies proliferated to make it possible for large sectors of the population to read a select canon of English literature as an emblem of national identity, including the works of Milton and Shakespeare. This model was not easily transferred beyond England's borders. As Du Ponceau's excerpt below suggests, American writers debated the legitimacy of American nationhood if they still relied exclusively on British literary precursors and, as Deborah Madsen's chapter traces, wrestled in myriad ways with the conflict between the democratic ideal and the patriarchal and enslaving reality of the newly formed United States.[44] For other nations of the British Isles the affiliation between popular culture and political rights was also fraught. For instance, in the Gaelic Literary Revival that spread across Ireland, Scotland, and Wales after 1780,[45] Gaelic-language culture was heralded as the true foundation of national identity that must be defended and rejuvenated for the nation to survive as such, part of a larger antiquarian movement that Wright discusses in her chapter. In the same period, anglicization was tied to the promise of modernity: economic prosperity, growing literacy rates, and, most explicitly for Ireland, a population capable of sovereignty because it was sufficiently well-educated to be self-governing and economically successful. These competing nativist and anglicizing pressures could be rationalized through a "national tale" in which national distinctiveness is preserved as an object of private study while the nation's public sphere moves forward into a more English modernity. Sir Walter Scott's *Waverley* is perhaps the best-known example of this kind of narrative, as the highlanders disappear leaving behind them artifacts that sit in the parlours of those reconciled to civil and economic progress on English terms, but it also appears in earlier Irish instances by Morgan and Maria Edgeworth. Identifying the core national identity with rural, agricultural, and relatively unlettered populations—as in Herder, Schiller, and Wordsworth—was complicated by the dominance of Adam Smith's "four stages" theory in which societies progress from hunting, to herding, to farming, and finally to commerce.[46] Consequently, while Romantic nationalists lauded the past for the naturalness of its culture and proximity to a mythic cultural origin, economic thought after the Enlightenment privileged progress and identified agrarian economies with social backwardness. A commercial—and increasingly an industrial—economy was the dominant sign of modernity, a modernity that could be read as a sign of national strength or of the nation's departure from its "natural" origins.

In the ensuing decades, the rise of modern capitalism fostered the very international movement that Anderson allies with the development of nationalism itself.[47] Hence, while globalization is seen as fundamentally transnational, even postnational, as Imre Szeman discusses in his chapter, its general impetus precedes the emergence of modern nationalism. Excerpts from Bradstreet, Cary, Kidd, and Du Ponceau as well as Sauer's, Madsen's, and Cabajsky's chapters that follow, speak to the problem of defining the nation for Europeans in the New World, particularly in the absence of the long history that was widely deemed to define the nation, while our extracts from Morgan's "Absenteeism" and "National Character" reflect the fact of migration within Europe as well. Even as concepts of national character, print culture, and emerging bureaucracies worked to homogenize the national space, the movement of national subjects across the borders that nationalism would privilege constitutes an ongoing irritant to this unifying project.

National Literature

While Raymond Williams traces the idea of national literature back to a German origin in the 1780s,[48] the phrase and its cognates appear even earlier in the British Isles: Thomas Campbell, writing of "the university of Dublin" in 1777, suggests that it "is by no means framed for supporting, augmenting, or extending the character of national literature," while Thomas Warton proposed in 1774 "to develope the dawnings of genius, and to pursue the progress of our national poetry, from a rude origin and obscure beginnings, to its perfection in a polished age."[49] In the 1770s, at the transition point between the Enlightenment and Romanticism, national literature as a critical concept, like nationalism itself as Smith notes,[50] emerges out of two contradictory ideas of culture: on the one hand, Enlightenment notions of progress in which increasing taste and learning are evidence of society's advancement; on the other, the Romantic idea of a national origin, a core cultural identity that should be preserved despite modernizing pressures. These dual influences on the early construction of "national literature" are still with us in the organization of textbooks and university classes on chronological lines to demonstrate cultural development but divided by nation to suggest insularly and distinctively national lines of development. We organize literature as if Edmund Spenser's *Faerie Queene* (1590, 1596) is as "English" as Philip Larkin's "Church Going" (1955), grasping one as emblematically early modern and the other as clearly part of the literary culture of the 1950s—while eliding regional identities, international influences, and, as Cabajsky's chapter demonstrates in the extreme example of bilingual Canada, different linguistic and literary cultures within one geographical space.

We can place writers such as Warton and Campbell in the Enlightenment tradition, in the sense that both understand literature and education as entwined projects in the development of the nation. In the nativist "Romantic" tradition, a seminal text appeared even earlier: Bishop Percy's *Reliques of Ancient English Poetry* (1765) linked the national past with the popular form of the ballad, offering "such specimens of ancient poetry" that "either shew the gradation of our language, exhibit the progress of popular opinions, display the peculiar manners and customs of former ages, or throw light on our earlier classical poets."[51] In the so-called "Celtic Periphery," Percy's work was extended by such studies and collections of verse as Edward Jones' *Musical and Poetical Relicks of the Welsh Bards* (1784), Charlotte Brooke's *Reliques of Irish Poetry* (1789), and Sir Walter Scott's *Minstrelsy of the Scottish Border* (1802). Against such nativist recoveries of pre-modern literature, almost exclusively poetry, Enlightenment anthologists stressed the progressive improvement of literature. While they differ on the merits of the remote past versus the much-improved present, these early anthologists of national literature shared the assumption that their collections would serve to vindicate the nation and educate readers on its merits. This premise continued into early literary criticism. For instance, in his essay, "On Some of the Characteristics of Modern Poetry" (1831), Arthur Henry Hallam declares, "The knowledge and power thus imbibed became a part of national existence; it was ours as Englishmen; and amidst the flux of generations and customs we retain unimpaired this privilege of intercourse with greatness."[52] In 1818, the anonymous essay, "Of a National Character in Literature," included here in its entirety, appeared in an early volume of the conservative periodical, *Blackwood's*. The essay opens with the suggestion, "It would appear, that the pleasure we receive from making ourselves acquainted with the literature of a people, and more especially with their literature of imagination, is intimately connected with an impression, that in their literature we see the picture of their minds" (p. 108). The *Blackwood's* author tends to represent the national character as static, so that the literature expresses an identity rather than a moment in the development of that identity, positing the Romantic idea of a national spirit that transcends historical progress: the reader through national literature can "own[] the power of their spirit–the very voice of their speech is in his ears" (p. 109). In 1830, American author William Ellery Channing draws on similar premises but connects that "spirit" to national reputation. He begins by defining national literature:

> We mean the expression of a nation's mind in writing. . . . We mean the manifestation of a nation's intellect in the only forms by which it can multiply itself at home, and send itself abroad. . . . We mean that a nation shall take its place, by its authors, among the lights of the world . . . and it is for the purpose of quickening all to join their labours for the public good, that we offer the present plea in behalf of a national literature.[53]

It is this view of literature in relation to the expression of national identity and to the development of the populace through nationally specific education that leads, ultimately, to the entrenchment of national literature as a key object of scholarship and advanced education.

In this context, cultural works, especially literature, play an important role in the nation-building process and canon-formation consolidates that process. Corse's chapter charts the evolution of nationalism through changes in conceptions of the value and purpose of literature and the late eighteenth-century formation of a canon that operated as a vehicle for transmitting a national culture.[54] Today canon-formation is largely associated with mechanisms of cultural reproduction, and in particular with publishing and marketing demands, as well as with the development of university curricula and syllabi. The "value" of writings is thus determined within institutional contexts, where they are continually reintroduced to new consumers and generations of readers. Correspondingly, the latest critical and theoretical movements have legitimized scholarship on a wide range of literary and extra-literary writings, effectively detaching the discipline of English literature from the canon, or so cultural critics such as John Guillory have argued. At the same time, by remaining largely within the national frame—even if only to economize via the convenience of the term "English Literature," as we do in our title—those of us in the discipline risk downplaying different national identities in the British Isles in favour of English writings, or re-nationalizing non-English writers, such as Swift, Robert Burns, and Dylan Thomas.

As Josephine M. Guy and Ian Small note, histories of English literary study as an academic discipline broadly agree that "the institutionalization of English studies in the late nineteenth century was instrumental in the construction of a form of national identity—a notion of Englishness—which in its turn was put to political uses," an operation that builds in part on what Bill Readings describes as a Victorian project of "placing literature instead of philosophy as the central discipline of the University and hence also of national culture."[55] The institutionalization of English, and the disciplinary division of literary study by nation and its metonym, language, is legible as the operation of Gramscian hegemony—of the use of universities to consolidate ideas of culture that serve the interests of the nation-state. While Readings suggests that "the stakes of the University's functioning are no longer essentially ideological, because they are no longer tied to the self-reproduction of the nation-state,"[56] we are still the inheritors of the Victorian discipline, along with its foundation in nationalist ideas of literature and education.

The "Modern Perspectives" essays in this *Reader* stress the relevance of reading the nation in relation to early modern and modern formations of the nation, canonicity, and intersecting developments of nationalism and globalism. We seek thereby to show the literary and theoretical means by which "the nation" was questioned, observed, and became a subject of meditation in the historical periods we study, in our disciplines, and in the classroom. We make no effort to be exhaustive but rather aim to encourage pedagogical and research-related explorations of early and current representations of the nation, by demonstrating how imaginative literature in particular can enrich our understanding of this fraught and fascinating subject.

Notes

1 B. Anderson, *Imagined Communities: Reflections on the Origin and Spread of Nationalism*, 1983, rev. edn., London and New York: Verso, 1991; E. Gellner, *Nations and Nationalism*, Ithaca: Cornell University Press, 1983 (also Oxford and Malden: Blackwell, 1983; 2nd edn., Blackwell, 2005); E. J. Hobsbawm, *Nations and Nationalism since 1780: Programme, Myth, Reality*, Cambridge: Cambridge University Press, 1990, 2nd edn., 1992, 1997; A. D. Smith (ed.), *Nationalist Movements*, London: Macmillan Press, 1976; Smith, *The Ethnic Origins of Nations*, Oxford: Blackwell, 1986; Smith, *National Identity*, Oxford: Oxford University Press, 1986 reprinted London: Penguin, 1991; Smith, *The Nation in History: Historiographical Debates about Ethnicity and Nationalism*, Hanover: University Press of New England, 2000. Literary studies on the early nation include R. Helgerson, *Forms of Nationhood: The Elizabethan Writing of England*, Chicago: University of Chicago Press, 1992; A. Hadfield, *Literature, Politics and National Identity: Reformation to Renaissance*, Cambridge: Cambridge University Press, 1994; C. McEachern, *The Poetics of English Nationhood, 1590–1612*, Cambridge: Cambridge University Press, 1996, 2006; W. Maley, *Nation, State and Empire in English Renaissance Literature: Shakespeare to Milton*, Houndsmill and New York: Palgrave Macmillan, 2003; A. Escobedo, *Nationalism and Historical Loss in Renaissance England: Foxe, Dee, Spenser, Milton*, Ithaca: Cornell University Press, 2004; P. Schwyzer, *Literature, Nationalism, and Memory in Early Modern England and Wales*, Cambridge: Cambridge University Press, 2004; U. J. Hebel (ed.), *The Construction and Contestation of American Cultures and Identities in the Early National Period*, Heidelberg: Carl Winter, 1999; D. Loewenstein and P. Stevens (eds), *Early Modern Nationalism and Milton's England*, Toronto: Toronto University Press, 2008; J. Kerrigan, *Archipelagic English: Literature, History, and Politics 1603–1707*, Oxford: Oxford University Press, 2008; J. E. DeCastro, *Mestizo Nations: Culture, Race, and Conformity in Latin American Literature*, Tucson: University of Arizona Press, 2002; D. A. Bell, *The Cult of the Nation in France: Inventing Nationalism, 1680–1800*, Cambridge, MA: Harvard University Press, 2001; J. M. Wright, *Ireland, India, and Nationalism in Nineteenth-Century Literature*, Cambridge: Cambridge University Press, 2007. See also note 20 below.

2 J. G. [von] Herder, *Outlines of a Philosophy of the History of Man* (1784–1791), trans. T. Churchill, London: J. Johnson, 1800, p. 197.

3 E. Burke, *Thoughts on the Prospect of a Regicide Peace*, London, 1796, p. 58.

4 The phrase is cited by B. Anderson, *The Spectre of Comparisons: Nationalism, Southeast Asia, and the World*, London: Verso, 1998, p. 59 (for the original, see Lord Acton, "Nationality," *The Home and Foreign Review*, 1, 1862, pp. 1–25).

5 A. D. Smith, *The Nation in History*; J. Leerssen, *National Thought in Europe: A Cultural History*, Amsterdam: Amsterdam University Press, 2006, p. 17.
6 Gellner, *Nations and Nationalism*; Anderson, *Imagined Communities*; Hobsbawm, *Nations and Nationalism*; A. D. Smith, "Neo-Classicist and Romantic Elements in the Emergence of Nationalist Conceptions," in Smith (ed.), *Nationalist Movements*, London: Macmillan, 1976, pp. 74–87; A. D. Smith, *Antiquity of Nations*, Cambridge: Polity Press, 2004.
7 Hobsbawm, *Nations and Nationalism*, pp. 10–11; Smith, *Nation in History*, pp. 61, 77, 60.
8 *The Spirit of Nation: Ballads and Songs by the Writers of "The Nation,"* Dublin: James Duffy, 1845, p. 72, ll. 9–10.
9 "1320 Letter of Barons of Scotland to Pope John XXII" (The Declaration of Arbroath), in G. Donaldson (ed.), *Scottish Historical Documents*, Edinburgh and London: Scottish Academic Press, 1970, pp. 56–57. Murray Pittock acknowledges that "Scottish national literature in the eighteenth century knew what it was doing when it re-encountered its own medieval period" ("Literature and Nationhood," in D. Womersley (ed.), *Companion to Literature from Milton to Blake*, Oxford: Blackwell, 2000, p. 115).
10 A. Hastings, *The Construction of Nationhood: Ethnicity, Religion and Nationalism*, Cambridge: Cambridge University Press, 1997, 1999, pp. 14–19.
11 L. Greenfeld, *Nationalism: Five Roads to Modernity*, Cambridge, MA: Harvard University Press, 1992, pp. 6–7.
12 Smith, *National Identity*, p. 14.
13 Leerssen, *National Thought in Europe*, p. 16. On ethnicity in early modern Britain, see C. Kidd, *British Identities before Nationalism: Ethnicity and Nationhood in the Atlantic World, 1600–1800*, Cambridge: Cambridge University Press, 1999. K. Kumar likewise maintains that nationalism post-dates the early modern era (*Making of English National Identity*, Cambridge: Cambridge University Press, 2003).
14 Smith, *Antiquity of Nations*, p. 185.
15 See D. Resnick, "John Locke and Liberal Nationalism," *History of European Ideas*, 15, 1992, pp. 511–17.
16 Certainly the nation has a long history of ambition, beginning in the sixteenth century and arguably much earlier. See A. Pagden, *Lords of All the World: Ideologies of Empire in Spain, Britain and France, c.1500–c.1800*, New Haven: Yale University Press, 1995, p. 14.
17 J. Habermas, *The Structural Transformation of the Public Sphere: An Inquiry into a Category of Bourgeois Society*, trans. T. Burger, Cambridge: MIT Press, 1989.
18 R. Helgerson (*Forms of Nationhood*, 1992) demonstrated that literary authors and popular writers were collectively concerned to articulate a national community, and that the nation represented the site of mediation between "their literary undertaking and the claims of the state" (pp. 1–2). Such a theory creates a state-nation binary, responded C. McEachern (*The Poetics of English Nationhood*, 1996, 2006), who argues for "the fellowship of literature and propaganda, and the expression in both alike of the state itself as a utopian structure" (p. 23).
19 Smith, *Antiquity of Nations*, pp. 11–12.
20 In addition to the sources cited in note 1 above, see the following seminal studies: A. Hastings, *The Construction of Nationhood*, 1997, 1999; R. D. Tumbleson,

Catholicism in the English Protestant Imagination: Nationalism, Religion, and Literature, 1660–1745, Cambridge: Cambridge University Press, 1998; J. E. Howard and P. Rackin, *Engendering a Nation: A Feminist Account of Shakespeare's English Histories*, New York: Routledge, 1997; P. Stevens, "Milton's Janus-faced Nationalism: Soliloquy, Subject, and the Modern Nation-state," *Journal of English and Germanic Philology*, 100, 2001, pp. 247–68; Stevens, "Donne's Catholicism and the Innovation of the Modern Nation-state," *John Donne Journal*, 20, 2001, pp. 53–70; Stevens, "Milton's Nationalism and the Rights of Memory," in E. J. Bellamy, P. Cheney, and M. Schoenfedt (eds), *Imagining Death in Spenser and Milton*, London: Palgrave Macmillan, 2003, pp. 171–84; D. J. Baker and W. Maley (eds), *British Identities and English Renaissance Literature*, Cambridge: Cambridge University Press, 2002; P. A. Palmer, *Language and Conquest in Early Modern Ireland: English Renaissance Literature and Elizabethan Imperial Expansion*, Cambridge: Cambridge University Press, 2001; A. Parker et al. (eds), *Nationalisms and Sexualities*, New York: Routledge, 1992; J. Lucas, *England and Englishness: Ideas of Nationhood in English Poetry, 1688–1900*, Iowa City: University of Iowa Press, 1990; Greenfeld, *Nationalism: Five Roads to Modernity*.

21 B. P. Levack, *The Formation of the British State: England, Scotland, and the Union, 1603–1707*, Oxford: Clarendon Press, 1987, p. 2.

22 W. Maley, *Nation, State and Empire*, p. 21. *Henry V* features a British nation of English, Welsh, Irish, and Scottish characters, and a final union between the English King Henry V and Katherine of France. The Jacobean tragedies *King Lear* and *Macbeth* dramatize uneasy constructions of nationhood, see Schwyzer, *Literature, Nationalism, and Memory*, chs. 5 and 6. Literary appropriations of Shakespeare transcended national identities while channeling nationalist sentiment into new forms. The 1775 advertisement to Philip Freneau's "A Voyage to Boston. A Poem" contained lines from Shakespeare's *Henry V* (3.1) to promote anti-British sentiment and champion American republicanism (K. C. Sturgess, *Shakespeare and the American Nation*, Cambridge: Cambridge University Press, 2004, p. 27).

23 On the British problem, see J. G. A. Pocock, "British History: A Plea for a New Subject," *Journal of Modern History*, 47, 1975, pp. 601–28, originally presented in 1973, and recently reprinted in *The Discovery of Islands: Essays in British History*, Cambridge: Cambridge University Press, 2005, pp. 24–43. Pocock argues for "an Age of the Three Kingdoms" that encompasses the whole early modern era. See also Maley's comprehensive bibliographic note in *Nation, State and Empire*, pp. 150–51 n8; and D. J. Baker, *Between Nations: Shakespeare, Spenser, Marvell, and the Question of Britain*, Stanford: Stanford University Press, 1997, in which English identity is established in relation to its neighbors; and see especially Kerrigan's magisterial *Archipelagic English*.

24 Hadfield, *Literature, Politics and National Identity*, p. 11.

25 D. J. Baker and W. Maley, "Introduction: An Uncertain Union," in Baker and Maley (eds), *British Identities and English Renaissance Literature*, p. 4.

26 C. McEachern, "Literature and National Identity," in D. Loewenstein and J. Mueller (eds), *The Cambridge History of Early Modern English Literature*, Cambridge: Cambridge University Press, 2002, p. 313. The four essays on "Literature and National Identity" in *The Cambridge History of Early Modern English Literature* do justice to the forms of nationhood across the British Isles.

27 See Anderson, *Imagined Communities*, p. 40; Gellner, *Nations and Nationalism*, pp. 40–41. Early modernists have been making this point for some time; see for example, C. Shrank, *Writing the Nation in Reformation England, 1530–1580*, Oxford: Oxford University Press, 2004, p. 8.
28 G. Viswanathan, "Milton and Education," in B. Rajan and E. Sauer (eds), *Milton and the Imperial Vision*, Pittsburgh: Duquesne University Press, 1999, p. 279.
29 J. Speed, "To the Reader," *The Theatre of the Empire of Great Britaine: Presenting an Exact Geography of the Kingdomes of England, Scotland, Ireland, and the Iles Adioyning*, London, 1611.
30 James I, *The True Law of Free Monarchies*, in Daniel Fischlin and Mark Fortier (eds), *James I, The True Law of Free Monarchies and Basilikon Doron: A Modernized Edition*, Toronto: Centre for Reformation and Renaissance Studies, 1996, p. 75.
31 Kumar, *Making of English National Identity*, p. 103.
32 J. Owen, *Indulgence and Toleration Considered in a Letter unto a Person of Honour*, London, 1667, p. 31.
33 C. Hill, "The Protestant Nation," in *The Collected Essays of Christopher Hill, Volume II: Religion and Politics in Seventeenth Century England*, Brighton: Harvester Press, 1986, p. 28; R. Trubowitz, "Body Politics in *Paradise Lost*," *PMLA*, 121, 2006, pp. 388–404.
34 See Sauer's and Madsen's chapters in Part II. See also A. Bradstreet's "A Dialogue between Old *England* and New" in this volume, and I. K. Steele, *The English Atlantic 1675–1740: An Exploration of Communication and Community*, New York: Oxford University Press, 1986.
35 See I. Watt, *The Rise of the Novel: Studies in Defoe, Richardson and Fielding*, Berkeley: University of California Press, 1957.
36 See E. C. Eze, *Race and the Enlightenment: A Reader*, Oxford: Blackwell, 1997; Eze's volume includes some key excerpts from writings on nation.
37 Smith, "Neo-Classicist," p. 83.
38 Gellner, *Nations and Nationalism*, pp. 48, 46.
39 Smith, "Neo-Classicist."
40 See L. Colley, *Britons: Forging the Nation, 1707–1837*, New Haven: Yale University Press, 1992.
41 See R. W. Jones, "Sheridan and the Theatre of Patriotism: Staging Dissent during the War for America," *Eighteenth-Century Life*, 26, 2002, pp. 24–45; J. Moskal, "English National Identity in Mariana Starke's 'The Sword of Peace': India, Abolition, and the Rights of Women," in C. Burroughs (ed.), *Women in British Romantic Theatre: Drama, Performance, and Society, 1790–1840*, Cambridge: Cambridge University Press, 2000, pp. 102–31; D. O'Quinn, *Staging Governance: Theatrical Imperialism in London, 1770–1800* (Baltimore: Johns Hopkins University Press, 2005).
42 W. Wordsworth, "Preface to *Lyrical Ballads*" (1802), in S. Gill (ed.), *William Wordsworth*, Oxford: Oxford University Press, 1984, p. 599.
43 F. Schiller, *On the Naive and Sentimental in Literature* (1795), trans. H. Watanabe-O'Kelly, Manchester: Carcanet New Press, 1981, p. 22.
44 W. Wordsworth, "Preface to *Lyrical Ballads*," p. 599.
45 S. Deane, *A Short History of Irish Literature*, Notre Dame: Notre Dame University Press, 1986.

46 For a useful overview, see M. Harkin, "Adam Smith's Missing History: Primitives, Progress, and Problems of Genre," *ELH*, 72, 2005, pp. 432–33.
47 Anderson, *Spectre of Comparisons*.
48 R. Williams, "Marxism, Structuralism and Literary Analysis," *New Left Review*, September–October, 129, 1981, pp. 51–66.
49 T. Campbell, *A Philosophical Survey of the South of Ireland*, London, 1777, p. 404; T. Warton, *The History of English Poetry*, London, 1774, 1: ii.
50 See Smith, "Neo-Classicist."
51 T. Percy, *Reliques of Ancient English Poetry* (1765), reprinted with an intro. by N. Groom, 3 vols, London: Routledge/Thoemmes Press, 1996, vol. 1: ix.
52 A. H. Hallam, "On Some of the Characteristics of Modern Poetry" (1831), in T. J. Collins and V. Rundle (eds), *The Broadview Anthology of Victorian Poetry and Poetic Theory*, concise edn., Peterborough: Broadview Press, 2000, p. 544.
53 W. E. Channing, *The Importance and Means of a National Literature*, London: Edward Rainford, 1830, pp. 3–4.
54 J. Guillory, *Cultural Capital: The Problem of Literary Canon Formation*, Chicago: University of Chicago Press, 1993. See also T. Ross's *The Making of the English Literary Canon*, Kingston and Montreal: McGill-Queen's University Press, 1998, which explores the medieval and early modern mimetic reproduction of literary and cultural values—the promotion of a national literature, and the employment of rhetorical habits of thought.
55 J. M. Guy and I. Small, *Politics and Value in English Studies: A Discipline in Crisis?* Cambridge: Cambridge University Press, 1993, p. 159; B. Readings, *The University in Ruins*, Cambridge, MA: Harvard University Press, 1996, pp. 15–16.
56 Readings, *University in Ruins*, p. 15.

Part I

WRITING THE NATION, c. 1550–1850

1 From *The Complaynt of Scotland* (1549?)

The author of this otherwise anonymous work was likely Robert Wedderburn, Vicar of Dundee and, from c. 1548–1550, Chamberlain to the Knights of St. John at Torphichen. While apologizing in the "Prolog to the Redar" for employing "domestic scottis langage," he draws on French and Latin literary models to ennoble the vernacular. The *Complaynt* consists of four parts, including the author's discourse on the affliction of his country and his dream of Dame Scotia's complaint against her three sons. In Chap. VII, which is a part of the *Complaynt*'s dream vision, Dame Scotia appears as a lady of noble extraction who is now aggrieved. The devices on her torn mantle represent the corrupt, wretched Nobility, Clergy, and Commons, her "native natural sons," whom she reproaches for vice and selfishness. Published not in Edinburgh but Paris, the *Complaynt* presents "a distinctly negative assessment" of this feminized but also defiant nation.[1]

The Complaynt of Scotland (Paris, 1549?).

The visione that aperit befor the actor in his sleipe. Chap. VII.

In my dullit dreyme ande sopit visione, i thocht that ther aperit to me, ane lady of excellent extractione ande of anciant genolygie,[2] makkand ane melancolius cheir, for the grite violens, that sche hed sustenit & indurit. it aperit be hyr voful contenens, that sche vas in grite dout ande dreddour,[3] for ane

1 D. Loades, "Literature and National Identity," in D. Loewenstein and J. Mueller (eds), *The Cambridge History of Early Modern English Literature*, Cambridge: Cambridge University Press, 2002, p. 216. In this transcription, original spelling and punctuation are largely preserved, as is the use of u/v, but abbreviations have been expanded.

2 The dreamer sees a lady of noble extraction.

3 As the political and ecclesiastical body of the nation, she was greatly troubled.

mair dolorus future ruuyne, that vas aperand to succumb hyr haistylye, in the maist extreme exterminatione. hyr hayr of the cullour of fyne gold, vas feltrit & trachlit out of ordour, hing and ouer [h]yr schuldirs. sche hed ane croune of gold, hingand & brangland, that it vas lyik to fal doune fra hyr hede to the cald eird.[4] sche bure ane scheild in the quhilk vas grauit ane rede rampand lyon in ane feild of gold, bordoryt about vi[th] doubil floure delicis. This rede lyon vas hurt in mony placis of his body. the acoutremetis ande clethyng of this dolorus lady vas ane syde mantil, that couurit al hyr body of ane meruelouse ingenius fassoune, the quhilk hed bene tissu ande vrocht be thre syndrye fassons of verkmenschips.[5] [On] the fyrst part quhilk vas the hie bordour of hyr mantil, there vas mony precius stanis, quhar in ther vas grauit, scheildis, speyris, sourdis bayrdit horse harnes ande al vthir, sortis of vaupynis ande munitions of veyr. in the middis of that mantil there vas grauit in carrecters beukis ande figuris, diuerse sciensis diuyne ande humain, vitht mony cheretabil actis ande supernatural miraclis. on the thrid part of that mantil, i beheld brodrut about al hyr tail, al sortis of cattel ande profitabil beystis, al sortis of cornis eyrbis, plantis, grene treis, schips, marchantdreis, a[n]de mony politic verkmanlumis for mecanyc craftis. This mantil quhilk hed bene maid & vrocht in ald tymys, be the prudent predecessours of this foyr said lady, vas reuyn & raggit in mony placis, that skantly mycht i persaue the storeis ande figuris that hed bene grauit vrocht ande brodrut in ald tymis in the thre partis of it.[6] for the fyrst part of it vantit mony of the scheildis ande harnes that vas fyrst vrocht in it ande ane vthir part of the scheildis & harnes var brokyn ande roustit, ande reddye to fal ande tyne furtht of the bordour of that mantil. Siklyik the pleisand verkmenschips that vas in the middis of hyr mantil, vas seperat fra vthirs, ande altrit fra the fyrst fassone, that na man culd etract ony profitabil sentens nor gude exempil furtht of ony part of it. Nou to speik of the thrid part of hyr mantil, it vas verst grathit, ande spylt be ane grit defferens nor vas the tothir tua partis of that mantil: for it aperit that al the grene treis cornis bestialite mecanyc craftis ande schips ande marchandreise, that hed bene curiouslye vrocht in ald tymis in the bordour of the tail of that mantil, vas spilt ande distroyit, ande the eird vas becum barran & stirril, ande that na ordinance of policye culd be persauit in it, nor esperance of relef. Nou to conclude of the fassone of this ladeis mantil, it vas baytht altrit in culour ande in beaulte, ande reuyn in mony placis, hingand doune raggit in pecis, in sic ane sort, that gyf thay hed bene present that vrocht ande maid it in the begynnyng, thai vald haue clair myskend it, be rasone that it vas sa mekil altrit fra the fyrst fassone. This affligit lady beand of this sort troublit ande disaguisit, ande al hyr gaye

4 Her hair was in disarray and her crown was on the verge of toppling from her head.

5 The description of her mantle and its three parts follows.

6 The mantle was ruined and ripped, for which the Three Estates and especially the commons, are held responsible.

clathis reuyn & raggit throucht the grite violens that sche hed sustenit: sche began to suspire lamentabil regrettis, vitht mony salt teyris distillant doune fra hyr piteous ene this desolt affligit lady, beand in this perplexite, ande disparit of remeid, sche began to contempil the vidthrid barran feildis, quhilkis in vthir tymis hed bene fertil in al prosperiteis, quhar she persauit cummand tourt hyr, thre of hyr auen natiue natural sonnis.[7] The eldest of them vas in harnes, traland ane halbert, behynd hym, beand al affrayit ande sleyit for dreddour of his lyue. The sycond of hyr sonnis vas sittand in ane chair, beand cle[t]hd in ane syde goune, kepand grite grauite, hessand ane beuk in his hand, the glaspis var fast lokkyt vitht rouste. hyr yongest sone vas lyand plat on his syde on the cald eird, ande al his clathis var reuyn ande raggit, makkand ane dolorus lamentatione, ande ane piteouse complaynt. he tuke grite pane to ryise vp on his feit, bot he vas sa greuouslye ouer set be violens, that it vas nocht possibil til hym, to stand rycht vp.[8] Than quhen this lady persauit hyr thre sonnis in that langorius stait, sche began to reproche them inuectyuely of ther neclegenes couuardeis ande ingratitude vsit contrar hyr. the quhilk reproche sche pronuncit vitht mony dolorus suspiris, the quhilk be aperens procedit fra ane trublit spreit, desolat of consolatione ande disparit of remede. than i beand in my sopit melancolius dreyme, i thocht that i inquirit of hyr stile, of hyr duelling place & of the dolorus cause of hyr lamentabil regrettis. Sche ansuert vitht ane dolorouse contenens, quod sche, my name is callit, the affligit lady dame scotia,[9] vthir tymis i haue tryumphit in gloir ande prosperite,[10] bot nou aduerse fortoune hes bene inuyful contrar my veil fayr, quhilk is the cause that my triumphant stait is succumbit in decadens, ther can nocht be ane mair vehement perplexite, as quhen ane person beand in prosperite at his hartis desire, ande syne dechays in miserabil aduersite. thir vordis maye be applyit ande conferrit vitht the dolorouse accidentis that hes persecutit me. for i that hes bene in maist fortunat prosperite, nou i am inuadit ande affligit be my ald mortal enemeis be the maist extreme assaltis that ther pouuer can exsecute, the quhilk i beleuit til haue resistit be the support ande supple of my thre so[n]nis that standis heir in my presens, be rason that thai ar oblist be goddis lau, ande be the lau of nature to be my deffens contrar al externe inuasions, bot thai haue schauen them self ingrat dissymilit ande couuardis in the iust deffens of my veil fayr: as thou sal heir be this reproche that i sal pronunce to them in thy presens as eftir follouis.

---

7 While contemplating her once prosperous state, the afflicted lady saw her sons approaching.

8 The youngest son was suffering so grievously that he couldn't stand.

9 She identifies herself and attributes her adverse state to her sons' betrayal of their mother through their divisiveness and abuse of natural law.

10 The *Complaynt* is ultimately an exercise in moral philosophy: Chapter 7 concludes with a marginal pronouncement from Cicero's *De Officiis* that is also repeated in Home below (see p. 93 n80).

2 From **John Foxe, *Actes and Monuments* (1563)**

Historian and martyrologist John Foxe produced what would become a key work outlining the Protestant nation's history of suffering. *Actes and Monuments of these latter days of the English Church*, also known as the "Book of Martyrs," detailed the narrative of the church in England in terms of the fight against Catholic authority and of national liberation achieved under Henry VIII. The multi-genre history was greatly expanded from its initial Latin installment: four vernacular editions were overseen by Foxe and his publisher John Day, and by 1684, nine editions had appeared. The reception history saw the identification of Foxe's England with a "peculiar, divinely appointed role in world history" even though Foxe's elect nation is more at one with the international Protestant church.[11]

A Reformist Protestant, Anne Askew, was interrogated by church and civil authorities in 1545–1546 before being burned as a heretic at Smithfield in London. In her published testimony she describes her interrogation and displays her command of scripture. *The Examinations of Anne Askew*, which she claimed to have written, was published in Basel shortly after her death by Johan Bale, an English émigré active in religious polemics. Askew's account was then mediated and printed for religious and polemical purposes by Foxe.

John Foxe, *Actes and Monuments of these latter and perillous dayes, touching matters of the Church, wherein ar comprehended and described the great persecutions horrible troubles, that have bene wrought and practised by the Romishe prelates, speciallye in this Realme of England and Scotlande . . .* (London, 1563).

TO THE QUENES MOSTE EXCELLENT Majestie Quene Elizabeth, by the grace of God Quene of England, Fraunce & Ireland, defendour of the faith, and supreme governour of the saide Realme of Englande and Irelande, next under the Lorde, as well in causes ecclesiasticall, as also to the temporall state appertaining, her humble subject JOHN FOX hartely wisheth and desireth with increase of Gods holy spirite and grace, long to florishe and reigne in perfect health, and much honour, through the mercie and favour of Christ Jesus, our Lorde and æternall Saviour, to the comfort of his churche, and glorie of his holy name. . . .

For first thinking with my selfe to wryte to your Majestie, as duetie byndeth in the Preface of this boke: then againe pondering with my selfe the famous actes, the memorable doinges, the Princely proceadinges of your

11 J. Lander, "Foxe's *Book of Martyrs*: Printing and Popularizing the *Acts and Monuments*," in C. McEachern and D. Shuger (eds), *Religion and Culture in Renaissance England*, Cambridge: Cambridge University Press, 1997, pp. 70–71. Notes from the original appear in this transcription in square brackets and are inserted directly into the text. The u/v convention is regularized and abbreviations are expanded.

grace, and conferringe the same, with the like valiaunt factes of that worthy Emperour [Constantine], I could not enter mention of the one, but must nedes wryte of the other. Such is the mercifull goodnes of almightie God upon his poore afflicted creatures, that though he suffer sometyme the Tyraunt to rage, and the Hypocrite to reigne for the iniquitie of the people, yet some tyme againe, the same hande of the Lorde whiche woundeth, healeth: that presseth, refre[s]heth: that striketh, salveth againe, to make amendes withall. what a sore and dreadfull hand of the Lorde in the primative tyme of the churche was sene under so many persecuting Emperours, and cruell consules? At length the Lord sent this mild Constantinus, to cease bloud, to staye persecutiom, to refreshe his people. In much like maner what bitter blastes, what smarting stormes have been felt in England duryng the space of certaine yeares, till at last Gods pitifull grace sent us youre Majestie to quenche fier brandes, to asswage rage, to releave innocentes. what a multitude of godly Martyrs were slayne before the tyme of the sayde Constantine, is partly above declared. And likewyse what a nomber also before your graces happie reigne were murdered, in this present historie here followyng is comprehended. Over and besides, to compare tyme with tyme, and place with place: what was in his tyme founde so happie, for whiche we have not as great cause nowe to blesse God in this so gracious a tyme of yours. For as God gave then great reaste to his Churche by the reigne of him: so hath it pleased the Lorde with no lesse aboundaunce of peace to blesse us by the meanes of you. . . .

The confession of the faith whiche Anne Askewe made in Newgate, before she suffred.

I Anne Askewe, of good memory, although my mercifull father hath geven me the bread of adversytie, and the water of trouble: yet not so muche as my synnes have deserved: confesse my selfe here a synner before the throne of hys heavenly majestie, desyryng his forgevenes & mercy. And for so muche as I am by the lawe unrightuously condemned for an evyl doer, concerning opinions, I take the same moste mercifull God of myne, whiche hathe made bothe heaven and earth, to recorde, that I holde no opynions contrarie to his mooste holye worde. And I trust in my mercyfull Lorde, whiche is the gever of all grace, that he wyll graciously assiste me against all euyll opinions, whiche are contrary to his blessed veritie. For I take hym to wytnesse, that I have done and wyll doo unto my lyves ende, utterly abhorre them, to the uttermoste of my power. But this is the heresye whiche they reporte me to holde, [The matter and cause why Anne Askew suffered death.] that after the priest hath spoken the wordes of consecration, there remayneth bread styll.

But they both saye, and also teache it for a necessarye artycle of faythe, that after those wordes be once spoken, there remayneth noo bread, but even the selfe same body, that hong upon the crosse on good fryday, both flesh, bloud and bone. To this belefe of theirs saye I naye: For then were our common Crede false, which sayeth that he sytteth on the ryghte hande of God the father almyghtie: And from thence shall come to judge the quicke and dead. Lo, this is the heresie that I holde. And for it must suffer the death. But as touchyng the holy and blessed supper of the Lorde, I beleve it to be a moste necessary remembraunce of his glorious sufferynges and death. Moreover, I beleve as muche therin, as my eternall and onely redemer, Jesus Christe would I should beleve. Finally I beleve all those scriptures to be true, whome he hath confyrmed with his moste precious bloud. Yea, and as S. Paule sayth, those scriptures are sufficient for our learning and salvation, that Christe hath left here with us. So that I beleve, we nede no unwrytten verities to rule his churche with. Therfore looke what he hathe sayde unto me with his owne mouthe, in his holy Gospell, that have I with Gods grace closed up in my harte. And my full trust is (as David sayth) that it shalbe a lanterne to my footesteppes. Psalm. xxviii. Ther be some do saye, that I denie the *Eucha-riste* or sacrament of thankes geving. But those people do untruely reporte of me. For I both saye and beleve it, that if it were ordered, lyke as Christe instituted it, and lefte it, a moste syngular comfort it were unto us all. [The masse abhominable Idol.] But as concerning your masse, as it is nowe used in our dayes, I do saye and beleve it, to be the mooste abhominable idoll that is in the worlde. For my God wyll not bee eaten with teeth, neither yet dyeth he agayne. And upon these wordes, that I have nowe spoken, wyll I suffer death. O Lorde, I have mo enemies nowe then there be heares on my head. Yet Lorde, let them never overcome me with vayn words, but fyght thou Lorde in my stede, for on the cast I my care[.] [W]ith all the spight they can imagine, they fall upon me, whiche am thy poore creature. [The praier of Anne Askewe.] Yet swete Lorde, lett me not sett by them whiche are against thee. For in thee is my whole delyght. And Lord I hartely desyre of thee, that thou wylt of thy moste mercifull goodnes forgeve them that violence, whiche they doo and have done unto me. Open also thou ther blynde hartes, that they may hereafter do that thyng in thy syght, whiche is only acceptable before thee. And to set fourth thy veritie aryght, without al vayne phantasies of synfull men. So be it. O Lorde so be it.

By me Anne Askewe.

Hetherto we have intreated of this good woman, now it remaineth that we touch somwhat as tou[c]hing her end & martyrdom. She beyng borne of such stock & kynred, that she might have lyved in great wealth & prosperitie, if she wold rather have folowed the world then Christ, but now she was so tormented, that she could neither live long in so great distres, neither yet by the adversaries be suffred to die in secret. wherfor the daie of her execution was appointed, & she brought into Smithfielde in a chayre, because she could not go on her feete, by meanes of her great tormentes, when she was brought unto the stake, she was tied by the middle with a chaine, that helde up her body, when all thinges were thus prepared to the fire, [Anne Askewe refused the kinges pardon.] the kinges letters of pardon were brought, wherby to offer her safe garde of her life if she would recant, which she would neither receave, neither yet vouchsafe once to loke upon. Shaxton also was there present who openly that day recanting his opinions, went about with a long oration to cause her also to turne, against whome she stoutly resisted. Thus she being troubled so many maner of waies, & having passed through so many torments, having now ended the long course of her agonies, being compassed in with flames of fire, as a blessed sacrifice unto God, she slept in the Lorde, in An. 1546. leaving behind her a singular example of Christen constancie for all men to folowe.

The description of Smythfielde with the order and maner of certayne of the Councell, sytting there at the burnyng of Anne Askewe and Lacels with the others.

John Lasselles, John Adams, and Nicolas Belenian.

There was at the same tyme also burnt together with her one Nicolas Belenian priest of Shropshyre, John Adams a tayler, and John Lasselles Gentleman of the Courte and housholde of kynge Henry. There is a certaine appologetical, or defensive Epistle extant, whiche this man briefly wrote, beyng in pryson, touchyng the Sacrament of the body and bloud, wherein it doth bothe confute the errour of them whiche not beyng contented with the spyritual receavyng of the Sacrament wyll leave no substaunce of bread therein, and also doth put of the synister interpretation of many thereupon. It happened well for them, that they died together with Anne Askewe. For albeit that of them selves they were strong and stout menne, yet through the example & praier of her, thei being the more boldned, receyved occasion of more greater comforte, in that so painfull and doolefull kynde of death, not only beholdyng her invincible constancie, but also oftentimes stirred up through her perswasions, they did set apart all kynde of feare. Thus they confyrming one another with mutuall exhortations, taried lookyng for the tormenter and fyre, whiche at the last flamyng round about them, consumed their blessed bodies in happie martyrdome, in the yeare of our salvation 1546. about the moneth of June.[12]

12 July 16, 1546 (E. Beilin (ed.), *The Examinations of Anne Askew*, Oxford: Oxford University Press, 1996, pp. xxxii, 192.)

3 From **Edmund Spenser,** ***A View of the State of Ireland*** **(1596)**

Edmund Spenser (c. 1552–1599), the celebrated London-born poet and author of *The Faerie Queene* (1590, 1596), became private secretary to Lord Grey of Wilton, the new lord deputy of Ireland, where he would spend the second half of his life. Composed as a dialogue, *A viewe of the presente state of Irelande*, as it was originally titled, urges the enforcement of English hegemony in Ireland. The treatise outlines what the main interlocutor Irenaeus (originally Irenius) calls the "evils" "most hurtfull to the common-weale of that land" in the late 1590s, and it advances solutions for addressing them. The original 1596 title contained the modifier "presente," referring to the late sixteenth-century proposal for the civilizing of the barbarous nation by the Protestant "New English," thus also rectifying the abuses of the earlier subjugators, the pre-Reformation "Old English." Irenaeus's catalogue of corruptions infesting colonial Ireland concentrates on the laws, customs, and religion of the natives. The solutions include the use of force, the reformation of Irish abuses, and the administration of the colony.[13] In the excerpt we see a discursively produced nation defined by the colonizer in terms of the history, ethnicity, customs, and culture of the barbarous nation he constructs.[14]

Edmund Spenser, *A View of the State of Ireland* (1596) in Sir James Ware, *History of Ireland*. Collected by Three Learned Authors, viz. Meredith Hanmer . . . Edmund Campion and Edmund Spenser (Dublin, 1633), 1–119.

From **"Preface" by James Ware**[15]

As for his worke now published, although it sufficiently testifieth his learning and deepe judgement, yet we may wish that in some passages it had bin tempered with more moderation.[16] The troubles and miseries of the time when

13 L. Gregerson, "Colonials Write the Nation: Spenser, Milton, and England on the Margins," in B. Rajan and E. Sauer (eds), *Milton and the Imperial Vision*, Pittsburgh: Duquesne University Press, 1999, pp. 169–90.

14 W. Maley, "Forms of Discrimination in Spenser's *A View of the State of Ireland* (1596; 1633): From Dialogue to Silence," in *Nation, State and Empire in English Renaissance Literature: Shakespeare to Milton*, New York: Palgrave Macmillan, 2003, pp. 63–91.

15 This transcription from the original is largely standardized according to the following conventions: original spelling, punctuation, and capitalization are preserved, but u/v, long s, and i/j are regularized, and superscripted letters are silently lowered and abbreviations expanded.

16 Marginalia in the Huntington Library copy of the 1633 *Historie of Ireland* reads: "Mr Spencer censured by Sr. James Wares mistake of immoderation for the Rebellion of Oct. 23. 1641. [j]ustified Spencers wisedome and deep insight into that barbarous nation."

he wrote it, doe partly excuse him, And surely wee may conceive, that if hee had lived to see these times, and the good effects which the last 30. yeares peace have produced in this land, both for obedience to the lawes, as also in traffique, husbandry, civility, & learning, he would have omitted those passages which may seeme to lay either any particular aspersion upon some families, or generall upon the Nation. . . .

From **A View of the State of Ireland, Written Dialogue-wise betweene Eudoxus and Irenaeus, by Edmund Spenser Esq. in the yeare 1596.**

Eudox.[17] BUT if that Countrey of *Ireland*, whence you lately came, bee of so goodly and commodious a soyle as you report, I wonder that no course is taken for the turning thereof to good uses, and reducing that[18] nation to better government and civility.

Iren. Marry so there have bin divers good plottes devised, & wise Councels cast already about reformation of that Realme, but they say, it is the fatall destiny of that Land, that no purposes whatsoever which are meant for her good, wil prosper or take good effect, which whether it proceed from the very *Genius* of the soyle, or influence of the starres, or that almighty God hath not yet appointed the time of her reformation, or that hee reserveth her in this unquiet state still, for some secret scourge, which shall by her come unto *England*, it is hard to be knowne, but yet much to be feared.

Eudox. Surely I suppose this but a vaine conceipt of simple men, which judge things by their effects, and not by their causes; for I would rather thinke the cause of this evill, which hangeth upon that Countrey, to proceed rather of the the unsoundnes of the Councels, and plots which you say have bin oftentimes laid for the reformation, or of faintnes in following & effecting the same, then of any such fatall course appointed of God, as you misdeeme, but it is the manner of men, that when they are fallen into any absurdity, or their actions succeede not as they would, they are alwayes readie to impute the blame thereof unto the Heavens, so to excuse their owne follies and imperfections. So have I heard it often wished also, (even of some whose great wisedomes in opinion should seeme to judge more soundly of so weighty a consideration) that all that land were a Sea poole: which kinde of speech,

17 Eudoxus likely comes from the Greek "of good repute, honored" while Irenius/Irenaeus probably is associated with the name for Ireland, Irena (R. Gottfried (ed.), *E. Spenser, A View of the Present State of Ireland, The Prose Works*, 1949, vol. 9 in E. Greenlaw et al. (eds), *The Works of Edmund Spenser: A Variorum Edition*, 10 vols in 11, Baltimore: Johns Hopkins University Press, 1932–1957, p. 278 n3).

18 The original text read "salvage nacion."

is the manner rather of desperate men farre driven, to wish the utter ruine of that which they cannot redress, then of grave Councellors, which ought to thinke nothing so hard but that thorough wisedome, it may bee mastered and subdued, since the *Poet* saith, that *the wiseman shall rule even over the Starres*, much more over the Earth, for were it not the part of a desperate Phisitian to wish his diseased Patient dead, rather then to apply the best indeavour of his skill, for his recovery. But since we are so farre entred, let us, I pray you, a little devise of those evils, by which that country is held in this wretched case, that it cannot (as you say) be recured. And if it be not painefull to you, tell us what things during your late continuance there, you observed to bee most offensive, and greatest impeachment to the good rule and government thereof.

Iren. Surely *Eudox*. the evils which you desire to be recounted are very many, & almost countable with those which were hidden in the basket of *Pandora*. But since you so please I will out of that infinite number, reckon but some that are most capitall, & commonly occurrant both in the life & conditions of private men, as also in the managing of publicke affaires and pollicy, the which you shall understand to be of divers natures, as I observed them: For some of them are of verie great antiquity and long continuance; others more late and of lesse indurance; others dayly growing and increasing continuallie by their evill occasions, which are every day offered.

Eudox. Tell them then, I pray you, in the same order that you have now rehearsed them, for there can be no better method then this which the very matter it selfe offereth. And when you have reckoned all the evils, let us heare your opinion for the redressing of them: After which there will perhaps of it selfe appeare some reasonable way to settle a sound and perfect rule of government, by shunning the former evils, and following the offered good. The which method we may learne of the wise Phisitians, which first require that the malady be knowne thoroughly, and discovered: Afterwards to teach how to cure and redresse it: And lastly doe prescribe a dyet with straight rule and orders to be dayly observed, for feare of relapse into the former disease, or falling into some other more dangerous then it.

Iren: I will then according to your advisement begin to declare the evils, which seeme to me, most hurtfull to the common-weale of that land; And first those (I say) which were most auncient and long growne. And they also are of three sorts: The first in the Lawes, the second in Customes, and the last in Religion. . . .

I will begin then to count their customes in the same order that I counted their Nations, and first with the *Scythian* or *Scottish* manners. Of the which there is one use, amongst them to keepe their cattle, and to live themselves the most part of the yeare in *Boolies*,[19] pasturing upon the mountaine, and waste wilde places; and removing still to fresh land, as they have depastured the former. The which appeareth plaine to be the manner of the *Scythians*, as you may read in *Olaus Magnus*, and *Joh: Boemus*,[20] and yet is used, amongst all the *Tartarians* and the people about the *Caspian Sea*, which are naturally *Scythians*, to live in heards as they call them, being the very same, that the *Irish Boolies* are, driving their cattle continually with them, and feeding onely on their milke and white meates.

Eudox. What fault can you finde with this custome: for though it be an old *Scythian* use, yet it is very behoofefull in this Country of *Ireland*, where there are great mountaines, and waste deserts full of grasse, that the same should be eaten downe, and nourish many thousands of cattle, for the good of the whole Realme, which cannot (me thinks) well be any other way, then by keeping those *Boolies* there, as yee have shewed.

Iren: But by this custome of *Boolying*, there grow in the meane time many great enormityes unto that Common-wealth. For first if there be any outlawes, or loose people, (as they are never without some) which live upon stealthes and spoyles, they are evermore succoured and finde releife only in these *Boolies*, being upon the waste places, whereas else they should be driven shortly to starve, or to come downe to the townes to seeke releife, where by one meanes or other, they would soone be caught. Besides such stealthes of cattle as they make, they bring commonly to those *Boolies*, being upon those waste places, where they are readily received, and the theife harboured from danger of law, or such Officers as might light upon him. Moreover the people that thus live in those Boolies, grow thereby the more barbarous, and live more licentiously then they could in Townes, using what manners they list, and practizing what mischeifes and villainies they will, either against the government there, by their combynations, or against private men, whom they maligne, by stealing their goods, or murdering themselves. For there they thinke themselves halfe exempted from law and obedience, and having once tasted freedome, doe like a steere, that hath beene long out of his yoke, grudge and repyne ever after, to come under Rule againe.

Eudox. By your speech *Iren*. I perceive more evill come by this use of *Boolies*, then good by their grasing: and therefore it may well be reformed: but that must be in his due course, doe you proceed to the next.

---

19 A booly refers to a company of wandering Irish herdsmen and to an enclosed place in the mountain pastures used to shelter cattle.

20 Olaus Magnus, *Historia de Gentibus Septentrionalibus* (1555) ("A History of the Northern Peoples"); Joannes Boemus, *Omnium Gentium Mores, Leges et Ritus* (1520) ("Manners, Laws, and Customes of all Nations").

Iren. They have another custome from the *Scythians*, that is the wearing of *Mantles*, and long *Glibbes*, which is a thicke curled bush of haire, hanging downe over their eyes, and monstrously disguising them, which are both very bad and hurtfull.

Eudox. Doe you thinke that the *Mantle* commeth from the *Scythians*? I would surely thinke otherwise, for by that which I have read, it appeareth that most Nations of the world auncienly used the *Mantle*. For the *Jewes* used it, as you may read of *Elyas Mantle*, &c. The *Chaldees* also used it, as yee may read in *Diodorus*.[21] The *Egyptians* likewise used it, as yee may read in *Herodotus*, and may bee gathered by the description of *Berenice*, in the *Greeke* Commentary upon *Callimachus*.[22] The *Greekes* also used it auncienly, as appeareth by *Venus Mantle* lyned with starrs, though afterwards they changed the forme thereof into their cloakes, called *Pallia*, as some of the *Irish* also use. And the auncient *Latines* and *Romans* used it, as you may read in *Virgil*, who was a very great Antiquary. That *Evander*, when *Æneas* came to him at his Feast, did entertaine and feast him, sitting on the ground, and lying on *Mantles*.[23] Insomuch that he useth the very word *Mantile* for a *Mantle*.

——*Humi mantilia sternunt*.[24]

So that it seemeth that the *Mantle* was a generall habite to most Nations, and not proper to the *Scythians* onely, as you suppose.

Iren. I cannot deny but that auncienly it was common to most, and yet sithence disused and laide away. But in this later age of the world, since the decay of the *Romane Empire*, it was renewed and brought in againe by those Northerne nations, when breaking out of their cold caves and frozen habitations, into the sweet soyle of *Europe*, they brought with them their usuall weedes, fit to sheild the cold, and that continuall frost, to which they had at home beene inured: the which yet they left not off, by reason that they were in perpetuall warres, with the Nations whom they had invaded, but still removing from place to place, carried alwayes with them that weed, as their house, their bed, and their garment, and, comming lastly into *Ireland*, they found there more speciall use thereof, by reason of the rawe cold climate, from whom it is now growne into that generall use, in which that people now have it. After whom the *Gaules* succeeding, yet finding the like necessitie of that garment, continued the like use thereof.

---

21 Elijah's mantle: II Kings 2:8; Diodorus, *Bibliotheca historica* (c. 60–30 BCE) ("Library of History").

22 Herodotus: fifth-century BCE Greek historian; Callimachus: third-century BCE Greek poet and scholar

23 Evander: a character in the *Aeneid* VIII by the Roman poet Virgil.

24 "They are spreading the mantles on the ground."

Eudox. Since then the necessity thereof is so commodious, as you alledge, that it is insteed of housing, bedding, & cloathing, what reason have you then to wish so necessarie a thing cast off?

Iren. Because the commoditie doth not countervaile the discomoditie: for the inconveniences which thereby doe arise, are much more many. For it is a fit house for an Out-law, a meet bed for a Rebell, & an apt cloake for a thiefe. First the Out-law being for his many crimes and villanyes, banished from the Townes & houses of honest men, & wandring in waste places, far from danger of law, maketh his Mantle his house, & under it covereth himselfe from the wrath of Heaven, from the offence of the Earth, & from the sight of men. . . .

Eudox. O evill minded man, that having reckoned up so many uses of a Mantle, will yet wish it to be abandoned! Sure I thinke *Diogenes* dish did never serve his Master more turnes, notwithstanding that he made it his Dish, his Cup, his Cap, his Measure, his Water-pot, then a Mantle doth an *Irish* man. But I see they be most[25] to bad intents, & therefore I will joyne with you in abolishing it. But what blame lay you to the glibbe? take heed (I pray you) that you be not too busie therewith for feare of your owne blame, seeing our *Englishmen* take it up in such a generall fashion to weare their haire so immeasurably long, that some of them exceed the longest *Irish* glibs.

Iren. I feare not the blame of any undeserved dislikes: but for the *Irish* glibbes,[26] they are as fit maskes as a mantle is for a theife. For whensoever he hath run himselfe into that perill of Law, that he will not be knowne, he either cutteth off his glibbe quite, by which he becommeth nothing like himselfe, or pulleth it so low downe over his eyes, that it is very hard to discerne his theevish countenance. And therefore fit to be trussed up with the Mantle.

Eudox. Truly these three *Scythian* abuses, I hold most fit to bee taken away with sharpe penalties, and sure I wonder how they have beene kept thus long, notwithstanding so many good provisions and orders, as have beene devised for that people.

Iren. The cause thereof shall appeare to you hereafter: but let us now go forward with our *Scythian* customes. Of which the next that I have to treat of, is the manner of raising the cry in their conflicts, & at other troublesome times

25 The original reads "all" rather than "most."

26 Omitted here is "I say that besides theire salvage brutishnes and loathly filthines which is not to be named." For a list of other telling differences between the early and late editions, see Gottfried, vol. 9, pp. 519 ff.

of uproare: the which is very natural *Scythian*, as you may read in *Diodorus Siculus*, & in *Herodotus*, describing the maner of the *Scythians & Parthians* comming to give the charge at battles: at which it is said that they came running with a terrible yell as if heaven & earth would have gone together, which is the very Image of *the Irish Hubub*, which their *Kerne*[27] use at their first encounter. Besides, the same *Herodotus* writeth, that they used in their battles to call upon the names of their Captains or Generals, & sometimes upon their greatest Kings deceased, as in that battle of *Thomyris* against *Cyrus*: which custome to this day manifestly appeareth amongst the *Irish*. For at their joyning of Battle, they likewise call upon their Captaines name, or the word of his Auncestours. As the under *Oneale* cry *Laundarg-abo*, that is, the bloody hand, which is *Oneales* badge. They under O Brien call *Launlaider*, that is, the strong hand. And to their ensample, the old *English* also which there remayneth, have gotten up their cryes *Scythian*-like, as *Crom-abo*, and *Butler-abo*. And here also lyeth open an other manifest proofe, that the *Irish* bee *Scythes* or *Scots*, for in all their incounters they use one very common word, crying *Ferragh, Ferragh*, which is a *Scottish* word, to wit, the name of one of the first Kings of *Scotland*, called *Feragus*, or *Fergus*, which fought against the *Pictes*, as you may read in *Buchanan, de rebus Scoticis*; but as others write, it was long before that, the name of their chiefe Captaine, under whom they fought against the *Africans*, the which was then so fortunate unto them, that ever sithence they have used to call upon his name in their battailes. . . . There be other sorts of cryes also used among the *Irish*, which favour greatly of the *Scythian* barbarisme, as their lamentations at their buryals, with dispairfull out-cryes, and immoderate waylings, the which Master *Stanihurst* might also have used for an Argument to proove them *Egyptians*.[28] For so in Scripture it is mentioned, that the *Egyptians* lamented for the death of *Joseph*. Others thinke this custome to come from the *Spaniards*, for that they doe immeasurably likewise bewayle their dead. But the same is not proper *Spanish*, but altogether Heathenish, brought in thither first either by the *Scythians*, or the *Moores* that were *Africans*, and long possessed that Countrey. For it is the manner of all *Pagans* and *Infidels* to be

27 Kerne: peasant or rustic.

28 The theory of the Egyptian roots of the Irish has a long history, the descendants of the Greek Gathelus and the Egyptian Scotia (1500 BC) having, according to John of Fordun and Hector Boece, conquered Ireland. The account of this origin was reinforced and contested by Spenser's contemporaries, including Richard Stanyhurst (1547–1618), identified in the excerpt as "Master *Stanihurst*." A descendant of the Old English settlement in Ireland who initially defended English hegemony in Ireland, Stanyhurst affirms the mythical history connection in *A Plaine and Perfect Description of Ireland* published in Holinshed's *Chronicle* but contests it in *De Rebus* (Gottfried, p. 335). George Buchanan's *Rerum Scoticarum historia* (1582) discredits Boece's account of Scottish origins.

intemperate in their waylings of their dead, for that they had no faith nor hope of salvation. And this ill custome also is specially noted by *Diodorus Siculus*, to have beene in the *Scythians*, and is yet amongst the Northerne *Scots* at this day, as you may reade in their Chronicles.[29]

Eudox. This is sure an ill custome also, but yet doth not much concerne civill reformation, as abuse in Religion.

Iren. I did not rehearse it as one of the abuses which I thought most worthie of reformation; but having made mention of *Irish* cryes I thought this manner of lewd crying and howling, not impertinent to be noted as uncivill and *Scythian*-like: for by these old customes, and other like conjecturall circumstances, the descents of nations can only be proved, where other monuments of writings are not remayning.

4 From **Richard Hakluyt, *The Principal Navigations, Voyages, Traffiques and Discoveries of the English Nation* (1599); *The Third and Last Volume* (1600)**

Richard Hakluyt's (1552?–1616) writing of the nation took the form of a highly influential history of British imperialism as the expression of national destiny. Haklyut served in various ecclesiastical capacities, including as a cleric at Bristol Cathedral and as a chaplain for Elizabeth I's ambassador to France, and at Oxford immersed himself in the study of travel narratives in classical and European languages. He emerged as the first major geographer, and contributed significantly to knowledge of history, natural and social sciences. The first edition of *The Principal Navigations* was published in 1589, and was followed by an enlarged edition in three volumes in which Hakluyt shifted the focus from America to the entire world and also added "Traffiques" to the title. Recognizing that England lagged behind other European nations in trade, Hakluyt sought to legitimize English nationhood not only on religious and international grounds but also on economic ones.

The Third and Last Volume of the Voyages, Navigations, Traffiques, and Discoveries of the English Nation . . . (London, 1600) gathers documents on voyages to North America, the West Indies, and world-round trips. Sir Humphrey Gilbert (c. 1539–1583), the founder of the first English colony in North America, took possession of the harbour of St. John Newfoundland in 1583 in hopes of

29 The discussion of the Irish people's ethnicity includes reference to the Scythians, who account for Irish savagery and nomadic existence, and the Spanish, enemies of Protestant England.

claiming America for the English. Though he died upon his return to Europe, an account of Gilbert's journey was documented by Edward Hayes, captain of "The Golden Hind," the only ship to reach England. Gilbert's plan for English domination was eventually realized.[30]

Richard Hakluyt, *The Principal Navigations, Voyages, Traffiques and Discoveries of the English Nation, made by Sea or overland . . . within the compasse of these 1600 yeres . . .*, 3 vols (London, 1599–1600).

From "A preface to the Reader as touching the principall Voyages and discourses in this first part"[31]

Having for the benefit and honour of my Countrey zealously bestowed so many yeres, so much traveile and cost, to bring Antiquities smothered and buried in darke silence, to light, and to preserve certaine memorable exploits of late yeeres by our *English* nation atchieved, from the greedy and devouring jawes of oblivion: to gather likewise, and as it were to incorporate into one body the torne and scattered limmes of our ancient and late Navigations by Sea, our voyages by land, and traffiques of merchandise by both: and having (so much as in me lieth) restored ech particular member, being before displaced, to their true joynts and ligaments; I meane, by the helpe of Geographie and Chronologie (which I may call the Sunne and the Moone, the right eye and the left of all history) referred ech particular relation to the due time and place: I do this second time (friendly Reader, if not to satisfie, yet at least for the present to allay and hold in suspense thine expectation) presume to offer unto thy view this first part of my threefold discourse. For the bringing of which into this homely and rough-hewen shape, which here thou seest; what restlesse nights, what painefull dayes, what heat, what cold I have indured; how many long & chargeable journeys I have traveiled; how many famous libraries I have searched into; what varietie of ancient and moderne writers I have perused; what a number of old records, patents, privileges, letters, &c. I have redeemed from obscuritie and perishing; into how manifold acquaintance I have entred; what expenses I have not spared; and yet what faire opportunities of private gaine, preferment, and ease I have neglected; albeit thy selfe canst hardly imagine, yet I by daily experience do finde & feele, and some of my entier friends can sufficiently testifie. Howbeit (as I

30 On Hakluyt's contribution to the forms of nationhood, see R. Helgerson's "The Voyages of a Nation," in *Forms of Nationhood: The Elizabethan Writing of England*, Chicago: University of Chicago Press, 1992, pp. 149–91.

31 In this excerpt, original spelling, punctuation, and capitalization are preserved, but u/v, long s, and i/j are regularized, and superscripted letters are silently lowered and abbreviations expanded. Marginal notes appearing in the original are here inserted into the text in square brackets.

told thee at the first) the honour and benefit of this Common weale wherein I live and breathe, hath made all difficulties seeme easie, all paines and industrie pleasant, and all expenses of light value and moment unto me. . . .

But that no man should imagine that our forren trades of merchandise have bene comprised within some few yeeres, or at least wise have not bene of any long continuance; let us now withdraw our selves from our affaires in *Russia*, and ascending somewhat higher, let us take a sleight survey of our traffiques and negotiations in former ages. First therefore the Reader may have recourse unto the 124 page of this Volume, & there with great delight and admiration, consider out of the judicial Historiographer *Cornelius Tacitus*, that the Citie of *London* fifteene hundred yeeres agoe in the time of *Nero* the Emperour, was most famous for multitude of merchants and concourse of people. In the pages folowing he may learne out of Venerable *Beda*, that almost 900. yeeres past, in the time of the *Saxons*, the said citie of *London* was *multorum emporium populorum*, a Mart-towne for many nations. There he may behold, out of *William* of *Malmesburie*, a league concluded betweene the most renoumed and victorious *Germane* Emperour *Carolus Magnus*, and the *Saxon* king *Offa*, together with the sayd *Charles* his patronage and protection granted unto all English merchants which in those dayes frequented his dominions. There may hee plainly see in an auncient testimonie translated out of the *Saxon* tongue, how our merchants were often woont for traffiques sake, so many hundred yeeres since, to crosse the wide Seas, and how their industry in so doing was recompensed. Yea, there mayest thou observe (friendly Reader) what privileges the *Danish* king *Canutus* obtained at *Rome* of Pope *John*, of *Conradus* the Emperour, and of king *Rudolphus* for our English merchants Adventurers of those times. Then if you shall thinke good to descend unto the times and ages succeeding the conquest, there may you partly see what our state of merchandise was in the time of king *Stephen* and of his predecessor, and how the Citie of *Bristol* (which may seeme somewhat strange) was then greatly resorted unto with ships from *Norway* and from *Ireland*. There may you see the friendly league betweene king *Henry* the second, and the famous *Germane* Emperour *Friderick Barbarossa*, and the gracious authorizing of both their mercha[n]ts to traffique in either of their dominions. And what need I to put you in mind of king *John* his favourable safe-conduct, whereby all forren merchants were to have the same privileges here in *England*, which our English merchants enjoyed abroad in their severall countreys.

From **The Third and Last Volume**

A report of the voyage and successe thereof, attempted in the yeere of our Lord 1583 by sir *Humfrey Gilbert* knight, with other gentlemen assisting him in that action, intended to discover and to plant Christian inhabitants in place convenient, upon those large and ample countreys extended

Northward from the cape of *Florida*, lying under very temperate Climes, esteemed fertile and rich in Minerals, yet not in the actuall possession of any Christian prince, written by *M. Edward Haies* gentleman, and principall actour in the same voyage, who alone continued unto the end, and, by Gods speciall assistance returned home with his retinue safe and entire.

Many voyages have bene pretended, yet hitherto never any thorowly accomplished by our nation of exact discovery into the bowels of those maine, ample and vast countreys, extended infinitely into the North from 30 degrees, or rather from 25 degrees of Septentrionall latitude, neither hath a right way bene taken of planting a Christian habitation and regiment upon the same, as well may appeare both by the little we yet do actually possesse therein, & by our ignorance of the riches and secrets within those lands, which unto this day we know chiefly by the travell and report of other nations, and most of the French, who albeit they cannot challenge such right and interest unto the sayd countreys as we, neither these many yeeres have had opportunity nor meanes so great to discover and to plant (being vexed with the calamities of intestine warres) as we have had by the inestimable benefit of our long and happy peace: yet have they both waies performed more, and had long since attained a sure possession and setled government of many provinces in those Northerly parts of *America*, if their many attempts into those forren and remote lands had not bene impeached by their garboils at home.

[The coasts from Florida Northward first discovered by the English nation.] The first discovery of these coasts (never heard of before) was well begun by *John Cabot* the father, and *Sebastian* his sonne, an Englishman borne, who were the first finders out of all that great tract of land stretching from the cape of *Florida* into those Islands which we now call the *Newfoundland*: all which they brought and annexed unto the crowne of *England*. Since when, if with like diligence the search of inland countreys had bene followed, as the discovery upon the coast, and out-parts thereof was performed by those two men; no doubt her Majesties territories and revenue had been mightily inlarged and advanced by this day. And which is more; the seed of Christian religion had bene sowed amongst those pagans, which by this time might have brought foorth a most plentifull harvest and copious congregation of Christians; which must be the chiefe intent of such as shall make any attempt that way; or els whatsoever is builded upon other foundation shall never obtaine happy successe nor continuance. . . .

[A fit consideration.] In the meane while, it behooveth every man of great calling, in whom is any instinct of inclination unto this attempt, to examine his owne motions: which if the same proceed of ambition or avarice, he may assure himselfe it commeth not of God, and therefore can not have confidence of Gods protection and assistance against the violence (else irresistible) both of sea, and infinite perils upon the land; whom God yet may use as an instrument to further his cause and glory some way, but not to build upon so bad a foundation.

Otherwise, if his motives be derived from a vertuous & heroycall minde, preferring chiefly the honour of God, compassion of poore infidels captived by the devill, tyrannizing in most wonderfull and dreadfull maner over their bodies and soules; advancement of his honest and well-disposed countrey-men, willing to accompany him in such honourable actions; relief of sundry people within this realme distressed; all these be honourable purposes, imitating the nature of the munificent God, wherewith he is well pleased, who will assist such an actour beyond expectation of man. [Probable conjectures in these lands North of Florida, are reserved for the English nation to possesse.] And the same, who feeleth this inclination in himselfe, by all likelihood may hope or rather confidently repose in the preordinance of God, that in this last age of the world (or likely never) the time is compleat of receiving also these Gentiles into His mercy, and that God will raise him an instrument to effect the same: it seeming probable by event of precedent attempts made by the Spanyards and French sundry times, that the countreys lying North of *Florida*, God hath reserved the same to be reduced unto Christian civility by the English nation. For not long after that *Christopher Columbus* had discovered the Islands and continent of the *West Indies* for *Spaine, John* and *Sebastian Cabot* made discovery also of the rest from *Florida* Northwards to the behoofe of *England.*

[The Spanyards prosperous in the Southerne discoveries, yet unhappy in these Northerne.] And whensoever afterwards the Spanyards (very prosperous in all their Southerne discoveries) did attempt anything into *Florida* and those regions inclining towards the North, they proved most unhappy, and were at length discouraged utterly by the hard and lamentable successe of many both religious and valiant in armes, endevouring to bring those Northerly regions also under the Spanish jurisdiction; as if God had prescribed limits unto the Spanish nation which they might not exceed: as by their owne gests recorded may be aptly gathered.

[The French are but usurpers upon our right.] The French, as they can pretend lesse title unto these Northerne parts then the Spanyard, by how much the Spanyard made the first discovery of the same continent so far Northward as unto *Florida*, and the French did but review that before discovered by the English nation, usurping upon our right, and imposing names upon countreys, rivers, bayes, capes, or headlands, as if they had bene the first finders of those coasts; which injury we offered not unto the Spanyards, but left off to discover when we approached the Spanish limits: even so God hath not hitherto permitted them to establish a possession permanent upon anothers right, notwithstanding their manifolde attempts, in which the issue hath bene no lesse tragicall then that of the Spanyards, as by their owne reports is extant. [The Fre[n]ch also unfortunate in those North parts of America.]

[A good incouragement for the English nation, to proceed in the conquests of the North of America.] Then seeing the English nation onely hath right unto these countreys of *America* from the cape of *Florida* Northward by the privilege of first discovery, unto which *Cabot* was authorised by regall authority, and set forth by the expense of our late famous king *Henry* the seventh: which right also seemeth strongly defended on our behalfe by the powerfull hand of almighty God, withstanding the enterprises of other nations: it may greatly incourage us upon so just ground, as is our right, and upon so sacred an intent, as to plant religion (our right and intent being meet foundations for the same) to prosecute effectually the full possession of those so ample and pleasant countreys apperteining unto the crowne of *England*: the same (as is to be conjectured by infallible arguments of the worlds end approaching) being now arrived unto the time by God prescribed of their vocation, if ever their calling unto the knowledge of God may be expected. [The best time approacheth bye all likelihood of calling these heathens unto Christianity. The word of God moveth circularly.] Which also is very probable by the revolution and course of Gods word and religion, which from the beginning hath moved from the East, towards, & at last unto the West, where it is like to end, unlesse the same begin againe where it did in the East, which were to expect a like world againe. But we are assured of the contrary by the prophesie of *Christ*, whereby we gather, that after his word preached thorowout the world shal be the end. And as the Gospel when it descended Westward began in the South, and afterward spread into the North of *Europe*: even so, as the same hath begunne in the South countreys of *America*, no lesse hope may be gathered that it will also spread into the North.

These considerations may helpe to suppresse all dreads rising of hard events in attempts made this way by other nations, as also of the heavy successe and issue in the late enterprise made by a worthy gentleman our countryman sir *Humfrey Gilbert* knight, who was the first of our nation that carried people to erect an habitation and government in those Northerly countreys of *America*. . . .

[The first and great preparation of sir Humphrey Gilbert.] When first Sir *Humfrey Gilbert* undertooke the Westerne discovery of *America*, and had procured from her Majesty a very large commission to inhabit and possesse at his choice all remote and heathen lands not in the actuall possession of any Christian prince, the same commission exemplified with many privileges, such as in his discretion he might demand, very many gentlemen of good estimation drew unto him, to associate him in so commendable an enterprise, so that the preparation was expected to grow unto a puissant fleet, able to encounter a kings power by sea. . . .

A brief relation of the New found lande, and the commodities thereof.

[New found land is an Island[] of broken lands] That which we doe call the *Newfound land*, and the Frenchmen *Bacalaos*, is an Iland, or rather (after the opinion of some) it consisteth of sundry Ilands and broken lands, situate[d] in the North regions of *America*, upon the gulfe and entrance of a great river called *S. Laurence* in *Canada*. Into the which, navigation may be made both on the South and North side of this Iland. The land lyeth South and North, containing in length betweene three & 400 miles, accounting from cape *Race* (which is in 46 degrees 25 minuts) unto the *Grand bay* in 52 degrees of Septentrionall latitude. The Iland round about hath very many goodly bayse and harbors, safe roads for ships, the like not to be found in any part of the knowen world. [Goodly roads and harbours.] . . .

We could not observe the hundreth part of creatures in those unhabited lands: but these mentioned may induce us to glorifie the magnificent God, who hath super abundantly replenished the earth with creatures serving for the use of man, though man hath not used the fift[h] part of the same, which the more doth aggravate the fault and foolish slouth in many of our nation, chusing rather to live indirectly, and very miserably to live & die within this realme pestered with inhabitants, then to adventure as becommeth men, to obtaine an habitation in those remote lands, in which Nature very prodigally doth minister unto mens endevours, and for art to worke upon. [Newfound land doth minister commodities abundantly for art & industrie.]

For besides these alreadie recounted and infinite moe, the mountaines generally make shew of minerall substance: Iron very common, lead, and somewhere copper. I will not averre of richer metals: albeit by the circumstances following, more then hope may be conceived thereof. . . .

The maner how our Admirall was lost.

[A]mongst very many difficulties, discontentments, mutinies, conspiracies, sicknesses, mortalitie, spoylings, and wracks by sea, which were afflictions, more then in so small a fleete, or so short a time may be supposed, albeit true in every particularitie, as partly by the former relation may be collected, and some I suppressed with silence for their sakes living, it pleased God to support this company, (of which onley one man died of a maladie inveterate, and long infested: the rest kept together in reasonable contentment and concord, beginning, continuing, and ending the voyage, which none els did accomplish, either not pleased with the action, or impatient of wants, or prevented by death[)].

Thus have I delivered the contents of the enterprise and last action of Sir *Humfrey Gilbert* knight, faithfully, for so much as I thought meete to be published: wherein may alwaies appeare,[Constancie in sir Humphrey Gilbert.] (though he be extinguished) some sparkes of his vertues, be remaining firme and resolute in a purpose by all pretence honest and godly, as was this, to discover, possesse, and to reduce unto the service of God, and Christian pietie, those remote and heathen Countreys of *America*, not actually possessed by Christians, and most rightly appertaining unto the Crowne of *England*[.]

5 From **The King James Bible (1611)**

The Bible is a collection of a national literature, represented by genres ranging from legal documents to poetry and prophecy. It serves as a model for the nation in terms of the unity of people, language, religion, territory, and government. Without it and its Christian interpretation and implementation, "nations and nationalism, as we know them, could never have existed."[32] The printing of the Bible generated a shared language used by English Protestants in the formation of their religion, culture, theories of literary expression, politics, foreign policy, and conception of nationhood. In a significant contribution to the discursive production of the nation, King James authorized a translation of the Bible in the vernacular based on former English translations. Richard Hakluyt and John Winthrop, for instance, feature Genesis and Deuteronomy respectively to justify dominion over creation and the English possession of the New World. Winthrop cites Deut. 30 in his 1630 *Modell of Christian Charity* to convey the transfer of Old Israel's chosen status and entitlement to the promised land of the English colonists.

THE HOLY BIBLE, Conteyning the Old Testament, and the New: Newly Translated out of the Originall tongues: & with the former Translations diligently compared and revised, by his Majesties speciall Co[m]mandement. Appointed to be read in Churches (London, 1611).

TO THE MOST HIGH AND MIGHTIE PRINCE, JAMES by the grace of God King of Great Britaine, France and Ireland, Defender of the Faith, &c.[33]

THE TRANSLATORS OF THE BIBLE, wish Grace, Mercie, and Peace, through JESUS CHRIST our LORD.

Great and manifold were the blessings (most dread Soveraigne) which Almighty GOD, the Father of all Mercies, bestowed upon us the people of ENGLAND, when first he sent your Majesties Royall person to rule and raigne over us. For whereas it was the expectation of many, who wished not well unto our SION, that upon the setting of that bright *Occidentall Starre* Queene ELIZABETH of most happy memory, some thicke and palpable cloudes of darkenesse would so have overshadowed this land, that men should have bene in doubt which way they were to walke, and that it should hardly be knowen,

32 A. Hastings, *The Construction of Nationhood: Ethnicity, Religion and Nationalism*, Cambridge: Cambridge University Press, 1997, 1999, p. 4.

33 In this edition, original spelling, punctuation, and capitalization are preserved, but u/v, long s, and i/j are regularized, and superscripted letters are silently lowered and abbreviations expanded. Original annotations are reproduced here in upper case letters and located at the end of verses rather than in the margins where they appeared in the 1611 edition.

who was to direct the unsetled State: the appearance of your MAJESTIE, as of the *Sunne* in his strength, instantly dispelled those supposed and surmised mists, and gave unto all that were well affected, exceeding cause of comfort; especially when we beheld the government established in your HIGHNESSE, and your hopefull Seed, by an undoubted Title, and this also accompanied with Peace and tranquillitie, at home and abroad.

But among all our Joyes, there was no one that more filled our hearts, then the blessed continuance of the Preaching of GODS sacred word amongst us, which is that inestimable treasure, which excelleth all the riches of the earth, because the fruit thereof extendeth itselfe, not onely to the time spent in this transitory world, but directeth and disposeth men unto that Eternall happinesse which is above in Heaven. . . .

There are infinite arguments of this right Christian and Religious affection in your MAJESTIE: but none is more forcible to declare it to others, then the vehement and perpetuated desire of the accomplishing and publishing of this Worke, which now with all humilitie we present unto your MAJESTIE. For when Your Highnesse had once out of deepe judgment apprehended, how convenient it was, That out of the Originall sacred tongues, together with comparing of the labours, both in our owne and other forreigne Languages, of many worthy men who went before us, there should be one more exact Translation of the holy Scriptures into the *English tongue*; your MAJESTIE did never desist, to urge and to excite those to whom it was commended, that the worke might be hastened, and that the businesse might be expedited in so decent a manner, as a matter of such importance might justly require.

And now at last, by the Mercy of GOD, and the continuance of our Labours, it being brought unto such a conclusion, as that we have great hope that the Church of *England* shall reape good fruit thereby; we hold it our duety to offer it to your MAJESTIE, not onely as to our King and Soveraigne, but as to the principall moover and Author of the Worke. Humbly craving of your most Sacred Majestie, that since things of this quality have ever bene subject to the censures of ill meaning and discontented persons, it may receive approbation and Patronage from so learned and judicious a Prince as your Highnesse is, whose allowance and acceptance of our Labours, shall more honour and incourage us, then all the calumniations and hard interpretations of other men shall dismay us. So that, if on the one side we shall be traduced by Popish persons at home or abroad, who therefore will maligne us, because we are poore Instruments to make GODS holy Trueth to be yet more and more knowen unto the people, whom they desire still to keepe in ignorance and darknesse: or if on the other side, we shall be maligned by selfe-conceited brethren, who runne their owne wayes, and give liking unto nothing but what is framed by themselves, and hammered on their Anvile; we may rest secure, supported within by the trueth and innocencie of a good conscience, having walked the wayes of simplicitie and integritie, as before the Lord; And sustained without, by the powerfull Protection of your Majesties grace and favour, which will ever give countenance to honest and Christian endevours, against bitter censures, and uncharitable imputations. . . .

The First Booke of Moses, Called GENESIS.

Chap. I

1 The creation of Heaven and Earth, 3 of the light, 6 of the firmament, 9 of the earth separated from the waters, 11 and made fruitfull, 14 of the Sunne, Moone, and Starres, 20 of fish and fowle, 24 of beasts and catell, 26 of Man in the Image of God. 29 Also the appointment of food.

1 In* the beginning God created the Heaven, and the Earth. *[Chap. I. Psal. 33.6. AND 136.5. ACTS. 14.15. AND 17.24. HEBR. 11.3.]
2 And the earth was without forme, and voyd, and darkenesse was upon the face of the deepe: and the Spirit of God mooved upon the face of the waters.
3 And God said, *Let there be light: and there was light. *[2. COR. 4.6.]
4 And God saw the light, that it was good: and God divided *the light from the darkenesse. *[HEBR. BETWEENE THE LIGHT AND BETWEENE THE DARKNESSE.]
5 And God called the light, Day, and the darkenesse he called Night: *and the evening and the morning were the first day. *[HEBR. AND THE EVENING WAS, AND THE MORNING WAS & C.]
6 And God said, *Let there be a +firmament in the midst of the waters: and let it divide the waters from the waters. *[PSAL. 136.5. JER. 10.12 AND 51.15.] +[HEBR. EXPANSION.]
7 And God made the firmament; and divided the waters, which were under the firmament, from the waters, which were above the firmament: and it was so.
8 And God called the *firmament, Heaven: and the evening and the morning were the second day. *[JER. 51.15.]
9 And God said, *Let the waters under the heaven be gathered together unto one place, and let the dry land appeare: and it was so. *[PSAL. 33.7. AND 136.5. JOB. 38.8.]
10 And God called the drie land, Earth, and the gathering together of the waters called hee, Seas: and God saw that it was good.
11 And God said, Let the Earth bring foorth *grasse, the herbe yeelding seed, and the fruit tree, yeelding fruit after his kinde, whose seed is in it selfe, upon the earth: and it was so. *[HEB. TENDER GRASSE.]
12 And the earth brought foorth grasse, and herbe yeelding seed after his kinde, and the tree yeelding fruit, whose seed was in it selfe, after his kinde: and God saw that it was good.

13 And the evening and the morning were the third day.
14 And God said, Let there bee *lights in the firmament of the heaven, to
divide +the day from the night: and let them be for signes and for seasons,
and for dayes and yeeres. *[DEU. 4.19. PSAL. 136.7.] +[HEBR. BETWEENE THE
DAY AND BETWEENE THE NIGHT.]
15 And let them be for lights in the firmament of the heaven, to give light
upon the earth: and it was so.
16 And God made two great lights: the greater light *to rule the day, and the
lesser light to rule the night: he made the starres also. *[HEBR. FOR THE RULE
OF THE DAY, &C.]
17 And God set them in the firmament of the heaven, to give light upon the
earth:
18 And to *rule over the day, and over the night, and to divide the light from
the darkenesse: and God saw that it was good. *[JER. 31.35.]
19 And the evening and the morning were the fourth day.
20 And God said, *Let the waters bring foorth aboundantly the +moving
creature that hath ++life, and foule that may flie above the earth in the #open
firmament of heaven. *[4. ESDR. 6.] +[OR, CREEPING.] ++[HEB. SOULE.]
#[HEB. FACE OF THE FIRMAMENT OF HEAVEN.]
21 And God created great whales, and every living creature that moveth,
which the waters brought forth aboundantly after their kinde, and every
winged foule after his kinde: and God saw that it was good.
22 And God blessed them, saying, *Be fruitfull, and multiply, and fill the
waters in the Seas, and let foule multiply in the earth. *[CHAP. 8.17. AND
9.1.]
23 And the evening and the morning were the fift day.
24 And God said, Let the earth bring forth the living creature after his
kinde, cattell, and creeping thing, and beast of the earth after his kinde: and
it was so.
25 And God made the beast of the earth after his kinde, and cattell after
their kinde, and every thing that creepeth upon the earth, after his kinde:
and God saw that it was good.
26 And God said, *Let us make man in our Image, after our likenesse: and
let them have dominion over the fish of the sea, and over the foule of the
aire, and over the cattell, and over all the earth, and over every creeping thing
that creepeth upon the earth. *[CHAP. 5.1. AND 9.6. 1. CORIN. 11.7. EPHES.
4.14. COL. 3.10.]
27 So God created man in his owne Image, in the Image of God created hee
him; *male and female created hee them. *[MATTH. 19. 4. WISD. 2.23.]
28 And God blessed them, and God said unto them, *Be fruitfull, and mul-
tiply, and replenish the earth, and subdue it, and have dominion over the
fish of the sea, and over the foule of the aire, and over every living thing that
+mooveth upon the earth. *[CHAP. 9.1.] +[HEB. CREEPETH.]
29 And God said, Behold, I have given you every herbe *bearing seede,

which is upon the face of all the earth, and every tree, in the which is the fruit of a tree yeelding seed, +to you it shall be for meat: *[HEBR. SEEDING SEED.] +[CHAP. 9.3.]

30 And to every beast of the earth, and to every foule of the aire, and to every thing that creepeth upon the earth, wherein there is *life, I have given every greene herbe for meat: and it was so. *[HEBR. A LIVING SOULE.]

31 And *God saw every thing that hee had made: and behold, it was very good. And the evening and the morning were the sixth day. *[CHAP. II. ECCLUS. 39.16.]

Chap. II

1 The first Sabbath. 4 The maner of the creation. 8 The planting of the garden of Eden, 10 and the river thereof. 17 The tree of knowledge onely forbidden. 19. 20 The naming of the creatures. 21 The making of woman, and institution of Mariage.

1 Thus the heavens and the earth were finished, and all the hoste of them.

2 *And on the seventh day God ended his worke, which hee had made: And he rested on the seventh day from all his worke, which he had made. *[EXOD. 20.11. AND 31.17. DEUT. 5.14. HEBR. 4.4.]

3 And God blessed the seventh day, and sanctified it: because that in it he had rested from all his worke, which God *created and made. *[HEB. CREATED TO MAKE.]

4 These are the generations of the heavens, & of the earth, when they were created; in the day that the LORD God made the earth, and the heavens,

5 And every plant of the field, before it was in the earth, and every herbe of the field, before it grew: for the LORD God had not caused it to raine upon the earth, and there was not a man to till the ground.

6 *But there went up a mist from the earth, and watered the whole face of the ground. *[OR, A MIST WHICH WENT UP FROM &C.]

7 And the LORD God formed man* +of the dust of the ground, & breathed into his nostrils the breath of life; and ++man became a living soule. *[HEB. DUST OF THE GROUND.] +[I. COR. 15.47.] ++[I. CORIN. 15.45.]

8 And the LORD God planted a garden Eastward in Eden; and there he put the man whom he had formed.

9 And out of the ground made the LORD God to grow every tree that is pleasant to the sight, and good for food: the tree of life also in the midst of the garden, and the tree of knowledge of good and evill.

10 And a river went out of Eden to water the garden, and from thence it was parted, and became into foure heads.

11 The name of the first is *Pison: that is it which compasseth the whole land of Havilah, where there is gold. *[ECCLUS. 24.29.]

12 And the gold of that land is good: There is Bdellium and the Onix stone.

13 And the name of the second river is Gihon: the same is it that compasseth the whole land of Ethiopia. *[Heb. Cush.]

14 And the name of the third river is Hiddekel: that is it which goeth *toward the East of Assyria: and the fourth river is Euphrates. *[Or, Eastward to Assyria.]

15 And the LORD God tooke *the man, and put him into the garden of Eden, to dresse it, and to keepe it. *[Or, Adam.]

16 And the LORD God commanded the man, saying, Of every tree of the garden thou mayest *freely eate. *[Hebr. eating thou shalt eate.]

17 But of the tree of the knowledge of good and evill, thou shalt not eate of it: for in the day that thou eatest thereof, thou shalt *surely die. *[Hebr. dying thou shalt die.]

18 And the LORD God said, It is not good that the man should be alone: I will make him *an helpe +meet for him. *[Ecclus. 17.5.] +[Hebr. as before him.]

19 And out of the ground the LORD God formed every beast of the field, and every foule of the aire, and brought them unto *Adam, to see what he would call them: and whatsoever Adam called every living creature, that was the name thereof. *[Or, the man.]

20 And Adam *gave names to all cattell, and to the foule of the aire, and to every beast of the fielde: but for Adam there was not found an helpe meete for him. *[Hebr. called.]

21 And the LORD God caused a deepe sleepe to fall upon Adam, and hee slept; and he tooke one of his ribs, and closed up the flesh instead thereof.

22 And the rib which the LORD God had taken from man, *made hee a woman, & brought her unto the man. *[Hebr. builded.]

23 And Adam said, This is now bone of my bones, and flesh of my flesh: she shalbe called woman, because shee was *taken out of man. *[1. Corin. 11.8.]

24 *Therefore shall a man leave his father and his mother, and shall cleave unto his wife: and they shalbe one flesh. *[Matt. 19.5 mar. 10.7. 1. corin. 6.16. ephe. 5.31.]

25 And they were both naked, the man and his wife, & were not ashamed.

Chap. III.

1 The serpent deceiveth Eve. 6 Mans shamefull fall. 9 God arraigneth
them. 14 The serpent is cursed. 15 The promised Seed. 16 The punishment
of Mankind. 21 Their first clothing. 22 Their casting out of Paradise.

1 Now the serpent was more subtill then any beast of the field, which the LORD God had made, and he said unto the woman, *Yea, hath God said, Ye shall not eat of every tree of the garden? *[Chap. III Heb. Yea, because, &c.]

2 And the woman said unto the serpent, Wee may eate of the fruite of the trees of the garden:

3 But of the fruit of the tree, which is in the midst of the garden, God hath
said, Ye shal not eate of it, neither shall ye touch it, lest ye die.
4 And the Serpent said unto the woman, Ye shall not *surely die. *[2. Cor.
11.3. 1. Tim. 2.14.]
5 For God doeth know, that in the day ye eat thereof, then your eyes shalbee
opened: and yee shall bee as Gods, knowing good and evill.
6 And when the woman saw, that the tree was good for food, and that it was
*pleasant to the eyes, and a tree to be desired to make one wise, she tooke
of the fruit thereof, +and did eate, and gave also unto her husband with her,
and hee did eate. *[Heb. a desire.] +[Ecclus. 25.26. 1. Tim. 2.14.]
7 And the eyes of them both were opened, & they knew that they were
naked, and they sewed figge leaves together, and made themselves *aprons.
*[Or, things to gird about.]
8 And they heard the voyce of the LORD God, walking in the garden in the
*coole of the day: and Adam and his wife hid themselves from the presence
of the LORD God, amongst the trees of the garden. *[Heb. wind.]
9 And the LORD God called unto Adam, and said unto him, Where art
thou?
10 And he said, I heard thy voice in the garden: and I was afraid, because I
was naked, and I hid myselfe.
11 And he said, Who told thee, that thou wast naked? Hast thou eaten of the
tree, whereof I commanded thee, that thou shouldest not eate?
12 And the man said, The woman whom thou gavest to be with mee, shee
gave me of the tree, and I did eate.
13 And the LORD God said unto the woman, What is this that thou hast
done? And the woman said, The Serpent beguiled me, and I did eate.
14 And the LORD God said unto the Serpent, Because thou hast done this,
thou art cursed above all cattel, and above every beast of the field: upon thy
belly shalt thou goe, and dust shalt thou eate, all the dayes of thy life.
15 And I will put enmitie betweene thee and the woman, and betweene thy
seed and her seed: it shal bruise thy head, and thou shalt bruise his heele.
16 Unto the woman he said, I will greatly multiply thy sorowe and thy con-
ception. In sorow thou shalt bring forth children: and thy desire shall be
*to thy husband, and hee shall +rule over thee. *[Or, subject to thy hus-
band.] +[1. Corin. 14.34.]
17 And unto Adam he said, Because thou hast hearkened unto the voyce
of thy wife, and hast eaten of the tree, of which I commanded thee, saying,
Thou shalt not eate of it: cursed is the ground for thy sake: in sorow shalt
thou eate of it all the dayes of thy life.
18 Thornes also and thistles shall it *bring forth to thee: and thou shalt eate
the herbe of the field. *[Heb. cause to bud.]
19 In the sweate of thy face shalt thou eate bread, till thou returne unto the
ground: for out of it wast thou taken, for dust thou art, and unto dust shalt
thou returne.

20 And Adam called his wives name *Eve, because she was the mother of all
living. *[Heb. Chauah.]
21 Unto Adam also, and to his wife, did the LORD God make coates of
skinnes, and cloathed them.
22 And the LORD God said, Behold, the man is become as one of us, to
know good & evill. And now lest hee put foorth his hand, and take also of
the tree of life, and eate and live for ever:
23 Therefore the LORD God sent him foorth from the garden of Eden, to
till the ground, from whence he was taken.
24 So he drove out the man: and he placed at the East of the garden of
Eden, Cherubims, and a flaming sword, which turned every way, to keepe
the way of the tree of life. . . .

Deuteronomie Chap. XXX

1 Great mercies promised unto the repentant. 11 The Commaundement is
manifest. 15 Death and life are set before them.

1 And it shall come to passe when all these things are come upon thee, the
blessing, and the curse, which I have set before thee, and thou shalt call them
to minde among all the nations whither the LORD thy God hath driven thee,
2 And shalt returne unto the LORD thy God, and shalt obey his voyce
according to all that I command thee this day, thou and thy children with al
thine heart, and with all thy soule:
3 That then the LORD thy God will turne thy captivitie, and have compas-
sion upon thee, and wil returne and gather thee from all the nations whither
the LORD thy God hath scattered thee.
4 *If any of thine be driven out unto the outmost parts of heaven, from
thence will the LORD thy God gather thee, and from thence will he fetch
thee. *[Nehe. 1.9.]
5 And the LORD thy God will bring thee into the land which thy fathers
possessed, and thou shalt possesse it: and he will doe thee good, and multiply
thee above thy fathers.
6 And the LORD thy God will circumcise thine heart, and the heart of thy
seed, to love the LORD thy God with all thine heart, and with all thy soule,
that thou mayest live.
7 And the LORD thy God will put all these curses upon thine enemies, and
on them that hate thee, which persecuted thee.
8 And thou shalt returne and obey the voice of the LORD, and doe all his
Commandements which I command thee this day.
9 *And the LORD thy God will make thee plenteous in every worke of thine
hand, in the fruit of thy body, and in the fruit of thy cattell, and in the fruit
of thy land, for good: for the LORD will againe rejoyce over thee for good,
as he rejoyced over thy fathers: *[Chap. 28.11.]

10 If thou shalt hearken unto the voyce of the LORD thy God to keepe his
Commandements, and his Statutes which are written in this booke of the
Law, and if thou turne unto the LORD thy God with all thine heart, and
with all thy soule.
11 For this Commaundement which I command thee this day, it is not
hidden from thee, neither is it farre off.
12 *It is not in heaven, that thou shouldest say, Who shal goe up for us to
heaven, and bring it unto us, that wee may heare it, and doe it? [ROM. 10.6.
&C.]
13 Neither is it beyond the sea, that thou shouldest say, Who shall goe over
the sea for us, and bring it unto us, that we may heare it, and doe it?
14 But the word is very nigh unto thee, in thy mouth, and in thy heart, that
thou mayest doe it.
15 See, I have set before thee this day, life and good, and death and evill:
16 In that I command thee this day to love the LORD thy God, to walke
in his wayes, and to keepe his Commandements, and his Statutes, and his
Judgements, that thou maiest live and multiply: and the LORD thy God
shall blesse thee in the land, whither thou goest to possesse it.
17 But if thine heart turne away, so that thou wilt not heare, but shalt bee
drawen away, and worship other gods and serve them:
18 I denounce unto you this day, that ye shall surely perish, and that yee
shall not prolong your dayes upon the land, whither thou passest over
Jordan, to goe to possesse it.
19 *I call heaven and earth to record this day against you, that I have set
before you life and death, blessing and cursing: therefore choose life, that
both thou and thy seed may live: *[CHAP. 4.36]
20 That thou maiest love the LORD thy God, and that thou mayest obey
his voyce, and that thou mayest cleave unto him: for he is thy life, and the
length of thy dayes, that thou mayest dwell in the land, which the LORD
sware unto thy fathers, to Abraham, to Isaac, and to Jacob, to give them.

6 John Lilburne, William Walwyn, Thomas Prince, Richard Overton, *An Agreement of the Free People of England* (1649)

The Levellers were among the dissenters whose history is limited to the Civil War and Interregnum eras of the mid-seventeenth century, their name having been coined by King Charles I after the Putney debates in 1647.[34] Visions of alternative

34 I. Gentles, "The *Agreements of the People* and their Political Contexts, 1647–1649," in M. Mendle (ed.), *The Putney Debates of 1647: The Army, The Levellers, and the English State*, Cambridge: Cambridge University Press, 2001, p. 152.

social and political structures and a fervent belief in universal grace and human rights underwrote their defence of the nation as the hallmark of civil and religious liberties. The collaborative undertaking that constituted the third *Agreement*, titled *An Agreement of the Free People* (May 1, 1649), presented the final version of the constitutional document whose authors, including John Lilburne, were prisoners at this time. Composed of thirty articles, *An Agreement* revealed the Levellers' confidence in popular representation. In turn they demanded annual parliaments and insisted that military power be made accountable to civil authority and that arbitrary power be curtailed. Pamphlets and newspapers of the day frequently cited the *Agreement*, which was printed in 20,000 copies. Its intentions were peaceful as the subtitle suggests, but the explosive historical events that coincided with its appearance, and that greatly influenced its initial reception and afterlife, rewrote the document.

John Lilburne, William Walwyn, Thomas Prince, Richard Overton, *An Agreement of the Free People of England. Tendered as a Peace Offering to this Distressed Nation* (London, 1649).

AN AGREEMENT of the Free People of England. Tendered as a Peace-Offering to this distressed Nation. By Lieutenant Colonel John Lilburne, Master William Walwyn, Master Thomas Prince, and Master Richard Overton, Prisoners in the Tower of London, May the I. 1649.

> Matth. 5. verse 9. Blessed are the Peace-makers for they shall be called the children of God.

A Preparative to all sorts of people.

If afflictions make men wise, and wisdom direct to happinesse, then certainly this Nation is not far from such a degree thereof, as may compare if not far exeed, any part of the world: having for some yeares by-past, drunk deep of the Cup of misery and sorrow. We blesse God our consciences are cleer from adding affliction to affliction, having ever laboured from the beginning, of our publick distractions, to compose and reconcile them: & should esteem it the Crown of all our temporal felicity that yet we might be instrumentall in procuring the peace and prosperity of this Common-wealth the land of our Nativity.

And therefore according to our promise in our late *Manifestation* of the 14 of *Aprill* 1649. (being perswaded of the necessitie and justnesse thereof) as a *Peace-Offering* to the Free people of this Nation, we tender this ensuing Agreement, not knowing any more effectuall means to put a finall period to all our feares and troubles.

It is a way of settlement, though at first much startled at by some in high authority; yet according to the nature of truth, it hath made its own way into the understanding, and taken root in most mens hearts and affections, so that we have reall ground to hope (what ever shall become of us) that our earnest desires and indeavours for good to the people will not altogether be null and frustrate.

The life of all things is in the right use and application, which is not our worke only, but every mans conscience must look to it selfe, and not dreame out more seasons and opportunities. And this we trust will satisfie all ingenuous people that we are not such wilde, irrationall, dangerous Creatures as we have been aspersed to be; This agreement being the ultimate end and full scope of all our desires and intentions concerning the Government of this Nation, and wherein we shall absolutely rest satisfied and acquiesce; nor did we ever give just cause for any to beleeve worse of us by any thing either said or done by us, and which would not in the least be doubted, but that men consider not the interest of those that have so unchristian-like made bold with our good names; but we must bear with men of such interests as are opposite to any part of this Agreement, when neither our Saviour nor his Apostles innocency could stop such mens mouthes whose interests their doctrines and practises did extirpate: And therefore if friends at least would but consider what interest men relate to, whilst they are telling or whispering their aspersions against us, they would find the reason and save us a great deale of labour in clearing our selves, it being a remarkable signe of an ill cause when aspersions supply the place of Arguments.

We blesse God that he hath given us time and hearts to bring it to this issue, what further he hath for us to do is yet only knowne to his wisedom, to whose will and pleasure we shall willingly submit; we have if we look with the eyes of frailty, enemies like the sons of *Anak*, but if with the eyes of faith and confidence in a righteous God and a just cause, we see more with us then against us,

From our causelesse captivity in the Tower of *London*, May I. 1649.

John Lilburn, Thomas Prince, William Walwyn, Richard Overton.

The Agreement it selfe thus followeth.

After the long and tedious prosecution of a most unnaturall cruell, homebred war, occasioned by divisions and distempers amongst our selves, and those distempers arising from the uncertaintie of our Government, and the exercise of unlimited or Arbitrary power, by such as have been trusted with Supreme and subordinate Authority, whereby multitudes of grevances and intolerable oppressions have been brought upon us.[35] And finding after eight yeares experience and expectation all indeavours hitherto used, or remedies hitherto applyed, to have encreased rather then diminished our distractions,

35 Civil Wars 1642–1646, 1648, followed by a military expulsion of royalist and Presbyterian members (Pride's Purge) and the establishment of the Rump or "Purged Parliament," which declared itself "the supreme power in this nation" on January 4, 1649, with powers to pass parliamentary legislation.

and that if not speedily prevented our falling againe into factions and divisions, will not only deprive us of the benefit of all those wonderful Victories God hath vouchsafed against such as sought our bondage, but expose us first to poverty and misery, and then to be destroyed by forraigne enemies.

And being earnestly desirous to make a right use of that opportunity God hath given us to make this Nation Free and Happy, to reconcile our differences, and beget a perfect amitie and friendship once more amongst us, that we may stand clear in our consciences before Almighty God, as unbyassed by any corrupt Interest or particular advantages, and manifest to all the world that our indeavours have not proceeded from malice to the persons of any, or enmity against opinions; but in reference to the peace and prosperity of the Common-wealth, and for prevention of like distractions, and removall of all grievances; We the free People of *England*, to whom God hath given hearts, means and opportunity to effect the same, do with submission to his wisdom, in his name, and desiring the equity thereof may be to his praise and glory; Agree to ascertain our Government, to abolish all arbitrary Power, and to set bounds and limits both to our Supreme, and all Subordinate Authority, and remove all known Grievances.

And accordingly do declare and publish to all the World,
that we are agreed as followeth,

I. That the Supreme Authority of *England* and the Territories therewith incorporate, shall be and reside henceforward in a Representative of the People consisting of four hundred persons, but no more; in the choice of whom (according to naturall right) all men of the age of one and twenty yeers and upwards (not being servants, or receiving alms, or having served the late King in Arms or voluntary Contributions) shall have their voices; and be capable of being elected to that Supreme Trust those who served the King being disabled for ten years onely. All things concerning the distribution of the said four hundred Members proportionable to the respective parts of the Nation, the severall places for Election, the manner of giving and taking of Voyces, with all Circumstances of like nature, tending to the compleating and equall proceedings in Elections, as also their Salary, is referred to be setled by this present Parliament, in such sort as the next Representative may be in a certain capacity to meet with safety at the time herein expressed: and such circumstances to be made more perfect by future Representatives.

II. That two hundred of the four hundred Members, and not lesse, shall be taken and esteemed for a competent Representative; and the major Voyces present shall be concluding to this Nation. The place of Session, and choice of a Speaker, with other circumstances of that nature, are referred to the care of this and future Representatives.

III. And to the end all publick Officers may be certainly accountable, and no Factions made to maintain corrupt Interests, no Officer of any salary Forces in Army or Garison, nor any Treasurer or Receiver of publick monies, shall (while such) be elected a Member for any Representative; and if any Lawyer shall at any time be chosen, he shall be uncapable of practice as a Lawyer, during the whole time of that Trust. And for the same reason, and that all persons may be capable of subjection as well as rule.

IIII. That no Member of the present Parliament shall be capable of being elected of the next Representative, nor any Member of any future Representative shall be capable of being chosen for the Representative immediately succeeding: but are free to be chosen, one Representative having intervened: Nor shall any Member of any Representative be made either Receiver, Treasurer, or other Officer during that imployment.

V. That for avoyding the many dangers and inconveniences apparantly arising from the long continuance of the same persons in Authority; We Agree, that this present Parliament shall end the first Wednesday in *August* next 1649, and thenceforth be of no power or Authority: and in the mean time shall order and direct the Election of a new and equall Representative, according to the true intent of this our Agreement: and so as the next Representative may meet and sit in power and Authority as an effectuall Representative upon the day following; namely, the first Thursday of the same *August*, 1649.

VI. We agree, if the present Parliament shall omit to order such Election or Meeting of a new Representative; or shall by any means be hindered from performance of that Trust:

That in such case, we shall for the next Representative proceed in electing thereof in those places, & according to that manner & number formerly accustomed in the choice of Knights and Burgesses; observing onely the exceptions of such persons from being Electors or Elected, as are mentioned before in the first, third and fourth Heads of this Agreement: It being most unreasonable that we should either be kept from new, frequent and successive Representatives, or that the supreme Authority should fall into the hands of such as have manifested disaffection to our common Freedom, and endeavoured the bondage of the Nation.

VII. And for pr[e]serving the supreme authority from falling into the hands of any whom the people have not, and shall not chuse,

We are resolved and agreed (God willing) that a *new Representative* shall be upon the first *Thursday* in *August* next aforesaid: the ordering and disposing of themselves, as to the choice of a speaker, and the like circumstances, is hereby left to their discretion: But are in the extent and exercise of Power, to follow the direction and rules of this agreement; and are hereby authorised and required according to their best judgements, to set rules for future equall distribution, and election of Members as is herein intended and enjoyned to be done, by the present Parliament.

VIII. And for the preservation of the supreme Authority (in all times) entirely in the hands of such persons only as shal be chosen thereunto—*we agree and declare*: That the next & al future Representatives, shall continue in full power for the space of one whole year: and that the people shall of course, chuse a Parliament once every year, so as all the members thereof may be in a capacity to meet, and take place of the foregoing Representative: the first *Thursday* in every *August* for ever if God so please; Also (for the same reason) that the next or any future Representative being met, shall continue their Session day by day without intermission for four monthes at the least; and after that shall be at Liberty to adj[ou]rn from two monthes to two months, as they shall see cause untill their yeer be expired, but shall sit no longer then a yeer upon pain of treason to every member that shall exceed that time: and in times of adj[o]urnment shall not erect a Councel of State but refer the managing of affairs in the intervals to a Committee of their own members giving such instructions, and publish them, as shall in no measure contradict this agreement.

IX. And that none henceforth may be ignorant or doubtfull concerning the power of the Supreme authority, and of the affairs, about which the same is to be conversant and exercised: we agree and declare, that the power of Representatives shall extend without the consent or concurrence of any other person or persons,

1 To the conservation of Peace and commerce with forrain Nations.
2 To the preservation of those safe guards, and securities of our lives, limbes, liberties, properties, and estates, contained in the Petition of Right, made and enacted in the third year of the late King.[36]
3 To the raising of moneys, and generally to all things as shall be evidently conducing to those ends, or to the enlargement of our freedom, redress of grievances, and prosperity of the Common-wealth.

For security whereof, having by wofull experience found the prevalence of corrupt interests powerfully inclining most men once entrusted with authority, to pervert the same to their own domination, and to the prejudice of our Peace and Liberties, we therefore further agree and declare.

36 The twice-mentioned "Petition of Right" in the *Agreement* refers to the 1628 *Petition exhibited to His Majesty by the Lords Spiritual and Temporal, and Commons in this present Parliament assembled, concerning divers Rights and Liberties of the Subjects*.

X. That we do not inpower or entrust our said representatives to continue in force, or to make any Lawes, Oaths, or Covenants, whereby to compell by penalties or otherwise any person to any thing in or about matters of faith, Religion or Gods worship or to restrain any person from the profession of his faith, or exercise of Religion according to his Conscience, nothing having caused more distractions, and heart burnings in all ages, then persecution and molestation for matters of Conscience in and about Religion:

XI. We doe not impower them to impresse or constraint any person to serve in war by Sea or Land every mans Conscience being to be satisfied in the justness of that cause wherein he hazards his own life, or may destroy an others.

And for the quieting of all differences, and abolishing of all enmity and rancour, as much as is now possible for us to effect.

XII. We agree, That after the end of this present Parliament, no person shall be questioned for any thing said or done in reference to the late Warres, or publique differences; otherwise then in persuance of the determinations of the present Parliament, against such as have adhered to the King against the Liberties of the people: And saving that Accomptants for publick moneys received, shall remain accomptable for the same.

XIII. That all priviledges or exemptions of any persons from the Lawes, or from the ordinary course of Legall proceedings, by vertue of any Tenure, Grant, Charter, Patent, Degree, or Birth, or of any place of residence, or refuge, or priviledge of Parliament, shall be henceforth void and null; and the like not to be made nor revived again.

XIIII. We doe not impower them to give judgment upon any ones person or estate, where no Law hath been before provided, nor to give power to any other Court or Jurisdiction so to do, Because where there is no Law, there is no transgression, for men or Magistrates to take Cognisance of; neither doe we impower them to intermeddle with the execution of any Law whatsoever.

XV. And that we may remove all long setled Grievances, and thereby as farre as we are able, take away all cause of complaints, and no longer depend upon the uncertain inclination of Parliaments to remove them, nor trouble our selves or them with Petitions after Petitions, as hath been accustomed, without fruit or benefit; and knowing no cause why any should repine at our removall of them, except such as make advantage by their continuance, or are related to some corrupt Interests, which we are not to regard.

We agree and Declare,

XVI. That it shall not be in the power of any Representative, to punish, or cause to be punished, any person or persons for refusing to answer questions against themselves in Criminall cases.

XVII. That it shall not be in their power, after the end of the next Representative, to continue or constitute any proceedings in Law that shall be longer then Six months in the final determination of any cause past all Appeal, nor to continue the Laws or proceedings therein in any other Language then English, nor to hinder any person or persons from pleading their own Causes, or of making use of whom they please to plead for them.

The reducing of these and other the like provisions of this nature on this Agreement provided, and which could not now in all particulars be perfected by us, is intended by us to be the proper works of faithful Representatives.

XVIII. That it shall not be in their power to continue or make any Laws to abridge or hinder any person or persons, from trading or merchandizing into any place beyond the Seas, where any of this Nation are free to Trade.[37]

XIX. That it shall not be in their power to continue Excise or Customes upon any sort of Food, or any other Goods, Wares, or Commodities, longer then four months after the beginning of the next Representative, being both of them extreme burthensome and oppressive to Trade, and so expensive in the Receipt, as the moneys expended therein (if collected as Subsidies have been) would extend very far towards defraying the publick Charges; and forasmuch as all Moneys to be raised are drawn from the People; such burthensome and chargeable wayes, shall never more be revived, nor shall they raise Moneys by any other ways (after the aforesaid time) but only by an equal rate in the pound upon every reall and personall estate in the Nation.

XX. That it shall not be in their power to make or continue any Law, whereby mens reall or personall estates, or any part thereof, shall be exempted from payment of their debts; or to imprison any person for debt of any nature, it being both unchristian in itself, and no advantage to the Creditors, and both a reproach and prejudice to the Common-wealth.

XXI. That it shall not be in their power to continue any Law, for taking away any mans life, except for murther, or other the like hainous offences

37 Article 18, opposing interference with foreign trade; Article 20, protesting imprisonment for debt; Article 21 contesting capital punishment; and Article 26, defending the eligibility of people of any Christian religion, except Catholicism, for public office, are new additions to the 1649 *Agreement*; for editions of the three *Agreements*, see D. M. Wolfe (ed.), *Leveller Manifestoes of the Puritan Revolution*, New York: Humanities Press, 1967; see also Gentles on the relationship of the *Agreements*.

destructive to humane Society, or for endevouring by force to destroy this our Agreement, but shall use their uttermost endeavour to appoint punishments equall to offences: that so mens Lives, Limbs, Liberties, and estates, may not be liable to be taken away upon trivial or slight occasions as they have been; and shall have speciall care to preserve, all sorts of people from wickedness misery and beggery: nor shall the estate of any capitall offendor be confiscate but in cases of treason only; and in all other capitall offences recompense shall be made to the parties damnified, as well out of the estate of the Malifactor,[sic] as by loss of life, according to the conscience of his jury.

XXII. That it shall not be in their power to continue or make any Law, to deprive any person, in case of Tryals for Life, Limb, Liberty, or Estate, from the benefit of witnesses, on his, or their behalf; nor deprive any person of those priviledges, and liberties, contained in the *Petition of Right*, made in the third yeer of the late King *Charls*.

XXIII. That it shall not be in their power to continue the Grievance of Tithes, longer then to the end of the next Representative; in which time, they shall provide to give reasonable satisfaction to all Impropriators: neither shall they force by penalties or otherwise, any person to pay towards the maintenance of the Ministers, who out of conscience cannot submit thereunto.

XXIV. That it shall not be in their power to impose Ministers upon any the respective Parishes, but shall give free liberty to the parishioners of every particular parish, to chuse such as themselves shall approve; and upon such terms, and for such reward, as themselves shall be willing to contribute, or shall contract for. Provided, none be chusers but such as are capable of electing Representatives.

XXV. That it shal not be in their power, to continue or make a law, for any other way of Judgments, or Conviction of life, limb, liberty, or estate, but onely by twelve sworn men of the Neighbor-hood; to be chosen in some free way by the people; to be directed before the end of the next Representative, and not picked and imposed, as hitherto in many places they have been.

XXVI. They shall not disable any person from bearing any office in the Common-wealth, for any opinion or practice in Religion excepting such as maintain the Popes (or other forraign) Supremacy.

XXVII. That it shal not be in their power to impose any publike officer upon any Counties, Hundreds, Cities, Towns, or Borroughs; but the people capable by this Agreement to chuse Representatives, shall chuse all their publike Officers that are in any kinde to administer the Law for their respective places, for one whole yeer, and no longer, and so from yeer to yeer: and this as an especial means to avoyd Factions, and Parties.

And that no person may have just cause to complain, by reason of taking away the Excise and Customs, we agree,

XXVIII. That the next, and all future Representatives shall exactly keep the publike Faith, and give ful satisfaction, for all securities, debts, arrears or damages, (justly chargeable) out of the publike Treasury; and shall confirm and make good all just publike Purchases and Contracts that have been, or shall be made; save that the next Representative may confirm or make null in part or in whole, all gifts of Lands, Moneys, Offices, or otherwise made by the present Parliament, to any Member of the House of Commons, or to any of the Lords, or to any of the attendants of either of them.

And for as much as nothing threateneth greater danger to the Commonwealth, then that the Military power should by any means come to be superior to the Civil Authority,

XXIX. We declare and agree, That no Forces shal be raised, but by the Representatives, for the time being; and in raising thereof, that they exactly observe these Rules, namely, That they allot to each particular County, City, Town, and Borrugh, the raising, furnishing, agreeing, and paying of a due proportion, according to the whole number to be levyed; and shall to the Electors of Representatives in each respective place, give Free liberty, to nominate and appoint all Officers appertaining to Regiments, Troops, and Companies, and to remove them as they shall see cause, Reserving to the Representative, the nominating, and appointing onely of the General, and all General Officers; and the ordering, regulating, and commanding of them all, upon what service shall seem to them necessary for the Safety, Peace, and Freedom of the Commonwealth.

And in as much as we have found by sad experience, That generally men make little or nothing, to innovate in Government, to exceed their time and power in places of trust, to introduce an Arbitrary, and Tyrannical power, and to overturn all things into Anarchy and Confusion, where there are no penalties imposed for such destructive crimes and offences.

XXX. We therefore agree and declare, That it shall not be in the power of any Representative, in any wise, to render up, or give, or take away any part of this Agreement, nor level mens Estates, destroy Propriety, or make all things Common: And if any Representative shall endevor, as a Representative, to destroy this Agreement, every Member present in the House, not entering or immediately publishing his dissent, shall incur the pain due for High Treason, and proceeded against accordingly; and if any person or persons, shall by force endevor to contrive, the destruction thereof, each person so doing, shall likewise be dealt withal as in cases of Treason.

And if any person shal by force of Arms disturb Elections of Representatives, he shall incurr the penalty of a Riot; and if any person not capable of being an Elector, or Elected, shal intrude themselves amongst those that are, or any persons shall behave themselves rudely and disorderly, such persons shal be liable to a presentment by a grand Inquest and to an indictment upon misdemeanor; and be fined and otherwise punish'd according to the discretion and verdict of a Jury. And all Laws made, or that shall be made contrary to any part of this Agreement, are hereby made null and void.

Thus, as becometh a free People, thankfull unto God for this blessed opportunity, and desirous to make use thereof to his glory, in taking off every yoak, and removing every burthen, in delivering the captive, and setting the oppressed free; we have in all the particular Heads forementioned, done as we would be done unto, and as we trust in God will abolish all occasion of offence and discord, and produce the lasting Peace and Prosperity of this Common wealth: and accordingly do in the sincerity of our hearts and consciences, as in the presence of Almighty God, give cleer testimony of our absolute agreement to all and every part hereof by subscribing our hands thereunto. Dated the first day of *May*, in the Yeer of our Lord 1649.

John Lilburn.
William Walwyn.
Thomas Prince.
Richard Overton.
April 30, 1649.

Imprimatur. Gilbert Mabbot.
FINIS
London, Printed for *Gyles Calvert* at the black spread-Eagle
at the West end of PAULS

7 Anne Bradstreet, "A Dialogue between Old *England* and New, concerning their present troubles. Anno 1642" (1650)

Anne Bradstreet (1612?–1672), née Anne Dudley, was born in Lincolnshire, England, and emigrated to Massachusetts Bay in 1630. The first volume of verse by a New World resident, *The Tenth Muse* was published allegedly without her consent, as John Woodbridge, who took the manuscript to London, acknowledges in his prefatory epistle. Composed in heroic couplets, "A Dialogue between Old *England* and New" features an exchange between the old country and the proto-nation at the outbreak of the English civil wars. The dialogue exhibits their interrelationship through the translation of Old English troubles across the Atlantic where they plague a feminized New England. Lamenting the disease of its physical and moral constitution, maternal England delineates the contours of nationhood in terms of relations within Britain,[38] inter-European and church–state relations, a monarchical history, Protestantism, parallels with ancient Israel, and a hierarchal relationship to New England, which partakes of the punishment exacted on its progenitor while also prophesying national redemption.

Anne Bradstreet, "A Dialogue between Old *England* and New, concerning their present troubles. Anno 1642," *The Tenth Muse lately sprung up in America. Or severall poems, compiled with great variety of wit and learning, full of delight . . . By a Gentlewoman in those parts* (London, 1650), pp. 180–90.

A Dialogue between Old *England* and New, concerning their present troubles

New England.
Alas, deare Mother, fairest Queen, and best,
With honour, wealth, and peace, happy and blest,
What ayles thee hang thy head, and crosse thine armes?
And sit i' th dust, to sigh these sad alarms?
What deluge of new woes thus over-whelme
The glories of thy ever famous Realme?
What meanes this wailing tone, this mourning guise?
Ah, tell thy Daughter, she may simpathize.

Old England.
Art ignorant indeed, of these my woes?
Or must my forced tongue these griefs disclose?
And must my selfe dissect my tatter'd state,
Which 'mazed Christendome stands wondring at?
And thou a childe, a Limbe, and dost not feele
My weakned fainting body now to reele?
This phisick-purging-potion I have taken,
Will bring Consumption, or an Ague quaking,
Unlesse some Cordial thou fetch from high,
Which present help may ease this malady.
If I decease, dost think thou shalt survive?
Or by my wasting state, dost think to thrive?

38 See C. Ivic, "'Our British Land': Anne Bradstreet's Atlantic Perspective," in P. Schwyzer and D. Mealor (eds), *Archipelagic Identities: Literature and Identity in the Atlantic Archipelago, 1550–1800*, Aldershot: Ashgate, 2004, pp. 195–204.

Then weigh our case, if 't be not justly sad,
Let me lament alone, while thou art glad.

New England.
And thus, alas, your state you much deplore,
In generall terms, but will not say wherefore:
What Medicine shall I seek to cure this woe,
If th' wound's so dangerous I may not know?
But you perhaps would have me guesse it out,
What, hath some *Hengist*, like that *Saxon* stout,
By fraud, and force, usurp'd thy flowring crown,
And by tempestuous Wars thy fields trod down?
Or hath *Canutus*, that brave valiant Dane,
The regall, peacefull Scepter from thee tane?
Or is't a *Norman*, whose victorious hand
With *English* blood bedews thy conquered Land?[39]
Or is't intestine Wars that thus offend?
Doe *Maud*, and *Stephen* for the Crown contend?[40]
Do Barons rise, and side against their King?
And call in Forreign ayde, to help the thing?
Must *Edward* be depos'd, or is't the houre
That second *Richard* must be clapt i' th' Tower?
Or is it the fatall jarre againe begun,
That from the red, white pricking Roses sprung?
Must *Richmonds* ayd, the Nobles now implore,
To come, and break the tushes of the Boar?[41]
If none of these, deare Mother, what's your woe?
Pray, do not fear *Spaines* bragging Armado?[42]
Doth your Allye, faire *France*, conspire your wrack?

39 Key figures associated with the first 500 years of English history: Hengist the Saxon who established a Kentish dynasty after fighting the Celts (died c. 455); Canutus or Canute, Danish king of England, Denmark, and Norway (died 1035); William of Normandy who conquered England in the Battle of Hastings in 1066.

40 The contest over the throne by the daughter of Henry I, Maud, and Stephen, King of England (1135–1154), that led to civil war. In the speech that follows, Old England presents a historical overview to New England, and refers to Stephen and Maud as "*Alcies* son and *Henries* Daughter."

41 A further tumultuous period of the English nation, characterized by a succession of monarchs, among whom Edward II and Richard II were murdered; the Boar: King Richard III, whose emblem was a boar, ruled England from 1483 to 1485 when he was defeated by the Earl of Richmond, Henry VII, a Lancaster and the first king of the Tudor dynasty; marriage of Henry and Edward IV's daughter Elizabeth, a York, ended the War of the Roses, uniting the houses of Lancaster and York.

42 England under Elizabeth I defeated the Spanish Armada in 1588.

Or, doth the *Scots* play false behind your back?
Doth *Holland* quit you ill, for all your love?
Whence is this storme, from Earth, or Heaven above?
Is't drought, is't Famine, or is't Pestilence?
Dost feele the smart, or feare the consequence?
Your humble Childe intreats you, shew your grief,
Though Armes, nor Purse she hath, for your relief:
Such is her poverty, yet shall be found
A supplyant for your help, as she is bound.

Old England.
I must confesse, some of those Sores you name,
My beauteous Body at this present maime;
But forraigne Foe, nor fained friend I feare,
For they have work enough (thou knowst) elsewhere;
Nor is it *Alcies* Son and *Henries* Daughter,
Whose proud contention cause this slaughter;
Nor Nobles siding, to make *John* no King
French *Lewis* unjustly to the Crown to bring;[43]
No *Edward, Richard,* to lose rule, and life,
Nor no *Lancastrians,* to renew old strife;
No Crook-backt Tyrant, now usurps the Seat,
Whose tearing tusks did wound, and kill, and threat:
No Duke of *York,* nor Earle of *March,* to soyle
Their hands in Kindreds blood, whom they did foyle:
No need of *Teder* [Tudor], Roses to unite,
None knowes which is the Red, or which the White:
Spaines braving Fleet a second time is sunke,
France knowes, how of my fury she hath drunk;
By *Edward* third, and *Henry* fifth of fame,[44]
Her Lillies in mine Armes avouch the same.
My Sister *Scotland* hurts me now no more,
Though she hath bin injurious heretofore.
What *Holland* is, I am in some suspense,
But trust not much unto his Excellence;
For wants, sure some I feele, but more I feare,
And for the Pestilence, who knowes how neare?
Famine, and Plague, two sisters of the Sword,
Destruction to a Land doth soone afford;
They're for my punishments ordain'd on high,

43 In 1216 Louis VIII invaded England governed by King John (1199–1216).

44 Edward III succeeded Edward II to the throne in 1327; King Henry's 1415 victory at Agincourt, France was dramatized in Shakespeare's *Henry V*.

Unlesse thy teares prevent it speedily.
But yet, I answer not what you demand,
To shew the grievance of my troubled Land;
Before I tell the effect, ile shew the cause,
Which are my Sins, the breach of sacred Lawes;
Idolatry, supplanter of a Nation,
With foolish superstitious adoration;
Are lik'd, and countenanc'd by men of might,
The Gospel is trod down, and hath no right;
Church Offices are sold, and bought, for gaine,
That Pope, had hope, to find *Rome* here againe;
For Oathes, and Blasphemies did ever eare
From *Beelzebub* himself, such language heare?
What scorning of the Saints of the most high,
What injuries did daily on them lye;
What false reports, what nick-names did they take,
Not for their owne, but for their Masters sake;
And thou, poore soule, wast jeer'd among the rest,
Thy flying for the Truth I made a jeast;
For Sabbath-breaking, and for Drunkennesse,
Did ever Land profanennesse more expresse?
From crying bloods, yet cleansed am not I,
Martyrs, and others, dying causelesly:
How many Princely heads on blocks laid down,
For nought, but title to a fading Crown?
'Mongst all the cruelties which I have done,
Oh, *Edwards* Babes, and *Clarence* haplesse Son,
O *Jane*, why didst thou dye in flowring prime,
Because of Royall Stem, that was thy crime;
For Bribery, Adultery, for Thefts, and Lyes,
Where is the Nation, I cann't parallize;
With Usury, Extortion, and Oppression,
These be the *Hydra*'s of my stout transgression;
These be the bitter fountains, heads, and roots,
Whence flow'd the source, the sprigs, the boughs, and fruits;
Of more then thou canst heare, or I relate,
That with high hand I still did perpetrate;
For these, were threatned the wofu'l day,
I mock'd the Preachers, put it faire away;
The Sermons yet upon record doe stand,
That cry'd, destruction to my wicked Land:
These Prophets mouthes (alas the while) was stopt,
Unworthily, some backs whipt, and ears crept;
Their reverent cheeks, did beare the glorious markes

Of stinking, stigmatizing, Romish Clerkes;
Some lost their livings, some in prison pent,
Some grossely fin'd, from friends to exile went:
Their silent tongues to heaven did vengeance cry,
Who heard their cause, and wrongs judg'd righteously,
And will repay it sevenfold in my lap,
This is fore-runner of my after clap,
Nor took I warning by my neighbours falls,
I saw sad *Germanie's* dismantled walls,
I saw her people famish'd, Nobles slain,
Her fruitfull land, a barren heath remain.[45]
I saw (unmov'd) her Armies foil'd and fled,
Wives forc'd, babes toss'd, her houses calcined,
I saw strong *Rochel* yeelding to her foe,[46]
Thousands of starved Christians there also.
I saw poore *Ireland* bleeding out her last,
Such cruelty as all reports have past.
My heart obdurate, stood not yet agast.
Now sip I of that cup, and just 't may be,
The bottome dregs reserved are for me.

New England.
To all you've said, sad mother, I assent
Your fearfull sinnes, great cause there's to lament,
My guilty hands (in part) hold up with you,
A sharer in your punishment's my due,
But all you say, amounts to this effect,
Not what you feel, but what you do expect.
Pray in plain termes, what is your present grief,
Then let's join heads, and hands for your relief.

Old England.
Well, to the matter then, there's grown of late,
'Twixt King and Peeres a question of state,
Which is the chief, the law, or else the King,
One saith its he, the other no such thing.
My better part in Court of Parliament,
To ease my groaning land shew their intent,
To crush the proud, and right to each man deal.
To help the Church, and stay the Common-Weal,

45 Thirty Years' War in Germany (1618–1648).

46 La Rochel[le]: a French Protestant stronghold.

So many obstacles comes in their way,
As puts me to a stand what I should say,
Old customs, new Prerogatives stood on,
Had they not held law fast, all had been gone,
Which by their prudence stood them in such stead,
They took high *Strafford* lower by the head,
And to their *Laud* be't spoke, they held i' th' Tower,[47]
All *Englands* Metropolitane that houre,
This done, an Act they would have passed fain,
No prelate should his Bishoprick retain;
Here tugg'd they hard indeed, for all men saw,
This must be done by Gospel, not by law.
Next the *Militia* they urged sore,
This was deny'd, I need not say wherefore.
The King displeas'd, at *York* himself absents,
They humbly beg return, shew their intents,
The writing, printing, posting to and fro,
Shews all was done, I'll therefore let it go.
But now I come to speak of my disaster,
Contention's grown 'twixt Subjects and their Master,
They worded it so long, they fell to blows,
That thousands lay on heaps, here bleeds my woes.[48]
I that no warres, so many years have known,
Am now destroy'd and slaughter'd by mine own,
But could the field alone this cause decide,
One battell, two or three I might abide,
But these may be beginnings of more woe,
Who knows, the worst, the best may overthrow;
Religion, Gospell, here lies at the stake,
Pray now, dear child, for sacred *Zions* sake,
Oh pity me, in this sad perturbation,
My plundered Townes, my houses devastation,
My ravisht virgins, and my young men slain,
My wealthy trading faln, my dearth of grain,
The seed time's come, but Ploughman hath no hope,
Because he knows not, who shall inn his crop:
The poore they want their pay, their children bread,
Their wofull mother's tears unpitied.
If any pity in thy heart remain,

47 In 1641 the Earl of Strafford, Thomas Wentworth, a chief minister of Charles I, was executed and the Archbishop of Canterbury, William Laud, committed to the Tower.

48 Events leading up to the breakout of the English Civil War, presented from a monarchist perspective.

Or any child-like love thou dost retain,
For my relief now use thy utmost skill,
And recompense me good, for all my ill.

New England.
Dear mother cease complaints, and wipe your eyes,
Shake off your dust, chear up, and now arise,
You are my mother, nurse, I once your flesh,
Your sunken bowels gladly would refresh:
Your griefs I pity much, but should do wrong,
To weep for that we both have pray'd for long,
To see these latter dayes of hop'd for good,
That Right may have its right, though't be with blood;
After dark Popery the day did clear,
But now the Sun in's brightnesse shall appear,
Blest be the Nobles of thy Noble Land,
With (ventur'd lives) for truths defence that stand,
Blest be thy Commons which for Common good,
And thine infringed Lawes have boldly stood.
Blest be thy Counties which do aid thee still
With hearts and states, to testifie their will.
Blest be thy Preachers, who do chear thee on,
O cry: the sword of God and *Gideon*:
And shall I not on those wish *Mero*'s curse,[49]
That help thee not with prayers, arms, and purse,
And for my self, let miseries abound,
If mindlesse of thy state I e'er be found.
These are the dayes, the Churches foes to crush,
To root out Prelates, head, tail, branch, and rush.
Let's bring *Baals* vestments out, to make a fire,
Their Myters, Surplices, and all their tire,
Copes, Rochets, Crossiers, and such trash,
And let their names consume, but let the flash
Light Christendome, and all the world to see,
We hate *Romes* Whore, with all her trumperie.
Go on brave *Essex*, shew whose son thou art,
Not false to King, nor Countrey in thy heart,
But those that hurt his people and his Crown,
By force expell, destroy, and tread them down:
Let Gaoles be fill'd with th' remnant of that pack,
And sturdy *Tyburn* loaded till it crack,

49 Gideon (Judges 6:11 ff); Mero: Meroz (Judges 5:23).

And yee brave Nobles, chase away all fear,
And to this blessed Cause closely adhere
O mother, can you weep, and have such Peeres.
When they are gone, then drown your self in teares.
If now you weep so much, that then no more,
The briny Ocean will o'rflow your shore,
These, these, are they (I trust) with *Charles* our King,
Out of all mists, such glorious dayes will bring,
That dazzled eyes beholding much shall wonder
At that thy setled Peace, thy wealth and splendour,
Thy Church and Weal, establish'd in such manner,
That all shall joy that thou display'dst thy banner,
And discipline erected, so I trust,
That nursing Kings, shall come and lick thy dust:
Then Justice shall in all thy Courts take place,
Without respect of persons, or of case,
Then bribes shall cease, and suits shall not stick long,
Patience, and purse of Clients for to wrong:
Then High Commissions shall fall to decay,
And Pursevants and Catchpoles[50] want their pay,
So shall thy happy Nation ever flourish,
When truth and righteousnesse they thus shall nourish.
When thus in Peace: thine Armies brave send out,
To sack proud *Rome*, and all her vassalls rout:
There let thy name, thy fame, and valour shine,
As did thine Ancestours in *Palestine*,
And let her spoils, full pay, with int'rest be,
Of what unjustly once she poll'd from thee,
Of all the woes thou canst let her be sped,
Execute to th' full the vengeance threatened.
Bring forth the beast that rul'd the world with's beck,
And tear his flesh, and set your feet on's neck,
And make his filthy den so desolate,
To th' 'stonishment of all that knew his state.
This done, with brandish'd swords, to *Turky* go,
(For then what is't, but English blades dare do)
And lay her wast, for so's the sacred doom;
And do to *Gog*, as thou hast done to *Rome*.[51]

---

50 Catchpole: pejorative term for bailiff.

51 In Ezek. 38–39 Gog is a ruler from Magog (land of Gog); in Rev. 20:8, Gog is a nation under Satan's dominion; also a statue in Guildhall, London, representing a giant supposedly occupying Britain in pre-Roman times.

Oh *Abrahams seed*[52] lift up your heads on high
For sure the day of your redemption's nigh;
The scales shall fall from your long blinded eyes,
And him you shall adore, who now despise,
Then fulnes of the Nations in shall flow,
And Jew and Gentile, to one worship go,
Then follows dayes of happinesse and rest.
Whose lot doth fall to live therein is blest:
No Canaanite shall then be found ith' land,
And holinesse, on horses bells shall stand,
If this make way thereto, then sigh no more,
But if at all, thou dist not see't before.
Farewell dear mother, Parliament, prevail,
And in a while you'l tell another tale.

8 From **John Milton,** ***A Defence of the People of England*** **(1651, 1692)**

John Milton (1608–1674) was an English poet, polemicist, and champion of the regicide, who would later compose the celebrated national epic in the lofty vernacular, *Paradise Lost*. Following the execution of Charles I in 1649 and the military victory of the revolutionaries, Milton was commissioned by the Council of State in his capacity as secretary of foreign tongues to produce a response to the anonymously published defence of absolute monarchical authority, *Defensio Regia* (1649) ("Defence of King Charles I") by Claude de Saumaise or Salmasius, an internationally renowned French classicist and Protestant scholar.

The first *Defence* was originally composed in Latin and had a domestic and continental readership in mind.[53] Chapter 3 cites the law of nature aligned with God's law—whereby all enjoy freedom from tyranny in a Christian commonwealth—to refute the claims outlined in *Defensio Regia*. Milton applies scriptural exegesis to challenge Salmasius' claim that Christ promoted subjection to secular power. The *Defence* is significant for its definition of the nation as a safeguard for Christian liberty, used here as part of the argument justifying opposition to kingship. Along with *Eikonoklastes* (1649)—Milton's commissioned retort to the most popular seventeenth-century work, Charles I's *Eikon Basilike* (1649)—*A Defence* was called in to be burnt by the common hangman in 1660. The 1692 English translation (excerpted below) of the 1651 *Pro Populo Anglicano Defensio* is testimony of the treatise's relevance for the political nation in the years

52 On the language of election in Old and New England, see Sauer's Part II chapter.

53 M. Dzelzainis, "Introduction," in M. Dzelzainis (ed.), John Milton, *Political Writings*, *Cambridge Texts in the History of Political Thought*, trans. Claire Gruzelier, Cambridge: Cambridge University Press, 1991, p. xix.

following the Glorious Revolution of 1688. The owner of one 1692 copy of the treatise was Gilbert Burnet, Bishop of Salisbury (1643–1715), a liberal-minded Scottish theologian and historian. Cut out of his copy (BL 8122.a.47) is the "Advertisement of the Reader" (cf. BL 8005.c.24.), which features royalist works, including two royalist defences of *Eikon Basilike* (1649).

John Milton, *A Defence of the People of England by John Milton . . . in answer to Salmasius's defence of the King*, translated by Joseph Washington (London?, 1692).

From **To the English reader.**

The Author of this Book is sufficiently known, and so is the Book it self, both at Home and Abroad, to the Curious and Inquisitive; but never having been rendred into English, many, whose Veneration for the Author would induce them to read any thing of his, and who could not master it in the Language in which he wrote it, were deprived of the pleasure of perusing it, and of the Information they might justly expect from it. To gratifie them it is, that this Translation, long since made, is now published[.]

From **The Author's Preface.**

ALTHO I fear, lest, if in defending the People of *England*, I should be as copious in Words, and empty of Matter, as most Men think *Salmasius* has been in his Defence of the King; I might seem to deserve justly to be accounted a verbose and silly Defender; yet since no Man thinks himself obliged to make so much haste, tho in the handling but of any ordinary Subject, as not to premise some Introduction at least, according as the weight of his Subject requires; if I take the same course in handling well-nigh the greatest Subject that ever was, without being too tedious in it, I am in hopes of attaining two things, which indeed I earnestly desire: The one, not to be at all wanting, as far as in me lies, to this most Noble Cause, and most worthy to be recorded to all future Ages. The other, That I shall appear to have avoided my self, that frivolousness of Matter, and redundancy of Words, which I find fault with in my Antagonist. For I am about to discourse of Matters, neither inconsiderable nor common, but how a most Potent King, after he had trampled upon the Laws of the Nation, and given a shock to its Religion, and was ruling at his own Will and Pleasure, was at last subdu'd in the Field by his own Subjects, who had undergone a long Slavery under him; how afterwards he was cast into Prison, and when he gave no ground, either by Words or Actions, to hope better things of him, he was finally by the Supreme Council of the Kingdom condemned to dye, and beheaded before the very Gates of the Palace.[54] I shall likewise

54 Charles I (1600–1649), King of Great Britain and Ireland, was executed at the Banqueting House at Whitehall.

relate, (which will much conduce to the easing mens minds of a great Superstition,) by what Right, especially according to our Law, this Judgment was given, and all these Matters transacted; and shall easily defend my Valiant and Worthy Countrymen, and who have extremely well deserved of all Subjects and Nations in the World, from the most wicked Calumities both of Domestick and Foreign Railers, and especially from the Reproaches of this most vain and empty Sophister, who sets up for a Captain and Ringleader to all the rest. For what King's Majesty sitting upon an Exalted Throne, ever shone so brightly, as that of the People of *England* then did, when shaking off that old Superstition, which had prevailed a long time, they gave Judgment upon the King himself, or rather upon an Enemy, who had been their King, caught as it were in a Net by his own Laws (who alone of all Mortals challenged to himself impunity by a Divine Right) and scrupled not to inflict the same punishment upon him himself, being guilty, which he would have inflicted upon any other. But why do I mention these things as performed by the People? which almost open their Voice themselves, and testify the Presence of God throughout. Who, as often as it seems good to his Infinite Wisdom, uses to throw down proud and unruly Kings, exalting themselves above the Condition of Humane Nature, and utterly to extirpate them and all their Family. . . .

Chap. III.

Having proved sufficiently that the Kings of the *Jews* were subject to the same Laws that the people were; That there are no exceptions made in Scripture; That 'tis a most false assertion, grounded upon no reason, nor warranted by any Authority, to say, That Kings may do what they list with Impunity; That God has exempted them from all humane Jurisdiction, and reserved them to his own Tribunal only: Let us now consider, whether the Gospel preach up any such Doctrine, and enjoyn that blind obedience which the Law was so far from doing, that it commanded the contrary; let us consider whether or no the Gospel, that Heavenly Promulgation, as it were, of Christian Liberty, reduce us to a condition of Slavery to Kings and Tyrants, from whose imperious rule even the old Law, that Mistress of Slavery, discharged the people of God, when it obtained. Your first argument you take from the person of Christ himself. But, alas! who does not know that he put himself into the condition, not of a private person only, but even of a servant, that we might be made free? Nor is this to be understood of some internal spiritual liberty only; how inconsistent else would that Song of his Mothers be with the design of his coming into the world, *He hath scattered the proud in the imagination of their heart, he hath put down the mighty from their seat, and hath exalted the humble and meek*?[55] How

55 Luke 1:52.

ill suited to their occasion would these expressions be, if the coming of Christ rather established and strengthened a Tyrannical Government, and made a blind subjection the duty of all Christians? Himself having been born and lived and died under a Tyrannical Government, has thereby purchased Liberty for us. As he gives us his Grace to submit patiently to a condition of Slavery, if there be a necessity of it; so if by any honest ways and means we can rid our selves, and obtain our Liberty, he is so far from restraining us, that he encourageth us so to do. Hence it is that St. *Paul* not only of an Evangelical, but a Civil Liberty, says thus, 1 Cor. 7. 21. *Art thou called being a servant, care not for it; but if thou maist be made free, use it rather; you are bought with a price, be not ye servants of men.*[56] So that you are very impertinent in endeavouring to argue us into Slavery by the example of our Saviour; who by submitting to such a condition himself, has confirmed even our Civil Liberties. He took upon him indeed in our stead the form of a servant, but he always retained his purpose of being a deliverer; and thence it was that he taught us a quite other notion of the right of Kings, than this that you endeavour to make good: You, I say, that preach up not Kingship, but Tyranny, and that in a Commonwealth; by enjoyning not a necessary only, but a Religious subjection to whatever Tyrant gets into the Chair, whether he come to it by Succession, or by Conquest, or chance, or any how. And now I'le turn your own weapons against you, and oppose you, as I use to do, with your own Authorities. When the Collectors of the Tribute-money came to Christ for Tribute in *Galilee*, he asked *Peter*, Mat. 17. *Of whom the Kings of the earth took custom or tribute, of their own children, or of strangers? Peter saith unto him, Of strangers; Jesus saith unto him, then are the children free; notwithstanding lest we should offend them,* &c *give unto them for thee and for me*[.][57] Expositors differ upon this place whom this Tribute was paid to; some say it was paid to the Priests, for the use of the Sanctuary; others that it was paid to the Emperour. I am of opinion that it was the Revenue of the Sanctuary, but paid to *Herod*, who perverted the Institution of it, and took it to himself. *Josephus* mentions divers sorts of Tribute which he and his Sons exacted, all which *Agrippa* afterwards remitted. And this very Tribute, though small in it self, yet being accompanied with many more, was a heavy burden; the *Jews*, even the poorest of them, in the time of their Commonwealth paid a Poll; so that it was some considerable oppression that our Saviour spoke of; and from hence he took occasion to Tax *Herod*'s Injustice, under whose Government, and within whose Jurisdiction he then was; in that, whereas the Kings of the Earth (who affect usually the Title of Fathers of their Country) do not use to oppress their own Children, that is, their own natural born Subjects with heavy and unreasonable Exactions, but lay such burdens upon strangers and

56 1 Cor. 7:21–23.

57 Matt. 17:24–27.

conquer'd enemies; he, quite contrary, oppressed not strangers, but his own people. But let what will be here meant by Children, either natural born Subjects, or the Children of God, and those the Elect only, or Christians in general, as St. *Augustine* understands the place; this is certain, that if *Peter* was a child, and therefore free, then by consequence we are so too, by our Saviour's own Testimony, either as *Englishmen*, or as Christans[sic]; and that consequently it is not the right of Kings to exact heavy Tributes from their own Countrymen, and those freeborn Subjects. Christ himself professeth, that he paid not this Tribute as a thing that was due, but that he might not bring trouble upon himself by offending those that demanded it. The work that he came into this World to do, was quite of another Nature. But if our Saviour deny, that it is the Right of Kings to burden their Free-born Subjects with grievous Exactions, he would certainly muchless allow it to be their Right to Spoil, Massacre, and Torture their own Countrymen, and those Christians too. He discoursed after such a manner of the Right of Kings, that those that he spoke to, suspected his Principles, as laying too great a restraint upon Sovereignty, and not allowing the License that Tyrants assume to themselves to be the Rights of Kings. It was not for nothing that the *Pharisees* put such Questions to him, tempting him; and that at the same time they told him, that he regarded not the Person of any Man; nor was it for nothing that he was angry when such Questions were proposed to him, *Matth*. 22.[58] If one should endeavour to ensnare you with little Questions, and catch at your Answers, to ground an Accusation against you upon your own Principles concerning the Right of Kings, and all this under a Monarchy, would you be angry with him? You'd have but very little reason. 'Tis evident, That our Saviours Principles concerning Government, were not agreeable to the Humour of Princes. His Answer too implies as much; by which he rather turn'd them away, than instructed them. He asked for the Tribute-money. *Whose Image and Superscription is it*, says he? They tell him it was *Caesar*'s. *Give then to Caesar*, says he, *the things that are Caesar's; and to God, the things that are God's*. And how comes it to pass, that the People should not have given to them the things that are theirs? *Render to all men their dues*, says St. *Paul*, *Rom*. 13.[59] So that *Caesar* must not ingross all to himself. Our Liberty is not *Caesar*'s; 'tis a Blessing we have received from God himself; 'tis what we are born to; to lay this down at *Caesar*'s feet, which we derive not from him, which we are not beholden to him for, were an unworthy Action, and a degrading of our very Nature. If one should consider attentively the Countenance of a Man, and enquire after whose Image so noble a Creature were framed; would not any one that heard him, presently make answer, That he was made after the Image of God himself? Being therefore peculiarly God's

58 Matt. 22:15–21.

59 Rom. 13:7.

own, and consequently things that are to be given to him; we are intirely free by Nature, and cannot without the greatest Sacrilege imaginable be reduced into a Condition of Slavery to any Man, especially to a wicked, unjust, cruel Tyrant. Our Saviour does not take upon him to determine what things are God's, and what *Caesar*'s; he leaves that as he found it. If the piece of Money which they shewed him, was the same that was paid to God, as in *Vespatian*'s time it was, then our Saviour is so far from having put an end to the Controversy, that he has but entangl'd it, and made it more perplext than it was before; for 'tis impossible the same thing should be given both to God, and to *Caesar*. But, you say, he intimates to them what things were *Caesar*'s; to wit, that piece of Money because it bore the Emperor's Stamp; and what of all that? How does this advantage your Cause? You get not the Emperor, or to your self, a Penny by this Conclusion. Either Christ allowed []nothing at all to be *Caesar*'s, but that piece of Money that he then had in his hand, and thereby asserted the Peoples Interest in every thing else; or else, if (as you would have us understand him) he affirms all Money that has the Emperor's stamp upon it, to be the Emperor's own. He contradicts himself, and gives the Magistrate a property in every Man's Estate, when as he himself paid his Tribute-money with a Protestation, that it was more than what either *Peter*, or himself was bound to do. The ground you rely on, is very weak; for Money bears the Prince's Image, not as a token of its being his, but of its being good Metal, and that none may presume to Counterfeit it. If the writing Princes Names, or setting their Stamps upon a thing, vest the property of it in them, 'twere a good ready way for them to invade all Property. Or rather, if whatever Subjects have, be absolutely at their Prince's disposal, which is your Assertion, that piece of Money was not *Caesar*'s, because his Image was stampt on it, but because of Right it belonged to him before 'twas coyn'd. So that nothing can be more manifest, than that our Saviour in this place never intended to teach our Duty to Magistrates (he would have spoke more plainly, if he had) but to reprehend the Malice and Wickedness of the hypocritical *Pharisees*. When they told him that *Herod* laid wait to kill him; did he return an humble, submissive Answer? *Go, tell that Fox*,[60] says he, *&c.* intimating, that Kings have no other Right to destroy their Subjects, than Foxes have to devour the things they prey upon. Say you, 'He suffered Death under a Tyrant.' How could he possibly under any other? But from hence you conclude, that he asserted it to be the Right of Kings to commit Murder, and act Injustice. You'd make an excellent Moralist. But our Saviour, tho he became a Servant, not to make us so, but that we might be free; yet carried he himself so with Relation to the Magistracy, as not to ascribe any more to them then their due. Now, let us come at last to enquire what his Doctrine was upon this Subject. The Sons of *Zebedee* were ambitious of Honour and

60 Luke 13:32.

Power in the Kingdom of *Christ*, which they persuaded themselves he would shortly set up in the World; he reproves them so, as withal to let all Christians know what Form of Civil Government he desires they should settle amongst themselves. *Ye know*, says he, *that the Princes of the Gentiles exercise dominion over them; and they that are great, exercise authority upon them; but it shall not be so among you; but whoso[e]ver will be great among you, let him be your Minister; and whosoever will be chief among you, let him be your servant.*[61] Unless you'd been distracted, you could never have imagined that this place makes for you: and yet you urge it, and think it furnishes you with an Argument to prove that our Kings are absolute Lords and Masters over us and ours. May it be our fortune to have to do with such Enemies in War, as will fall blind-fold and naked into our Camp instead of their own: as you constantly do, who alledge that for your self, that of all things in the World makes most against you. The *Israelites* asked God for a King, such a King as other Nations round about them had. God dissuaded them by many Arguments, which our Saviour here gives us an Epitomy of; *You know that the Princes of the* Gentiles *exercise Dominion over them*. But yet, because the *Israelites* persisted in their desire of a King, God gave them one, tho in his Wrath. Our Saviour, lest Christians should desire a King, such a one at least, as might Rule as, he says, the Princes of the *Gentiles* did, prevents them with an Injunction to the contrary; *but it shall not be so among you*. What can be said plainer than this? That stately, imperious Sway and Dominion that Kings use to exercise, shall not be amongst you; what specious Titles soever they may assume to themselves, as that of Benefactors, or the like. *But he that will be great amongst you*, (and who is greater than the Prince?) *let him be your Servant.*[62] So that the Lawyer, whoever he be, that you are so smart upon, was not so much out of the way, but had our Saviour's own Authority to back him, when he said that Christian Princes were indeed no other than the Peoples Servants; 'tis very certain that all good Magistrates are so. Insomuch that Christians either must have no King at all, or if they have, that King must be the People's Servant. Absolute Lordship and Christianity are inconsistent. *Moses* himself, by whose Ministry that seviler Oeconomy of the old Law was instituted, did not exercise an Arbitrary, Haughty Power and Authority, but bore the burden of the People, and carried them in his Bosom, as a Nursing Father does a sucking Child, *Numb.* 11.[63] and what is that of a Nursing Father, but a Ministerial Employment? *Plato* would not have the Magistrates called Lords, but Servants and Helpers of the People; nor the People Servants, but Maintainers of their Magistrates, because they give Meat, Drink, and Wages to their Kings themselves. *Aristotle* calls the Magistrates, Keepers and Ministers of the Laws. *Plato*, Ministers and servants. The

61 Matt. 20:25–27.

62 Luke 22:25–26.

63 Num. 11:12.

Apostle calls them Ministers of God; but they are Ministers and Servants of the People, and of the Laws, nevertheless for all that; the Laws and the Magistrates were both created for the good of the People[.]

9 From **Daniel Defoe, *The Original Power of the Collective Body of the People of England, Examined and Asserted* (1702)**

Daniel Defoe (1660–1731) was born Daniel Foe in London, England. He was briefly trained as a Presbyterian minister, but left his studies and, like his father, went into trade. A Dissenter, he participated in Monmouth's Rebellion (1685) and was pardoned two years later. Much of his early writing deals with political and religious rights, including *An Inquiry into Occasional Conformity* (1698), *Shortest Way with Dissenters* (1702), and *The Original Power of the Collective Body of the People of England* (1702), from which the following is excerpted. Throughout the essay, Defoe quotes from his long verse satire, *The True-Born Englishman* (1701), but it is centrally a response to Sir Humphrey Mackworth's *A Vindication of the Rights of the Commons of England* (1701), which argued that "the several and respective Powers Vested in the *King*, *Lords*, and *Commons*, are *Mutual Checks and Mutual Boundaries to one another*, but are not to be Limited by any Authority besides their own."[64] His best-known works were published near the end of his career, including *Robinson Crusoe* (1719), *Moll Flanders* (1722), *Journal of the Plague Year* (1722), and a three-volume guide-book, *A Tour Through the Whole Island of Great Britain* (1724–1726).

[Daniel Defoe] *The Original Power of the Collective Body of the People of England, Examined and Asserted* (London, 1702).

The Defence of the Rights of the Representative Body of the People, understood by the Name of the Commons of *England* in Parliament, *is a great Point*; and so plain are their Rights, that 'tis no extraordinary Task to defend them: But for any Man to advance, that they are so August an Assembly that no Objection ought to be made to their Actions, nor no Reflection upon their Conduct, though the Fact be true; and that it is not to be examin'd whether the Thing said be true, but what Authority the Person speaking has to say it, *is a Doctrine wholly new*, and seems to be a Badge of more Slavery to our own Representative than ever the People of *England* owes them, or than ever they themselves expected.

64 Sir H. Mackworth, *A Vindication of the Rights of the Commons of England*, London, 1701, p. 5.

This therefore, together with some Invasions of the Peoples Rights made publick by several Modern Authors, are the Reasons why I have adventur'd, *being wholly Disinterested and Unconcerned either for Persons or Parties*, to make a short Essay at declaring the Rights of the People of *England*, not Representatively but Collectively considered.

And with due Defference to the Representative Body of the Nation, I hope I may say, *it can be no Diminution of their Rights*, to assert the Rights of that Body from whom they derive the Powers and Priviledges of their House, and which are the very Foundation of their Being. For if the Original Right of the People be overthrown, the Power of the Representative, which is subsequent and subordinate, must dye of it self.

And because I have to do rather with Reason and the Nature of the Thing, than with Laws and Precedents, I shall make but very little use of Authors, and Quotations of Statutes, since Fundamentals and Principles both in Law and Argument, are superiour to Laws or Examples.

To come directly to what I design in the following Papers, 'tis necessary to lay down some Maxims, other than what a late[65] Author has furnish'd us with.

1. That *Salus Populi suprema Lex*, all Government, and consequently our whole Constitution, was originally design'd, and is maintain'd, for the Support of the Peoples Property, who are the Governed.

2. That all the Members of Government, whether King, Lords or Commons, if they Invert the Great End of their Institution, the Publick Good cease to be in the same Publick Capacity,

> "And Power retreats to its Original."
>
> *True-Born Englishman*[66]

3. That no Collective or Representative Body of Men whatsoever, in Matters of Politicks any more than Religion, *are or ever have been Infallible*.

4. That Reason is the Test and Touch-stone of Laws, and that all Law or Power that is contradictory to Reason, is *ipso facto* void in it self, and ought not to be obeyed. . . .

The Good of the People Governed is the End of all Government, and the Reason and Original of Governours; and upon this Foundation it is that it has been the Practice of all Nations, and of this in particular, That if the

---

65 Sir *H. M.* Vindication of the House of Commons (Defoe's note).

66 D. Defoe, *The True-Born Englishman*, in P. N. Furbank and W. R. Owen (eds), *The True-Born Englishman and Other Writings*, Markham: Penguin, 1997, l. 819.

Male Administration of Governours have extended to Tyranny and Oppression, to Destruction of Right and Justice, overthrowing the Constitution, and abusing the People, the People have thought it Lawful to Reassume the Right of Government into their own Hands, and to reduce their Governours to Reason.

The present Happy Restoring of our Liberty and Constitution is owing to this Fundamental Maxim, according to a late Author,

> "That Kings, when they descend to Tyranny,
> Dissolve the Bond, and leave the Subject free."
>
> *Trueborn Englishman*[67] . . .

That Power which is Original, is Superior; *God is the Fountain of all Power, and therefore is the Supreme*: And if we could suppose a Prior and Original of the Divine Power, *that Original would be God*, and be Superiour; for all subsequent Power must be subject and inferiour to the precedent.

The Power vested in the Three Heads of our Constitution, is vested in them by the People of *England*, who were a People before there was such a Thing as a Constitution. . . .

The People of *England* have Delegated all the Executive Power *in the King*, the Legislative in the *King, Lords and Commons*, the Sovereign Judicature in the *Lords*, the Remainder is reserv'd in themselves, and not committed, no not to their Representatives: All Powers Delegated are to one great End and Purpose, and no other, and that is *the Publick Good.* If either or all the Branches to whom this Power is Delegated invert the Design, the End of their Power, the Right they have to that Power ceases; and they become Tyrants and Usurpers of a Power they have no Right to.

The Instance has been visible as to Kings in our Dayes; and History is full of Precedents in all Ages, and in all Nations; particularly in *Spain*, in *Portugal*, in *Swedeland*, in *France*, and in *Poland.*

But in *England*, the late Revolution is a particular Instance of the Exercise of this Power.

King *James* on the Approach of a Foreign Army, and the general recourse of the People to Arms, fled out of the Kingdom. What must the People of *England* do? They had no Reason to run after him to be Govern'd there; there was no Body to call a Parliament, so the Constitution was entirely Dissolved.

The Original of Power, *the People*, Assembled in Convention, to consider of Delegating New Powers for their future Government, and accordingly made a New Settlement of the Crown, a New Declaration of Right, and a

---

67 Defoe, *True-Born Englishman*, ll. 804–5.

New Representative of the People; *and some have thought they ought to have given a New Sanction to all precedent Laws.*

It remains to argue from hence, But what Course must the People of *England* take, if their Representatives exercise the Power intrusted with them to the Ruine of the Constitution?

It has been advanced, That every Man must submit, and not presume to argue against it upon any Supposition of Mismanagement.

I can see no Reason given to confirm such a Position; for unless we will place the Original of Power in the persons Representing, not in the persons Represented, it cannot be made out that there ought to be no Complaint upon the score of Mismanagement.

It is not the Design of this Discourse to lessen the Authority of Parliament: But all Power must Centre some where. If it is in the Three Branches of the Constitution, 'tis there inherently and originally, or it is there by Deputation. If it be there by Deputation, then there must be a Power Deputing, and that must be both *Prior*, and consequently Superiour to the Deputed, *as before.*

If we will come off of this, we must fly to the old weak Refuge of a Power *Jure Divino*, a Doctrine which the most famous Pretenders to, have lived to be ashamed of; and whose Foundation is so weak, that 'tis not worth while to Expose it.

I should therefore have been very glad, that for the Perfecting the Defence of the *English* Constitution, the Gentlemen who have begun so well, would have gone forward to Recognize the Power of the People of *England*, and their undoubted Right to judge of the Infractions made in their Constitution, by either Parties abusing the particular Powers vested in them; and inverting them, by turning them against the People they are designed to defend. . . .

The *Genius* of this Nation has always appear'd to tend to a Monarchy, a legal limited Monarchy; and having had in the late Revolution a full and uninterrupted Liberty, to Cast themselves into what Form of Government they pleas'd: There was not discovered the least Inclination in any Party towards a *Commonwealth*, tho' the Treatment they met with from their last two Kings, had all in it that could be, to put them out of Love with Monarchy.

A Commonwealth can never be introduc'd, but by such Invasions of Right as must make our present Constituted Government impracticable: The Reason is, because Men never willingly change for the Worst; and the People of *England* enjoy more Freedom in our Regal, than any People in the World can do in a Popular Government.

The People of *England* can never chuse a Commonwealth Government, till they come to desire less Liberty than they now enjoy; that is, till they come to be blind to their own Interest. 'Tis true, Example is no Argument; but I might freely appeal to the Friends of the Last Republick in *England* to answer this Question. . . .

The People assembled in a Universal Mob to take the Right of Government upon themselves, are not to be supposed to give their personal Suffrages to every Article, but they may agree to a Convention of such Persons as they think fit to Intrust, to Constitute *de Novo*, and may Delegate their Power, or part of it to such a Convention; and in such Case a general Concurrence is to be suppos'd, unless there be a publick Dissent.

Now suppose the general Collective Body of the People should not unanimously agree, 'tis owned the Power could not be universally Delegated, and there a Division would follow; but in such Case, those who Dissented from such an Agreement, must declare their Dissent, and agree to any other Form of Government for themselves, and so divide from the other Body, and if they do not divide, they in effect do not Dissent. . . .

Yet is there no Fear of such a Division in a Country so depending on its several Parts as this is, because the rest would render them so uneasie, that Interest would compel them to comply.

I do not place this Right upon the Inhabitants, but upon the *Freeholders*; the *Freeholders* are the proper Owners of the Country: It is their own, and the other Inhabitants are but Sojourners, like Lodgers in a House, and ought to be subject to such Laws as the Freeholders impose upon them, or else they must remove; because the Freeholders having a Right to the Land, the other have no right to live there but upon sufferance.

In former Days the Freehold gave a Right of Government to the Freeholder, and Vassalage and Villinage was deriv'd from this Right, that every Man who will live in my Land shall be my Servant; if he wont, let him go about his Business, and live somewhere else. And 'tis the same still in right reasoning.

And I make no question but that Property of Land is the best Title to Government in the World; and if the King was universal Landlord, he ought to be Universal Governour of Right, and the People so living on his Lands ought to obey him, or go off of his Premises.

And if any single Man in *England* should at any time come to be Landlord of the whole Freehold of *England*, he could indeed have no Right to Dispossess the King, till the present Legal Settlement of the Crown fail'd, because it was settled by those that had then a Right to settle it.

But he would immediately be the full Representative of all the Counties in *England*, and might Elect himself Knight of the Shire for every County, and the Sheriff of every County must Return him accordingly.

He would have all the Baronies and Titles of Honour which are entail'd upon Estates devolv'd upon him, and upon any Expiration of the Settlement would be King by natural Right.

And he would be King upon larger Terms, than ever any Man was legally King of *England*; for he would be King by inherent Right of Property.

When therefore I am speaking of the Right of the People, I would be understood of the Freeholders, for all the other Inhabitants live upon Sufferance, and either are the Freeholders Servants, or having Money to pay Rent live upon Conditions, and have no Title to their living in *England*, other than as Servants, but what they must pay for.

Upon this foot it is that to this Day our Law suffers not a Foreigner to Purchase any of the Freeholds of *England*: For if a Foreigner might Purchase, your Neighbours (having Money to spare) might come and buy you out of your own Country, and take Possession by a legal and indisputable Right.

10 From **Jonathan Swift,** ***A Letter to the Whole People of Ireland*** **(1724)**

Jonathan Swift (1667–1745) was born in Dublin, Ireland, and educated at Kilkenny College and then Trinity College Dublin. He was ordained in 1695 and was Dean of St. Patrick's Cathedral in Dublin from 1713 until 1742. Before taking up his position as Dean, he wrote myriad pieces for *The Examiner* in support of Tory policies; political interests also dominated his (mostly satiric) writing while he was Dean. The *Drapier's Letters* (1724–1725) is the name given to a series of anonymous pamphlets by Swift responding to a patent granted to William Wood, an English ironmaster, to produce coins for Ireland. The debased coinage would have undermined the Irish economy, according to Swift and others, and the patent was eventually withdrawn because of wide protests in Ireland. The excerpt below is from Swift's fourth pamphlet (October 22, 1724); a reward of £300 was offered for the identity of this pamphlet's author, but Swift was not exposed. Other major works by Swift include *The Battle of the Books* (1704), *Gulliver's Travels* (1726), *A Modest Proposal* (1729), *Verses on the Death of Dr. Swift* (1731), and *The Lady's Dressing Room* (1732).

[Jonathan Swift] *A Letter to the Whole People of Ireland.* By M. B. Drapier. Author of the Letter to the Shop-Keepers, &c, 2nd edn. Corrected (Dublin, 1724).

My Dear Countrymen,
HAVING already written Three *Letters*, upon so disagreeable a Subject, as Mr. *Wood* and his *Half-pence*; I conceived my Task was at an End: But I find, that Cordials must be frequently apply'd to weak Constitutions, *Political* as well as *Natural*. A People long used to Hardships, lose by Degrees the very Notions of *Liberty*, they look upon themselves as Creatures at Mercy, and that all Impositions laid on them by a stronger Hand, are, in the Phrase of the *Report*, *Legal* and *Obligatory*. Hence proceeds that *Poverty* and *Lowness of Spirit*, to which a *Kingdom* may be subject as well as a *Particular Person*. And when *Esau came fainting from the Field at the Point to Die*, it is no wonder that he *Sold his Birth-Right for a Mess of Pottage*.[68]

68 Gen. 25:29–34.

I thought I had sufficiently shewn to all who could want Instruction, by what Methods they might safely proceed, whenever this *Coyn* should be offered to them: And I believe there hath not been for many Ages an Example of any Kingdom so firmly united in a Point of great Importance, as this of Ours is at present, against that detestable Fraud. But however, it so happens that some weak People begin to be allarmed anew, by Rumours industriously spread. *Wood* prescribes to the News-Mongers in *London* what they are to write. In one of their Papers published here by some obscure Printer (and probably with no good Design) we are told, that *the Papists*[69] *in* Ireland *have entered into an Association against his Coyn*, although it be notoriously known, that they never once offered to stir in the Matter; so that the Two Houses of Parliament, the Privy Council, the great Number of Corporations, the Lord Mayor and Alderman of *Dublin*, the Grand-Juries, and Principal Gentlemen of several Counties are stigmatized in a Lump under the Name of *Papists*.

This Impostor and his Crew do likewise give out, that, by refusing to receive his Dross for Sterling, we *dispute the King's Prerogative, are grown Ripe for Rebellion, and ready to shake off the Dependancy of* Ireland *upon the Crown* of England. To countenance which Reports he hath publish'd a Paragraph in another News-Paper, to let us know, that *the Lord Lieutenant*[70] *is ordered to come over immediately to settle his Half-pence*.

I intreat you, my dear Countrymen, not to be under the least Concern upon these and the like Rumours, which are no more than the last Howls of a Dog dissected alive, as I hope he hath sufficiently been. These Calumnies are the only Reserve that is left him. For surely our continued and (almost) unexampled Loyalty will never be called in Question, for not suffering our selves to be Robbed of all that we have, by one obscure *Iron-Monger*.

As to disputing the King's *Prerogative*, give me Leave to explain to those who are Ignorant, what the meaning of that word *Prerogative* is.

The Kings of these Realms enjoy several Powers, wherein the Laws have not interposed: So they can make War and Peace without the Consent of Parliament; and this is a very great *Prerogative*. But if the Parliament doth not approve of the War, the King must bear the Charge of it out of his own Purse, and this is as great a Check on the Crown. So the King hath a *Prerogative* to Coin Money without Consent of Parliament. But he cannot compel the Subject to take that Money except it be Sterling, Gold or Silver; because herein he is Limited by Law. Some Princes have indeed extended their *Prerogative* further than the Law allowed them: Wherein however, the Lawyers of Succeeding Ages, as fond as they are of *Precedents*, have never dared to Justifie them. But to say the Truth, it is only of late Times that *Prerogative* hath been fixed and ascertained. For whoever Reads the Histories of *England*, will

69 A pejorative term for Catholics.

70 The King's representative in Ireland.

find that some former Kings, and these none of the worst, have upon several Occasions ventured to controul the Laws with very little Ceremony or Scruple, even later than the Days of Queen *Elizabeth*.[71] In her Reign that pernicious Council of sending *Base Money* hither, very narrowly failed of Losing the Kingdom, being complained of by the Lord Deputy, the Council, and the whole Body of the *English* here: So that soon after her Death it was recalled by her Successor, and Lawful Money paid in Exchange.

Having thus given you some Notion of what is meant by the King's *Prerogative*, as far as a *Tradesman* can be thought capable of Explaining it, I will only add the Opinion of the great Lord *Bacon*; That *as God governs the World by the settled Laws of Nature, which he hath made, and never transcends those Laws but upon High Important Occasions: So among Earthly Princes, those are the Wisest and the Best, who govern by the known Laws of the Country, and seldomest make Use of their* Prerogative.[72]

Now, here you may see that the Vile Accusation of *Wood* and his Accomplices, charging us with *Disputing the King's Prerogative* by refusing his Brass, can have no Place, because compelling the Subject to take any Coin which is not Sterling is no Part of the King's *Prerogative*, and I am very confident if it were so, we should be the last of his People to dispute it, as well from that inviolable Loyalty we have always paid to his Majesty, as from the Treatment we might in such a Case justly expect from some who seem to think, we have neither *Common Sense* nor *Common Senses*. But God be thanked, the Best of them are only our *Fellow Subjects*, and not our *Masters*. One great Merit I am sure we have, which those of *English* Birth can have no Pretence to, That our Ancestors reduced this Kingdom to the Obedience of ENGLAND, for which we have been rewarded with a worse Climate, the Priviledge of being governed by Laws to which we do not consent, a Ruined Trade, a House of *Peers* without *Jurisdiction*, almost an Incapacity for all Employments; and the Dread of *Wood's* Half-pence. . . .

There is one comfortable Circumstance in this Universal Opposition to Mr. *Wood*, that the People sent over hither from *England* to *fill up our Vacancies Ecclesiastical, Civil and Military*, are all on our Side: *Money*, the great *Divider* of the World, hath by a strange Revolution, been the great *Uniter* of a most *Divided* People. Who would leave a Hundred Pounds a Year in *England* (*a Country of Freedom*) to be paid a Thousand in *Ireland* out of *Wood's* Exchequer. The *Gentleman*[73] *They* have lately made *Primate* would never quit his Seat in an *English* House of Lords, and his Preferments at *Oxford* and *Bristol*, worth Twelve hundred Pounds a Year, for Four times the Denomination here, but not half the Value; therefore I expect to hear he will be as

71 Elizabeth I of England (1533–1603).

72 Francis Bacon (1561–1626).

73 Hugh Boulter (1672–1742) became Primate of the Church of Ireland in 1724; in 1725, he actively opposed Wood's Halfpence.

good an *Irish* Man, upon *this Article*, as any of his Brethren, or even of *Us* who have had the *Misfortune* to be born in this Island: For those, who, in the common Phrase, do not *come hither to learn the Language*, would never change a better Country for a Worse, to receive *Brass* instead of *Gold*.

Another Slander spread by *Wood* and his Emissaries is, that by opposing him we discover an Inclination to *shake off our Dependance upon the Crown of* England. Pray observe how Important a Person is this same *William Wood*, and how the Publick Weal of Two Kingdoms is involved in his Private Interest. First, all those who refuse to take his Coyn *are Papists*; for he tells us that *none but Papists are associated against him*; Secondly, They *dispute the King's Prerogative*; Thirdly, *They are Ripe for Rebellion*, and Fourthly, They are going to *shake off their Dependance upon the Crown of* England; That is to say, *they are going to chuse another King*: For there can be no other Meaning in this Expression, however some may pretend to strain it.

And this gives me an Opportunity of Explaining, to those who are Ignorant, another Point, which hath often *Swelled in my Breast*. Those who come over hither to us from *England*, and some *Weak* People among our selves, whenever in Discourse we make mention *of Liberty* and *Property*, shake their Heads, and tell us, that *Ireland* is a *Depending Kingdom*, as if they would seem, by this Phrase, to intend that the People of *Ireland* is in some State of Slavery or Dependance different from those of *England*: Whereas a *Depending Kingdom* is a *Modern Term of Art*, unknown, as I have heard, to all antient *Civilians*, and *Writers upon Government*; and *Ireland* is on the contrary called in some Statutes an *Imperial Crown*, as held only from God; which is as High a Style as any Kingdom is capable of receiving. Therefore by this Expression, a *Depending Kingdom*, there is no more understood than that by a Statute made here in the 33d Year of *Henry* 8th.[74] *The King and his Successors are to be Kings Imperial of this Realm as United and Knit to the Imperial Crown of* England. I have looked over all the *English* and *Irish* Statutes [without] finding any Law that makes *Ireland depend* upon *England*, any more than *England* does upon *Ireland*. We have indeed obliged our selves to have the *same King with them*, and consequently they are obliged to have *the same King with us*. For the Law was made by *our own Parliament*, and our Ancestors then were not such *Fools* (*whatever they were in the Preceding Reign*) to bring themselves under I know not what *Dependance*, which is now talked of without any Ground of *Law, Reason* or *Common Sense*.

74 The Crown of Ireland Act (1542); the next sentence largely repeats wording from the Act.

11 From **David Hume, "Of National Characters" (1748)**

David Hume (1711–1776) was born in Edinburgh, Scotland, and became a key figure in the Scottish Enlightenment for his writings in philosophy and history. His major works include *A Treatise of Human Nature* (1739), *Essays, Moral and Political* (1741–1742), *An Enquiry Concerning Human Understanding* (1748, 1756), and *The History of Great Britain* (1754–1761, known as *The History of England*). Hume's *Essays* went through many different editions, and the essay "Of National Characters" in particular went through significant changes. Most notably, in 1760 he added, for a "new edition" of his collected essays, what is now a notorious footnote beginning, "I am apt to suspect the negroes, and in general all the other species of men (for there are four or five different kinds), to be naturally inferior to the whites,"[75] qualifying his essay's argument for "moral" (cultural and political) causes over "physical causes" as determinants of "national character" by presenting "race" as a key factor.

David Hume, "Of National Characters," *Essays, Moral and Political* (London, 1748), pp. 267–88.

The Vulgar are very apt to carry all *national Characters* to Extremes; and having once establish'd it as a Principle, that any People are knavish, or cowardly, or ignorant, they will admit of no Exception, but comprehend every Individual under the same Character. Men of Sense condemn these undistinguish'd Judgments; tho' at the same Time, they allow, that each Nation has a peculiar Set of Manners, and that some particular Qualities are more frequently to be met with among one People than among their Neighbours. The common People in *Swisserland* have surely more Probity than those of the same Rank in *Ireland*; and every prudent Man will, from that Circumstance alone, make a Difference in the Trust he reposes in them. We have Reason to expect greater Wit and Gaiety in a *Frenchman* than in a *Spaniard*; tho' *Cervantes* was born in *Spain*. An *Englishman* will naturally be supposed to have more Knowledge than a *Dane*; tho' *Tycho Brahe* was a Native of *Denmark*.[76] Different Reasons are assign'd for these *national Characters*; while some account for them from *moral* and others from *physical* Causes. By *moral* Causes, I mean all Circumstances, which are fitted to work on the Mind as Motives or Reasons, and which render a peculiar Set of Manners habitual to us. Of this Kind are, the Nature of the Government, the Revolutions of public Affairs, the Plenty or

75 D. Hume, *Essays and Treatises on Several Subjects*, 4 vols, new edn., London, 1760, 1: 337n.

76 Spanish author Miguel de Cervantes Saavedra (1547–1616); Danish astronomer Tycho Brahe (1546–1601).

Penury in which the People live, the Situation of the Nation with Regard to its Neighbours, and such like Circumstances. By *physical* Causes, I here mean those Qualities of the Air and Climate, which are supposed to work insensibly on the Temper, by altering the Tone and Habit of the Body, and giving a particular Complexion, which, tho' Reflection and Reason may sometimes overcome, yet will it prevail among the Generality of Mankind, and have an Influence on their Manners.

That the Character of a Nation will very much depend on *moral* Causes must be evident to the most superficial Observer; since a Nation is nothing but a Collection of Individuals, and the Manners of Individuals are frequently determined by these Causes. As Poverty and hard Labour debase the Minds of the common People, and render them unfit for any Science and ingenious Profession; so where any Government becomes very oppressive to all its Subjects, it must have a proportional Effect on their Temper and Genius, and must banish all the liberal Arts from amongst them. Instances of this Nature are very frequent in the World.

The same Principle of moral Causes fixes the Character of different Professions, and alters even that Disposition, which the particular Members receive from the Hand of Nature. A Soldier and a Priest are different Characters, in all Nations, and all Ages; and this Difference is founded on Circumstances, whose Operation is eternal and unalterable. . . .

As to *physical* Causes, I am inclin'd to doubt altogether of their Operation in this particular; nor do I think, that Men owe any thing of their Temper or Genius to the Air, Food, or Climate. I confess, that the contrary Opinion may justly, at first Sight, seem very probable; since we find, that these Circumstances have an Influence over every other Animal, and that even those Creatures, which are fitted to live in all Climates, such as Dogs, Horses, *&c.* do not yet attain the same Perfection in all. The Courage of Bull-Dogs and Game-Cocks seems peculiar to *England. Flanders* is remarkable for large and heavy Horses: *Spain* for Horses light, and of good Mettle. And any Breed of these Creatures, transported from one Country into another, will soon lose the Qualities, which they deriv'd from their native Climate. It may be ask'd, Why not the same with Men?

There are few Questions more curious than this, nor which will occur oftener in our Enquiries concerning human Affairs; and therefore it may be proper to give it a serious Examination.

The human Mind is of a very imitative Nature; nor is it possible, for any Set of Men, to converse often together, without acquiring a Similitude of Manners, and communicating to each other their Vices as well as Virtues. The Propensity to Company and Society is strong in all rational Creatures; and the same Disposition, which gives us this Propensity, makes us enter deeply into each other's Sentiments, and causes like Passions and Inclinations to run, as it were by Contagion, thro' the whole Club or Knot of Companions. Where a Number of People are united into one political Body, the

Occasions of their Intercourse must be so frequent, for Defence, Commerce, and Government, that, along with the same Speech or Language, they must contract a Resemblance in their Manners, and have a common or national Character, as well as a personal one, peculiar to each Individual. Now tho' Nature produces all Kinds of Temper and Understanding in great Abundance, it follows not that she always produces them in like Proportions, and that in every Society the Ingredients of Industry and Indolence, Valour and Cowardice, Humanity and Brutality, Wisdom and Folly will be mixt after the same Manner. In the Infancy of Society, if any of these Dispositions be found in greater Abundance than the rest, it will naturally prevail in the Composition, and give a Tincture to the national Character. Or should it be asserted, that no Species of Temper can reasonably be presum'd to predominate, even in those contracted Societies, and that the same Proportions will always be preserv'd in the Mixture; yet surely the Persons in Credit and Authority, being a more Contracted Body, cannot always be presum'd to be of the same Character; and their Influence on the Manners of the People, must, at all Times, be very considerable. If on the first Establishment of a Republic, a *Brutus*[77] should be plac'd in Authority, and be transported with such an Enthusiasm for Liberty and public Good, as to overlook all the Ties of Nature, as well as private Interest; such an illustrious Example will naturally have an Effect on the whole Society, and kindle the same Passion in every Bosom. Whatever it be that forms the Manners of one Generation, the next must imbibe a deeper Tincture of the same Dye; Men being more susceptible of all Impressions during Infancy, and retaining these Impressions as long as they remain in the World. I assert, then, that all national Characters, where they depend not on fixt *moral* Causes, proceed from such Accidents as these, and that physical Causes have no discernible Operation on the human Mind.

If we run over the whole Globe, or revolve all the Annals of History, we shall discover every-where Signs of this Sympathy or Contagion of Manners, and none of the Influence of Air or Climate.

First. We may observe, that where a very extensive Government has been establish'd for many Centuries, it spreads a national Character over the whole Empire, and communicates to every Part a Similitude of Manners. Thus the *Chinese* have the greatest Uniformity of Character imaginable; tho' the Air and Climate, in different Parts of that vast Empire, admit of very considerable Variations.

Secondly. In small Governments, which are very contiguous, the People have notwithstanding a different Character, and are often as distinguishable in

77 Lucius Junius Brutus (c. 509 BCE), founder of the Roman Republic and purported ancestor of Marcus Junius Brutus (85–42 BCE); both were known for their civic virtue.

their Manners as the most distant Nations. *Athens* and *Thebes* were but a short Day's Journey from each other; tho' the *Athenians* were as remarkable for Ingenuity, Politeness, and Gaiety, as the *Thebans* for Dulness, Rusticity, and a phlegmatic Temper. *Plutarch*, discoursing of the Effects of Air on the Minds of Men, observes that the Inhabitants of the *Piræum*, possest very different Tempers from those of the higher Town of *Athens*, which was distant about four Miles from it.[78] But I believe no one attributes the Difference of Manners, in *Wapping* and St. *James's*,[79] to a Difference of Air or Climate.

Thirdly. The same national Character commonly follows the Authority of the Government to a precise Limit or Boundary; and upon crossing a River, or passing a Mountain, one finds a new Set of Manners along with a new Government. The *Languedocians* and *Gascons* are the gayest People of all *France*; but whenever you go over the *Pyrenees*, you are among *Spaniards*. Is it conceivable, that the Qualities of the Air should change so exactly with the Limits of an Empire, which depend so much on the Accidents of Battles, Negotiations, and Marriages?

Fourthly. Where any Set of Men, scatter'd over distant Nations, have a close Society or Communication together, they acquire a Similitude of Manners, and have but little in common with the Nations amongst whom they live. Thus the *Jews* in *Europe*, and the *Armenians* in the East, have a peculiar Character; and the former are as much noted for Fraud, as the latter for Probity. The *Jesuites*, in all *Roman-Catholic* Countries, are also observ'd to have a Character peculiar to themselves.

Fifthly. Where any Accident, as a Difference of Language or Religion, keeps two Nations, inhabiting the same Country, from mixing with each other, they will preserve a distinct and even opposite Set of Manners for several Centuries. The Integrity, Gravity, and Bravery of the *Turks* form an exact Contrast to the Levity, Deceit, and Cowardice of the modern *Greeks*.

Sixthly. The same Set of Manners will follow a Nation, and adhere to them over the whole Globe, as well as the same Laws and Language. The *Spanish*, *English*, *French*, and *Dutch* Colonies are all distinguishable, even betwixt the Tropics.

Seventhly. The Manners of a People change very considerably from one Age to another; either by great Alterations in their Government, by the Mixtures of new People, or by that Inconstancy, to which all human Affairs are subject.

---

78 Greek historian and biographer Plutarch (c. 46–120); cities in classical Greece.

79 Districts of London, England, presenting a contrast in wealth.

The Ingenuity and Industry of the ancient *Greeks* have nothing in common with the Stupidity and Indolence of the present Inhabitants of those Regions. Candour, Bravery, and Love of Liberty, form'd the Character of the ancient *Romans*; as Subtilty, Cowardice, and a Slavish Disposition do that of the modern. The old *Spaniards* were restless, turbulent, and so addicted to War, that many of them killed themselves, when they were depriv'd of their Arms by the *Romans*. One would find an equal Difficulty, at present, (at least fifty Years ago) to rouze up the modern *Spaniards* to Arms. The *Batavians* were all Soldiers of Fortune, and hir'd themselves into the *Roman* Armies. Their Posterity make use of Foreigners for the same Purpose that the *Romans* did their Ancestors. Tho' some Strokes of the *French* Character be the same, which *Cæsar* has ascrib'd to the *Gauls*; yet what Comparison betwixt the Civility, Humanity and Knowledge of the modern Inhabitants of that Country, and the Ignorance, Barbarity and Grossness of the ancient?

Eighthly. Where several neighbouring Nations have a very close Communication together, either by Policy, Commerce, or Travelling, they acquire a Similitude of Manners, proportion'd to the Communication. Thus all the *Franks* seem to have a uniform Character to the Eastern Nations. The Differences among them are like the particular Accents of different Provinces, which are not distinguishable, except by an Ear accustom'd to them, and which commonly escape a Foreigner.

Ninthly. We may often remark a wonderful Mixture of Manners and Character in the same Nation, speaking the same Language, and subject to the same Government: And in this Particular, the *English* are the most remarkable of any People, that ever were in the World. Nor is this to be ascrib'd to the Mutability and Uncertainty of their Climate, or to any other *physical* Causes; since all these Causes take Place in their neighbouring Kingdom of *Scotland*, without having the same Effect. Where the Government of a Nation is altogether republican, it is apt to beget a particular Set of Manners. Where it is altogether monarchical, it is more apt to have the same Effect; the Imitation of Superiors spreading the national Manners faster among the People. If a State consists altogether of Merchants, such as *Holland*, their uniform Way of Life will form their Character. If it consists chiefly of Nobles and landed Gentry, like *Germany, France,* and *Spain*, the same Effect follows. The Genius of a particular Sect or Religion is also apt to mould the Manners of a People. But the *English* Government is a Mixture of Monarchy, Aristocracy, and Democracy. The People are compos'd of Gentry and Merchants. All Sects of Religion are to be found amongst them. And the great Liberty and Independency, which they enjoy, allows every one to display the Manners, which are peculiar to him. Hence the *English*, of any People to the Universe, have the least of a national Character; unless this very Singularity be made their national Character.

If the Characters of Men depended on the Air and Climate, the Degrees of Heat and Cold should naturally be expected to have a mighty Influence; since nothing has a greater Effect on all Plants and irrational Animals. And indeed, there is some Reason to think, that all the Nations, which live beyond the polar Circles or betwixt the Tropics, are inferior to the rest of the Species, and are utterly incapable of all the higher Attainments of the human Mind. The Poverty and Misery of the northern Inhabitants of the Globe, and the Indolence of the southern, may, perhaps, account for this remarkable Difference, without having Recourse to *physical* Causes. This however is certain, that the Characters of Nations are very promiscuous in the temperate Climates, and that almost all the general Observations, which have been form'd of the more southern or more northern Nations in these Climates, are found to be uncertain and fallacious.

12 From **Henry Home,** ***Sketches of the History of Man*** **(1774)**

Henry Home (1696–1782) was born in Scotland and received most of his early education through private tutors. He later trained for the law and became an advocate in 1723. His first publications were on legal subjects as he rose through the ranks, entered the judiciary and became Lord Kames in 1752. It was about this time that, like other authors of the Scottish Enlightenment, he began publishing on larger social and cultural questions, including *Essays upon Several Subjects Concerning British Antiquities* (1747) and the controversial *Essays on the Principles of Morality and Natural Religion* (1751). He continued to publish on the law, creating an impressive body of work across his career, but arguably his major works are *Elements of Criticism* (1762), a comprehensive treatise on rhetoric, poetics, and other literary devices from which he quotes below, and *Sketches of the History of Man* (1774), a series of essays on society, culture, and government from which the following "Sketch" is taken.

Henry Home, "Sketch VII: Rise and Fall of Patriotism," *Sketches of the History of Man*, 2 vols (Edinburgh and London, 1774), 1, pp. 439–54.

From **SKETCH VII: Rise and Fall of Patriotism**

The members of a tribe, in their original state of hunting and fishing, being little united but by a common language, have no notion of a *patria*; and scarce any notion of society, unless when they join in an expedition against an enemy, or against wild beasts. The shepherd-state, where flocks and herds are possessed in common, gives a clear notion of a common interest; but still none of a *patria*. The sense of a *patria* begins to unfold itself, when a people leave off wandering, to settle upon a territory which they call their own. Agriculture connects them together; and government still more: they become fellow-citizens; and the territory is termed the *patria* of every person born in it. It is so ordered by Providence, that a man's country, and his countrymen, are to him in conjunction an object of a peculiar affection, termed *amor patriæ*, or *patriotism*; an affection that rises high among a people intimately connected by regular government, by husbandry, by commerce, and by a common interest. "Cari sunt parentes, cari liberi, propinqui, familiares; sed omnes omnium caritates patria una complexa est; pro qua quis bonus dubitet mortem oppetere?"[80]

Social passions and affections, beside being greatly more agreeable than selfish, are those only which command our esteem.[81] Patriotism stands at the head of social affections; and stands so high in our esteem, that no actions but what proceed from it are termed grand or heroic. When that affection appears so agreeable in contemplation, how sweet, how elevating, must it be in those whom it inspires! Like vigorous health, it beats constantly with an equal pulse: like the vestal fire, it never is extinguished. No source of enjoyment is more plentiful than patriotism, where it is the ruling passion: it triumphs over every selfish motive, and is a firm support to every virtue. In fact, where-ever it prevails, the morals of the people are found to be pure and correct.

These are illustrious effects of patriotism with respect to private happiness and virtue; and yet its effects with respect to the public are still more illustrious. A nation in no other period of its progress is so flourishing, as when patriotism is the ruling passion of every member: during that period, it is invincible. Atheneus remarks, that the Athenians were the only people in the world, who, tho' clothed in purple, put formidable armies to flight at Marathon, Salamine, and Platea.[82] But at that period patriotism was their ruling passion; and success attended them in every undertaking. Where patriotism rules, men do wonders, whatever garb they wear. The fall of Saguntum is a grand scene; a people exerting the utmost powers of nature, in defence of their country.[83] The city was indeed destroyed; but the citizens were not subdued. The last effort of the remaining heroes was, to burn themselves, with their wives and children, in one great funeral pile. . . .

Patriotism at the same time is the great bulwark of civil liberty; equally abhorrent of despotism on the one hand, and of licentiousness on the other.

80 "Our parents are dear to us; so are our children, our relations, and our friends; all these our country comprehends; and shall we fear to die for our country?" (Home's translation). The passage is from Cicero's *De Officiis* ("On Duties," 1, ch. 17; 44 BCE), a book of practical morals.

81 *Elements of Criticism*, vol. I p. 113 edit. 5 (Home's note).

82 Atheneus (or Athenaeus), Greek author active around 200 AD; these were the sites of major battles in the Greco-Persian wars (490–448 BCE).

83 Saguntum, in Spain, fell to Hannibal after a lengthy siege in 219 BCE; it was the subject of a play by Philip Frowde in 1727.

While the despotic government of the Tudor family subsisted, the English were too much depressed to have any affection for their country. But when manufactures and commerce began to flourish in the latter end of Elizabeth's reign, a national spirit broke forth, and patriotism made some figure. That change of disposition was perhaps the chief cause, tho' not the most visible, of the national struggles for liberty, which were frequent during the government of the Stewart family, and which ended in a free government at the Revolution.

Patriotism is too much cramped in a very small state, and too much relaxed in an extensive monarchy. But that topic has already been discussed in the first sketch of this book.

Patriotism is enflamed by a struggle for liberty, by a civil war, by resisting a potent invader, or by any incident that forcibly draws the members of the state into strict union for the common interest. The resolute opposition of the seven provinces to Philip II. of Spain, in the cause of liberty, is an illustrious instance of the patriotic spirit rising to a degree of enthusiasm.[84] Patriotism, roused among the Corsicans by the oppression of the Genoese, exerted itself upon every proper object. Even during the heat of the war, they erected an university for arts and sciences, a national bank, and a national library; improvements that would not have been thought of in their torpid state. Alas! they have fallen a victim to thirst of power, not to superior valour. Had Providence favoured them with success, their figure would have been considerable in peace as in war.[85]

But violent commotions cannot be perpetual: one party prevails, and prosperity follows. What effect may this have on patriotism? I answer, that nothing is more animating than success after a violent struggle: a nation in that state resembles a comet, which in passing near the sun, has been much heated, and continues full of motion. Patriotism made a capital figure among the Athenians, when they became a free people, after expelling the tyrant Pisistratus.[86] Every man exerted himself for his country: every man endeavoured

---

84 The Union of Utrecht (1579) united the seven provinces of the Spanish Netherlands against Spanish rule; Philip II (1527–1598).

85 The elevation of sentiment that a struggle for liberty inspires, is conspicuous in the following incident. A Corsican being condemned to die for an atrocious crime, his nephew with deep concern addressed Paoli in the following terms. "Sir, if you pardon my uncle, his relations will give to the state a thousand zechins, beside furnishing fifty soldiers during the siege of Furiali. Let him be banished, and he shall never return." Paoli, knowing the virtue of the young man, said to him. "You are acquainted with the circumstances of that case: I will consent to a pardon, if you can say, as an honest man, that it will be just or honourable for Corsica." The young man, hiding his face, burst into tears, saying, "I would not have the honour of our country sold for a thousand zechins" (Home's note).

86 Pisistratus, despite being overthrown twice, ruled Athens for most of the period 560–528 BCE.

to excell those who went before him: and hence a Miltiades, an Aristides, a Themistocles,[87] names that for ever will figure in the annals of time. While the Roman republic was confined within narrow bounds, austerity of manners, and disinterested love to their country, formed the national character. The elevation of the Patricians above the Plebians,[88] a source of endless discord, was at last remedied by placing all the citizens upon a level. This signal revolution excited an animating emulation between the Patricians and Plebians; the former, by heroic actions, labouring to maintain their superiority; the latter straining every nerve to equal them: the republic never at any other period produced so great men in the art of war.

But such variety there is in human affairs, that tho' men are indebted to emulation for their heroic actions, yet actions of that kind never fail to suppress emulation in those who follow. An observation is made above,[89] that nothing is more fatal to the progress of an art, than a person of superior genius, who damps emulation in others: witness the celebrated Newton,[90] to whom the decay of mathematical knowledge in Britain is justly attributed. The observation holds equally with respect to action. Those actions only that flow from patriotism are deemed grand and heroic; and such actions, above all others, rouse a national spirit. But beware of a Newton in heroism: instead of exciting emulation, he will damp it: despair to equal the great men who are the admiration of all men, puts an end to emulation. After the illustrious achievements of Miltiades, and after the eminent patriotism of Aristides, we hear no more in Greece of emulation or of patriotism. Pericles was a man of parts, but he sacrificed Athens to his ambition. The Athenians sunk lower and lower under the Archons, who had neither parts nor patriotism; and were reduced at last to slavery, first by the Macedonians, and next by the Romans.[91] The Romans ran the same course, from the highest exertions of patriotic emulation, down to the most abject selfishness and effeminacy.

And this leads to other causes that extinguish patriotism, or relax it. Factious disorders in a state never fail to relax it; for there the citizen is lost, and every person is beheld in the narrow view of a friend or an enemy. In the contests between the Patricians and Plebians of Rome, the public was totally

87 Three military leaders in Athens during the Greco-Persian wars.

88 In Rome, Patricians were the nobility and Plebians the workers, farmers, merchants and so forth; the third major division of Roman society was that of slaves.

89 Book I. sketch 5. § I. (Home's note). In this section of *Sketches*, "Useful Arts," Home writes, "As the progress of arts and sciences toward perfection is greatly promoted by emulation, nothing is more fatal to an art or science than to remove that spur, as where some extraordinary genius appears who soars above rivalship."

90 English scientist Isaac Newton (1642–1727).

91 Pericles, another leading Athenian about the time of the Greco-Persian wars, promoted the arts and public works as well as advanced democracy (c. 460–429 BCE). The Archons were elected officials who ruled Athens.

disregarded: the Plebians could have no heart-affection for a country where they were oppressed; and the Patricians might be fond of their own order, but they could not sincerely love their country, while they were enemies to the bulk of their countrymen. Patriotism did not shine forth in Rome, till all equally became citizens.

To support patriotism, it is necessary that a people be in a train of prosperity: when a nation becomes stationary, patriotism subsides. The ancient Romans upon a small foundation erected a great empire; so great indeed, that it fell to pieces by its unwieldiness. But the plurality of nations, whether from their situation, from the temper of their people, or from the nature of their government, are confined within narrower limits; beyond which their utmost exertions avail little, unless they happen to be extraordinary favourites of fortune. When a nation becomes thus stationary, its pushing genius is at an end: its plan is to preserve, not to acquire: the members, even without any example of heroism to damp emulation, are infected with the languid tone of the state: patriotism subsides; and we hear no more of bold or heroic actions. The Venetians are a pregnant instance of the observation. Their trade with Aleppo and Alexandria did for centuries introduce into Europe the commodities of Syria, Egypt, Arabia, Persia, and India. The cities of Nuremberg and Augsburg in particular, were supplied from Venice with these commodities; and by that traffick became populous and opulent. . . .

No cause hitherto mentioned hath such influence in depressing patriotism, as inequality of rank and riches in an opulent monarchy. A continual influx of wealth into the capital, generates show, luxury, avarice, which are all selfish vices; and selfishness, enslaving the mind, eradicates every fibre of patriotism.[92] Asiatic luxury, flowing into Rome in a plentiful stream, produced a universal corruption of manners, and metamorphos'd into voluptuousness the warlike genius of that great city. The dominions of Rome were now too extensive for a republican government, and its generals too powerful to be disinterested. Passion for glory wore out of fashion, as austerity of manners had done formerly: power and riches were now the only objects of ambition: virtue seemed a farce; honour, a chimera; and fame, mere vanity. . . .

Successful commerce is not more advantageous by the wealth and power it immediately bestows, than it is hurtful ultimately by introducing luxury and voluptuousness, which eradicate patriotism. In the capital of a great monarchy, the poison of opulence is sudden; because opulence there is seldom acquired by reputable means: the poison of commercial opulence is slow, because commerce seldom enriches without industry, sagacity, and fair dealing. But by whatever means acquired, opulence never fails soon or late to smother patriotism under sensuality and selfishness. . . .

92 France is not an exception. The French are vain of their country, because they are vain of themselves. But such vanity must be distinguished from patriotism, which consists in loving our country independent of ourselves (Home's note).

It is deplorable, that in English public schools, patriotism makes no branch of education; young men, on the contrary, are trained up to selfishness. *Keep what you get, and get what you can*, is the chief lesson inculcated at Westminster, Winchester, and Eaton.[93] Students put themselves in the way of receiving vails from strangers; and that dirty practice continues, tho' far more poisonous to manners, than the giving vails to menial servants, which the nation is now ashamed of. The Eaton scholars are at times sent to the highway to rob passengers. The strong without control tyrannize over the weak, subjecting them to every servile office, wiping shoes not excepted. They are permitted to trick and deceive one another; and the finest fellow is he who is the most artful. Friendship indeed is cultivated, but such as we find among robbers: a boy would be run down, if he had no associate. In a word, the most determined selfishness is the capital lesson.

When a nation, formerly warlike and public-spirited, is depressed by luxury and selfishness, doth nature afford no means for restoring it to its former state? The Emperor Hadrian declared the Greeks a free people; not doubting, but that a change so animating, would restore the fine arts to their pristine lustre.—A vain attempt: for the genius of the Greeks vanished with their patriotism; and liberty to them was no blessing. With respect to the Portuguese, the decay of their power and of their commerce, have reduced them to a much lower condition, than when they rose as it were out of nothing. At that time, they were poor, but innocent; at present they are poor, but corrupted with many vices. Their pride in particular swells as high as when masters of the Indies. . . . To enable these nations to recommence their former course, or any nation in the same situation, I can discover no means but pinching poverty. Commerce and manufactures taking wing, may leave a country in a very distressed condition: but a people may be very distressed, and yet very vitious; for vices generated by opulence are not soon eradicated. And tho' other vices should at last vanish with the temptations that promoted them, indolence and pusillanimity will remain for ever, unless by some powerful cause the opposite virtues be introduced. A very poor man, however indolent, will be tempted for bread to exert some activity; and he may be trained gradually from less to more by the same means. Activity at the same time produces bodily strength; which will restore courage and boldness. By such means a nation may be put in motion with the same advantages it had originally; and its second progress may prove as successful as the first. Thus nations go round in a circle, from weakness to strength, and from strength to weakness. The first part of the progress is verified in a thousand instances; but the world has not subsisted long enough to afford any clear instance of the other.

I close this sketch with two illustrious examples of patriotism; one ancient,

93 Elite schools in contemporary England ("Eaton" is better known as Eton).

one modern; one among the whites, and one among the blacks. Aristides the Athenian is famed above all the ancients for love to his country. Its safety and honour were the only objects of his ambition; and his signal disinterestedness made it the same to him, whether these ends were accomplished by himself or by others, by his friends or his foes. One conspicuous instance occurred before the battle of Marathon. Of the ten generals chosen to command the Athenian army, he was one: but sensible that a divided command is subjected to manifold inconveniencies, he exerted all his influence for delegating the whole power to Miltiades; and at the same time zealously supported the proposal of Miltiades, of boldly meeting the Persians in the field. His disinterestedness was still more conspicuous with regard to Themistocles, his bitter enemy. Suspending all enmity, he cordially agreed with him in every operation of the war; assisting him with his counsel and credit, and yet suffering him to engross all the honours of victory. In peace he was the same, yielding to Themistocles in the administration of government, and contenting himself with a subordinate place. In the senate and in the assembly of the people, he made many proposals in a borrowed name, to prevent envy and opposition. He retired from public business in the latter part of his life; passing his time in training young men for serving the state, instilling into them principles of honour and virtue, and inspiring them with love to their country. His death unfolded a signal proof of the contempt he had for riches: he who had been treasurer of Greece during the lavishment of war, left not sufficient to defray the expence of his funerals: a British commissary in like circumstances, acquires the riches of Crœsus.[94]

The scene of the other example is Fouli, a negro kingdom in Africa.[95] Such regard is paid there to royal blood, that no man can succeed to the crown, but who is connected with the first monarch, by an uninterrupted chain of females: a connection by males would give no security, as the women of that country are prone to gallantry. In the last century, the Prince of Sambaboa, the King's nephew by his sister, was invested with the dignity of Kamalingo, a dignity appropriated to the presumptive heir. A liberal and generous mind, with undaunted courage, rivetted him in the affections of the nobility and people. They rejoiced in the expectation of having him for their King. But their expectation was blasted. The King, fond of his children, ventured a bold measure, which was, to invest his eldest son with the dignity of Kamalingo, and to declare him heir to the crown. Tho' the Prince of Sambaboa had for him the laws of the kingdom, and the hearts of the people, yet he retired in silence to avoid a civil war. He could not however prevent men of rank

94 Croesus, King of Lydia (c. 595–547 BCE), was proverbially rich and defeated by the Persians.

95 *The Modern Part of an Universal History* (vol. 17, London, 1760), which Home closely echoes throughout this paragraph, describes Fouli as a substantial kingdom in eastern Africa.

from flocking to him; which the King interpreting to be a rebellion, raised an army in order to put them all to the sword. As the King advanced, the Prince retired, resolving not to draw his sword against an uncle, whom he was accustomed to call father. But finding that the command of the King's army was bestowed on his rival, he made ready for the battle. The Prince obtained a complete victory: but his heart was not elated: the horrors of a civil war stared him in the face: he bid farewell to his friends, dismissed his army, and retired into a neighbouring kingdom; relying on the affections of the people to be placed on the throne after his uncle's death. During banishment, which continued thirty tedious years, frequent attempts on his life, put his temper to a severe trial; for while he existed, the King had no hopes that his son would reign in peace. He had the fortitude to stand every trial; when, in the year 1702, beginning to yield to age and misfortunes, his uncle died. His cousin was deposed; and he was called by the unanimous voice of the nobles, to reign over a people who adored him.

13 From **Thomas Cary**, ***Abram's Plains: A Poem*** **(1789)**

Thomas Cary (1751–1823) was born near Bristol, England, and spent some time working for the East India Company before arriving in Canada, likely about the time of the American Revolutionary War.[96] After an unsuccessful stint in trade, he turned to government work, eventually, though only briefly, working as the secretary to the Governor (1798–1799). He then returned to the private sector, establishing a newspaper, *Quebec Mercury*, and running a reading room stocked with European and American publications. *Abram's Plains*, nearly 600 lines of rhyming couplets, is one of the leading works of eighteenth-century Canadian verse and commemorates one of the key battles of the Seven Years' War: the Battle of the Plains of Abraham, Quebec, took place in 1759 and was a turning point in the British defeat of French forces in New France, territory formally ceded to Britain at the end of the Seven Years' War (1763). Cary celebrates British rule in Canada, suggesting that even the French settlers who remain prefer the post-1763 dispensation under George III of England (reigned 1760–1820): "Grateful, ye peasants, own your mended state, / And bless, beneath a GEORGE, your better fate" (450–51).

Thomas Cary, *Abram's Plains: A Poem* (Quebec, 1789).

96 F. G. Halpenny, *Dictionary of Canadian Biography*, vol. 6, Toronto: University of Toronto Press, 1966, p. 123.

Preface

At a time when literature seems to be emerging from the closet to illuminate our horizon, I venture to usher into day the following little poem, the offspring of a few leisure hours; which I hope will not be unpleasing to the lovers of polite learning.

If I may be allowed to judge from experience, I must pronounce descriptive poetry, that exhibits a picture of the real scenes of nature, to be the most difficult to excel in. To vary, harmonize, soften and add the necessary graces to description to make it palatable to a judicious and poetical reader require no small genius and skill. I think far more than are requisite to any thing of the fabulous kind, whose fabric is the sole work of imagination and where the fancy has full play.

Convinced of this difficulty, I cannot enough admire those writers who have excelled in this kind of writing. At the head of whom, amongst the moderns, Thomson, the harmonious Thomson stands unrivalled.[97] Much as I admire that great refiner of English verse Pope, I cannot help feeling a preference for Thomson, so strikingly unparalleled and inimitable are the beauties of his numbers.[98] It must be observed that it is only Pope's descriptive poetry, such as his Windsor-Forest, that I here bring into comparison, Thomson having wrote nothing of the nature of his ethics or satires. It may be said that their comparative merits, even in description, cannot but with difficulty be ascertained, the one having wrote in blank verse the other in rime. It is true that Thomson has the advantage of not being fettered by rime, but to excel in blank verse, in my opinion, requires a far more poetical fancy as well as greater strength of imagination than are requisite to please in rime, where correctness of numbers often passes on the generality of readers for every thing. I cannot avoid making this avowal however it may operate against myself.

Before I began this Poem I read Pope's Windsor-Forest and Dr. Goldsmith's Deserted Village,[99] with the view of endeavouring, in some degree, to catch their manner of writing; as singers in country-churches in England, to use a simple musical comparison, modulate their tones by the prelusive sound of a pitch-pipe. How far I have succeeded I must leave to my readers to determine; trusting, however, for a favourable decision more to their good-nature than to my deserts.

Quebec, 24th Jan. 1789

---

97 James Thomson (1700–1748), English topographical poet best known for *The Seasons* (1728–1730); Cary's misspelling has been silently corrected.

98 Alexander Pope (1688–1744), English poet, author of "Windsor-Forest" (1713).

99 Oliver Goldsmith (1728–1774), Irish author of "The Deserted Village" (1770), a work which influenced a generation of Canadian poets, including his distant relative, another Oliver Goldsmith, author of *The Rising Village* (1825).

From *Abram's Plains*

Thy Plains, O *Abram!* and thy pleasing views,
Where, hid in shades, I sit and court the muse,
Grateful I sing. For there, from care and noise,
Oft have I fled to taste thy silent joys:
There, lost in thought, my musing passion fed,
Or held blest converse with the learned dead.
Else, like a steed, unbroke to bit or rein,
Courting fair health, I drive across the plain;
The balmy breeze of Zephyrus inhale,
Or bare my breast to the bleak northern gale.
Oft, on the green sod lolling as I lay,
Heedless, the grazing herds around me stray:
Close by my side shy songsters fearless hop,
And shyer squirrels the young verdure crop:
All take me for some native of the wood,
Or else some senseless block thrown from the flood.
Thy flood Saint Lawrence, in whose copious wave
The Naiades of a thousand riv'lets lave:
Through whom, fresh seas, from mighty urns descend,
And, in one stream their many waters blend.
Thee, first of lakes![100] as *Asia's Caspian* great,
Where congregated streams hold icy state.
Huron, distinguish'd by its thund'ring bay,
Where full-charg'd clouds heav'ns ord'nance ceaseless play.
Thee *Michigan*, where learned beavers lave,
And two great tribes divided hold thy wave.
Erie for serpents fam'd, whose noisome breath,
By man inhal'd, conveys the venom'd death.
The streams thence rushing with tremendous roar,
Down thy dread fall, *Niagara*, prone pour;
Back foaming, in thick hoary mists, they bound,
The thund'ring noise deafens the country round,
Whilst echo, from her caves, redoubling sends the sound.
'Twixt awe and pleasure, rapt in wild suspense,
Giddy, the gazer yields up ev'ry sense.
So have I felt when Handel's heavenly strains,
Choral, announce the great Messiah reigns:

---

100 Lake *Superiour*. One quality of whose waters is to be remarkably cold under the surface (Cary's note). Cary details major waterways of the region: the St. Lawrence river; the Great Lakes; Niagara Falls, between the Great Lakes Erie and Ontario.

Caught up by sound, I leave my earthly part,
And into something more than mortal start.
Now, in *Ontario's* urn, spacious they spread,
By added waters, from *Oswego*, fed;
Thence down the *Cataraqui* rolling on,
Or gliding gently to the Naiades' song;
Who, in full chorus, vocal, join their lays,
To chant, in chearful carols, Ceres' praise:
Whose yellow harvests, nodding, glad the shore,
Where Dryades, midst wild deserts, reign'd before.
Where prowl'd the wolf, the bear and fox obscene,
Now grateful kine, loud lowing, graze the green.
Such are thy blessings peace! superior far
To specious conquests of wild-wasting war.
Destructive war! at best the good of few,
Its dire effects whilst millions dearly rue.
How blest the task, to tame the savage soil,
And, from the waters, bid the woods recoil!
But oh! a task of more exalted kind,
To arts of peace, to tame the savage mind;
The thirst of blood, in human breasts, to shame,
To wrest, from barb'rous vice, fair virtue's name;
Bid tomahawks to ploughshares yield the sway,
And skalping-knives to pruning hooks give way;
In *Circe's*[101] glass bid moderation reign,
And moral virtues humanize the plain!
Here, shelter'd from the storm of civil broils,
The loyal sufferer renews his toils:
Again, from the unclog'd responsive earth,
Calls a new patrimony into birth.
By British magnanimity repaid,
The foe triumphant dare no more upbraid:
But wish he had so lost so to have gain'd,
Pleas'd with the *now*, the *past* no more had pain'd.
Thus mariners wreck'd on some distant shore
Their homes, their all, sunk in the deep, deplore;
'Till with sad step, they inland bend their way
Where mines of gold their loss amply repay.

101 Figure of classical myth associated with transformation.

14 Anna Letitia Barbauld, "To a Great Nation" (1793)

Anna Letitia Aikin (1743–1825), Barbauld after her marriage in 1774, was born to an English Dissenting family with strong literary connections. Her brother, author John Aikin, edited the influential *Monthly Magazine*, to which Barbauld was a frequent contributor; her poetry began to appear in print in the 1760s. In the 1790s, she published essays praising the French Revolution and opposing British participation in the slave trade, and her poetry often repeated these themes. In 1812, her successful literary career was effectively ended by her devastating critique of British imperialism in *Eighteen Hundred and Eleven*. "To a Great Nation," was later retitled, "On the Expected General Rising of the French Nation in 1792," suggesting that it refers to the period before the "Terror" in which the royal family and others were executed by guillotine; relevant events in late 1792 include the arrest of the King and the abolition of monarchy, the "Edict of Fraternity" which declared common cause with other peoples wishing to overthrow monarchies, and the defeat of an attempted invasion of France.

[Anna Letitia Barbauld] "To a Great Nation," *The Cambridge Intelligencer*, November 2, 1793, n.p.

"To a Great Nation"

Rise mighty nation! in thy strength,
And deal thy dreadful vengeance round;
Let thy great spirit rous'd at length,
Strike hordes of Despots to the ground.

Devoted land! thy mangled breast,
Eager the r---l vultures tear:
By friends betray'd, by foes oppress'd,
And virtue struggles with despair.

The tocsin sounds! arise, arise,
Stern o'er each breast let country reign;
Nor virgins plighted hand, nor sighs
Must now the ardent youth detain.

Nor must the hind who tills thy soil,
The ripen'd vintage stay to press,
'Till rapture crowns the flowing bowl,
And Freedom boasts of full success.

Briareus like,[102] extend thy hands,
    That every hand may crush a foe;
In millions pour thy generous bands,
    And end a warfare by a blow.

Then wash with sad repentant tears,
    Each deed that clouds thy glory's page;
Each phrensied start impell'd by fears,
    Each transient burst of headlong rage.

Then fold in thy relenting arms
    Thy wretched outcasts where they roam;
From pining want and war's alarms,
    O call the child of Misery home.

Then build the tomb—O not alone,
    Of him who bled in freedom's cause;
With equal eye the martyr own,
    Of faith revered and antient laws.

Then be thy tide of glory stay'd,
    Then be thy conquering banners furl'd,
Obey the laws thyself hast made,
    And rise—the model of the world!

15 From **William Drennan,** ***Letter to the Right Honorable William Pitt*** **(1799)**

William Drennan (1754–1820), born in Belfast, was a Presbyterian and successful medical doctor in 1790s Dublin who became one of the leaders of the nationalist Society of United Irishmen, a group that sought legislative independence for Ireland and argued for an end to religious intolerance at a time when Irish Catholics (and Dissenters such as Drennan) could not vote, hold political or government office, or take a university degree. Drennan was also a poet, and his nationalist ballads appeared in United Irishmen publications. He left the United Irishmen shortly before the 1798 Uprising, but published pamphlets arguing against the Act of Union (1800) that followed the suppression of the uprising, the first of which was the *Letter* excerpted below, addressed to the current Prime Minister of Britain, William Pitt. Under the Act of Union, the Irish Parliament was

102 *Briareus* was a giant of ancient fable, represented with a hundred hands, and fifty heads (Barbauld's note).

abolished and Ireland was given a group of seats in the British Parliament. Drennan continued to publish in the 1800s, and collected his work in *Fugitive Pieces in Verse and Prose* (1815), a volume that includes one of his anti-Union essays. He returned to Belfast where he helped to found the Belfast Academical Institution and *Belfast Monthly Magazine*.

William Drennan, *Letter to the Right Honorable William Pitt* (Dublin: James Moore, 1799).

A great change is imperiously called for. The rooted moral and national evil, which must ever stand in the way of social improvement, and has been the peculiar curse of this country, is an HABITUAL CONTEMPT (worse than injury) of the common people, generated at first from the spirit of conquest, and nursed by the same spirit transfused into penal codes, systems of monopolism, and creeds of ascendancy, until it has grown into a disease, that affects all the higher orders with hereditary contamination. It is the scrophula of the proud and powerful, which has totally relaxed and loosened all the joints of society. It has spread its acrimony among the patriots of party, the philosophers of schools, and the most sequacious professions.—The standing exception even to the barren benevolence of general speculation is—their native country; and thus it has necessarily happened that the extended family feeling, which ought to bind the different ranks of society into one neighbourhood, is resolved into an anarchy of separate interests, producing for many years past periodical and partial insurrection, and, of late, more connected and premeditated rebellion.

The system of conquest, which gathers the fruit by cutting down the tree; the system of mercantile monopoly, which withdraws the manure from the roots; the system of influence, which blasts and withers the branches, or occasions such partial circulation of vital juice, as is seen strangely to bloom and blossom in the midst of barrenness and decay; all these systems rendering the great tree of society sapless and unproductive, are finally resolvable into that *inveterate contempt* of the lower community, which has hitherto counteracted, and must ever counteract the establishment of free, equal, and *reciprocal* society.—A great change *is* required, and *must* prove salutary from whatever quarter it comes—"*J'accepteroi le bien public des mains d'Arimaine même.*"[103]

Ireland has been kept in a state of *savage* independence; in such a state as might best break down, and destroy that *mutual* dependence, from which flows the happiness of the individual, and the true wealth of nations. The inhabitants were insulated to keep the country subjugated; the former in a state of nature; the latter an imperial slave. Under the combined oppression

103 "I would accept the public good from the hands of Arimanes himself." Arimanes is a Persian deity, associated with evil.

of manners and of laws, the country throve into a sort of barbarous independence and public servility—no want of capital, but a partial distribution of it—much wealth, but no common wealth—much labour acquiring little property.—The palsy of indolence from the absence of that diffusible stimulus, property; and an incapability, turned at last into an unwillingness, of transforming and fixing labour into durable possession, and capital stock.—Irregular, inordinate, and exhausting *labour*, produced by and for intoxication (the source of revenue) instead of *industry* creating a little stock, slowly and regularly adding to it; always receiving, always repaying; the happiness of the individual, the real and imperishable wealth of the community. . . .

I aver, Sir, in your *hearing*, that as it was the bigotry of the Protestant which generated the Papist, and the partiality of ascendancies which begot civil distraction, it is now the time for all parties here to break through the suspicions of ignorance, and instead of looking at the world through Britain, to look at Britain through the world. Sir, for my own part, I will follow the genuine principles of the British Constitution, even when they emigrate into France; and I will glory in my estrangement from your island, whenever the dogmas of French despotism are transfused into Britain. When, under such auspices, or rather the shade of such omens, I see a plan handed from an English minister to an English-Irish minister, like to you in nothing, I know of, but in being young, thin, and self-sufficient; when I see, not an East-India bill, but a *West-Britain* bill preparing for dissolving not only all principles of constitution, but the constituency itself; for removing the seat of government *for ever* from the soil, and eternizing the provinciality and servitude of my country, under an administration unalterably English, and everlastingly conforming to the interests, prejudices, and jealousies of the seat of sovereignty, leaving us a lease of lives renewable for ever of all the *abuses* of our wretched administration, and taking from us the fee-simple of our country, making it utterly, and ever impracticable for Ireland to manage her own affairs in the way she judges most suitable to her own interest; *when* I see all this leze nation attempted, and about to be executed, merely because this mill-stone war is tied round the neck of the minister, and that *he* wants both Islands not so much to stand or fall together, as to sink both to the bottom with himself, if I could not suddenly untie the knot which bound me to him, I should wish, not for the dagger of Aristogiton, which I detest, but for the cutting sword of Alexander.[104] I should say to my king, let not

104 Aristogiton and his lover Harmodius killed an Athenian tyrant, but without popular support; Harmodius was killed, and Aristogiton tortured and then executed, but they were later celebrated as heroes; see J. Aikin and W. Enfield, vol. 1 of *General Biography; or Lives, Critical and Historical, of the Most Eminent Persons of All Ages, Countries, Conditions, and Professions* (London: G. G. and J. Robinson, 1799), pp. 376–77. Alexander the Great (356–323 BCE), military leader and ruler who conquered much of Asia.

this infuriate minister drive you to the breach of your coronation oath, by subverting a constitution, which you have sworn to defend; and I should say to the people, for liberty can never wholly be destroyed without the wilful and treacherous co-operation of the people, unite or die.

Push away the invading minister, as you have done the invading foe. Drive him into the ocean. Let not either republic or monarchy, transgressing their limits, cajole or conquer your country. While I breathe this short breath of life, I will uphold, as my strength can uphold, and an honest man is a strong one, the republican part of the British constitution, nor shall it be the commentaries of an academician, or the fashion of the day, which shall make the principles of John Locke[105] wither in my hand, or in my heart; but I would neither give up my country to a directory, or to a divan, to millions of men or to a single man, who happens to be sole minister. And when I figure in fancy the Genius of my beloved and calumniated country taking his station on some mountain of our western coast, that, in calm majesty, sees the great Atlantic break at its feet, and casting his eyes on the geographical pre-eminence, and general aspect of his island, set as a jewel in the most temperate part of the temperate zone, gifted with the fair and overflowing fertility of nature, with such well tempered air, such safe and large ports and havens courting the trade of the world, such rivers, and such lakes, I should not be surprised that if a little minister should send to him for such a country, he would answer, —COME AND TAKE IT—YES—YES—my country, "most choice, forsaken; and most loved, despised;" you shall yet have your avengers.

Sir, I do think and I do say, that if the cruel alternative be proposed to me, unite for ever with England, or separate for ever, I would say—*separate*, in the name of God and nature. If such be the alternative, let no little pert pre-eminence say to me, "look at the map," and attempt to reconcile the perfidy of policy to the policy of geography—Why I would answer—If I look on the *map*, Britain belongs to Ireland, but I detest this property of nations, and, in return for an Irishman insulting his own country, I shall assert that the separation of the governments would accomplish the *Union* of the British and Irish people. Good God! what a paradox!—true—but a paradox is not always contrary to truth; it is only contrary to received opinion. The true system of the world was long a paradox to philosophers as well as to the people, and when the Genoese pilot, in pursuit of the East Indies, steered due *west*, he steered most paradoxically, but, while he was losing one world, he made another. I will venture the paradox, and steering due *west*, I will assert that the interest of *Britain* lies in the real and absolute independence of Ireland, on the immediate renunciation of all governmental connexion, a just compensation for past treatment, but also the truest wisdom, by securing our friendship in a *solitary* world. The stranger, the foreigner, the supposed foe

105 John Locke (1632–1704), English philosopher.

would then become fellow countrymen, fellow citizens, and brothers; and our greater population and capacity to purchase would produce to Britain a better market, (to *her* supreme felicity,) for there is not a country, which grows and increases, that does not, in its collateral consequences, augment the industry of the whole world.

The inherent sovereignty of Ireland *might* become the salvation of Britain; an Union *will* accelerate her destruction. What is this wished-for monopolism? The monopolist of the whole world would turn it into a desert, and were any one, or any people, to purchase as it were the whole lottery of life, they would, in the end, be a loser. I shall not now enter farther into the subject, but I do assert that the great perfection of this sublunary system would be such a law of nations, recognized and supported, as might cover the universality of *independent* countries, fulfilling their duties and asserting their rights, with its tutelary authority, defending the weakest from the most ambitious, and guaranteeing to all the full possession of their independence, under the ægis of a common power—and hear me for once, Ireland! when I say—happiness never can be had by a people whose sovereignty does not rest—WITHIN THEMSELVES.

16 "Of a National Character in Literature" (1818)

This essay appeared in *Blackwood's Edinburgh Magazine* in 1818, anonymously as was usual for articles in periodicals at the time, though it was later attributed to John Wilson. The magazine dealt with various subjects, from current events to book reviews to original poetry and satires, but was generally associated with a conservative social and political outlook.

"Of a National Character in Literature," *Blackwood's Edinburgh Magazine*, 3, September 1818, pp. 707–9.

It would appear, that the pleasure we receive from making ourselves acquainted with the literature of a people and more especially with their literature of imagination, is intimately connected with an impression, that in their literature we see the picture of their minds. Every people has, to our conception, its own individual character; and in virtue of that character, is the interest inspired by their fortunes. Even that strong sympathy which waits upon the events of life, is not sufficient in itself entirely to attract us; and our interest in their history is imperfect, except when the distinct individual conception of their character as a people accompanies the relation. Whatever the nature of that interest may be which is thus demanded even by our human sympathy, it is far more important towards constituting that peculiar power which a people hold over our imagination, or over our mind altogether. Every one who has applied himself with interest to the theory of a nation's literature, will, on looking back to the impressions with which he engaged in it, and to the feelings by which he was led on, recognise in himself the effect of such persuasion. He will most probably remember, that in the works he then read, there seemed opening up to him, not the mind of a new author, but the mind of another nation; that he seemed to make himself acquainted with a people of whom he had heard, but whom he had not known; that his pleasure was more than belonged to the beauty,–as he could discern it,–of the works; that their interest and importance were far beyond what their intrinsic character and kind would justify. He will recollect, that besides the thoughts which were unfolded to his intelligence–and the appeal of feeling and passion to his sensibilities–besides the hold on his imagination which belonged to the events which he had read, and to the genius under which perhaps he was held captive–that beyond and above all these, there was a charm thrown over him–a new and strange feeling of visiting an unknown land, and of standing for the first time among an unknown people. What he then felt resembled that wild and delightful impression with which a traveller finds himself on a foreign shore, where all that he sees is alike strange–with one entire power subverts his previous associations, and violently, as it were, throws open his mind to a sense of new existence, and to the apprehension of a new world. In such a situation, there is something that so calls the imaginative faculty out of the mind into the midst of open realities, that even the ordinary life of men seems a scene of enchantment,–and thought, feeling, purpose, and desire, are all suspended in mere wondering sight. Something, faint indeed in comparison, yet assuredly of the same kind, accompanies the mind on its intellectual voyage, visiting and exploring a new people.

It is not the dignity–the beauty–the importance of what it sees, that alone demands the interest and admiration of the delighted mind. That which is unimportant and common, is invested with an indescribable charm, while that which is inherently great and beautiful, appears in a still more gorgeous light flung over it by our own imagination. It is the sense of treading in another region–of beholding and knowing another mighty race of mankind–that possesses the spirit, and throws into all their life, and over all its appearances, the same power with which nature has endowed the people, and the land which she has given to be their seat. That spell which holds the traveller–by which he walks in high imagination through the paths of common life, is granted to the still and solitary student when his mind goes forth on its adventurous speculation, ranging the records of men. To him new scenes are disclosed–a new people arise. He owns the power of their spirit–the very voice of their speech is in his ears–and his imagination fills itself from their life, from the emotions of their bosoms, from their whole world of existence. These feelings, in more or less force, according to the character of the mind, attend upon the communication and intercourse which, through their language, is opened up to us with another people. They are an essential part of the interest with which we pursue such studies, though frequently they are not so fully unfolded or developed, and almost rest in the mere strong general impression of communication held with another people.

In whatever way, however, such impression is made, it is very powerful. It is one independent altogether of literature, and belongs to the feelings with which, as men, we look upon men. In literature, it assumes a modification especial to the faculties that are there in play. It enters with deep power into the imagination, and blends itself in subtle combination with the subtlest workings of intelligence. The language itself–the instrument–the express work and mirror of the mind, invests itself, especially to the intellectual thought, with this character, and takes the interest of these feelings. It is so directly the voice of the mind–it so shapes its subtle being, and receives its colours from the very breath that gives it forth, that it cannot but speak to the mind of the mind from which it springs. Fine, shadowy, and evanescent, as the motions of apprehension are which accompany the flow of language through the mind,–inapplicable perhaps to intellect, and scarcely to be retraced, even by imagination returning upon itself–yet, these most faint, light, delicate arts of mind answering to mind, are all deeply impregnated with the great feeling of communion with another race. Let the thoughtful and feeling scholar tell–for he only knows–how curiously minute these impressions are in their blending with language. He knows, indeed, beyond what he can tell, how language has discovered to his thought its wonderful being; how intimately he has beheld its minute intricate structure,–how, to intuitive and unconscious analysis, to apprehension that seemed almost fanciful in its exceeding subtlety, the properties, relations, and powers of language, its intense, complex, infinitely divided, and yet comprehensive significance of mind have been disclosed. He knows this far beyond what he can tell: he knows it in degrees, which, if he were to attempt to speak of them, would appear quite illusory and fantastical. He knows, too, that with this extreme metaphysical division of the acts of mind in language, there exists the feeling, strong and entire, that this language is the language of the mind of another people.

If it be true, that even in these extreme abstractions of intellectual thought, there is no separation effected of this peculiar feeling from the perception of language, far less can it be separated from those stronger, fuller, more embodied acts of the mind, into which imagination enters in its own dimensions, into which sentiment and passion infuse their living blood,–those acts of the aroused, kindling, agitated intellect,–those workings of the moved soul which attend upon the creations of the highest arts, and upon all the imaginative literature of a people, upon their eloquence, and their poetry.

The strong interest of this feeling of knowing and discerning the mind of another people, arises not merely out of a precedent knowledge of the greatness of that people–it is not the offspring of former associations–but it springs up at the moment, instinct with life of its own, from present discernment of their character. The mind is not merely satisfying itself in acquiring new evidence of what it believed before: it is making discovery of what it did not know–it is creating its knowledge by its own momentary acts–it apprehends, discerns, reads the mind which it had never apprehended, contemplated, studied before. What is this feeling–this interest? What is the strong power by which, as human beings, we are held in the contemplation of individual character? Why are those qualities of the mind, which are visibly its own,–those virtues, powers, which seem to have their birth within itself, and to be the living inherent tendencies of its own nature,–why are these so peculiarly beautiful? What is that charm of a native grace that is felt in them all? Why, in short, is every manifestation of the unforced, uncontrolled, self-developement of the soul so strangely interesting? We all know, at least, that it is so. And we see, therefore, a principle in our nature sufficiently cooperative and powerful to explain (if the fact be so) the strong interest that is felt in discerning and considering the native character of a people in their native literature.

If what has now been advanced be true, in any thing like the extent to which we believe it to be true, we have a reason why no access can ever be obtained to the wealth of a people's literature in any language but their own. All argument for or against the cultivation of classical literature is vain and idle. If it be of importance that we should know who and what the Greeks and Romans were, and what they did, it is of importance that we know their language. Without that knowledge, all else that is worth being known is to us dark as night.

A reason also springs out of this speculation, much more essential than the mere difficulties of language, why the early study of language is often so repulsive to minds of imagination and sensibility? It is because they have not yet enough of acquired intelligence to discern in that language its characters of life. They afterwards come to possess that intelligence, and then the study of language changes to them its nature.

We also perceive a reason much deeper than lies in our clearer intelligence merely, why no language can ever exert over us the power of our own. In none can there be to us such deep consciousness and such subtle apprehension of the acts of another mind, as in that which, from the dawning of life, has been blended with all the thoughts and feelings of our own.

If there be this power in native language and native literature, two questions seem to arise, which we may afterwards discuss at some length,–first, What is it that gives such force to the principle in our nature now alluded to, our delight in our individual character? And, secondly, How are we to estimate the benefit to the literature of a people from the influx upon them of the literature of another, even though that other have far surpassed them in all intellectual cultivation?

17 From **Lady Sydney Morgan, "Absenteeism.—No. III" (1825)**

Lady Morgan (c. 1783–1859) was born Sydney Owenson, according to her own legend, in the middle of the Irish sea while her parents were crossing to Ireland. Morgan was tutored for a time by the Irish poet Thomas Dermody, and then sent to boarding-school; thereafter, she briefly worked as a governess, a job that put her into contact with some of the Irish aristocracy who, along with her mentor Alicia Sheridan Lefanu, assisted her writing career by, for instance, giving her access to their libraries. She is best known now as a novelist, a key contributor to the genre of the "national tale" with *The Wild Irish Girl* (1806), *O'Donnel* (1814), and *The O'Briens and the O'Flahertys* (1827). But much of her writing in the 1820s was non-fiction prose in liberal periodicals. Her three-part anonymous essay "Absenteeism" (1824–1825) on the ongoing problem of Irish landlords living outside of Ireland, leaving the management of their estates to hired agents, elicited so much interest that a book-version of the essay was published, under her name, in 1825.

Lady Sydney Morgan, "Absenteeism.—No. III," *New Monthly Magazine*, 10, 1825, pp. 162–76.

The Irish press!—and who that now knows the capital of Ireland, and beholds its utter incompetency to support the publication of even *one* trifling periodical work, will believe that Ireland *once had a press*!—the Irish press then teemed with native literary productions; which if as mere "*piece de circonstance*,"[106] thrown off at a heat, they might sometimes want the higher finish of more elaborate composition, were still stamped with the ardour of the national spirit, and "faithful to its fires." The frequent and "keen encounter of the wits" upon great questions, produced an animated competition, which even the statesman-like sobriety of English viceroys could not always resist. The Draper's letter of Lord Chesterfield (an imitation of Swift), and the political caricatures of Lord Townshend,[107] written at a later period, were proofs that Ireland was not always governed by the dull and the dogged, and that her metropolis once boasted of a society which *obliged* the representatives of majesty as well as the representatives of the people to cultivate the suffrages of the public, by means never addressed to an uncivilized or an illiterate community. Politics and polemics then alike fell to the discussion of humour and talent. The public journals, though few, were fair; their editors were responsible both by their property and their personal consideration;

106 "Occasional piece."

107 Philip Dormer Stanhope (1694–1773) and George Townshend (1724–1807) were both viceroys of Ireland.

and their contributors were frequently the most brilliant members of Irish society, the most learned sons of the Irish alma mater. Swift, Dr. Sheridan, Lucas, Flood, Burgh, Yelverton, Courtenay, Jephson, Bishop Marley, Grattan, Curran, and others equally notable, if not equally noted, contributed successively a portion of their luminous intellects to illustrate the pages of that mighty engine of public feeling—the PERIODICAL PRESS.[108] Whatever side was advocated,—the country or the court, patriotism or power,—it does not appear that any journal was set up on a merely sordid principle, or an utter disregard of all truth and decency. There was then no waylaying with indiscriminate ruffianism the feelings of private individuals, no exhibition of the sacred details of the domestic life of political characters, as a means of existence to some outcast of society, who wanted the courage to seek a less dishonourable bread on the public highway. For when the genuine and educated gentry of Ireland, her hereditary senators and native legislators, made up the larger portion of the reading public of her capital, a journal edited by the nefarious and the base, by the hired assassin of reputation or the paid pander of ribald passions, would have been hunted down with one common feeling of national indignation and manly contempt. Where is the land, so lost in its degradation, so insensible to all its higher interests, as to endure that such a "damning witness" should go forth to the world and bear testimony to its moral, social, and literary depravity? Alas that there should be one! Alas that the land of wit and feeling should furnish forth readers, even from its high and official classes, to reward and encourage the instruments of its own disgrace! Alas for the country, where the hired servants of the government club their quota to propagate the rancorous overflowings of the vilest and most antisocial passions; where the ordained ministers of religion, subscribe for the dissemination of the grossest and most mischievous falsehoods; where the magistrate chuckles privately over the libel he is publicly bound to punish; and where to be pre-eminent in villainy and matchless in audacity, is the short road to command sympathy and ensure subsistence.

But if a reduction of absenteeism, if the permanent residence of the major part, of the wealth, the nobility, and above all, and more precious than all, of the EDUCATION of the country, produced these blessed effects, the greater good, the "last best gift,"[109] which congregated interests and intellects could bestow on a community, Public Spirit, fell like dew in the desert upon the renovating nation. Men who had learned to feel and to think, now, in the consciousness and confidence of their associated strength, first ventured to speak and to act: at once inspiring and inspired, they spoke as prophets and acted as patriots. The talent of the free suddenly burst into existence, as if

108 Irish writers and politicians, including a number allied with Townshend (above) or Henry Grattan.

109 John Milton, *Paradise Lost*, in M. Y. Hughes (ed.), *John Milton: Complete Poems and Major Prose*, New York: Macmillan, 1957, 5.19.

by a divine miracle in the land of the enslaved; and eloquence, the inherent characteristic of the nation, which had occasionally broken forth in the rude but exciting harangues of the O'Donnels and the O'Neils,[110] now shone out brilliantly, with a lustre which Athens in her best, and Rome in her greatest days, scarcely surpassed. . . . Oh! these were times to live in and men to live among—when the capital of the kingdom was something better than a garrison or an assize town! when its fashionable assemblies were not thrown upon the eleemosinary contributions of barracks and boarding-schools, of military exquisites who "*never dance*," and harmless young gentlemen who do nothing else! These were times, when the men were all at home, and their spirits all abroad! when the rush from the senate was sure to fill the drawing-room; and they who boldly fought in the one for the liberties of their country, came to lay their own liberty at the feet of beauty in the other. . . .

But to return. When penal statutes and all that is intended by the false policy of shallow and self-interested legislators to disqualify man for the knowledge and assertion of his political rights, still continued to check the progress of civil liberty in Ireland, the combined efforts of a portion of the liberal and educated resident gentry were found sufficient to make head against a government which the sternest upholder of English power, and he too an Irish chancellor,[111] declared "was enough to crush any nation on earth;" and which one of the wisest and best philanthropists of that or any age[112] has defined to have been "such a combination of rapine, treachery, and violence as would have disgraced the name of government in the most arbitrary country in the world."

18 Adam Kidd, "Preface" and "Cathleen" from *The Huron Chief, and Other Poems* (1830)

Adam Kidd (1802–1831) was born in Tullynagee, Ireland, and emigrated to Canada sometime between 1818 and 1824, the year his poetry began to appear in Quebec periodicals. His best-known poem is *The Huron Chief*, a long poem that draws extensively on Irish poet Thomas Moore's orientalist critique of religious intolerance and empire-building, *Lalla Rookh* (1817). Kidd was explicit about his debts to Moore, dedicating *The Huron Chief, and Other Poems* (1830)

---

110 Irish families celebrated earlier in the text, particularly their Elizabethan scions.

111 Lord Clare (Morgan's note). John Fitzgibbon (1748–1802), first earl of Clare, and Lord Chancellor of Ireland (1789–1802); according to legend, he was so disliked that people threw dead cats at his funeral procession.

112 Dr. Franklin (Morgan's note). Benjamin Franklin (1706–1790), American politician; the passage she cites appears in *An Address to the Good People of Ireland on Behalf of America* (1778).

"To Thomas Moore, the most popular, most powerful, and most patriotic poet of the nineteenth century, whose magic numbers have vibrated to the hearts of nations." Kidd, as his Preface makes clear, was strongly interested, both culturally and politically, in native peoples; like other Irish-Canadian authors (Thomas D'Arcy McGee, for instance), he both praised British rule in Canada, often in order to criticize the US, and condemned British rule in Ireland. As in other early Canadian writing, the landscape is associated with a sublime wildness in explicit distinction to more cultivated Europe.

Adam Kidd, *The Huron Chief, and Other Poems* (Montreal, printed at the Office of the HERALD and NEW GAZETTE, 1830).

Preface

At a time when Poetry has received the highest polish, from the master hands of a BYRON and a MOORE,[113] it seems almost rashness in a youthful bard to attempt to cull, from the banks of Helicon, even one leaf of the immortal *baccalia*, to adorn his aspiring brow—while the consequences may prove as serious before the ordeal of Criticism as the efforts of Pliny, who perished in the fire of Vesuvius, while searching into the cause of the beauteous, but destructive element.[114]

The little birch canoe, in which I have safely glided through the tranquil lakes of the Canadas, could not securely venture on the boiling surge, and foaming breakers, over which Childe Harold and Lalla Rookh[115] triumphantly rode in their magnificent Gondolas.

It is not, however, my intention to trouble the readers of the "HURON CHIEF" with useless apologies for the defects that it may possess, knowing that a poem of such length can scarcely be free from errors; and, particularly, when written, without much opportunity for correction, on the inner rind of birch bark, during my travels through the immense forests of America, and under many difficulties and privations, arising from causes that I must, for the present, avoid mentioning. The innocent, and unassuming, friendly treatment that I experienced among the Indians, together with the melancholy recital of the deep wrongs which they received from those calling themselves "*Christians*," induced me to undertake this dramatic poem.

From the days of the American Revolution until this very hour, the poor Indians have been so cruelly treated, and driven from their homes and

113 Irish poet Thomas Moore (1779–1852) and British poet George Gordon, Lord Byron (1778–1824).

114 The Helicon is a mountain in Greece associated with poetry; "baccalia" refers to laurel, traditionally used to crown poets; the author Pliny the Elder (23–79 AD) died in the eruption of Mount Vesuvius in Italy.

115 Byron's *Childe Harold's Pilgrimage* (1812–1818) and Moore's *Lalla Rookh* (1817).

hunting-grounds, by the boasted freemen of the United States, that the MOHICANS, the NARAGANSETTS, the DELAWARES, and others, once powerful Tribes, have now become totally extinct—while the remaining Nations are daily dwindling away, and in a few years hence will scarcely leave a memorial to perpetuate their names, as the once mighty rulers of the vast American regions.

I am fully aware, that the "HURON CHIEF" will draw on me the censure of many—but this is no consideration, since I can fairly and honestly plead the *correctness* of my observations. Many of the Indian Tribes have emigrated into Canada—and are now prospering, and happily enjoying the manly protection of the British Government.

The miscellaneous poems, which follow the "HURON CHIEF," with the exception of the one to Polyphemus, were written for amusement, during the leisure hours necessarily abstracted from a long round of professional studies, the benefits of which I have never yet reaped, owing to an accidental fall from the cloud-capped brows of a dangerous Mountain, over which I had heedlessly wandered, with all that open carelessness which is so peculiarly the characteristic of poetic feeling.[116]

In the lines addressed to the Rev. Polyphemus, perhaps I have been too severe, having written them at a moment when my every feeling was deeply touched by a sad and a serious disappointment. Let such be my apology!

The liberal and friendly encouragement with which my first attempt has been so highly favoured, and particularly in the Canadas—fifteen hundred copies being already called for—will induce me to follow up, in a more extensive volume, the *Tales* and *Traditions* of the Indians, which I have personally collected among them, together with local descriptions of the numerous cascades, stupendous cataracts, and majestic scenery of the country, which for beauty and grandeur remain unrivalled in the universe.

The poem of the HURON CHIEF has made such an impression on the Indian warriors to whom it has been communicated, that it will shortly be translated into their respective tongues, by SAWENNOWANE, and other Chiefs, equally celebrated and intelligent, who speak and write several languages.

Cathleen

Over her tearful eyes hung loose her disordered locks—
She wept for her own green land.—OSSIAN.[117]

---

116 Archdeacon George Mountain; see D. M. R. Bentley, Introduction, *The Huron Chief by Adam Kidd* (London: Canadian Poetry Press, 1987). Available at http://www.uwo.ca/english/canadianpoetry/longpoems/huron/introduction.htm.

117 James Macpherson, author of what purport to be *The Works of Ossian* (1765), a legendary Celtic poet. Kidd is liberally revising, or misremembering, *Ossian* here.

Upon a lonely bank, against whose base
Saint Lawrence wildly heaves, she sat and wept
Her sad misfortune—that dark misfortune,
Which thus had forced her from her native cot,
And doomed her in a distant land to seek
A scanty pittance from a hand unknown.

A sun more fierce than ever yet has flung
Its scorching beams upon her own green hills,
Had marked her care-worn cheek with brownest hue,
And tinged her brow with deep Canadian die—
To me she told the story of her woes,
And hopes of other times, which never more
Can wake one spark of joy in her dark soul.
Yet, CATHLEEN, though a wreck, seemed lovely still,
And kindled feelings of a finer stamp
Than pity or compassion e'er hath known.

Her plaintive tale was such, as Erin's child,
No matter where he strays to find a home,
Might well divine.—But as my pen, too oft,
Has freely strayed from that allegiance,
Which some may say it owes to England's king,
I'll here restrain its open willingness,
And check its *blamed* impetuosity!

Yet, quite too soon, the chequered path of life
Thy young and gentle heart must enter on,
Without a guide—save the All-ruling Power,
Which, at the call of stainless purity,
Is ever ready—and confers a boon,
On worth and innocence so chaste as thine.
Deep, deep, unseen like Bakou's ardent fire,[118]
Lie all the sympathies that merit praise
In man's proud breast, till sadly once he sees—
Too true an image of his country's fate—
The child of impulse weep, and drag the chain—
Then all the soft emotions of his heart—
As spirits flash resentment on the foe—
Quick swell to rage—he strikes, and takes revenge.

118 Another reference to *Lalla Rookh* where Moore refers to naptha at Baku (in modern Azerbaijan) as "everlasting fire."

Oh, Cathleen! I can truly share thy grief,
And fain would hope, that yet a brighter day
May shine with all its wonted cheerfulness,
And give to Erin's Isle what Heaven designed;—
Come then with me, the portion of my roof,
Which, though but scanty, thou shalt freely share—
And when the shell of joy has once proclaimed
Loved Erin free, I'll cross the ocean wave,
And to thy mountain-cot thyself restore.

19 From **Peter Du Ponceau,** ***A Discourse on the Necessity and the Means of Making our National Literature Independent of that of Great Britain*** **(1834)**

Peter Du Ponceau (1760–1844) was born Pierre-Etienne Du Ponceau in France but emigrated to the United States in 1777 as secretary to Baron von Steuben. Briefly a captain and aide-de-camp in the Revolutionary army during the US War of Independence, he became US under-secretary for foreign affairs (1781–1783) and then studied law, becoming a lawyer in Philadelphia in 1785. He is best known for his wide-ranging linguistic work, particularly on Amerindian languages, but also published legal tracts and translations.

Peter Du Ponceau, *A Discourse on the Necessity and the Means of Making our National Literature Independent of that of Great Britain, Delivered before the Members of The Pennsylvania Library of Foreign Literature and Science on Saturday, February 15, 1834* (Philadelphia: E. G. Dorsey, 1834).

Gentlemen of the Foreign Library Company,—

Among the various institutions that exist in this country for the cultivation and promotion of knowledge, there is none more likely to redound to the honour as well as the advantage of our citizens, than that which you have lately established. It is a novelty of its kind. In no part of the world, I believe, is there a public library, devoted entirely to foreign literature and science, to the exclusion of books written in the vernacular tongue. But to no country, also, is such a library so well suited as it is to ours. It seems called for by our peculiar situation, to enable us at the same time to vindicate our intellectual character from the misrepresentations which have become so fashionable among a certain class of writers in a certain quarter of Europe, and to free us from the shackles of a kindred, yet foreign literature, which prevent us from fully displaying that individuality which is the characteristic of a truly independent nation.

The success which this association has hitherto experienced; the number of subscribers, the choice of books, the avidity with which they are sought after, and the constant call for more, are a sufficient answer to the aspersions which superficial and flippant travellers delight to throw upon our country. They prove that there are those among us, and not a few of those, who have minds to understand and hearts to feel the beauties of Corneille and of Racine; of Petrarch and of Dante; of Schiller and Goethe, and of Cervantes and Calderon.[119] And mind, that it is not in the great commercial city of New York, where foreigners abound, that this society is established; but here, in Philadelphia, in the *Quaker city*,[120] as it has been called, where it is well known that strangers are comparatively few, and they in general, not persons devoted to literature and science. There would be no necessity for a library like this, if there were not readers of the works that it contains; and unless it were absolutely necessary to gratify the public taste, it would be absurd and ridiculous for any man of sense to dream for a moment of its establishment. I regret that I was not one of those who first conceived this happy idea; but I rejoice that it has been acted upon, and I congratulate you on the success it has hitherto obtained, and which justifies our most sanguine hopes for the future.

The two objects that I have mentioned, and the attainment of which this institution will greatly promote, are not the only good effects that it will produce. I could enumerate many more, but the limits of this discourse will not permit me to expatiate upon them. I shall, therefore, confine myself to those to which I have already adverted. I hope I shall be able to prove to you that the advancement of our literature absolutely requires that we should cease to look up so exclusively as we have hitherto done to the literature of Great Britain, as the model of our own, and that a more intimate acquaintance with that of other countries will not only enlarge our ideas, but as I shall undertake to show you, will even preserve the purity of our language. It hardly requires an argument to prove that this institution will raise our intellectual reputation, at least among those who might receive their impressions from the misrepresentations of foreign travellers. As to men of real knowledge and sound judgment, they are not to be worked upon by the ephemeral productions of those writers; availing themselves of the benefits which this library offers to them, they will see nothing in it but what might naturally have been expected from the progress of mental improvement in our country.

When I speak of misrepresentations of foreign travellers, I do not mean to advert to those who, conscientiously attached to the constitution and government of their country, view our republican institutions with a prejudiced eye, and represent them in a false light to their countrymen; these have

119 These pairs of writers are French, Italian, German, and Spanish, respectively.

120 Philadelphia was founded by William Penn, a Quaker.

their excuse in *amor patriæ*,[121] an honourable feeling, in which we do not less indulge than other nations; much less shall I take notice of those, who, laying hold of some national peculiarities differing from those to which they have been accustomed, seem to take pleasure in presenting to the world a caricature of our manners; the former are often respectable, the latter are always contemptible.

But when an author, not unknown in the literary world, after receiving in our country all the attentions to which a respectable stranger is entitled, affects to sink our nation to a low rank in the scale of intellect, and tauntingly reproaches us with the respect that we have long cherished for the literature of his country, which he represents as a humiliating servitude, we are bound, at least, to take warning from him, and free ourselves from those shackles which he boasts that his nation has imposed upon us.

The writer that I speak of is the author of a Book of Travels in the United States which he has entitled "Men and Manners in America."[122] I leave to reviewers the unfair description of our manners, with which his work abounds; I confine myself to what has a direct relation to the subject of this discourse. "In the present generation of Americans," says he, "I see no symptoms of improving taste or increasing *elevation of intellect*. The recorded specimens of this period (the period subsequent to our revolution) indicate a sad deficiency of taste, originality and imaginative power." He adds that we have degenerated, even from our immediate ancestors. Such is the cruel stigma which this author has attempted to fix upon our country. It is our duty to repel it.

That our literature cannot stand a comparison with that of Great Britain, is what I am willing freely to admit; and what none of us is disposed to deny; but that may be easily accounted for, without recurring to a want of elevation of mind or a deficiency of mental powers. Our existence in the colonial and independent state dates from a little more than two hundred years; during the first century and a half, our country consisted of infant settlements, devoted entirely to agriculture, with a scanty population, scattered through immense forests, and debarred of intercourse with all mankind, except Great Britain and her dependencies. Those were not times in which science or literature could flourish. Literature has never flourished *any where* under a colonial system of government. Yet at the latter end of that period, Franklin arose and shone like a brilliant meteor amidst the darkness that surrounded him. As Britain justly boasts of her Newton, America is equally proud of her Franklin.[123]

The next period of between thirty and forty years, from the commencement of our revolution to the last peace with Great Britain, was also unfavourable to literature. It languished even in Europe. In this country, the first part of

---

121 "Love of country."

122 Thomas Hamilton, *Men and Manners in America* (1833).

123 Scientists and authors Benjamin Franklin (1706–1790) and Isaac Newton (1642–1727).

it was consumed in the struggle with the mother country for our independence, and in organizing a bold and novel style of government, which other nations have since adopted as a model; during the latter part of it, we were distracted by the intrigues of France and Great Britain, and ruined by the piracies of Great Britain and France, which ended in a war with the former, in which we came off victorious. I must also acknowledge, that during the whole of that period, such was the force of ancient prepossessions, that we had not yet even thought of shaking off the mental yoke which had so long weighed upon us; we seemed to be satisfied with our political emancipation, and despaired ever to be able to wrestle with great Britain in the fields of literature and science. . . .

We have had, in fact, no literature until the peace of December, 1814. The war which preceded it, inspired us with a spirit we had never felt before. We had resisted in arms, unaided by friends or allies, the whole force of Great Britain; we now thought for the first time of an independent literature. The task was not an easy one; what cost Great Britain centuries to achieve, we could not expect to perform in twenty years; but we have begun, and are gradually advancing. Before the time that I speak of, it might, perhaps, not improperly have been asked: Who reads an American book? In less than twenty years after our first beginning, we have produced books that are read all over the world, that are translated into various languages, and are honourably noticed in the scientific and literary journals of all Europe. As the writers of these books are almost all living, I abstain from alluding particularly to any of them. Those have been (with a few honourable exceptions) our first efforts, and yet the colonial spirit which has borne so long upon us, is not quite extinguished. We have still to prove to foreigners that we are in every respect an independent people. . . .

Nothing can be more certain than that if we confine ourselves in any art to the imitation of a particular school, (excellent as it may be,) we shall never be able to have a school of our own. Imitation destroys genius; it narrows the range of our imaginations and the field of our conceptions. That we follow too closely the British models, and that our compositions are not sufficiently stamped with originality, is what I am not prepared to deny, and we cannot too much blame the satirist for giving it the name of *mental dependance*, though the imputation comes with a very ill grace from that quarter.

The reasons which have produced this *mental dependance*, (if it can be so called) are too well known, that I should take up much of your time in explaining them. The similarity of language, the constant influx of British books and literary productions of every description, which are reprinted here as fast as they appear, the natural indolence of man which makes him pursue the object easiest to be gained, in preference often to the most valuable; a long cherished congeniality of manners, habits and literary opinions with the nation whose language we speak, and whose descendants we, or the great majority of us, are; a filial respect, which, in spite of parental injuries, is not yet extinguished; all these circumstances together have produced that *mental thraldom* with which we are reproached by those whom it most honours, and from which we are warned by them that it is at last time to free ourselves. The question now occurs, how this is to be done; and it is not difficult of solution. When we were struggling with Great Britain for our political independence what did we do? We sought foreign alliances, and obtained them. I do not mean to say that without their aid we should not have succeeded; but with their aid we did succeed, and in a shorter time than we should otherwise have done: the same course is now to be pursued. Let us seek foreign alliances in the literature and science of other nations than Great Britain, and we may expect similar success.

20 "National Character," *The Nation* (1843)

The Nation was a weekly Irish newspaper, founded by secular nationalists who sought the Repeal of the Act of Union (1800) which had abolished the Irish Parliament and brought Ireland under the direct control of the British Parliament. Under the stewardship of Charles Gavan Duffy, the newspaper was an influential forum for nationalist thought, publishing articles and poems on the Irish past, political essays, reports of British military failures, profiles of Irish writers, and notices from correspondents outside of Ireland. It also published many of the major Irish poets of the era, including James Clarence Mangan and Lady Wilde. While the newspaper generally argued for a non-sectarian, liberal, modern state, with an educated and politically autonomous populace, it also fostered a cultural nationalism that occasionally exhibited the exclusionary, even racist, gestures of such thought. A recurring subject in *The Nation* was the difference between Celts and Saxons (or Goths) as the indigenous peoples of western Europe and the Germanic invaders who became the Anglo-Saxons of England.

"National Character," *The Nation*, 1.48, September 9, 1843, p. 763.

Lycurgus[124] sought to make his countrymen unlike all other people. By making them peculiar, their characteristics became strong. Opposition has a tendency to force its object to concentration, for resistance long-continued grows into hard unflinching unyieldingness, else it is converted into obsequious compliance. This peculiarity in the characteristics of a nation breeds dislike in foreigners. Foreign antipathy begets domestic love of fatherland. An isolated family of Indian Pariahs[125] cherish a sentiment of fireside affection fervid as the hatred

124 Lycurgus (c. 700 BCE), Spartan statesman famed for instituting laws that shaped Spartan society.

125 A low-ranking caste in India.

which 'mediately gives it birth. He who has only one home loves it intensely. Men who find themselves at home in one island or state, must yearn to live where they will not be miserable. The Jewish lawgiver seems to have weighted its truth. Jews are still a peculiar race. National peculiarity in the sons of Jacob rivetted them to their rites by links which no fires could sunder. It fiercely excited the bitter scorn of others, but the patient Jew only clung with a more convulsive grasp to the subject of alien contempt.

What is that held the Chinese together during the lapse of unnumbered ages? Time has grown old, while to his destructive flight, which elsewhere is so disastrous, China calmly bids defiance; and China now is what Time beheld it in its youth. This is a nation which seems exempted from the common fate of great communities. It knows no decline, no decadence, and, we trust, will experience no fall. It was invested with all the glorious attributes of independent nationality when its English enemies were naked savages in the wilds of Holstein.[126] It is yet wealthier, as well as more venerable, after the flight of four thousand years, than it was in anterior epochs of its history. My heart yearned within me when I read that the hills of China bear patriarchal names whose meaning is understood by the inhabitants. Alas! there is another country whose wizard streams and mountains have names which the natives can interpret; but she is not independent, and we will name her not.

Robber-kingdoms, those confederacies of banditti, cannot read the titles inscribed by the hand of primeval topography on their fresh green meadows, which they wrested with the sword from aboriginals. It is only the primal people who can tell why an extremity of England was named Kent, the headland; or why the Garonne of France, as it keeps on its course, deserves that picturesque name of Gara, rough; Avon, the river. It is only the Celts, who yielded their solemn woodlands, clear flowing rivers, and wide domains, to the barbarian Goths–it is the Celts alone who can tell why those patriarchal titles were conferred on the hills of Europe by the "world's gray fathers."[127] Those military brigands who slaughtered, devastated, or enslaved us, knew not why the graphic and poetic genius of the ancient primitive ancestors of Europe coined their beautiful epithets, or crowned the towering cliffs with descriptive appellatives to last them for ever. It was reserved for the gentle and yielding Celt to come from the caves and howling wilds to which truculent, victorious barbarism relegated him–'twas for him to point to the hills, and, like the Hebrew seer in the Assyrian's presence, interpret the words which time had only chiselled deeper.[128] He has done so; every mountain has vindicated his claims to primogeniture, despite the malignant grin of envious

126 Part of a region of Germany once known as Old Saxony; the author is referring to the Saxons before they invaded England in the 5th century CE.

127 Thomas Campbell, "To the Rainbow" (1821).

128 Dan. 5.

incredulity; and they who were sceptics in other times, are now believers. To return: the natives of China, like the European Celts, construe the names of their provinces, a circumstance which proves that the primitive invaders or occupants spoke the same tongue, and that the same human family holds it now which first engrossed it. However (let it be said in passing), the fate of the Chinese has always been different from that of the European Celts. The infernal spirit which dictated to our fiery zealots their fanatic war-cry, and which cruelly offered to the conquered brave the appalling option between hell and Connaught,[129] was not breathed by the nursling of the Tartarian deserts.

We should ask ourselves, to what are the Chinese indebted for their political indissolubility, so wonderful as to be apparently inexplicable? The Chinese are indebted for their political indissolubility to their national idiosyncracy. So it is with all communities or nations which have had any considerable longevity. The various conquerors of Persia failed to destroy either the religion or the devotees of Mythra.–Every traveller in the East sees, at each successive sunrise, the Persian bow his face in solemn veneration, and extend his arms in grateful thanksgiving to the source of light. This tenacity of life in human communities, on which the tyrant breaks his sword vainly, is begotten of that palladium of a people–idiosyncracy. The mobile Greeks of chameleon character were too imitative in their constitution to impose (like iron Rome) their sway permanently on Asia. The burning lava torrent of irresistible Islamism which the prophet poured out on the fiery sands of Arabia, the headlong fury of which precipitated itself on the writhing and vanquished inhabitants of three continents, overturned all obstacles, and bore the crescent at the same time to the pillars of Hercules and to the Ganges.[130] Its success resulted from the distinctive stamp of permanent peculiarity, which has not yet entirely forsaken the Arab. No nation can become great, if it be not peculiar. Nations must esteem themselves; 'tis this political faith in itself–this illusion of national being, which tyrants would willingly remove. They would attach to the physiognomy of nations the mask of a slavish uniformity, lest the brotherhood of freemen should recognise their kin–lest we should remember that Italians cannot be Germans, Flemings Dutch, nor Celts Saxons. They would drive the ponderous rolling-stone, as it were, over the different families of man, to render more facile their own regal tread over prostrate human nature.

"What is your purpose?" said Napoleon to the Portuguese; "what are your views–do you wish to be Spaniards?" "They sought not to be Spaniards," they replied; "they had been independent, and they sought to continue so."[131]

---

129 The phrase "To Hell or Connaught" reputedly originates with Cromwell and his conquest of Ireland. Irish (Catholic) landowners were offered execution or exile to Clare or Connaught under an order of the English Parliament in 1654.

130 That is, from the Strait of Gibraltar to a river in India.

131 Peninsular War (1807–1814).

Thus those conquerors would bray us down as in a mortar,[132] because the stumbling-block of conquerors consists of the self-association of nations. But freedom and her votaries cherish these distinctive moral and physical features which cause us to know ourselves and one another. The Poles will not be Russians. Nature repudiates and forbids the coercive transmutation. The stubborn impatience of a pigmy state, "that small infantry," frustrates for a time the march "o'er the hearts of the free" which humanity denounces as accursed. The modern conqueror, who, with the men of the nineteenth century, endeavoured to effect the feats of Genghis Khan, the late Emperor of France,[133] divided the whole human species into two classes merely–monogamists and polygamists. "There is no other true distinction," said the great master of European kings; "the Asiatic polygamists are a family apart from the European monogamists–the wide earth contains no third family." Thus they speak because the fortune of a man biasses his mind, influences his views, and warps his thoughts. They and we have no community of feeling. Fortune renders those our masters alien to their kind. Irrespective of our traditionary attachments and hereditary prejudices, they would fain make nations assume, like mercenaries, a uniform. They are not our peers, and they judge of us falsely. Their prosperous fortune colours all objects with a peculiar tinge, and invests them with a hue which is foreign and strange, and exists not in us but in themselves. When the thunder of an *emeute*[134] broke in, in tones of terrific violence, on one of those cream-faced princes of Bourbon, he falteringly, and with glaring eye-balls, asked what was the matter. The pale inquirer heard in astonishment that the hungry people of France fiercely required bread. "Bread," he exclaimed, with large eyes and exalted eye-brows–"Bread! good God, bread! Why, can they not eat pie-crust?"[135]

21 From **Giuseppe Mazzini, "Europe: Its Condition and Prospects" (1852)**

Giuseppe Mazzini (1805–1872) was born in Genoa, Italy, but lived primarily in England after 1837. He studied at Genoa University and soon became a nationalist active in Italian political movements to unify Italy. The Congress of Vienna (1814–1815) had restored a pre-Napoleonic dispensation in Europe, including the division of Italy into a number of small states, many indirectly or directly controlled by Austria or France. Mazzini's support of Italian independence and

---

132 Prov. 27:22.

133 Genghis Khan, Mongol emperor (c. 1162–1227); the "modern conqueror" is likely Napoleon I (1769–1821), but the quotation which follows is untraced.

134 Uprising.

135 This passage refers to a remark by Queen Maria Theresa, mother of Marie Antoinette (incorrectly credited with a variation on her mother's words, "Let them eat cake").

unification thus ran afoul of most of western continental Europe: he was exiled from Sardinia in 1831 and subsequently sentenced to death in absentia. In exile in France in 1831, he founded the nationalist movement, Young Italy, and launched attempted insurrections in northern Italy. In 1834 he was thrown out of Switzerland, and then required to leave France for England where he moved in early 1837. With the founding of a republic in Rome (1849), Mazzini returned to Italy and was named triumvir but left after the republic's collapse. He published a number of political treatises, but particularly important was the widely translated *Duties of Man* (first appearing in English in 1862). The essay excerpted here appeared in a London magazine, and responds to the European Revolutions of 1848 which took place in France, Italy, Germany, Poland, Hungary, and elsewhere.

Giuseppe Mazzini, "Europe: Its Condition and Prospects," *Westminster Review*, 62, April 1852, pp. 236–50.

The literature of the Continent during the last few years has been essentially political, revolutionary, and warlike. Out of ten historical works, seven at least speak to us, from a favourable point of view or otherwise, of a revolution now extinct; out of ten polemical, political, economical, or other works, seven at least proclaim or combat a revolution about to take place. The first bear the impress of terror, the last are full of gigantic hopes, though most imperfectly defined. Calm has fled from the minds of writers. Poetry is silent, as if frightened by the storm now gathering in the hearts of men. Romance becomes rarer every day; it would find no readers. Pure art is a myth. Style itself is changed; when it is not commonplace, when it retains something of that individual originality which every style ought to have, it is sharp, cutting, biting. The pen seems, as it were, sword-shaped; all the world thinks and writes as if it felt itself on the eve of a battle. . . .

For sixty years Europe has been convulsed by a series of political struggles which have assumed all aspects by turns, which have raised every conceivable flag, from that of pure despotism to that of anarchy, from the organization of the bourgeoisie in France and elsewhere as the dominant caste, to the *jacqueries* of the peasants of Gallicia. Thirty revolutions have taken place. Two or three royal dynasties have been engulfed in the abyss of popular fury. Nations have risen, like Greece, from the tombs where they had been for ages buried; others, like Poland, have been erased from the map.[136] Forgotten, almost unknown races, the Sclavonian race, the Roumaine race, silent until now, have disinterred their traditionary titles and demanded to be represented in the Congress of nations. Kings and Queens have gone to die in

136 Greek War of Independence (1821–1832); in the late eighteenth century, Poland was annexed by Russia, Prussia, and Austria.

exile. The Austrian Empire, the China of Europe, has been on the brink of destruction. A Pope, drawn along by the popular current, has been obliged to bless a national insurrection, and then to fly under favour of disguise from the capital of the Christian World.[137] Vienna has twice been covered with barricades. Rome has seen the republican banner float above the Vatican. Governments, attacked and overthrown, have ten, twenty times recovered strength, drawn closer their alliances, overrun the half of Europe with their armies, annihilated revolutions, effaced by the sword, the scaffold, prison and exile, entire generations of revolutionary spirits, and crushed, as they term it, the hydra of disorder and anarchy. . . .

Europe no longer possesses unity of faith, of mission, or of aim. Such unity is a necessity in the world. Here, then, is the secret of the crisis. It is the duty of every one to examine and analyze carefully and coolly the probable elements of this new unity. But those who persist in perpetuating, by violence, or by jesuitical compromise, the external observance of the old unity, only perpetuate the crisis, and render its issue more violent.

Europe—we might say the world, for Europe is the lever of the world—no longer believes in the sanctity of royal races; she may still accept them here and there as a guarantee of stability, as a defence against the encroachments of some other dangerous element; but she no longer believes in the *principle*, in any special virtue residing in them, in a divine right consecrating and protecting them. Wherever they reign despotically, she conspires against them; wherever liberty exists under their sway, in however small a degree, she supports them under a brevet of impotence. She has invented the political axiom, "Kings reign without governing;" wherever they govern and govern badly, she overthrows them. Europe no longer believes in aristocracy, the royalty of several; she no longer believes in the inevitable physical transmission, in the perpetual inheritance of virtue, intelligence, and honour: she believes in it no longer, either scientifically or practically. Wherever an aristocracy acts well—if that ever happens to be the case—she follows its lead, not as an aristocracy, but as a doer of good; wherever it drags itself along in the pride of its old traditions—idle, ignorant, and decayed—she rids herself of it; she destroys it, either by revolutions or by ridicule. The carnival on the Continent looks to the historical order of patricians for its masks. Europe no longer believes in the Papacy; she no longer believes that it possesses right, mission, or capacity for spiritual education or guidance; she no longer believes in the immediate revelation, in the direct transmission of the designs and laws of Providence, by virtue of an election, to any individual whatsoever; five years ago she was seized with enthusiasm for a Pope who seemed disposed to bless the progress of the human race, and to constitute

137 In February 1849, Pope Pius IX, by tradition the ruler of the city of Rome, was overthrown and a Republic established; disguised as a monk, Pius IX fled to Naples.

himself the representative of the most advanced ideas of his age; she despised him as soon as he retraced his steps and recommenced the brutal career of his predecessors. Europe no longer believes in privilege, be it what it may, except in that which no one can destroy, because it comes from God,—the privilege of genius and virtue; she desires wealth, but she despises or hates it in the persons of those who possess it, when it is not the price of labour, or when it arrogates to itself rights of political monopoly.

Now look at the organization of Europe—is it not altogether based upon privilege, by whatever name it may be known? How then can one wonder at the struggle which is engendered within it?

Let it, then, be openly declared by every honest man, that this struggle is sacred, sacred as liberty, sacred as the human soul. It is the struggle which has for its symbol, since the commencement of the historical world, the great type of Prometheus;[138] which has for its altar, in the midst of the march of the human race, the cross of Jesus; which has for its apostles almost all the men of genius, the thousand pillars of humanity. This war-cry which rises from the ranks of the Proletaire is the cry of our fathers, the Hussites: *The cup for all, the cup for all!*[139] It is the logical consequence of the doctrine common to us all, the unity of God, and, therefore, of the human race. It is an effort to realize the prayer of Christ: *Thy will be done, on earth as it is in heaven!*[140] Yesterday we worshipped the priest, the lord, the soldier, the master; to-day we worship MAN, his liberty, his dignity, his immortality, his labour, his progressive tendency, all that constitutes him a creature made in the image of God,—not his colour, his birth, his fortune—all that is accidental and transitory in him. We believe that every man ought to be a temple of the living God; that the altar upon which he ought to sacrifice to God is the earth, his field of trial and of labour; that the incense of his sacrifice is the task accomplished by him; that his prayer is love, his power—love realized—Association. . . .

There are in Europe two great questions; or, rather, the question of the transformation of authority, that is to say, of the Revolution, has assumed two forms; the question which all have agreed to call social, and the question of nationalities. The first is more exclusively agitated in France, the second in the midst of the other peoples of Europe. We say, *which all have agreed to call social*, because, generally speaking, every great revolution is social, in this,

138 Greek demi-god who stole fire for humanity and was chained to a rock as punishment; sometimes viewed as prefiguring Christ.

139 "Proletaire" means "the common people." The Hussites were a religious group in 15th-century Bohemia with some nationalist overtones who anticipated the Protestant Reformation in key respects; one of their Four Articles of Prague (1420) demanded that the laity would have access to Communion, not just the bread or host but also the cup (chalice with wine).

140 Matt. 6:10.

that it cannot be accomplished either in the religious, political, or any other sphere, without affecting social relations, the sources and the distribution of wealth. But that which is only a secondary consequence in political revolutions, is now the cause and the banner of the movement in France. The question there is now, above all, to establish better relations between labour and capital, between production and consumption, between the workman and his employer.

It is probable that the European initiative, that which will give a new impulse to intelligence and to events, will spring from the question of nationalities. The social question can, in effect, although with difficulty, be partly resolved by a single people; it is an internal question for each, and the French Republicans of 1848 so understood it, when, determinately abandoning the European initiative, they placed Lamartine's manifesto by the side of their aspirations towards the organization of labour.[141] The question of nationality can only be resolved by destroying the treaties of 1815, and changing the map of Europe and its public Law.[142] The question of *Nationalities*, rightly understood, is the Alliance of the Peoples, the balance of powers based upon new foundations, the organization of the work that Europe has to accomplish.

We should be wrong, however, to separate the two questions; they are indissolubly connected. The men who plead the cause of the Nationalities well know that revolutions, necessarily supporting themselves on the masses, ought to satisfy their legitimate wants; they know that a revolution is sacred whenever it has for its object the progress of the millions, but that it is an unpardonable crime when it has only for its object the interest of a minority, of a caste, or of a monopoly; they know that the problem now to be resolved is, the association of all the faculties, of all the forces of humanity towards a common end, and that no movement can at the present time be simply political.

By dividing into fractions that which is in reality but one thing, by separating the social from the political question, a numerous section of French socialists has powerfully contributed to bring about the present shameful position of affairs in France. The great social idea now prevailing in Europe may be thus defined: the abolition of the proletariat; the emancipation of producers from the tyranny of capital concentrated in a small number of hands; re-division of productions, or the value arising from productions, in proportion to the work performed; the moral and intellectual education of the operative; voluntary association between workmen gradually and peacefully, as much as possible, for individual labour paid at the will of the capitalist. This sums up all the reasonable aspirations of the present time. It is not

141 Alphonse de Lamartine's "Manifesto to Europe" (March 1848).

142 The Congress of Vienna (1814–1815) largely reinstated pre-Napoleonic boundaries in Europe, but also reassigned some smaller regions to the major powers which negotiated the treaty.

a question of destroying, abolishing, or violently transferring property from one class to another; it is a question of extending the circle of consumers, of consequently augmenting production, of giving a larger share to producers, of opening a wide road to the operative for the acquisition of wealth and property, in short, of putting capital and the instruments of labour within reach of every man offering a guarantee of good will, capacity, and morality. These ideas are just; and they are destined eventually to triumph; historically, the time is ripe for their realization. To the emancipation of the *slave* has succeeded that of the *serf*; that of the serf must be followed by that of the *workman*. In the course of human progress the patriciate has undermined the despotic privilege of royalty; the bourgeoisie, the financial aristocracy, has undermined the privileges of birth; and now the people, the workers, will undermine the privilege of the proprietary and moneyed bourgeoisie; until society, founded upon labour, shall recognise no other privilege than that of virtuous intelligence, presiding, by the choice of the people enlightened by education, over the whole development of its faculties and its social capabilities. . . .

It was not for a material interest that the people of Vienna fought in 1848; in weakening the empire it could only lose power. It was not for an increase of wealth that the people of Lombardy fought in the same year; the Austrian Government had endeavoured in the year preceding to excite the peasants against the landed proprietors, as they had done in Gallicia; but everywhere they had failed. They struggled, they still struggle, as do Poland, Germany, and Hungary, for country and liberty, for a word inscribed upon a banner, proclaiming to the world that they also live, think, love, and labour for the benefit of all. They speak the same language, they bear about them the impress of consanguinity, they kneel beside the same tombs, they glory in the same tradition, and they demand to associate freely, without obstacles, without foreign domination, in order to elaborate and express their idea, to contribute their stone also to the great pyramid of history. It is something moral which they are seeking; and this moral something is at the bottom, even politically speaking, the most important question in the present state of things. It is the organization of the European task. It is no longer the savage, hostile, quarrelsome nationality of two hundred years ago which is invoked by these people. The nationality which Ancillon founded upon the following principle—*whichever people, by its superiority of strength, and by its geographical position, can do us an injury, is our natural enemy; whichever cannot do us an injury, but can by the amount of its force and by its position injure our enemy, is our natural ally*,—is the princely nationality of aristocracies or royal races.[143] The nationality of the peoples has not these dangers; it can only

143 Friedrich Ancillon (Prussian writer and politician), *Tableau des révolutions du système politique de l'Europe depuis le XVe siècle* (1803–1805).

spring from common effort and a common movement; sympathy and alliance ought to be its consequence. In principle, as in the ideas formally laid down by the men influencing every national party, nationality ought only to be to humanity that which the division of labour is in a workshop, the recognised symbol of association, the assertion of the individuality of a human group called by its geographical position, its traditions, and its language, to fulfill a special function in the European work of civilization.

The map of Europe has to be re-made. This is the key to the present movement; here lies the initiative. Before acting, the instrument of action must be organized; before building, the ground must be one's own. The social idea cannot be realized under any form whatsoever before this reorganization of Europe is effected, before the peoples are free to interrogate themselves, to express their vocation, and to assure its accomplishment by an alliance capable of substituting itself for the absolutist league which now reigns supreme.

Take the map of Europe. Study it synthetically in its geographical structure, in the great indications furnished by the lines of mountains and rivers, in the symmetrical arrangement of its parts. Compare the previsions of the future which this examination suggests, with the existing collocation of the principal races and idioms. Open the page of history, and seek for the signs of vitality, for the different populations, resulting from the *ensemble* of their traditions; listen, in short, to the cry which rises from the consciousness of these populations through their struggles and their martyrs.

Part II

READING THE NATION, c. 1550–1850

1

THE NATION IN THE RENAISSANCE

Andrew Hadfield

The age of mass nationalism in Europe can be dated to the eighteenth century, with the advent of a reading public and the rise of the newspaper.[1] But, of course, nations existed before nationalism. A strong case can be made that literature played a crucial role in constructing a public sphere before the advent of mass literacy, one in which the nation was not only debated but imagined and defined. Indeed, authors who claimed that they were speaking for and to a nation had to fabricate their audience within the confines of their work, in the absence of what we recognise as the form and signs of a nation's existence. And, given the carefully circumscribed nature of political debate in sixteenth-century England—Elizabeth was keen to prevent discussion of numerous topics, especially foreign policy and the succession—literary works, especially drama, often represented and discussed matters of significant national import, such as the succession crisis, court scandals and key events.[2] Literature was at the forefront of establishing different versions of an English national identity, a fact that can be overlooked or obscured if it is thought that literature only really plays this role later on when there is a mass nation to represent.[3] Furthermore, it could be argued that the hard work and thought takes place before the nation exists as an easily imagined community, when authors had to imagine who they were writing for and what they were actually writing about. We should not be surprised if we encounter texts that have very different, often inconsistent, conceptions of the nation, in particular, divergent ideas of what constitutes that nation. Writers sometimes conceive the nation as one huge community of citizens; and, at others, as a select group of people who have the right to rule the populace.

The anxiety is also expressed in political works, notably Sir Thomas Smith's posthumously published *De Republica Anglorum*, which appeared in 1583 but was written in 1565, a work that sought to catalogue contemporary England in terms of Roman, including republican, models. Smith divides Englishmen into four categories: gentlemen (which includes all the nobles), citizens and burgesses, yeomen, and "the fourth sort of men which doe not rule", i.e., those who have no right to take part in any of the means of governing the state, from local councillors and Justices of the Peace, to Members of Parliament and state counsellors who have the ear of the monarch. The men who do not rule are the largest category, the proletariat "which the olde Romans called *capite censij proletarij* or *operae*" and consists of "day labourers, poore husbandmen, yea marchantes or retailers which have no free lande, copiholders, and all artificers, as Taylers, Shoomakers, Carpenters, Brickemakers, Bricklayers, Masons, &c", men who do not own any land and therefore have no stake in the country. Smith argues that "These have no voice nor authoritie in our common wealth, and no account is made of them but onelie to be ruled, not to rule other, and yet they be not altogether neglected."[4]

Smith's comment reveals a great deal about early modern conceptions of the nation, who it represents and who represents it. England is governed by a relatively inclusive class but, even so, there are clear limits to who has a right to rule the nation. As Smith's words make clear, attention must be paid to the lower classes who need to have some stake in the nation and not to feel alienated or excluded. *De Republica Anglorum* demonstrates that even if we feel confident enough to be able to divide early modern authors into monarchists and republicans, there is no obvious correlation between republicanism and a more inclusive and democratic conception of the state. Monarchists and divine right theorists often paid far more attention to the landless than aristocratic republicans did, indicating that questions of political organisation and theory cannot be separated from the conception of the nation.[5] We should not be surprised to find these cross-currents in an era before the establishment of the institutions that constitute a nation.

The same issues of nation and class also help determine the course of English literature in the sixteenth century. John Skelton's aggressively polemical anti-Wolsey poems, "Colin Clout" and "Why Come Ye Nat to Courte?" are an attempt to seize a national political agenda in exposing Wolsey as the figure who has exploited and oppressed the honest labouring folk of the nation, precisely the sort of workers who Smith represents in his treatise because they cannot represent themselves.[6] Skelton's poems are part of a long tradition of estates satire based on the oppositional figure of the noble English plowman.[7] But not all writers and literary theorists were quite so sanguine about the value of writing for or about the ordinary people. George Puttenham, whose *Arte of Poesie* (published 1589, probably written c. 1565) was an attempt to account for the history and types of poetry produced in England as a way of constructing a tradition and cataloguing the ways of developing it by inspiring new writers to produce English verse, is very clear about the need for social hierarchy. His chapter, "Of the high, low, and mean subject" provides an instructive counterpoint to Smith's analysis, and needs to be quoted at length:

> The matters therefore that concern the gods and divine things are highest of all other to be couched in writing; next to them the noble gests and great fortunes of Princes, and the notable accidents of time,

> as the greatest affairs of war and peace. These be all high subjects, and therefore are delivered over to the poets hymnic and historical, who be occupied either in divine lauds or in heroical reports. The mean matters be those that concern mean men, their life and business, as lawyers, gentlemen, and merchants, good householders and honest citizens, and which sound neither to matters of state nor of war, nor leagues, nor great alliances, but smatch all the common conversation, as of the civilier and better sort of men. The base and low matters be the doings of the common artificer, servingman, yeoman, groom, husbandman, day-labourer, sailor, shepherd, swineherd, and such like of homely calling, degree, and bringing up. So that in every of the said three degrees not the selfsame virtues be equally to be praised, nor the same vices equally to be dispraised, nor their loves, marriages, quarrels, contracts, and other behaviours be like high, nor do require to be set forth with the like style, but every one in his degree and decency.[8]

Puttenham's taxonomy of class stratification closely resembles that of Smith, showing that political and literary categories were thought of in similar ways in the middle years of the sixteenth century, resulting from a common culture of rhetorical argument, perhaps derived from the pioneering work of Peter Ramus and his systems for classifying ideas and arguments.[9] As will also be clear from the move from high to low subjects, Puttenham has in mind the great, epic deeds of nations as the proper subject of serious poetry, so that the acts of war and peace are to be represented in heroic, hymnic and the historical style. Class and nation are inextricably bound together. The nation needs serious poets skilled in the high style to narrate its mighty deeds. More homely subjects require more lowly style and do not, in Puttenham's scheme, represent the nation's identity.

Puttenham is hardly consistent in his theorising. Elsewhere in his treatise he disrupts his neat classificatory scheme and admits that pastoral poetry is not quite as simple as it might appear and that the "rude speeches" of the "homely persons" represented in such works are counterfeit. Pastoral poets "insinuate and glaunce at greater matters, and such as had not bene safe to haue beene disclosed in any other sort."[10] This disjunction between style and subject matter suggests that it was not as easy to classify a nation's poetry as Puttenham claimed. If authors adopted a disguised form of commentary on important events by making lowly shepherds stand for the high and mighty, then the nation was clearly being divided in the process between those who ruled and those who felt they had the right and duty to comment on the nation's political affairs but were prevented from doing so by the former group. While the political rulers were encouraging songs of praise for the nation's heroes, its cunning poets were undermining their confidence in the prevailing order through their oblique commentary, and so avoiding censorship.

These considerations are especially relevant to the career of the greatest non-dramatic English poet of the sixteenth century, Edmund Spenser. Spenser wrote a complex, involved and critical volume of pastoral poetry early in his career, before adopting the mantle of the poet "historical", and writing the sort of elevated and serious poem that Puttenham sees as appropriately representing the heroic deeds of the nation. *The Shepheardes Calender* (1579) is a hard work to classify and has bewildered commentators eager to get to grips with its elusive and slippery text. On the one hand Spenser is clearly imitating the career of Virgil, starting out his poetic career with a work of homely style which points towards the greater tasks that he will set himself in the future. But, on the other, he produces a text that deliberately combines ambition and a sense of entitlement, one that marks him out as the best poet writing in English (a judgement that Sir Philip Sidney endorsed), deserving an edition that resembles the great humanist works of scholarship of major Latin poets and able to comment on the great affairs of state.[11] As this might indicate, *The Shepheardes Calender* is an extraordinarily cheeky work, showing no respect for poetic tradition or the dignity of the ruling class, and, by implication, asserting the right of the poet to comment on the affairs of state, a conception of his role he was to develop throughout his writing career. In the March, May, July and September eclogues Spenser commented on the state of the church in England.[12] In the April and November eclogues he commented on the projected marriage of Elizabeth to François, Duc of Alençon, a match that was fiercely condemned by the Sidney circle at court and other influential Protestant groups who felt that the queen was exposing England to the domination of French Catholicism and potentially visiting the horror of the Massacre of Saint Bartholomew's Day (August 23, 1572) and the subsequent religious civil war on her subjects.[13] The dazzling array of poetic styles on display in the volume indicate that, for Spenser, poetry and politics could not be separated and that he was demonstrating that good poetry which would make the nation great was also free to criticise the ruling powers and suggest how things should and should not be done.

Such ambitious notions of poetry are developed in *The Faerie Queene* (1590, 1596), the great unfinished epic-romance of Elizabethan England, where Spenser claims the title of "Poet historicall" in the "Letter to Ralegh" appended to the first edition.[14] There is an elegiac quality to the poem which is often missed by readers who have often seen it as a triumphalist work celebrating the reign and achievements of Elizabeth. The problem is that Spenser is describing a world that has gone, a past that never happened the absence of which has determined the gloomy state of the present. Elizabeth is represented in many forms throughout the poem, but what seems like praise of her status as the virgin queen becomes more and more critical as the narrative progresses. By the time the poem was published in 1590, Elizabeth was 57, the oldest ruling monarch since Henry III (1207–1272), some 300 years earlier. Not only was she past the age of child-bearing but she was expected to die at any moment and had been for a decade. The Tudor dynasty was doomed and although there were candidates who could start a new regime, the future looked frightening and uncertain to most Elizabethans. We should never lose sight of the fact that patriots and nationalists are often the harshest critics of the status quo.

Spenser's criticisms of Elizabeth are both harsh and clear. Most of the powerful women represented in the poem can be read as types and antitypes of Elizabeth, reflecting on what the queen has and has not done. These range from Duessa and Lucifera in Book I, gaudy figures of pride whose vanity and scheming threatens to undermine all forms of stability, to the commanding figure of Britomart, the Amazonian Knight of Chastity.[15] Britomart might seem to be the more obvious figure of Elizabeth, a woman warrior and a mighty queen who struggles hard to guard the future of the nation. However, given that Britomart will marry Artegall and produce a line of kings and queens that will ensure the future of Faerieland, as revealed to her in Merlin's magic mirror (Book II, canto iii), the path she has chosen to ensure the fate of her nation is the direct opposite of the one Elizabeth selected. Britomart reminds readers of what Elizabeth could—and, probably in Spenser's eyes—should have done, ensured a suitable match that would have protected her subjects. Spenser uses his self-appointed role as "Poet historicall" to comment on affairs of state, in line with Puttenham's conception of the function of "poets hymnic and historical." As the "Letter to Ralegh" explains

> In that Faery Queene I meane glory in my generall intention, but in my particular I conceiue the most excellent and glorious person of our soueraigne the Queene, and her kingdome in Faery land. And yet in some places els, I doe otherwise shadow her. For considering she beareth two persons, the one of a most royall Queene or Empresse, the other of a most vertuous and beautifull Lady, this latter part in some places I doe expresse in Belphoebe, fashioning her name according to your own excellent conceipt of Cynthia (Phoebe and Cynthia being both names of Diana) (p. 716).[16]

The poem announces that its aim is to "fashion a gentleman or noble person in vertuous and gentle discipline" (p. 714), words that have inspired a whole school of thought and writing about early modern identity.[17] Clearly one of the key ways of doing this is to fashion the queen to make the gentleman reader understand how the nation is, has and should be governed, through a series of positive and negative examples. Spenser, following Sidney, carefully distinguishes between the historian and the poet: "For an Historiographer discourseth of affayres orderly as they were donne, accounting as well the times as the actions, but a Poet thrusteth into the middest, euen where it most concerneth him, and there recoursing to the thinges forepaste, and diuining of thinges to come, maketh a pleasing Analysis of all" (pp. 716–17).[18] The historian is tied to a description of real events. But a poet can use historical events in a more flexible way, referring to the past, present and future, and, the implication is, counter-factual narratives in order to represent the real truth of the nation and inspire the reader to help shape its future. Poetry becomes a critical space in which real advice and comment can be provided, more political than the cautious, compromised and limited language of politics. Spenser's conception of the poet and his work had considerable influence in shaping the style and purpose of seventeenth century poetry, particularly in inspiring a generation of poets who also argued that they could speak for a nation that had gone soft and abandoned the ideals of militant Protestantism.[19]

For Spenser the queen was the problem and the political effects of her stubborn refusal to marry endangered the safety of those she was supposed to protect. This was especially true in Ireland where Spenser was a colonial planter on the Munster Plantation, having acquired his estate, Kilcolman—which he named Hap-Hazard—in 1589 after the defeat of the rebellion of the earl of Desmond.[20] Spenser, as his prose dialogue, *A View of the Present State of Ireland* (c. 1596) demonstrates, ceased to be English, and became acutely conscious of his status as an Englishman in Ireland, defining and defending an identity which he had been forced to adopt.[21] In Ireland it is especially obvious that the bio-politics of the queen's private life determines the lives of her subjects, as Spenser makes clear with reference to his own life and marital status, with a series of inter- and intra-textual references made through his works. In the ending to the 1590 version of *The Faerie Queene*, published just after Spenser acquired his estate, Britomart is cast as the witness to the joyful union of Scudamore and Amoret, who she has helped rescue from the enchanter, Busirane:

> Had ye them seene, ye would haue surely thought,
> That they had beene that faire *Hermaphrodite*,
> Which that rich *Romane* of white marble wrought,
> And in his costly Bath causd to bee site:
> So seemd those two, as growne together quite,
> That *Britomart* halfe enuying their blesse,
> Was much empassiond in her gentle sprite,
> And to her selfe oft wisht like happinesse,
> In vaine she wisht, that fate n'ould let her possesse.
>
> (III.xii.46)

Britomart is envious of the lovers and, as the adjective "empassiond" suggests, inflamed by their actions. The last lines describing her frustrated desires refer much more aptly to those of Elizabeth. Britomart, we already know, will eventually marry Artegall, and the poem will tell their story. Elizabeth, the antitype of Britomart, will not marry and experience such joys, a failure that does not bode well for the future lives of her subjects. The direct address in the first line of the stanza, like an aside from a character on stage, draws the reader into this intimate scenario and invites him or her to consider carefully what is going on. The moment might seem like a voyeuristic one, as the reader is invited to be a consumer of pornography (and it is not obvious that the wealthy Roman is to be admired for his artistic taste). However, sex is never simply sex in Spenser, and we know that the fate of nations hangs on the private lives of the mighty. In the "Two Cantos of Mutabilitie", posthumously published in 1609 from what appears to be a fragment of an unfinished seventh book, Spenser makes a more direct reference to Elizabeth (as Cynthia) as old and capricious, on the very point of death: "her face and countenance euery day / We changed see" (VII.vii.50, ll. 6–7). Elizabeth could have had the life of Britomart but she chose that of Cynthia.

Near the end of the *Epithalamion*, written to celebrate his marriage to Elizabeth Boyle—probably in Cork—on June 11, 1594, Spenser recycles the moment of Britomart's scopic desire:

> Who is the same, which at my window peepes?
> Or whose is that faire face, that shines so bright?
> Is it not Cinthia, she that neuer sleepes,
> But walkes about high heauen al the night?
> O fayrest goddesse, do thou not enuy
> My loue with me to spy:
> For thou likewise didst loue, though now vnthought,
> And for a fleece of woll, which priuily,
> The Latmian shepherd once vnto thee brought,
> His pleasures with thee wrought.
> Therefore to vs be fauourable now;
> And sith of wemens labours thou hast charge,
> And generation goodly dost enlarge,
> Encline thy will t'effect our wishfull vow,
> And the chast wombe informe with timely seed,
> That may our comfort breed:
> Till which we cease our hopefull hap to sing,
> Ne let the woods vs answere, nor our Eccho ring.[22]

Here, Cynthia, like Britomart, stares at the united lovers with envy, the word providing a clear connection between the two episodes. It was the monarch's duty to protect her subjects and, read superficially, this might appear to be what she is doing, in her allegorical guise as the goddess who protects women. But her jealousy of her subjects' bliss, followed by details of her own past loves, reminds us forcefully of what Elizabeth/Cynthia did not do, i.e., marry and have children to secure the Tudor dynasty. There is a savage irony in Spenser asking Elizabeth to bless his marriage: one reason why she never sleeps is because she has no one to sleep with. Elizabeth has failed to provide a proper future for her subjects by neglecting her marital duties, which is why she looks through the window, a neat reversal of the myth of Actaeon, used frequently by Spenser in various ways in his poetry, who was transformed into a stag and then torn to pieces by his hounds after he came across Diana bathing naked. The myth of Diana's fierce self-protectiveness has also been transformed: she has turned herself into Actaeon and put herself and her subjects in danger of being torn apart by the sort of civil war that could result from a contested succession, exactly the type of war that had bedevilled England in the fifteenth century before the Tudors came to power and which had been represented on the stage so graphically in Shakespeare's first tetralogy only a few years earlier.[23]

Spenser's lines may contain a certain sympathy for Elizabeth whose decision not to marry anyone was based on a fear of making her own subjects over-mighty or subjecting England to foreign rule, as her half-sister was believed to have done.[24] But they also remind readers that the bio-politics of the monarch determined the lives of his or her subjects. Individuals could and did think about nations and their place within them in a variety of ways and it is a mistake to imagine that all patriotic arguments support the status quo. Many writers outside the close circle around the monarch—and even some within it—imagined the nation in terms of a more republican or inclusive form of political entity than currently existed. *The Faerie Queene* is an excellent example of this conception of national form, one that explores, often in complicated and critical terms, the relationship between the monarch and the territories which she ruled.[25] But, in the end, how the monarch lived, as well as how he or she ruled, really mattered. In the early modern nation the personal was indeed the political.

Notes

1 B. Anderson, *Imagined Communities: Reflections on the Origin and Spread of Nationalism* (1983), reprinted London: Verso, 1991; J. Raymond, *The Invention of the Newspaper: English Newsbooks, 1641–1649*, Oxford: Clarendon Press, 1996.

2 D. Bevington, *Tudor Drama and Politics: A Critical Approach to Topical Meaning*, Cambridge, MA: Harvard University Press, 1968; M. Axton, *The Queen's Two Bodies: Drama and the Elizabethan Succession*, London: Royal Historical Society, 1977.

3 A. Hadfield, *Literature, Politics and National Identity: Reformation to Renaissance*, Cambridge: Cambridge University Press, 1994; C. McEachern, *The Poetics of English Nationhood, 1590–1612*, Cambridge: Cambridge University Press, 1996, 2006.

4 Sir T. Smith, *De Republica Anglorum: A Discourse on the Commonwealth of England* (1906), L. Alston (ed.), reprinted in Shannon: Irish Academic Press, 1972,

p. 46. For comment, see C. Shrank, *Writing the Nation in Reformation England, 1530–1580*, Oxford: Oxford University Press, 2004, ch. 4; J. Richards, *Rhetoric and Courtliness in Early Modern Literature*, Cambridge: Cambridge University Press, 2003, ch. 3.

5 For reflections on this issue, see J. F. McDiarmid (ed.), *The Monarchical Republic of Early Modern England: Essays in Response to Patrick Collinson*, Aldershot: Ashgate, 2007.

6 J. Skelton, *The Complete Poems*, John Scattergood (ed.), Harmondsworth: Penguin, 1983. For comment, see A. Hadfield, *Literature, Politics and National Identity*, ch. 1; G. Walker, *John Skelton and the Politics of the 1520s*, Cambridge: Cambridge University Press, 1988, ch. 3.

7 J. Dean (ed.), *Six Ecclesiastical Satires*, Kalamazoo: Medieval Institute Publications, 1991.

8 Cited in B. Vickers (ed.), *English Renaissance Literary Criticism*, Oxford: Oxford University Press, 1999, pp. 230–31.

9 W. J. Ong, *Ramus, Method, and the Decay of Dialogue: From the Art of Discourse to the Art of Reason*, Cambridge, MA: Harvard University Press, 1958; P. Mack, *Elizabethan Rhetoric: Theory and Practice*, Cambridge: Cambridge University Press, 2002, chs. 1–3.

10 Cited in G. Smith (ed.), *Elizabethan Critical Essays*, 2 vols, Oxford: Clarendon Press, 1904, II, p. 40.

11 For Sidney's comment, see *An Apology for Poetry (or The Defence of Poesy)*, G. Shepherd (ed.), revised and expanded by R. Maslen, Manchester: Manchester University Press, 2002, p. 110.

12 See P. E. McLane, *Spenser's Shepheardes Calender: A Study in Elizabethan Allegory*, Notre Dame: Notre Dame University Press, 1961, chs. 7–14.

13 K. Duncan-Jones, *Sir Philip Sidney: Courtier Poet*, London: Hamish Hamilton, 1991, pp. 159–65; McLane, *Spenser's Shepheardes Calender*, chs. 2–6.

14 E. Spenser, *The Faerie Queene* (1590), A. C. Hamilton (ed.), rev. edn., Harlow: Longman, 2001, p. 716. All subsequent references to this edition are in parentheses in the text.

15 McEachern, *Poetics of English Nationhood*, ch. 2.

16 Spenser is referring to Raleigh's allegorical poem, "The Ocean to Cynthia."

17 The foundational work is S. Greenblatt, *Renaissance Self-Fashioning from More to Shakespeare*, Chicago: Chicago University Press, 1980. Greenblatt's assumptions that individuals create and determine their own identities has been criticised and developed in various ways, but his work remains inspirational, especially for discussions of Spenser.

18 See Sidney, *Apology*, pp. 82–83.

19 See M. O'Callaghan, *The "Shepheardes Nation": Jacobean Spenserians and Early Stuart Political Culture, 1612–1625*, Oxford: Clarendon Press, 2000.

20 W. Maley, *A Spenser Chronology*, Basingstoke: Macmillan, 1994, p. 55, *passim*.

21 For more discussion, see A. Hadfield, *Spenser's Irish Experience: Wilde Fruyt and Salvage Soyl*, Oxford: Clarendon Press, 1997.

22 E. Spenser, "Epithalamion", in R. A. McCabe (ed.), *The Shorter Poems*, Harmondsworth: Penguin, 1999, pp. 437–49, ll. 372–89.

23 For comment, see A. Hadfield, *Shakespeare and Republicanism*, Cambridge: Cambridge University Press, 2005, ch. 3.

24 See S. Doran, *Monarchy and Matrimony: Courtships of Elizabeth I*, London: Routledge, 1995.

25 See, for example, T. H. Cain, *Praise in "The Faerie Queene,"* Lincoln: University of Nebraska Press, 1978.

2

THE PECULIAR STATUS OF EARLY MODERN ENGLAND

Elizabeth Sauer

Through divine intervention, order was restored to a divided nation in the sixteenth century; thus John Lyly declares, "So tender a care hath [God] alwaies had of that *England*, as of a new *Israel*, his chosen and peculier people.[1] "Peculiar" connects Old Testament Israelites with the elect of the New. 1 Peter 2:9 refers to "a chosen generacion, a royal Priesthode, an holie nacion, a peculiar people."[2] The prerogatives of ancient Israel are thereby applied to the early Christians; "a chosen generacion" is derived from a people divinely "chosen" (Isaiah 44:1 ff.); "a royal Priesthode" from "a kingdome of Priests" (Exod. 19:6); "a holie nacion" from Exodus 19:6 and "an holy nation" (Deut. 14:2); "a peculiar people" from "a precious people" (Deut. 14:2; 26:18). 1 Peter 2:16 also describes the chosen as a liberated people, though answerable to civil authority (1 Peter 2:13). The bible thus supplied the English with a pattern for national self-fashioning by modelling "a unity of people, language, religion, territory, and government."[3] "English nationalism," as Hans Kohn affirmed, "was born in the great decisive hour of its history by repeating the experience of the chosen people and of the Covenant," earlier characterized by Ernest Barker as "a kind of Hebraic exclusive nationalism."[4] Nationalists in turn translated a belief in election into their own political and national mythology.

A nascent English nationalism had surfaced before the early modern era, in a rivalry with France whose election was justified through its papal legitimization of royal power. The effort to emulate France's national status involved the cultivation of a royal mystique and a "political theology," prominently featuring a providential narrative.[5] Interpreted in relation to an international Reformation movement, English nationhood was characterized by a resistance to the universal acclaims of continental Catholic powers allied with Rome.[6] The Tudor revolution of the 1530s saw Henry VIII in expression of theological independence, renouncing the foreign jurisdiction of the Papacy and assuming the title of Supreme Head of the Church of England by the first Act of Supremacy in 1534.[7] Following Henry's death, the imprisoned Sir Thomas Smith declared the transference of elect status through the succession of divinely ordained British monarchs at a time when the kingdom was "outwardly *with* foreyne enemies assailed, and *within* sore shaken *with* this cyvil dissencion":

> This Realme, o Lord, shuld be and is a chosen Realme to thee, to which thou haest vouchsaved to give the true knowledge of thi veritie and gospell, first by the late King of most famous memorie, Henrie the Eight, and now more amply by his most swete sonne, the Kings Majestie, that now reigneth.[8]

Originally and inextricably tied to monarchical authority, as Smith protests, the evolving concept of English nationhood would come to reflect a reformed relationship, one whose "democratic and libertarian connotations of nationality were strengthened."[9] Early modern rulers failed to recognize the increasing association of Englishness with the liberty of the subject that would ultimately lead to the nation's independence from an institutional and state identity.[10]

It is true that peculiar status was not originally and automatically associated in England with a national identity and, as Patrick Collinson recently reminded us, God's Englishness was not first voiced by a Protestant.[11] In fact even by Shakespeare's time "probably only a small minority were infected with [the virulence of Protestant nationalism] as decisively shaping their outlook."[12] Foxe himself was at least if not more an internationalist than a nationalist.[13] It took an additional century, Adrian Hastings continues, before the majority of the English identified with a Protestant nationhood. Thus early scholarship on the nation misleadingly charts a march toward nationalism through John Foxe, to John Aylmer, to the Golden Speech of Elizabeth I, and then to "the chauvinist rhetoric of John Milton."[14] Still in the later decades of the early modern era, the meaning of peculiar status shifts from Protestant internationalism to Protestant English nationalism as the universal designations of election become particularized and associated with a liberated people. This essay focuses on the consolidation and galvanizing of national sentiment around the concept of liberty as an expression of Protestant election. Of particular concern will be the celebrated work of the English literary canon, the national epic of John Milton, with whom arguably, "the full force of the new form of England's nationalism appears."[15]

The mid-seventeenth-century British kingdom that was imagined in the interregnum was largely the work of Oliver Cromwell. In "His Highnesse the Lord Protector's speech to the Parliament . . . the 4th of September, 1654" Cromwell appeals to the first Protectoral Parliament to uphold the interests of the three nations "with the territories belonging to them" and at the same time "the interest of all the Christian people in the world."[16] The remembrance of the nation's recent history, which culminates in a plea for "healing and settling" (3:435) of national affairs, particularizes a reference made by Dr. Thomas Goodwin in a sermon, delivered just before session that day: "the only parallel of God's dealing with us that I know in the world [is] . . . Israel's bringing out of Egypt through a wilderness, by many signs and wonders towards a place of rest." "The only parallel" offers a model for reading the nation's recent past as well for justifying its international mission and prophesying its destiny.[17] The translation of the statement from the sermon to Cromwell's political address is also a translation of the biblical to the national English context, anticipated by John Spittlehouse in his 1653 suggestively titled *A Warning-Piece Discharged . . . As also, A brief and full Parallel betwixt the History of Israel and our late and present Series of Affairs. In which Simile, Our present General is compar'd with Moses, as he was their Deliverer, Judge, and General.*[18]

Certainly Cromwell and his contemporaries still exhibited a nationalism not readily distinguishable from internationalism. Thus two years after the September 1654 address, Cromwell announces at the opening of Parliament that God's "peculiar interest in the world . . . [is] more extensive than the people of all these three nations." Yet in this divinely favoured community of Protestants, the British once again stand out: The Spaniard who is "providentially" predisposed to strike at "the very Being and interest" of Protestant nations, is especially intent on destroying "the interest of the people of God in these nations" (4:261). Cromwell's justifications for his war against Spain included the internal threat posed by the enemy: "The Papists in England they have been accounted, ever since I was born, Spaniolised"; worse yet, they "shake hands" with the English Cavaliers (4:264). While confessional identifications of chosenness continued to override national boundaries, the historical and political contingencies to which Protestantism was subject and the anti-Catholic momentum by which it was defined, as well as the ideas of liberty—God's most "glorious" gift— with which Englishness became associated, reestablished those bounds from within and without (3:436–37).

The future civil servant of the Cromwellian government and architect of the nation, John Milton claimed God as "Brittain's God" who "hath yet ever had this Iland under the speciall indulgent eye of his providence."[19] Several years later in a rousing statement on national potential, Milton recalls England's history of liberation enabled through the early Reformers:

> The favour and the love of heav'n we have great argument to think in a peculiar manner propitious and propending towards us. Why else was this Nation chos'n before any other, that out of her as out of *Sion* should be proclam'd and sounded forth the first tidings and trumpet of Reformation?
>
> (*CPW* 2:552)

Such sentiments were not unqualified: certainly Milton acknowledged the nation's moral vicissitudes. His treatise on church government announces the peculiar status of England while also pointing to a need for further reformation: how does it happen, he asks in 1641,

> that *England* (having had this *grace* and *honour* from GOD to bee the first that should set up a Standard for the recovery of *lost Truth*, and blow the first *Evangelick Trumpet* to the *Nations*, holding up, as from a Hill, the new Lampe of *saving light* to all Christendome) should now be last, and most unsettl'd in the enjoyment of that *Peace*, whereof she taught the way to others.
>
> (*CPW* 1:525)

Self-interest ultimately led the monarchy astray: "HENRY the 8. was the first that rent this *Kingdome* from the *Popes* Subjection totally; but his Quarrell being more about *Supremacie*, then other faultinesse in *Religion* that he regarded, it is no marvell if hee stuck where he did" (*CPW* 1:528). Even a century later, belief in national election and the coming of the kingdom constantly demanded readjusting. The "only parallel" would give way to a national history of intolerance in which the scriptural paradigm of nation-formation is not, however, invalidated but recast.

In 1649 Milton declared his opposition to monarchy on the basis that it was the obstacle to the advancement of a Reformation nation, which "seems much to favour two things to [kings] so dreadful, Liberty and Equality" (*CPW* 3:509). The identification of the nation with the people of God offered leverage to opponents of monarchy. Ironically the nation was torn by the terms of its origination as opposition to the royal mystique that launched a nationalist movement, seeded a new form of nationalism through a corresponding discourse on liberty. Milton's England–Israel identifications as correlative and antithetical[20] correspond with England's fluctuating commitment to Christian liberty. While it certainly has universal applications, the parallel as applied by Milton is designed to reflect the conditions of English nationhood and its moral character.

Historical awareness being a central feature of a national awareness, Milton's epic poem "doctrinal to the nation" relies on the prophetic mode for rescripting Israel's past. Revelation in particular supplied what Claire McEachern characterizes as "a narrative pattern for the internal unity so instrumental to the nation."[21] Sowing the seeds of nationhood, Milton's prophet-historian leads Adam up the "Hill / Of Paradise" to display what amounts to a *Pisgah-Sight* of Hebrew history.[22] The prospect of the worldly civilizations and monarchies launches a visual and verbal narrative that culminates in an apocalypse. A chronological series of vignettes then invests the nation with its moral and historical bearings, exposing tensions between its chosen status and the millennia-long cycles of depravity and political decline. The struggles for tolerance amidst persecution are set in a context of Israel's idolatry, disobedience, and betrayed election. The Israelites' disinheritance is prefigured by God's iconoclastic act in book 11 of reducing Eden to a wasteland (11.834). Possession of the Promised Land as a rightful inheritance, a permanent and binding arrangement is rendered conditional on the Israelites' fluctuating worthiness.[23] Having been deliberately composed in the mother tongue to reinforce the connection between the writing of the nation and a key feature in that endeavour—the use of the vernacular, *Paradise Lost* in its final books registers a corresponding linguistic change: the epic language and figures drop out, leaving in their place a comparatively unadorned language.

Adam learns that the favour bestowed on the "one peculiar Nation" (12.111) springs from Abraham in whose "Seed / All Nations shall be blest" (12.125–26). The "Race elect," "Safe towards *Canaan* from the shore advance[s]" (12.214–15), though the pilgrimage is constantly diverted as they wander "[t]hrough the wild Desert, not the readiest way," Michael warns Adam (12.216). The journey involves for the pilgrims a confrontation with the limitations of the Law, which "can discover sin, but not remove" (12.290) and which "Cannot appease" "peace / Of Conscience" (12.296–98). In due course, "long wander'd man" will be brought back "[t]hrough the worlds wilderness" to the "eternal Paradise of rest" (12.313–15). "Meanwhile [the Israelites] in their earthly *Canaan* plac't / Long time shall dwell and prosper, but when sins / National interrupt thir public peace, / Provoking God to raise them enemies" (12.315–18). The interim creates a place for liberty of conscience in terms of the testing thereof. At the same time, the postlapsarian context determines that liberty can only be known by its engagement with its opposite, its proximity to trial and persecution.

"[T]he failure of the godly revolution in England . . . [having given] the North American colonists a new sense of their special status," the Israelite paradigm of nationhood was transplanted to the New World and specifically New England by a host of émigrés from John Winthrop to Thomas Shepard, Samuel Danforth, Samuel Sewall, Cotton Mather, Anne Bradstreet, Edward Johnson, and Michael Wigglesworth.[24] While writers in turn assigned the peculiar status of the Old Israelites to the elect of the New World, each also submitted the parallel to the contingencies and frustrations of historical conditions. Biblical typology enables the formation of a national memory but the teleological providential narrative is readily diverted. Delivered from bondage in Old England, American Puritans nationalized their millenarianism in a historical mission, their errand into the wilderness. The collapse of the New World into an Old World model—a prospect that many émigrés were at pains to refute—brought to the fore questions of liberty, which were so central to Milton's own uses of the paradigm in his polemical and poetical work on English nationhood. Given the threats to liberty of conscience in a post-lapsarian England, Milton's polemical and poetic appeals are largely rooted in a negative conception thereof. In this regard Milton's national epic *Paradise Lost* imaginatively compels a reassessment of English nationhood and its moral and philosophical underpinnings, as well as of the millenarian history of the Puritan pilgrims who adapted the paradigm in transgressing national bounds.[25]

The commonplace of the pilgrimage connects the Old and New World historical, literary narratives. Milton in turn emerges as an important contributor to writing the early nation in terms of the literary models in the vernacular he develops for what George Sensabaugh described in *Milton in Early America* as "a country seeking national identity."[26] As the received tradition of *Paradise Lost* reveals, Milton would also eventually be drawn into the literary and national culture of the New World. The national epic supplied a language—albeit a lofty one—that appealed to those compelled to leave England for being denied the opportunity to be English, as Greenfeld calls it, that is, to enjoy liberty.[27] Numbering among the Puritans who left what Hans Kohn characterized as "indelible traces on the character of nationalism in Great Britain and even more in New England,"[28] Anglo-American writers from Bradford to Williams compared the deliverance of the Israelites to God gathering his "elect" (Matt. 24:31), leading them to the New World and specifically New England. William Bradford in *Of Plymouth Plantation*, the first sustained literary work of New England, wrote: "it is ever to be remembered that where the Lord begins to sow good seed, there the envious man will endeavour to sow tares" and since the Lord's blessing attracts all sorts, "a 'mixed multitude' came into the wilderness with the People of God out of Egypt of old (Exodus xii.38)."[29] In his letter on "New Englands lament," the Cambridge Massachusetts minister Thomas Shepard castigates Old England for the "cracks and flawes" in the "new building of Reformation" especially those produced by radicals who "cut off the hand of the Magistrate from touching men for their consciences." Contrasting Old with New England, he announces that the latter "never banished any for their consciences"; thus, he dismisses any "reports of the divisions in New-England" as "fables."[30]

Both the features of English peculiar status and the conditions of its backsliding are transplanted into the New World to create an American exceptionalism that is often compromised.[31] The prospect of New England becoming an intolerant Old England, which Shepard's defence of the former indirectly betrays, and which many New Englanders were at pains to refute, was intimately tied to the question of liberty of conscience, both by the supporters and detractors thereof. Perhaps the most adamant tolerationist in his day, Roger Williams condemned violence in Old and New England committed under the pretense of advancing Christendom: the dizzying "*Turnings* and *Turnings* of the body of this *Land* in point of Religion in few yeares" is due to the abuses of religion by English monarchs:

> From halfe-Protestantisme halfe-Popery under Henry the eight, to absolute Protestanisme under Edward the sixth: from absoluer Protestation under Edward the sixt to absalute [sic] popery under Quegne Mary, and from absolute Popery under Queene Mary, (just

> like the Weather-cocke, with the breath of every Prince) to absolute Protestantisme under Queene Elizabeth &c.

Likewise a witness to the "monstrous and most inhumane conversions" forced on the New England Natives, Williams judged that "*America* (as *Europe* and all nations) lyes dead in sin and trespasses." John Clarke's *Ill Newes from New-England, or, A Nar[r]ative of New-Englands Persecution wherin is declared that while old England is becoming new, New-England is become Old*, which is addressed to Parliament and the Council of State, rehearses

> a tragicall story . . . of strangers, and wayfaring-men that were passing by, and . . . men professing the fear of the Lord . . . who together for liberty of their consciences, and worship of their God, as their hearts were persuaded, long since fled from the persecuting hands of the Lordly *Bishops*, your adversaries and ours.

But the "peace and settlement" both of the three nations and the lands occupied by the British depend on the magistrates distinguishing between "these two administrations of Christ's power here on earth"—the secular and the spiritual or conscience. However, accuses Edward Burrough, on the "head" of the New England magistrates "lies the blood of our brethren."[32] There is much irony in the fact that, as James Truslow Adams recognized nearly a century ago, "An English Opposition Becomes a New England Oligarchy," as the appeals in the New World for "religious toleration, for civil liberty, and for a religion of love [are] silenced."[33]

The New England tracts on liberty and emerging concepts of nationhood can shed light on these conjunctions—and the tentativeness thereof—in *Paradise Lost*. Milton's work in turn exhibited what Sensabaugh discussed as an effort "to carve a new nation out of a new land," to develop "an idiom to celebrate New World experience."[34] As the epic's prophetic history shows, the betrayal of freedom, of what Milton calls "true Liberty" which "with right Reason (conscience) dwells / Twinn'd" (12.83–85) and which includes for Milton free will, is equally repressive and unconscionable as persecution. Onto the Jews' history, Milton inscribed a pilgrim's progress, constituting in *Paradise Lost* an exodus story of "strangers and pilgrims."[35] The wandering in the wilderness does result in the founding of the Israelites' "government, and thir great Senate" (*PL* 12.224–25), and consequently laws for "Civil justice" and "Religious rites" (231) through which they establish a republican-styled government.[36] But the Old Testament nation must give way to the abrogation of Deuteronomic law by what Michael foretells as "peace/ Of Conscience, which the Law by Ceremonies / Cannot appease" (12.296–98). Granted "a better cov'nant" (302), the Israelite nation acquires new underpinning only to turn on itself, constraining conscience and disassembling the house of God. In *Areopagitica* the Reformation nation is featured as a monument extolling national diversity and comprised of "many schisms and many dissections" (*CPW* 2:555). The builders are heretical opponents of prohibitions of rights and liberty. In the Restoration epic, the imposition "On every conscience" of "Spiritual Laws by carnal power" (12.521–22) is described as "unbuilding" God's "living Temples, built by Faith to stand / Thir own Faith not anothers" (12.526–28). The encroachment of secular into religious matters violates liberty of conscience. The catalogue of the persecuted extends beyond those who are directly or indirectly named in the final books of *Paradise Lost* to include all the faithful. In prophesying the abuses of temporal authority, Michael warns that "the Spirit of Grace itself" and "His consort Liberty" are bound (12.525–26), leading to the oppression of the righteous: "heavy persecution shall arise / On all who in the worship persevere / Of Spirit and Truth" (12.531–33).

Milton in turn developed a language and place for conscience in relation to a concept of a nation, whose election is continually frustrated. Out of the prophesied persecutory history that spans the Old and New Testaments emerges what John Coffey, in studying cases for toleration in the seventeenth-century Puritan movement, characterizes as a counter-cultural, anti-establishment community, "an *ecclesia* called out from among the nations, not a community coterminous with national populations."[37] The new nation is revealed by Michael in terms of "New heav'ns, new Earth, Ages of endless date / Founded in righteousness and peace and love" (12.549–50), the psychological, spiritual, and poeticized manifestation thereof being a "paradise within thee" (12.587) that Michael instructs Adam to cultivate, and which establishes the foundation of the true church, the invisible church. In the meantime, Adam and Eve go forth in a spirit of independence and interdependence, though N. H. Keeble suggests, perhaps overoptimistically, that "limitless opportunities for discovery and joy" await them.[38] The epic's final lines "They hand in hand with wand'ring steps and slow, / Through *Eden* took thir solitary way" (12.648–49) recall the account of the Israelites' plight in Psalm 107.4: "They wandred in the wildernesse and strayed from the way: And found no citie where to dwell." The lines also force a reassessment of Cromwell's only parallel and the teleological advancement once implied by his assurance that the New Israel under his direction was moving "towards a place of rest," later corrected by his admission that the nation had chosen a captain "to lead us back again into Egypt."[39]

At a time when national interests were again identified with unity and conformity and as "peculiar" increasingly acquired secular overtones and Englishness would become couched in political and civic terms, Milton designed a place for conscience in a nation distinguished by its commitment to Christian liberty. Constraint of conscience was "inconsistent with a Commonwealth that hath the Liberty of her own Conscience, or that is not Popish," as James Harrington testified on the eve of the Restoration.[40] For Milton and his Puritan contemporaries, the sinews of the nation are religious, prophetic, literary discourses—in the vernacular—that expound New Testament values, gospel equity, and liberty of conscience. The subject of the nation is answerable to spiritual power, the will of God alone, and independent of temporal state authority. Accordingly, *Paradise Lost* also proposes a reassessment of the millenarian history of the Puritan pilgrims by historicizing and prophesying the complications of what Puritan pastor Samuel Danforth in an election day sermon in Massachusetts called New England's errand into the "waste and howling Wilderness."[41] While the intolerance of Old England, like the judgment of Mosaic Law, drives the nonconformist into the wilderness, the pilgrimage he undertakes—as the literary evidence offered in Milton's epic suggests—interrogates the Israel/England paradigm and frustrates both typological advancement and the ready and easy way to establish a free commonwealth in the native country and the New World.

Notes

1 J. Lyly, *Euphues* (1580) in R. W. Bond (ed.), *The Complete Works of John Lyly*, 3 vols, Oxford: Clarendon Press, 1967, vol. 2, p. 205.

2 *The Bible and Holy Scriptures Conteyned in the Olde and Newe Testament*, Geneva, 1560.

3 A. Hastings, *The Construction of Nationhood: Ethnicity, Religion and Nationalism*, Cambridge: Cambridge University Press, 1997, 1999, p. 18.

4 H. Kohn, *The Idea of Nationalism: A Study in Its Origins* (1967), reprinted Edison, NJ: Transaction Books, 2005, p. 176; E. Barker, *Oliver Cromwell and the English People*, Freeport, NY: Books for Libraries Press, 1971, p. 24.

5 J. W. McKenna, "How God Became an Englishman," in D. J. Guth and J. W. McKenna (eds), *Tudor Rule and Revolution: Essays for G. R. Elton from his American Friends*, Cambridge: Cambridge University Press, 1982, pp. 27, 42.

6 A. D. Smith, *National Identity*, Oxford: Oxford University Press, reprinted London: Penguin, 1991, pp. 56–57.

7 Act of Supremacy (1534), National Archives c65/143, m. 5, nos. 8 and 9, on exhibit at the British Library (May 2009); see also L. B. Smith, "This Realm of England Is an Empire," *This Realm of England: 1399 to 1688*, 7th edn., Lexington, MA: D. C. Heath and Co., 1996, pp. 112–30.

8 T. Smith, *Certaigne Psalmes or Songues of David Translated into Englishe Meter, Literary and Linguistic Works*, vol. 1, B. Danielsson (ed.), *Stockholm Studies in English*, vol. 12, Stockholm: Almqvist and Wiksell, 1963, p. 33. See also C. Shrank, *Writing the Nation in Reformation England 1530–1580*, Oxford: Oxford University Press, 2004, p. 10.

9 L. Greenfeld, *Nationalism: Five Roads to Modernity*, Cambridge, MA: Harvard University Press, 1992, p. 71. Modern theorists of the nation have traditionally underplayed the role of religion in narratives of nation formation, see Greenfeld, *Nationalism*, p. 70. Published in the same year as this, R. Helgerson's *Forms of Nationhood: The Elizabethan Writing of England*, Chicago: Chicago University Press, 1992 presents a different narrative, in which the "language of politics was most often the language of religion" (p. 252) and not vice versa. See also A. D. Smith, "Nationalism and Religion," *Chosen Peoples: Sacred Sources of National Identity*, Oxford: Oxford University Press, 2003, reprinted 2008, pp. 9–18.

10 C. Hill, "The Protestant Nation," *The Collected Essays of Christopher Hill, Volume Two: Religion and Politics in Seventeenth Century England*, Brighton: Harvester Press, 1986, pp. 28–29. See also E. H. Kantorowicz, *The King's Two Bodies; A Study in Mediaeval Political Theory*, 1957, reprinted in Princeton: Princeton University Press, 1970.
11 On God's English identity, see W. Haller, *Foxe's Book of Martyrs and the Elect Nation*, London: Jonathan Cape, 1963, p. 245; cf. C. Hill, *The English Bible and the Seventeenth-Century Revolution*, London: Penguin, 1993, p. 266, and Collinson, "Biblical Rhetoric," p. 21.
12 Hastings, *Construction of Nationhood*, p. 60.
13 Lander, "Foxe's *Book of Martyrs*: Printing and Popularizing the *Acts and Monuments*," in C. McEachern and D. Shuger (eds), *Religion and Culture in Renaissance England*, Cambridge: Cambridge University Press pp. 70–71.
14 McKenna, "How God Became an Englishman," p. 43.
15 Hastings, *Construction of Nationhood*, p. 57.
16 O. Cromwell, *The Writings and Speeches of Oliver Cromwell*, W. C. Abbott (ed.), 4 vols, New York: Russell & Russell, 1970, vol. 3, p. 434.
17 Cromwell, *Writings and Speeches of Oliver Cromwell*, vol. 3, p. 435. See also H. Kohn, *Idea of Nationalism*, p. 176.
18 C. J. Spittlehouse, *A Warning-Piece Discharged*, London, 1653, pp. 7ff.
19 Milton, *Animadversions* (1641), in D. M. Wolfe (ed.), *Complete Prose Works of John Milton*, 8 vols, New Haven: Yale University Press, 1953–1982, vol. 1, p. 704. All citations from Milton's prose are to this edition and marked "*CPW*."
20 C. McEachern cites B. K. Lewalski's concept of the "'correlative type'" of England as an Israel which is at once "the heathen alien and the model of election to be identified with and imitated" (*Poetics of English Nationhood*, p. 31).
21 McEachern, *Poetics of English Nationhood*, p. 31.
22 J. Milton, *Paradise Lost*, in M. Y. Hughes (ed.), *John Milton: Complete Poems and Major Prose*, New York: Macmillan, 1957, 11.377–78.
23 See Hill, *English Bible*, p. 374.
24 Hill, *English Bible*, p. 266.
25 My reading of Milton's national epic supplements the scholarship of J. Hale, who charts the gradual disuse of the parallel in Milton's later works, as well as of J. Rosenblatt, A. Guibbory, and J. Shoulson who consider the anti-Jewish implications of the Biblical precedent in Milton (J. Hale, "England as Israel in Milton's Writings," *Early Modern Literary Studies*, 2:2, 1996, 3:1–54; J. Rosenblatt, "Eden, Israel, England: Milton's Spiritual Geography," in J. McVeagh (ed.), *All Before Them: Attitudes to Abroad in English Literature 1660–1780*, London: Ashfield, 1990, pp. 49–63; A. Guibbory, "England, Israel, and the Jews in Milton's Prose, 1649–1660," in D. A. Brooks (ed.), *Milton and the Jews*, Cambridge: Cambridge University Press, 2008, pp. 1–34; J. S. Shoulson, *Milton and the Rabbis: Hebraism, Hellenism and Christianity*, New York: Columbia University Press, 2001. In this chapter, I also demonstrate the value of inflecting English literary treatments of the New World with the language of nationhood and liberty. On Milton and the New World, see also J. M. Evans' *Milton's Imperial Epic: "Paradise Lost" and the Discourse of Colonialism*, Ithaca: Cornell University Press, 1996.
26 G. Sensabaugh, *Milton in Early America*, Princeton: Princeton University Press, 1964, p. ix.
27 Greenfeld, *Nationalism*, p. 71.
28 Kohn, *Idea of Nationalism*, p. 177.
29 W. Bradford, *Of Plymouth Plantation, 1620–1647: The Complete Text*, S. E. Morison (ed. and intro.), New York: Alfred A. Knopf, II, 1952, ch. 32

(1642), pp. 321, 322 (first published in 1856 under the title "History of Plymouth Plantation").

30 T. Shepard, *New Englands Lamentation for Old Englands Present Errours and Divisions*, London, 1645, pp. 2, 3, 5.

31 See D. Madsen's "From Colony to Republic: Building the American Nation" in this volume (Part II).

32 R. Williams, "Christenings Make Not Christians," in P. Miller (ed.), *The Complete Writings of Roger Williams*, 3rd edn., 7 vols, New York: Russell & Russell, 1963, vol. 7, pp. 36, 37; J. Clarke, *Ill Newes from New-England*, London, 1652, A2r, A4r, A4r; E. Burrough, *A declaration of the sad and great persecution and martyrdom of the people of God, called Quakers, in New-England*, London, 1661. See also the edition of A. Bradstreet, "A Dialogue between Old *England* and New" in this critical reader.

33 J. T. Adams, *The Founding of New England*, New York: Atlantic Monthly Press, 1921, p. 174.

34 Sensabaugh, *Milton in Early America*, p. xi.

35 Exod. 6:4; Heb. 11:13; The First Epistle of Peter 2:11.

36 L. Gregerson, "Colonials Write the Nation," in B. Rajan and E. Sauer (eds), *Milton and the Imperial Vision*, Pittsburgh: Duquesne University Press, 1999, p. 187; D. Quint, *Epic and Empire: Politics and Generic Form from Virgil to Milton*, Princeton: Princeton University Press, 1993, p. 306.

37 J. Coffey, "Puritanism and Liberty Revisited: The Case for Toleration in the English Revolution," *The Historical Journal*, 41.4, 1998, p. 973.

38 N. H. Keeble, *Literary Culture of Nonconformity in Later Seventeenth-Century England*, Leicester: Leicester University Press, 1987, p. 277.

39 Cromwell, *Writings and Speeches of Oliver Cromwell*, vol. 4, p. 263.

40 J. Harrington offers a corrective to the latter; see *Aphorisms Political*, London, 1659, nos. 35, 37, 38 in D. M. Wolfe (ed.), *Complete Prose Works of John Milton*, 8 vols, New Haven: Yale University Press, 1953–1982, vol. 7, p. 521.

41 S. Danforth, *A Brief Recognition of New-Englands Errand into the Wilderness; Made . . . at Boston in N. E.*, Cambridge, MA, 1671, p. 10.

3

NATIONHOOD IN THE AGE OF ENLIGHTENMENT

Terence N. Bowers

A readable nation

How are nations and nationalism different in the age of Enlightenment than in earlier periods? I would like to begin to address this question by looking at the term "nation-state." The rapid rise of nation-states during the Enlightenment profoundly changed Europe. If we glance back at Renaissance Europe, we see a complex patchwork of "some five hundred more or less autonomous political units," consisting of such entities as principalities, city-states, fiefdoms, and so on, but this number "by 1900 had shrunk to about twenty-five," consisting almost entirely of nation-states.[1] Not only did the rise of nation-states eliminate many of these older "political units," but it also changed the internal structure of the societies within them. Thus to talk about nationhood in the age of Enlightenment, it is useful first to talk about "nation-states."

What is a nation-state and how is it different from older forms of statehood? In Max Weber's classic definition, the state is a "community that (successfully) claims the *monopoly of the legitimate use of physical force* within a given territory."[2] What distinguishes nation-states from traditional states is that a nation-state achieves "an *administrative* monopoly over a territory with demarcated boundaries," something pre-modern states could not do.[3] Traditional states could control their territories through the use (or threat) of violence and some ability to monitor them, but that ability was limited by the difficulties of gathering and sending information over large geographical expanses. This is why Anthony Giddens claims that if "'government' means a concern of the state with the regularized administration of territory, then '*[t]raditional states did not govern.*'"[4] Traditional states left local communities alone so long as they paid taxes and tribute.

The limitations of traditional states to exercise greater control over their lands largely stemmed from an inability to *read* their territories, to gather information about them. Thus Louis XIV may have fancied himself the absolute ruler of France, but his actual control was far less all encompassing in part because the French state possessed limited means of knowing what was happening in its territories.[5] Nation-states thus emerge when the state significantly enhances its information gathering capacity. For the state to possess this capacity, two key developments must happen: good transportation networks must be built and effective systems of documentation must be established. It is thus no wonder that Louis XIV, in an effort to close the gap between the theoretical power he possessed and the actual power he wielded, started to invest in infrastructure and administrative capacity. But perhaps the greatest advances in these areas happened in Great Britain: during the eighteenth century, the dynamic of capitalism helped create an extensive turnpike road system, canal networks, and a reliable postal system, all of which greatly facilitated the circulation of goods, information, and (if needed) troops.[6] Equally impressive was the British state's development of various apparatus to collect, collate, and store data about the communities in Britain. According to John Brewer, the key figures in Britain's rise to power in the eighteenth century were not chiefly its military heroes (Marlborough, West, Nelson), but its clerks—"transcribers, copyists and record-keepers"—whose numbers underwent "an unprecedented expansion." It was these "prodigies of penmanship" who made Britain *legible* to the state, which in turn allowed the state to know what resources the nation possessed, to collect taxes efficiently, to allocate and track funds, supplies, and manpower effectively. This heightened administrative power ultimately enabled the state to wage war effectively.[7]

A nation of readers

So far our story has been that of the elimination of smaller "political units" by larger hegemonic ones and of growing state power, particularly its power to track people and things and to wage war. One could extend this story along still grimmer lines by talking about the state's expansion of the prison system, the creation of a modern police force, the increasing sequestration of undesirables (the criminal, the insane, the sick), and the growth of "disciplinary power."[8] This is the dark version of the Enlightenment. But there is another story that can be told that involves the articulation of natural rights applicable to all human beings—as seen, for example, in the writings of John Locke, Thomas Paine, Mary Wollstonecraft (to name a few on the British side)—the expansion of citizenship, and the legitimization of new value-givers within egalitarian visions of the nation.

We can outline this story by first observing that as Great Britain became readable to the state, it also became readable to many of its inhabitants, which allowed them to monitor both the state and the nation it presided over. For example, the government data to which Parliament had access also became increasingly available to the *reading public*,[9] which grew throughout the eighteenth century, thanks to rising literacy rates and an expanding print culture. By mid-century, literacy rates in Great Britain reached unprecedented levels—around 60 percent overall, and nearly 100 percent among "males from the middle class."[10] Further, at the start of the eighteenth century, a well developed and growing print culture was in place. Already in 1702 London had a daily newspaper (by contrast France did not have one until the latter part of the century), by the 1730s it had six, and by the 1780s there were sixty newspapers printed throughout Britain,[11] all catering to a large reading public hungry for information.[12] Newspapers in particular functioned as a kind of day-to-day-tracking of the nation's life and involved readers in the events of the nation, even though those events may have been remote from the personal affairs of many readers.[13] Further, the dynamic of this print culture helped form what Jürgen Habermas calls the "authentic public sphere" in that it allowed readers to understand themselves as collectively constituting a new kind of community, whose views ("public opinion") could claim to represent the *entire nation* because they seemed to transcend the narrow interests of any single group and were arrived at through reason, open communication, and critical discussion—all core Enlightenment ideals. In this respect, the formation of the public sphere profoundly influenced politics because it generated "through the vehicle of public opinion" criticism of the state.[14]

What we see in the Enlightenment then—certainly in Great Britain and to some extent in France—is a dynamic dialectic between an expanding state apparatus and "the public" (also expanding), and greater numbers of people reflecting on and attempting to shape the nation, sometimes in ways antithetical to the state's aims and to how the nation had traditionally been understood. This expanded involvement, even "mass participation," in the life of the nation is what made nations and nationalism in the Enlightenment *different* from earlier periods,[15] and what made nationalism specifically so powerful as a force of sociopolitical change.

Ways of reading/seeing the nation

As has been suggested, the Enlightenment not only made the nation readable and created more readers of the nation; it also created new ways of reading or envisioning the nation. But before embarking on this topic, it is worth defining the word "nation." In the term nation-state, "nation" refers to a territory, and in most modern definitions, it is associated with a "homeland." But a nation also means more than land. To use Benedict Anderson's well known but evocative definition, nations are "imagined communities": they are "imagined because the members of even the smallest nation will never know most of their fellow-members . . . yet in the minds of each lives the image of their communion."[16] Anderson's use of the word "communion," with its connotation of sacred fellowship, is not accidental because in the modern world the nation becomes the object of intense collective emotional devotion that hitherto only God could command. If nations are the products of affective bonds, then the formation of nation-states in the eighteenth century is not simply an issue of power, state expansion, and administrative control, but also one of culture—or of creating "image[s] of communion" that allow diverse people separated from each other (by geography, customs, language) to feel connected to the point that they are "willing to die for" their "imagined community."[17]

Anderson's term "imagined" also captures the made-up nature of nations, which contradicts the way nationalists typically view their nations (as natural, ancient, even God-given). Though there is disagreement as to when nations come into existence and how artificial they are—some, such as Anthony Smith and Adrian Hastings, see Western European nations as having deep roots, while others, such as Ernest Gellner and Eric Hobsbawm, see them as post-1700 fabrications[18]—it is useful to recall Anderson's suggestion that what matters is not their "falsity" or "genuineness," or (we might add) when they arise, but "the style in which they are imagined."[19] The forms in which nations are imagined, the tropes and images of nationhood, merit special attention for how nations are imagined determines their limits and internal structure. Whether one represents the nation as a geographical entity, as a machine, or as a body helps determine the kind of social order that constitutes the nation. Such tropes determine who is included in the community, who is excluded, who may play an active role in directing the nation and speak for it, and who may not. They also determine whether it will be organized predominantly along a vertical (hierarchical) axis or a horizontal (egalitarian) axis, and what kinds of social interactions are permissible.

While most scholars seem to agree that a strong sense of English nationhood existed since the sixteenth century, new accents and tropes of nationhood appear in the Enlightenment. But before examining these, we should note that even enduring bases of English nationalism received different emphases and applications in the eighteenth century. For example, Protestantism, which had formed the foundation of English nationalism since the mid-sixteenth century, was extended to form the basis of *British* nationalism, allowing, as Linda Colley has shown, "Great Britain"—a mere "would-be nation" when created in the 1707 Act of Union as a way to prevent the Catholic James Edward Stuart from claiming the throne—to be successfully "forged."[20] Moreover, that key Protestant text of English Protestant nationalism—John Foxe's *Book of Martyrs* (1563)—was not just reprinted, but "re-packaged" as a series of "cheap installments" that working-class families could afford.[21] This text and others—such as almanacs that delivered a crude interpretation of history from an aggressively Protestant perspective and outsold all other kinds of books—provided an image of Britons as God's chosen people battling the malevolent forces of Catholicism led mainly by France. Such texts provided a potent unifying "image of communion" for many in Great Britain, who in other respects were divided geographically, linguistically, and culturally.[22] The major developments mentioned earlier—rising literacy rates, an exploding print culture, expanding communication networks—insured a deep saturation of these texts (and the "image of communion" they supported) throughout Great Britain.

A different but important trope of British nationhood that developed in the eighteenth century was that of the body geographic. To emphasize the islandness of Great Britain as the foundation of nationhood implicitly undermined older ways of conceiving nationhood, such as ecclesiastic or monarch-centered conceptions, which saw the nation as hierarchically structured.[23] Thus in these latter conceptions—which existed in France and England—individuals conceived their connection to the larger world through a series of vertical links. While dynastic paradigms reinforced a stratified view of the cosmos, with the king as a high center in the great chain of being and a crucial link to the divine, geography tended to flatten things out, bringing one's sights down to the land, directing one's view horizontally, and allowing one to see one's connection to others inhabiting the same space. This form of nationhood thus suggested a more egalitarian social order.

A key text in promoting a geographic conception of British nationhood is Daniel Defoe's frequently reprinted *A Tour Thro' the Whole Island of Great Britain* (1724–1726). While the English had a sense of England's identity as an island going back at least to Shakespeare, Defoe was instrumental in fleshing out the ideological implications of the nation as a geographic body. Moreover, he wrote in a period when maps had wide circulation (as they had not in Shakespeare's day) and when individuals had, in J. R. Hale's words, developed "the habit of conceptualising space" cartographically.[24]

The space that Defoe's *Tour* helps his readers conceptualize is that of a dynamically integrated island, in which all parts materially and economically depend on each other. Readers receive a detailed picture of how "Every Part of the Island" contributes to the well being of the whole—how Newcastle supplies the nation with coal, how Scotland provides it with cattle, how Kent supplies hops, Derbyshire tin, and so on. Defoe also uses the metaphor of the body geographic with trade as the lifeblood of the nation, London as the pumping heart, and the roads, rivers, and canals as the veins through which the blood circulates to provide life to the entire nation. Such a metaphor ideologically reworks the traditional body politic metaphor, which divides the social order into a tiny minority of leaders (king/nobility as head) and masses of workers (as arms, legs, stomach). The body geographic implies a different structure that dramatically expands the nation's value-givers. This idea of the nation prizes those involved in the production and circulation of goods (manufacturers, tradesmen, shopkeepers, farmers), and sees them as the nation's "true Patriots."[25] Traditionally, birth, land, and leisure were required for civic and national leadership; trade and work disqualified one. But in Defoe's reading of the nation, these latter abilities are what matter. Moreover, instead of a social order organized around ascriptive roles and hierarchical social relationships based on the paternalistic system of obligation and obedience, the nation in Defoe's construct is composed of contractual relationships among free, autonomous equals, as Locke articulated in his *Second Treatise of Government* (1690).

Besides the *Tour*, Defoe's vision of the nation was expressed in other key texts, such as the *Review* (1704–1713), a pioneering journal where he first used the body geographic trope; *The Complete English Tradesman* (1726), where he continued to promote the view that "the wealth of the nation . . . lies chiefly among the trading part of the people";[26] and *A Plan of the English Commerce* (1728), which outlined the island's economic relationships with other parts of the world. In these texts, Defoe presented a vision of the nation consisting of freeholders, tradesmen, and "shopkeepers so numerous that they cannot be counted,"[27] who, as the *Tour* pointed out in detail, were not numerically represented in Parliament. The works of the 1720s are thus the documentary equivalent of Defoe's political polemic, *The Original Power of the Collective Body of the People of England* (1701), in which he argued that the King, Lords, and Commons do not ultimately possess the nation's political authority, but "the people" (by which he meant "freeholders" or property owners),[28] who may depute it to representatives, but who retain the right to retrieve it, with force if necessary.

We should note, too, that a common feature in Defoe's writings—especially during the 1720s—is their abundance of information: they constitute storehouses of data that allow their audiences to take conceptual possession of the nation and to become empowered within it. In this respect, they mirror what the state itself was doing. And just as the state was developing new systems of organizing data, so too did Defoe instruct his readers in the techniques of gathering, arranging, and using data. After Defoe, later writers produced numerous similar works—such as *The General Shop Book or Tradesman's Universal Director* (1756)—that, like his texts, did more than just present compilations of data: they enabled readers to situate themselves within larger contexts and articulated "a new vision of state and society."[29]

Representing Britain: national symbols and the national character

In addition to the promotion of new constructs of the nation—which continued, it must be stressed, to compete with older ones—the eighteenth century saw the emergence of symbols that did double work in defining English/British national identity. These included the songs "Rule Britannia" and "God Save the King" (both 1745); the image of a roast beef (for instance, William Hogarth's painting *Calais Gate, or the Roast Beef of Olde England*, 1749), which symbolized the prosperity, health, and robustness of a free people, in contrast to the French, who were seen as enslaved (by absolutism and Catholicism), ill-fed, and scrawny; and the figure of John Bull, who came to embody the national character. Often accompanied in pictures with a bulldog (his pugnacious canine counterpart), which also became a national symbol, John Bull was depicted as plain spoken and blunt (because he was free and independent), healthy and stout (because he was well fed on roast beef), masculine (that is, not French, deemed effeminate), and full of common sense.[30]

What a nation's character is and how it is formed were questions that concerned many Enlightenment thinkers (such as Hume, Montesquieu, and

Voltaire), and had important political implications because they went to the issue of who represents the nation and speaks for it. The idea of the national character is typically Janus-faced, being at once exclusive, but potentially allowing for greater inclusiveness and change. It is inevitably exclusive in that those who do not resemble the national character are not seen as part of the nation. Women, for example, were typically seen in the period as helping to form but not actually embodying the national character. Likewise, laboring folk were excluded from most eighteenth-century depictions of the national character. Additionally, those depictions were Anglo-centric, requiring Scots and Irish to "pass" as English in order to be accepted as Britons, resulting in what one scholar calls a "crisis of acculturation and assimilation."[31] In a letter to a fellow Scot, David Hume spoke poignantly of this problem: "Am I, or you, an Englishman? Will they allow us to be so?"[32]

In some respects, however, the literary expressions of national identity were expansive and challenged traditional social hierarchies. Michael Ragussis, for example, claims that the theater brought about a "legitimization of ethnic identity" within Great Britain.[33] Moreover, conceptions of the national character increasingly re-centered cultural authority below the patrician elite, as seen, for example, in the immensely popular periodical the *Spectator* (1711–1714), where the plain-speaking merchant Sir Andrew Freeport embodies a kind of Defovian Briton, or in *The Drapier's Letters* (1724–1725), where Swift adopts the persona of a cloth seller, a tradesman, to speak for all of Ireland.

The most significant effort, however, to identify the national character with non-patricians sprang from the sustained mid-century critique of the aristocracy as the nation's traditional value-givers. This critique, which was expressed in many different media (painting, graphic art, novels, travel literature), took the form of an attack on all things French, but it essentially attacked the aristocracy as a class, who, in their absorption of French culture (in dress, manners, art, food), were portrayed as parasitic, un-British, and culturally treasonous.[34] The aristocracy's adoption of French culture, it should be noted, was not a modish fad, but linked to a systematic strategy of social differentiation by which it separated itself from other classes, reproduced itself as the nation's elites, and attached itself to Europe's cosmopolitan governing class.[35] In this respect, the attack on French culture constituted an attack not only on the cultural and political authority of the aristocracy, but also on the class- and culture-divided social formation of traditional states (mentioned at the start of the essay), which consisted of elites who ruled over communities that were culturally *un*like them.

Here we can see that concerns about the national character manifested the potentially transformative power of nationalism, which is hostile to the class- and culture-divided societies of traditional states. In this regard, the proponents of the modernist view of nationalism perhaps offer an important insight. According to Gellner, nationalism occurs when literacy is universalized and access to knowledge and high culture ceases to be monopolized by one class—a process that is driven, he argues, by the dynamic of industrial society with its growth of the professions, its need for a literate and mobile workforce, and promise of progress. When this happens "the relationship of culture and polity changes radically," resulting in the erosion of class barriers and promotion of "egalitarianism."[36]

Concerns over the national character in the age of Enlightenment were thus politically fraught. No more dramatic example can be found than in France, where the goal of "changing the national character" was seen as "fundamental" to the Revolution and its project of remaking the nation.[37] In Great Britain, concerns about the national character also generated change, but the outcome was different. In the last quarter of the century, the aristocracy managed to retain its authority by making an enormous cultural transformation: they stopped imitating French cosmopolitan ways, began to dress differently, created new rituals that proclaimed their Britishness (so, for example, the Tour of Britain replaced the Grand Tour), and cultivated an ethos of masculine toughness.[38] In short, they became John Bulls. In so doing, British patricians retained their authority that would serve them well during the socio-political convulsions and intense nationalism generated by the French Revolution and radical Enlightenment thought at the end of the century.

Notes

1 A. Giddens, *A Contemporary Critique of Historical Materialism: Vol. 1 Power, Property and State* (1981), reprinted Berkeley: University of California Press, 1987, p. 187. Giddens also identifies the absolutist state of the seventeenth century as a transition from the traditional state to the modern nation-state (*The Nation-State and Violence: Volume Two of a Contemporary Critique of Historical Materialism*, Berkeley: University of California Press, 1987, pp. 83–121).

2 M. Weber, *Politics as a Vocation* (1919), in H. H. Gerth and C. Wright Mills (eds), *From Max Weber: Essays in Sociology*, New York: Oxford University Press, 1946, p. 78 (Weber's italics).

3 Giddens, *Contemporary*, p. 190 (my italics).

4 Giddens, *Nation-State*, p. 57 (Giddens' italics).

5 See W. Beik, *Absolutism and Society in Seventeenth-Century France: State Power and Provincial Aristocracy in Languedoc*, Cambridge: Cambridge University Press, 1985. Beik remarks that Louis XIV's absolutist regime "must be seen, not as a modern state . . . but as the political aspect of . . . feudal society" (p. 339).

6 See E. Pawson, *Transport and Economy: The Turnpike Roads of Eighteenth-Century Britain*, London: Academic Press, 1977; and P. Langford, *A Polite and Commercial People: England 1727–1783*, Oxford: Oxford University Press, 1989, pp. 391–417.

7 J. Brewer, *The Sinews of Power: War, Money, and the English State, 1688–1783*, New York: Knopf, 1989, p. xvi.

8 M. Foucault, *Discipline and Punish: The Birth of the Prison* (1975), trans. A. Sheridan, New York: Vintage, 1979.

9 Brewer, *Sinews*, p. 227.

10 T. C. W. Blanning, *The Culture of Power and the Power of Culture: Old Regime Europe 1660–1789*, Oxford: Oxford University Press, 2003, p. 113; R. Porter, *English Society in the Eighteenth Century*, Harmondsworth: Penguin, 1982, p. 183.

11 L. Colley, *Britons: Forging the Nation 1717–1837*, New Haven: Yale University Press, 1992, p. 41.
12 "The sheer volume of printed matter," as Langford notes, "produced in the period is striking testimony to the extent of the reading market" (*Polite*, p. 91).
13 Colley, *Britons*, p. 41.
14 J. Habermas, *The Structural Transformation of the Public Sphere: An Inquiry into a Category of Bourgeois Society*, trans. T. Burger with F. Lawrence, Cambridge, MA: MIT Press, 1989, pp. 27, 31.
15 P. Schwyzer, *Literature, Nationalism, and Memory in Early Modern England and Wales*, Cambridge: Cambridge University Press, 2004, pp. 8–9.
16 B. Anderson, *Imagined Communities: Reflections on the Origin and Spread of Nationalism*, London: Verso, 1983, p. 6.
17 Anderson, *Imagined*, p. 7.
18 A. D. Smith, *National Identity*, Oxford: Oxford University Press, 1986; reprinted London: Penguin, 1991; A. Hastings, *The Construction of Nationhood: Ethnicity, Religion, and Nationalism*, Cambridge: Cambridge University Press, 1997; E. Gellner, *Nations and Nationalism*, Ithaca: Cornell University Press, 1983 (2nd edn., 2005); E. Hobsbawm, *Nations and Nationalism since 1780: Progamme, Myth, Reality*, New York: Cambridge University Press, 1990.
19 Anderson, *Imagined*, p. 6.
20 Colley, *Britons*, pp. 11–12.
21 Colley, *Britons*, p. 26.
22 On these divisions, which go beyond well differences among the Scots, Welsh, and English, see Colley, *Britons*, pp. 14–16.
23 R. Helgerson, *Forms of Nationhood: The Writing of England*, Chicago: University of Chicago Press, 1992, pp. 105–47.
24 Quoted in J. B. Harley, "Meaning and Ambiguity in Tudor Cartography," in S. Tyacke (ed.), *English Map-Making 1500–1650*, London: British Library, 1983, p. 26.
25 D. Defoe, *A Tour Thro' the Whole Island of Great Britain*, London: Frank Cass, 1968, p. 686.
26 D. Defoe, *The Complete English Tradesman* (Letter III), in J. T. Boulton (ed.), *Daniel Defoe*, New York: Schocken Books, 1965, pp. 232.
27 P. Backscheider, *Daniel Defoe: His Life*, Baltimore: Johns Hopkins University Press, 1989, pp. 510 and 515.
28 "[T]he other inhabitants," he says, "are but sojourners, like lodgers in a house" (*The Works of Daniel De Foe*, Vol. III, London: John Clements, 1843, p. 14).
29 Brewer, *Sinews*, pp. 228–29.
30 For more on these symbols, see B. Rogers, *Beef and Liberty: Roast Beef, John Bull, and the English Nation*, London: Chatto and Windus, 2003.
31 M. Ragussis, "Jews and Other 'Outlandish Englishmen': Ethnic Performance and the Invention of British Identity under the Georges," *Critical Inquiry*, 26, 2000, p. 775.
32 Quoted in J. A. Smith, "Some Eighteenth-Century Ideas of Scotland," in N. T. Phillipson and R. Mitchison (eds), *Scotland in the Age of Improvement*, Edinburgh: Edinburgh University Press, 1970, p. 109.
33 Ragussis, "Outlandish," p. 790.
34 G. Newman, *The Rise of English Nationalism: A Cultural History 1740–1830*, rev. ed., New York: St. Martin's Press, 1997, pp. 63–86.
35 See T. N. Bowers, "Reconstituting the National Body in Smollett's *Travels through France and Italy*," *Eighteenth-Century Life*, 21 (n.s.), 1997, pp. 4–8.
36 Gellner, *Nations and Nationalism*, esp. chapters 3 and 6; quotations pp. 18 and 24.
37 D. A. Bell, *The Cult of the Nation in France: Inventing Nationalism, 1680–1800*, Cambridge, MA: Harvard University Press, 2001, p. 142.
38 Colley, *Britons*, pp. 155–77.

4

NATIONALIST DISCOURSES IN THE BRITISH ISLES, 1780–1850

Julia M. Wright

"With an enthusiasm incidental to my natural and national character, I visited the western part of the province of Connaught."[1] So begins an 1807 footnote that details Sydney Owenson's visit to a rural part of Ireland then associated with the survival of traditional Irish-language culture. Owenson's note concisely highlights the key features of what is often termed "romantic nationalism": a conflation of the natural with the national, so that the members of a nation are both organically connected as parts of a larger whole and naturally similar, alike extensions of the national "spirit"; the association of rural spaces with more authentic nationality; an identification of nationalism with intense feeling that motivates action ("enthusiasm"). In 1843, a writer for the Irish newspaper *The Nation* used this view to both authorize Irish sovereignty and critique empire by connecting language, land, and people through the naming of places:

> it is the Celts alone who can tell why those patriarchal titles were conferred on the hills of Europe by the "world's gray fathers." Those military brigands who slaughtered, devastated, or enslaved us, knew not why the graphic and poetic genius of the ancient primitive ancestors of Europe coined their beautiful epithets, or crowned the towering cliffs with descriptive appellatives to last them for ever.[2]

The people belong to the land and the land belongs to the people, a sense of belonging rooted in affection that is emotionally powerful, intrinsic and embedded in their daily lives through language. To separate people from the homeland or ask them to reframe their affection for it is to violate their sense of self. This view is seductively simplistic, resolving demographic, ideological, and other differences within the nation's population into an unassailable myth of fundamental unity that is grounded in feeling, "the invisible commerce of hearts and minds," as the English translation of J. G. von Herder puts it.[3]

But what is "the nation" here? The British Isles—an archipelago that includes Britain, Ireland, and dozens of smaller islands (from the Channel Islands to the

Hebrides)—were settled by various groups and then invaded and briefly conquered, in part, by several more. Imperial Rome controlled much of (what is now) England for centuries, Viking invasions hit nearly every region of the archipelago, and the Norman Conquest of 1066 ended Anglo-Saxon rule in England. French, not English, was the elite language of England for centuries, part of a politicized cultural division between the conquering French and the conquered Saxons. Trade and military support circulated across the British Isles, part of a complicated and shifting array of political allegiances in the medieval era. English border skirmishes with Wales and Scotland and the invasion of parts of Ireland (then divided into various kingdoms) followed well into the Early Modern period. With the rise of interest in the past motivated by romantic nationalism, all of this became the subject of both antiquarian scholarship and literary treatment. Sir Walter Scott in particular returned again and again to the "national" divisions within the British Isles in his poetry and his historical fiction, but he was joined in this literary enterprise of imagining the meaning of "nation" and national difference by scores of others.[4] This British Isles patchwork of conflict and competing interests up to about 1500 was followed by consolidation: first Wales and England formally unified in 1536; Scotland joined the "union" in 1707; and Ireland was incorporated via the Act of Union (1800) after a failed uprising in 1798. At each step, this consolidation led to parliamentary representation for the absorbed region in the pre-existing Parliament in London, defining political union through centralized government and uniform laws—dominated not generally by the English but specifically by the wealthy elite based in London. This centralization was supported through the location of other key institutions in London: banking, much of the print industry, and trading groups (including those that built the foundations of the Victorian-era British Empire, such as the East India Company). Disentangling a distinctively Scottish, Welsh, Irish, or Welsh (or Manx or Cornish) "nation" with a unique history, language, and culture as well as a clearly delineated "land" for the people is no easy feat in this context.

Romantic nationalism turned instead to what might better be termed "myth"—a selective historical view of the nation's origin and development that served particular ideological ends and was pursued through "antiquarian" research as well as fiction and verse. In particular, in the so-called "Celtic Periphery" of Scotland, Wales, and Ireland, there was marked attention to a remote age in which the nation was led by masculine heroes and cultivated bards who both advised and commemorated the nation's warriors:

> Oh! may his [Pendragon's] great example fire
> My noble patron to aspire
> To deeds like his! Impetuous fly,
> And bid the Saxon squadrons die:
> So shall thy laurel'd bard rehearse

Thy praise in never dying verse;
Shall sing the prowess of thy sword,
Beloved and victorious Lord.[5]

Other forms of nationalism avoided the problem by defining the nation on other terms. In the 1790s, the United Irishmen, for instance, argued for "a beloved principle, which takes in every individual of the Irish nation, casts an equal eye over the whole island, embraces all that think, and feels for all that suffer; the catholic cause is subordinate to our cause, and included in it, for, as United Irishmen, we adhere to no sect but society, to no creed but christianity, to no party but the whole people."[6] Echoing the Enlightenment principles of the newly formed United States, such a nationalism is democratic and concerned with popular sovereignty—both as individual choice and national autonomy—rather than rooted in a mythic past concerned with heredity and tradition. It looks forward to a modern nation-state and citizenry on terms that recall Anthony D. Smith's argument about the neoclassical influence on modern nationalism: "Neo-classicism presented a number of ideals and aspirations which gave meaning and direction to th[e] idea of an 'educated public'," including the "agree[ment] to live under common laws and institutions, as 'citizens' enjoying equal rights and common duties."[7]

Romantic nationalism, by contrast, stressed similitude rather than diversity (by eighteenth-century standards) through individual self-development. Romantic nationalism is widely tied to German Romanticism as an ideology that saw in language and region a basis for national cohesion and legitimacy, when what is now "Germany" was a collection of smaller states divided among the central European empires of Prussia and Austria. As Friedrich Schiller suggested in 1795, "They [rural and ancient peoples] are what we *were*; they are what we *should become again*. We were natural like them."[8] Like their Italian contemporaries, German nationalists in the period faced a double problem of consolidating the different regional groups within "Germany" and prying those regions away from more powerful empires. Romantic nationalism offered a basis for unity (shared language, and hence shared culture) and a foundation for sovereignty (the land belongs to the people native to it). A nationalism for emerging nation-states, however, also needed a developmental component. As Smith suggests,

> Fichte and other German Romantics gave Herder's organic culturalism a specifically political dimension by arguing that true freedom consists in the absorption of individual self-determining wills in the collective Will of the community or the state. This was to be achieved by the correct determination of individual wills through a process of national education in the vernacular language. Only through education and national struggle could individuals realize their authentic selves in the national self.[9]

The work of the Grimm brothers on folk tales is perhaps the best known cultural articulation of this ideological project, but Herder's work on nationalism, available in English by 1800, would become foundational to ideas of the nation as affective, rooted in profound feeling rather than habit or obligation.[10]

While scholars in the social sciences stress German Romanticism in this context, it is easy to find evidence of this approach in the British Isles, particularly in the circulation of national literatures as the foundation of "national education in the vernacular." In 1774, Thomas Warton offered his *History of English Poetry* "to pursue the progress of our national poetry, from a rude origin and obscure beginnings, to its perfection in a polished age."[11] As I have argued elsewhere, British anthologies were produced and widely published in the early nineteenth century to distribute to the newly literate classes a national literary canon.[12] Similarly, Irish writers across the Romantic period argued for national education: in 1799, William Drennan declared, "Plans of national education ought to be co-extensive with the nation"; in 1844, Thomas Osborne Davis published an essay in the nationalist newspaper, *The Nation*, arguing for "National Schools"; in 1845, Thomas D'Arcy McGee, Irish nationalist and father of Canadian Confederation, opens his "Glance at the Future Destiny of Ireland" by celebrating advances in religious and national education in Ireland.[13] Antiquarian works throughout the Celtic periphery sought to revive the language and literatures of the region before anglicization, in a "Celtic Revival" from about 1780–1880.[14]

Nationalism on these terms could both sanction the nation as it exists or argue that the nation needs to be changed—approaches that Stephen Behrendt connects to the genres of epic and prophecy, respectively, but which cut across the literary and non-fiction divide, as essays and histories as well as poems and novels railed for or against the state of the nation.[15] Robert Southey's orientalist and antiquarian long poems as well as William Blake's *Jerusalem* engage with nationalist epic in different ways, Southey following heroic models and Blake taking a more mystic and allegorical tack, but both on empire-friendly terms: in Blake's epic, for instance, "In the Exchanges of London every Nation walkd / And London walkd in every Nation mutual in love & harmony / Albion coverd the whole Earth, England encompassd the Nations."[16] In poems such as "Fears in Solitude" by S. T. Coleridge and "Eighteen Hundred and Eleven" by Anna Letitia Barbauld, English writers take a prophetic stance to critique the British government for its military interventions beyond the British Isles and suggest that the nation has departed from its proper, moral path: Coleridge's speaker exclaims, "We have offended, Oh! My countrymen! / We have offended very grievously, / And been most tyrannous," while Barbauld's warns, "Britain, know, / Thou who hast shared the guilt must share the woe."[17] On the subject of literature, Barbauld marks a carefully negotiated distinction, accepting the hegemonic view that British literature was exceptionally worthy while detaching it from the nation in order to underscore her point that the nation cannot survive under the government's current policies. She thus imagines the transplantation of still-great British letters to North America:

Nations beyond the Appalachian hills
Thy [Britain's] hand has planted and thy spirit fills:
Soon as their gradual progress shall impart
The finer sense of morals and of art,
Thy stores of knowledge the new states shall know,
And think thy thoughts, and with thy fancy glow . . .
And Milton's tones the raptured ear enthrall,
Mixt with the roar of Niagara's fall.[18]

Just as Britons read Virgil and Homer, future Americans will read John Milton, James Thomson, and Joanna Baillie, as London, like the classical world before it, falls into ruin.[19]

Such works also draw on organic metaphors to stress that the national is natural, to again use Owenson's terms. Coleridge ties his proper national subject to the natural space after he separates that proper subject from a misguided nation-state:

O native Britain! O my Mother Isle!
How shouldst thou prove aught else but dear and holy
To me, who from thy lakes and mountain-hills,
Thy clouds, thy quiet dales, thy rocks and seas,
Have drunk in all my intellectual life,
All sweet sensations, all ennobling thoughts . . .
There lives nor form nor feeling in my soul
Unborrowed from my country.[20]

Barbauld, conversely, uses an organic metaphor to argue for the inevitable decline that will follow British military expansion:

But fairest flowers expand but to decay;
The worm is in thy core, thy glories pass away;
Arts, arms and wealth destroy the fruits they bring;
Commerce, like beauty, knows no second spring.[21]

Melding Romantic organicism with nationalist ideas of the individual's ties to place (Coleridge) or of national progress/decline (Barbauld), such passages reveal the rising power of "nature" to authorize ideological positions on the nation, including careful critiques of the nation's current direction in marked distinction to an essential notion of the nation that transcends particular governments and policies.

Organic nationalism, an offshoot of Romantic nationalism, stresses the natural determinisms of nation and the trope of the national body in which individuals are important as constitutive members of the nation first and foremost. Daniel J. O'Neil suggests that such models facilitate the individual's self-abnegation before the needs of the nation: "The implication of organismic thinking is that the sacrifice of an individual or one generation for the collective well-being is not an unreasonable request."[22] Thomas De Quincey notes the conflict generated by such a subordination of the value of individual life in a passage on London celebrations after first news of British victory after the Battle of Waterloo in a "grand national sympathy" before news of casualties arrives: "A poor woman, who too probably would find herself, in a day or two, to have suffered the heaviest of afflictions by the battle, blindly allowed herself to express an exultation so unmeasured in the news, and its details, as gave to her the appearance which amongst Celtic Highlanders is called *fey*," "fey" here meaning "fated to die, doomed to death."[23] De Quincey undercuts this moment of national harmony by acknowledging the price through the figure of a woman who has yet to learn of the death of her son or husband, and highlights the un-national implications of such an acknowledgment by tying this anticipation to a not-quite British concept (both Scottish and unfamiliar to his English readers), the "Celtic" "fey." De Quincey thus recognizes the incompatibility of interest in particular lives with participation in the "grand national sympathy" that follows Waterloo. On practical terms, soliciting such national sentiment helps the nation-state to pursue its military objectives,[24] especially necessary in a period dominated by an almost endless set of costly conflicts that included the American War of Independence (1776–1783) and the four Anglo-Mysore wars in India in the last third of the eighteenth century, the French Revolutionary Wars (1792–1801) and then the Napoleonic Wars (1803–1815), and in the face of significant uprisings and mutinies across the emerging Empire: the Vellore Mutiny in India (1806); the Mutiny on the Bounty (1789) and the more dangerous mutinies at Spithead and the Nore (1797), which left the southern English coast largely undefended for weeks; and the Irish Uprising (1798).

Organicism's solicitation of self-sacrifice is only one of the ways in which its naturalizing framework defines individual value in relation to the nation. It also, for instance, authorizes racial ideas of nationality that are both deterministically exclusive, insisting that heredity undergirds nationality, and limiting to individuals in pathologizing deviation from national norms as unnatural. An essay in *The Nation* argues for the importance of national pride on the basis of national distinctiveness:

> No nation can become great, if it be not peculiar. Nations must esteem themselves; 'tis this political faith in itself—this illusion of national being, which tyrants would willingly remove. They would attach to the physiognomy of nations the mask of a slavish uniformity, lest the

> brotherhood of freemen should recognise their kin—lest we should remember that Italians cannot be Germans, Flemings Dutch, nor Celts Saxons.[25]

While this rejects the British assimilatory project, it also rejects Lockean ideas of citizenship in which individuals can choose their nations: "Italians cannot be Germans." Ironically, as Marlon B. Ross notes, the organic metaphor of growth also meant, at a national level, the necessity of the "folk" leaving their proper place, the national landscape, to serve the imperial project of the nation:

> How does a nation grow to become itself? Must it seek its limits by expanding to the point of its own potential dissolution, losing its sense of oneness demarcated originally by the closeness of its geographical borders and loosening its bonds to that indigenous tradition that initially marked its sense of self-identity? This question, a specter haunting Britain at the verge of the nineteenth century, appears on the threshold of Britain's modernization of itself as a nation-state.[26]

How, in other words, is Britain to be a modern trading and imperial nation if its people belong within the island's borders? This question had myriad answers, including the straightforward claim that expansion is unhealthy for British subjects—a point in the Coleridge and Barbauld poems mentioned above, as well as, for instance, Matthew Lewis's gothic tale, "The Anaconda." Defending empire on nationalist terms was less straightforward.

Take the case of an 1822 poem by Felicia Hemans, "England's Dead." The poem rather ghoulishly reimagines the world through the dispersal not of English colonists but of dead Englishmen. In the fifth, expanded edition of Edward Hughes' *Select Specimens of English Poetry* (1856), advertised on its title page as being "For the Use of Schools and Private Reading," the poem was included in a section entitled "Poems of Home and Country," with the addition of an epigraph from Thomas Carlyle's *Chartism* (1840):

> Of a truth, whosoever had, with the bodily eye, seen Hengist and Horsa mooring on the mud-beach of Thanet, on that spring morning of the year 449, and then, with the spiritual eye, looked forward to New York, Calcutta, Sydney Cove, across the ages and oceans, and thought what Wellingtons, Washingtons, Shaksperes, Miltons, Watts, Arkwrights, William Pitts, and David Crocketts had to issue from that business, and do their several taskworks so,—*he* would have said these leather boots of Hengist's had a kind of cargo in them—a genealogical mythus.[27]

In the same work, Carlyle writes,

> Crowds of miserable Irish darken all our towns. . . . American forests lie untilled across the ocean; the uncivilized Irishman, not by his strength but the opposite of strength, drives out the Saxon native, takes possession in his room. There abides he, in his squalor and unreason, in his falsity and drunken violence, as the ready-made nucleus of degradation and disorder. . . . And yet these poor Celtiberian Irish brothers, what can they help it? They cannot stay at home, and starve. It is just and natural that they come hither as a curse to us.[28]

Carlyle ties the "Saxon" not only to truth, reason, strength, and nature (and the Irish to the direct opposites, as Carlyle tended to do), but also to a pioneering mission: the Saxons have "cleared" "This soil of Britain" and "made it arable,"[29] while the Irish, he suggests, enter already-populated urban spaces instead of venturing to North America where "forests lie untilled." Carlyle identifies the Saxons with a colonizing, pioneering mission, from the arrival of Hengist and Horsa in fifth-century England to American expansion through "Davy Crocketts." Choosing the racial term "Saxon" (as part of a "genealogical mythus") rather than the national term "English" allows Carlyle to envision a "race" that sweeps the globe as well as pathologize the Irish as inevitably disruptive to order and production. Race, in other words, resolves the contradiction that Ross traces in Romantic literature: the Saxon "race" is by definition imperial, always expanding from "the mud-beach of Thanet" to the American frontier and beyond. And yet Carlyle's vision of an essential Saxon expansion is used in Hughes' anthology to introduce a poem in which Hemans traces not new farmland but new graves:

> Go, stranger, track the deep,
> Free, free the white sail spread!
> Wave may not foam, nor wild winds sleep,
> Where rest not England's dead.
>
> On Egypt's burning plains,
> By the pyramid o'ersway'd,
> With fearful power the noonday reigns,
> And the palm-trees yield no shade.
>
> But let the angry sun
> From heaven look fiercely red,
> Unfelt by those whose task is done!—
> There sleep England's dead[30]

In 1822, Hemans paints an inhospitable world with English graves everywhere, a vivid image of the price of imperial expansion. In 1856, Hughes takes her poem and suggests that teachers "point out the position" of Egypt "on the Map" and compare such adjectives as "Mighty" and "Loud."[31] The self-sacrifice demanded by organic nationalism is so accepted by Hughes as to become invisible: "England's Dead," for Hughes, marks the inevitability of Saxon global expansion, traceable across over 1400 years of Saxon history, a poem of "Home and Country" in which men prove their Saxon vigor by working and dying everywhere but England. Hughes, it should be noted, is listed on the title page of his *Specimens* as "Head Master of the Royal Naval Lower School, Greenwich Hospital," linking Hughes directly to the training of those who would be sent out to achieve this expansion.

At the same time, the Romantic linking of land and people was also popularized, in part through the rising validation of William Wordsworth as a national poet and what Wendy Joy Darby argues is a Romantic intensification of eighteenth-century pastoral literature in which the rural landscape was "freighted . . . with even more national sentiment" and became the site of public participation in, as well as exclusion from, the nation, through walking groups on the one hand and enclosures on the other.[32] The recreational experience of the British landscape was granted the potential to renew a land-based nationality for necessarily urban workers in industrialized Britain. In Ireland, poets adapted Wordsworthian principles for the Irish landscape. In "A Walk by the Bay of Dublin," for instance, Denis Florence MacCarthy represents the personally restorative properties of the Irish landscape while also noting its history as the site of attempted invasion—the landscape, despite the violence done to it, retains its power to heal its citizens.[33]

Nationalism between 1780 and 1850 thus takes a wide variety of forms: English, Scottish, Irish, Welsh, British, "Saxon"; in support of or opposed to the present direction of the nation-state; stressing cultural traditions, the landscape, and/or biological determinisms, or invoking a Lockean ideal of civic citizenship. This array of nationalisms reveals the degree to which nationalism is a cultural construct that can proliferate, and motivate, even at a time of intense public debate about what the nation is, and should be, and for whom. The literature of the Romantic period reveals the degree to which the nation was very far from a self-evident truth.

Notes

1 S. Owenson, *Lay of an Irish Harp*, Philadelphia: T. S. Manning, 1807, p. 17n.

2 The full essay appears above.

3 J. G. [von] Herder, *Outlines of a Philosophy of the History of Man* (1784–1791), trans. T. Churchill, London: J. Johnson, 1800, p. vi.

4 See, for instance, W. Scott's novels *The Antiquary* (1816) on Roman invasion, *Ivanhoe* (1819) on Norman colonization in Saxon England, *Waverley* (1814) on English–Scottish conflicts, and his poem *Lay of the Last Minstrel* (1805) on skirmishes along the Scottish–English border.

5 "Ode to Glendwr," in E. Jones, *Musical and Poetical Relicks of the Welsh Bards*,

London, 1784, p. 23. For a useful discussion of myriad novels in the British Isles and North America that build on such ideas of the remote past, see K. Trumpener, *Bardic Nationalism: The Romantic Novel and the British Empire*, Princeton: Princeton University Press, 1997.

6 A United Irishmen Declaration originally published in *The Hibernian Journal*, and quoted in the 1794 indictment of William Drennan for "seditious libel," reproduced in J. F. Larkin (ed.), *The Trial of William Drennan*, Dublin: Irish Academic Press, 1991, p. 41.

7 A. D. Smith, "Neo-Classicist and Romantic Elements in the Emergence of Nationalist Conceptions," in A. D. Smith (ed.), *Nationalist Movements*, London: Macmillan Press, 1976, p. 78.

8 F. Schiller, *On the Naive and Sentimental in Literature* (1795), trans. H. Watanabe-O'Kelly, Manchester: Carcanet New Press, 1981, p. 22.

9 A. D. Smith, *The Nation in History: Historiographical Debates about Ethnicity and Nationalism*, Hanover: University Press of New England, 2000, p. 10.

10 Herder, *Outlines of a Philosophy of the History of Man*.

11 T. Warton, *The History of English Poetry*, vol. 1, London: J. Dodsley, 1774, p. ii.

12 See J. M. Wright, "'The Order of Time': Nationalism and Literary Anthologies, 1774–1831," *Papers on Language and Literature*, 33, 1997, pp. 339–65.

13 W. Drennan, *Letter to the Right Honorable William Pitt*, Dublin: James Moore, 1799, p. 14; T. Davis, "Influences of Education," in *Literary and Historical Essays* (1846), reprinted Washington: Woodstock Books, 1998, pp. 246–52; T. D. McGee, *Historical Sketches of O'Connell and his Friends, with a Glance at the Future Destiny of Ireland*, 3rd edn., Boston: Donahoe and Rohan, 1845. Davis's essay appeared first in *The Nation* (October 5, 1844); see J. Kelly, Introduction, *Literary and Historical Essays*, n.p.

14 S. Deane provides this dating for the Revival in *A Short History of Irish Literature*, Notre Dame: University of Notre Dame Press, 1986.

15 S. C. Behrendt, "'The Consequence of High Powers': Blake, Shelley, and Prophecy's Public Dimension," *Papers on Language and Literature*, 22, 1986, pp. 255–57.

16 W. Blake, *Jerusalem*, in D. V. Erdman (ed.), *Complete Poetry and Prose of William Blake*, New York: Doubleday, 1988, 24.44. For discussions of Blake's *Jerusalem* on these terms, see, for instance, S. Clark, "*Jerusalem* as Imperial Prophecy," in S. Clark and D. Worrall (eds), *Blake, Nation and Empire*, New York: Palgrave Macmillan, 2006, pp. 167–85; S. Matthews, "Jerusalem and Nationalism," in J. Lucas (ed.), *William Blake*, New York: Longman, 1998, p. 99; J. M. Wright, *Blake, Nationalism, and the Politics of Alienation*, Athens, Ohio: Ohio University Press, 2004. On Southey and nationalist epic, see, for instance, C. Bolton, "*Thalaba the Destroyer*: Southey's Nationalist Romance," *Romanticism on the Net*, 32–33, 2003, n.p.; L. Pratt, "Patriot Poetics and the Romantic National Epic: Placing and Displacing Southey's *Joan of Arc*," in P. J. Kitson (ed.), *Placing and Displacing Romanticism*, Aldershot: Ashgate, 2001, pp. 88–105.

17 A. L. Barbauld, "Eighteen Hundred and Eleven," in W. McCarthy and E. Kraft (eds), *Anna Letitia Barbauld: Selected Poetry and Prose*, Peterborough, Ontario: Broadview Press, 2002, ll. 45–46; S. T. Coleridge, "Fears in Solitude," in W. Keach (ed.), *Coleridge: The Complete Poems*, New York: Penguin, 1997, pp. 41–43.

18 Barbauld, "Eighteen Hundred," ll. 83–88, 95–96.

19 Barbauld, "Eighteen Hundred," ll. 95, 97, 101; on ruin, see for instance ll. 205–14.

20 Coleridge, "Fears in Solitude," ll. 182–87, 192–93.

21 Barbauld, "Eighteen Hundred," ll. 313–17.
22 D. J. O'Neil, "The Cult of Self-Sacrifice: The Irish Experience," *Éire-Ireland*, 24, 1989, p. 92.
23 T. De Quincey, "The English Mail Coach," in J. Faflak (ed.), *Confessions of an English Opium-Eater*, Peterborough, ON: Broadview Press, 2009, pp. 255, 256, 256n.
24 See L. Colley, *Britons: Forging the Nation, 1707–1837*, New Haven: Yale University Press, 1992.
25 See p. 124 above.
26 M. B. Ross, "Romancing the Nation-State: The Poetics of Romantic Nationalism," in J. Arac and H. Ritvo (eds), *Macropolitics of Nineteenth-Century Literature: Nationalism, Exoticism, Imperialism*, Philadelphia: University of Pennsylvania Press, 1991, p. 56.
27 E. Hughes, *Select Specimens of English Poetry*, London: Longman, Brown, Green, and Longmans, 1856, p. 83.
28 T. Carlyle, *Chartism*, London: James Fraser, 1840, pp. 28–29.
29 Carlyle, *Chartism*, p. 29.
30 F. Hemans, "England's Dead," in Hughes, *Specimens*, p. 83. For a modern edition of Hemans, see G. Kelly (ed.), *Felicia Hemans: Selected Poems, Prose and Letters*, Peterborough: Broadview Press, 2002.
31 Hughes, *Specimens*, p. 83.
32 W. J. Darby, *Landscape and Identity: Geographies of Nation and Class in England*, New York: Berg, 2000, p. 86; on the "politics of access," see Darby, pp. 105–81.
33 D. F. MacCarthy, "A Walk by the Bay of Dublin," in J. M. Wright (ed.), *Irish Literature, 1750–1900: An Anthology* (Oxford: Blackwell, 2008).

5

FROM COLONY TO REPUBLIC

Building the American Nation

Deborah L. Madsen

The first nations in North America were communities of indigenous peoples, such as the Iroquois Confederation or "the Five Nations" (comprised of Cayuga, Mohawk, Oneida, Onondaga, and Seneca nations; later, the Confederation was known as the Six Nations after the Tuscarora joined), though the latinate term "nation" was not applied by those groups to themselves; they referred to the Nations as the "Haudenosaunee" or "People of the Longhouse."[1] The term "First Nations" is used now to designate the indigenous peoples of Canada rather than the United States, though tribes territorially located within the US are, as Craig Womack describes, "legally defined political entities that exist in government-to-government relationships with the United States."[2] The Iroquois Confederation, which was established probably in the early twelfth century and lasted through to the Revolutionary War, was characterized by practices attributed to a national entity. These practices included a shared system of law, cognate languages within the Iroquoian family, a common origin narrative, a shared belief system, and a political structure that enabled the creation of treaties with various European settler groups. This Iroquoian system of governance, as Susan Kalter and others before her suggest, may have inspired the understanding of American democracy proposed by some of the Founding Fathers.[3]

The nation we now know as the United States is the result of a long history of colonial territorial acquisition. At the time of European contact in the late fifteenth century, North America was home to many indigenous tribal nations. The human cost of establishing the modern US is disputed but it is always counted in the millions of indigenous lives.[4] Through a lengthy process of conquest, genocide, and annexation European colonial powers established settlements that became the nation. Consequently, the "America" referenced in a seventeenth-century text is different to that found in an eighteenth-century work, and even in a nineteenth-century text what is referred to as "America" or the United States probably is not what we envision from a twenty-first century perspective. Therefore, this account of the emergence of the US nation begins with an overview of the process of territorial expansion that formed the contemporary nation-state.

The English hegemony of early America was established with the terms of the Treaty of Paris (1763) which displaced French and Spanish colonial interests east of the Mississippi. At the time of the Revolution, the Thirteen British Colonies comprised Georgia, the Carolinas (North and South), Virginia, Maryland, Delaware, Pennsylvania, New Jersey, New York, Connecticut, Rhode Island, Massachusetts, and New Hampshire. What later became Maine was at that time part of Massachusetts; further to the north Nova Scotia was held by the British and the Hudson Bay region was claimed by both Britain and France; France held territory to the east of Nova Scotia as New France and south of the Great Lakes as French Louisiana; New Spain occupied the area south of and including what is now Texas. As the United States expanded westward in the course of the nineteenth century, anxieties became acute concerning the need to sustain the Anglicized character of American culture (particularly against Spanish influences) while at the same time developing a distinctive American civilization. The Louisiana Purchase of 1803 brought into the United States all territories from the 49th parallel to the Gulf of Mexico; Florida was ceded by Spain in 1819; Britain ceded the Oregon Territory in 1846; Texas was annexed in 1845 and the 1848 Treaty of Guadalupe Hidalgo, which brought the Mexican–American War to an end, together with the Gadsden Purchase of 1853, completed the acquisition of the entire continental United States. By 1912 the forty-eight mainland states comprised the nation-state. Alaska was purchased from Russia in 1867; Hawai'i was annexed in 1898: both became US states in 1959. As these various land acquisitions with their communities (both indigenous and settler) were incorporated into the US the tensions that characterized literary representations of America from the beginning were heightened. The dominance of English-language literature, in the British tradition but expressive of an American national sensibility, remains at issue in debates concerning American multiculturalism and transnational cultural relations.

The first European literary texts to reference North America are the Norse sagas *The Saga of Eric the Red* and the *Saga of the Greenlanders*, dating from around 1000 AD. The permanent European colonization of the Americas began with Columbus's voyage of 1492; the English followed when John Cabot and his sons were awarded a royal patent by Henry VII in 1496 to seek a trade route to the Indies. The early exploration literature introduced to metropolitan writers a symbolic vocabulary, not so much of nation as of empire, that was extensively used in texts ranging from Edmund Spenser's allegorical epic *The Faerie Queene* (1590) to William Shakespeare's *The Tempest* (1611). The Jamestown colony in Virginia, which was founded in 1607, became the second successful European settlement in North America, following the Spanish settlement of St. Augustine, in Florida, in 1565. Captain John Smith's writings, particularly *A Description of New England* (1616) and

The Generall Historie of Virginia, New England and the Summer Isles (1624), were influential promotional narratives that encouraged further English migration to North America by emphasizing the abundance of New World nature. Where earlier narratives published by men such as Richard Hakluyt were focussed upon promoting a political will to extend the nascent English Empire by colonizing North America, Smith helped to inaugurate a long-standing style of promotional writing that was aimed at potential immigrants rather than investors. The second important English colony in North America, at Plymouth in Massachusetts, was settled in 1620 for primarily religious reasons. The Plymouth region was located outside the charter granted the Virginia Company and, in response to the potential absence of legitimate governing structures, the company signed the Mayflower Compact almost immediately upon landing. In some respects, the Mayflower Compact was a precursor to John Winthrop's sermon "A Modell of Christian Charity," which he preached on board the *Arbella* in 1630 to the first group of Puritan colonists who were bound for Boston.[5] These texts establish a colonial style of writing that culminates in the core documents of the American Republic: the Declaration of Independence, the Bill of Rights, and the Constitution.

Winthrop's "A Modell of Christian Charity" not only sets out the terms of the social compact into which the colonists entered; it also explains what is at stake in this venture. He uses the now famous image of the colony as "a Citty upon a Hill" to describe their experiment in Christian theocracy upon which the eyes of the world will be fixed. If they should succeed in creating a perfectly reformed Church then all the blessings of this world and the next will be upon them. Should they fail, however, they will become more than a global laughing stock: they will have failed to bring about the latest phase of a sacred history that has been unfolding since the creation. Winthrop's image of the city upon a hill refers to the three historical locations central to this history: the holy city of Jerusalem, Calvin's city of Geneva, and the city that is to come in Massachusetts. This future scene, like its symbolic predecessors, will be the scene of revelation, Winthrop suggests. He interprets the future anticipated by the colonists through the lens of scripture, seeing the Puritan New World as the fulfillment of prophecies laid down in the symbolic texture of the Old and New Testaments. This mode of scriptural interpretation, known as typology, dates back to the earliest interpretations of the New Testament and was common in the seventeenth century. Typology was favored among New England colonists who explained the hardships they faced (disease, starvation, Indian attacks) in terms of tests sent by God to prove them worthy of the exceptional destiny assigned to them. The popular genre of colonial captivity narratives, the best-known of which is perhaps Mary Rowlandson's *Sovereignty and Goodness of God* (1682), made extensive use of this typological rhetoric. Among Winthrop's contemporaries he was interpreted as the fulfillment of biblical promises that a leader would emerge to lead persecuted Puritans out of Anglican-dominated England into a Promised Land.

Like Moses leading his people out of bondage in Egypt into the freedom of Canaan, so Winthrop was interpreted as a liberating agent of God, and Massachusetts was his Canaan. Consequently, the initial generations of settlers saw their community as a divinely ordained "errand into the wilderness."[6] This dominant view persisted despite the failure of Cromwell's Puritan Commonwealth and the restoration of the English monarchy in 1660 and has come to be called "American exceptionalism": the idea that the New World (and specifically that part of it which became the United States) has been singled out above all other nations for a distinctive destiny.

New World exceptionalism was legitimated and supported by the assumption that North America represented a land of opportunity: economic opportunity for the landless of Europe and religious opportunity for those who sought a haven from persecution. In fact, from the early colonial period both sets of assumptions were false: Puritans persecuted the Quakers of the Pennsylvania colony and the Catholics of Maryland, for instance, and land was increasingly concentrated in the hands of wealthy settlers through the operation of land grants. We can see in this history a distinction between the actual conditions of life and the mythologizing of the New World, in which literature played a key role. Colonial literature offered an interpretive medium or lens through which the meaning of everyday life could be read in providential or exceptionalist terms. In typological texts the contrast or conflict between the real and the ideal could be reconciled.

American exceptionalism has proved to be a long-lived national mythology, especially when represented in the form of the "American Dream." The Statue of Liberty, which marks the 1876 centenary of the Declaration of Independence, for example, was designed to welcome immigrants arriving by sea from Europe. The inscription inside the base of the statue, Emma Lazarus's sonnet "The New Colossus," designates the torch-bearing woman as "Mother of all Exiles." The poem concludes,

"Keep ancient lands, your storied pomp!" cries she
With silent lips. "Give me your tired, your poor,
Your huddled masses yearning to breathe free,
The wretched refuse of your teeming shore.
Send these, the homeless, tempest-tost to me,
I lift my lamp beside the golden door!"[7]

This notion of North America as a haven for the landless and the persecuted was a theme, from the early colonial period onward, in promotional writings that aimed to encourage migration. The promise that hard work will be rewarded with material affluence is repeated in promotional rhetoric throughout the colonial period and provides the structuring principle in one of the major texts of republican nationalism: Benjamin Franklin's *Autobiography* (written between 1771 and 1788).

Franklin links his own success both to nurture and nature: to his embrace of the values of common sense, practicality, and industry, and also to his descent from a line of religious dissenters. His family legacy is represented as a willingness to rebel against injustice, an insistence upon self-determination, and a passionate commitment to freedom. These same qualities are attributed, in the *Autobiography*, to the fledgling American nation. The narrative is structured in such a way that Franklin emerges as a model citizen of the new Republic. In the third of his *Letters from an American Farmer* (1782), Hector St. John de Crèvecoeur asks "What is an American?" Franklin offers an answer: he begins life as a colonist and subject of the British Crown yet dies a citizen of his own nation; he is born into poverty and obscurity but becomes wealthy and internationally famous. Franklin offers himself not only as an exemplary American. The didactic tone of the narrative is directed towards a reader who is encouraged to follow Franklin's model and to avoid that offered by characters who fail to meet the demands of the new nation: such as the incompetent, cheating printer Samuel Keimer, who eventually moves to Barbados.

While Franklin describes a New World that offers opportunity he also acknowledges that not everyone is capable of realizing the advantages offered to them. In contrast, Crèvecoeur's initial description of the new American citizen evokes a much more compelling image of what he calls "the great American asylum."[8] Crèvecoeur moves quickly to the issue of how a settler population, derived from all the nations of Europe, can be transformed into a nation. Though the Treaty of Paris (1763) had paved the way for the creation of an English nation-state, it is in the multi-national context of continental North America that Crèvecoeur invents the image of the "melting pot" to describe the unique national qualities of the American:

> He is an American, who by leaving behind him all his ancient prejudices and manners, receives new ones from the new mode of life he has embraced, the new government he obeys, and the new rank he holds. He becomes an American by being received in the broad lap of our great Almer Mater. Here individuals of all nations are melted into a new race of men, whose labours and posterity will one day cause great changes in the world.[9]

The absence of aristocracy, the availability of land to be farmed, and above all the democratic republican government of America provide the foundation for the new national character. Crèvecoeur imagines the demographic emergence of "the American" through intermarriage among people of many nations. However, the problem of defining what an American is in the present rather than the future is much more difficult. The frontiersmen to the west, and southern slavery, together with the fearful imminence of Revolution and anarchic warfare, complicate the myth of national innocence by exposing an ugly historical context. Crèvecoeur describes an ambivalent national character: consequently, the political and moral values represented as distinctively American in colonial writings bore a debatable relation to American demography.

Much of the literature of the revolutionary period emphasized independence as separation from Britain. Royall Tyler's play *The Contrast* (1787), for example, sets up a series of unflattering comparisons between American patriots and English-influenced dandies. However, the play betrays one of the deep contradictions of early republican literature: while the US had rejected English government and national identity, there was no distinctive "American" culture with which to replace it. Consequently, literature of the early national period tends to favor exaggerated nationalist content rather incongruously expressed in literary forms that are derived from metropolitan English models. Tyler's play is a case in point: he uses the dramatic structure of Richard Brinsley Sheridan's *A School for Scandal*, which was first performed in London in 1777, but "Americanizes" the subject matter. Joel Barlow's *The Hasty Pudding*, a satirical mock-epic after the fashion of Alexander Pope's *The Rape of the Lock* (1712), is another example of this literary contradiction. The desire for a national literature was strong; early nationalists were aware that they lacked a culture that would match the political innovations represented by US republicanism.

In the post-1776 period, republican ideas centered upon the values of liberty and individual rights. The republic was envisioned as a collectivity of independent citizens who would engage voluntarily in civic duties. In contrast to the feudalism that represented all that the Founding Fathers wished to repudiate, US republicanism was to be based not upon a sovereign ruler but upon the sovereignty of the entire people. The relationship between United States nationhood and republicanism is complex and it is useful here to speculate whether the US may constitute not so much a nation-state as a state-nation. In the nation-state, a community sharing common descent and language precedes the creation of governing structures; in a state-nation, however, the principles of governance come first and prescribe the terms for national identity within an "imagined community."[10] Seen from this perspective, formation of the US republican state apparatus preceded the nation, an historical sequence that explains why writers such as Franklin were at such pains to promote a particular way of becoming a citizen of the new American nation. The semantic relations between the American republic and nation have been central to literary-critical interrogations of the racial, gendered, and class assumptions that structure the story of American national formation. These relations have been put into question by scholars such as Cathy Davidson, Lawrence Buell, Nina Baym, and Jay Fliegelman, and more recently by Teresa Goddu's work on American Gothic, Bruce Burgett's study of liberalism and republicanism, and Eve Allegra Raimon's work on the figure of the tragic mulatta. To this body of work we must add Malini

Johar Schueller's important work on postcolonial contexts for early American literature.

These critics question the assumption that early literary expressions of nationalism are characterized by a style of expression that conveys the "self-evident truths" or "common-sense" valued in revolutionary republican writings, paradigmatic of which is Thomas Paine's *Common Sense* (1776). Rather, this style and its reception is treated in the manner of the interpretive lens I mention above, as a cultural form that disguises truth as myth or state governance as subjective national identity. Early American literature has benefitted from the acquisition of foundational status, but early writers have also suffered as less-than-literary national institutions. William Spengemann notes this in his revisionist effort to define the concept of a national American literature in such a way that the value of colonial writers can be appreciated. Spengemann argues that the body of pre-revolutionary literature is too easily dismissed as neither American nor good literature because of the narrow parameters that are applied to it. Rather, by resisting the urge to evaluate these texts by the standard of a national US culture that had yet to come into being, critics can see colonial literature as "an important phase in the evolution of the language that conditions all of our literary and historical judgments."[11]

The language of democratic republicanism is the focus of Bruce Burgett's revisionary efforts as he reads a variety of early texts, from George Washington's "Farewell Address" to the sentimental narratives of Hannah Foster's fiction and Harriet Jacobs' account of slavery. Burgett is interested in the ways in which sentiment, the embodied experience of a reader who is also a citizen-subject, binds the individual to the state through the idea of democratic self-government. The Enlightenment ideals of rationality and reason that underpin democratic political theory were critiqued by popular early American novelistic forms, particularly sentimental fiction and Gothic novels, which then act as agents in contemporary debates about defining the nation rather than as early engagements in a developing literary canon. Teresa Goddu isolates one of the basic issues confronting the American Gothic: namely, that "it is an historical mode operating in what appears to be an historical vacuum" (1997: 9). However, through her analysis of the Gothic as a style that returns obsessively to a repressed history, she contests an American literary canon that has been constructed to obscure this reality of US imperial history. It is this history that the American Gothic engages in contrast to that found in the European Gothic style. As Charles Brockden Brown observes in the preface to *Edgar Huntley* (1799), "incidents of Indian hostility, and the perils of the western wilderness, are far more suitable" to the American context than superstition, haunted castles, and ghosts.[12]

This emphasis upon repressed histories, twinned with a sensationalist or sentimental style of writing, is applied to the relationship between the US nation and commercial republicanism in Brockden Brown's novel *Arthur*

Mervyn (1800). This narrative, through a symbolic interplay between "gold fever" and an outbreak of "yellow fever," takes up the debate about the place of commerce within the new Republic: whether it will inhibit the development of a US culture by promoting greed rather than egalitarian republican ideals. Commercial republicanism had replaced the earlier agrarian ideal celebrated by Crèvecoeur. The idea that in the free *laissez faire* market the pursuit of individual self-interest will serve the public good raised the spectre of conflict between economic interests and civic duty. The civilizing potential of commerce was placed in contrast with the national cost of commercial endeavors. This contrast was especially acute in relation to slavery, where individual economic self-interest proved insufficient to protect rights and liberty.

Race, and especially slavery, haunts the early national self-image and the debate about the self-contradiction embodied in the term "American slavery" is engaged repeatedly in the popular early republican form of the Gothic novel. Slavery was seen as a regional (Southern) rather than national issue, though it also worked to define by opposition (South versus North) the nature of the new nation. This tension between region and nation is not reserved for the Gothic; in his classic study of the American historical romance (1987), George Dekker traces the influence of Sir Walter Scott's *Waverley*-model upon the romance tradition, from the work of James Fenimore Cooper onwards. Dekker identifies a characteristic dynamic or tension between a universalizing, nationalizing impulse on the one hand and regionalizing pressures on the other. The forces of historical progress and reaction shape the contours of what for Dekker emerges as an ambivalent genre. In her study, *The "Tragic Mulatta" Revisited*, Raimon attends to what she calls "the nation's long struggle to delineate racial boundaries" and the racial tensions between region and nation that this struggle seeks to repress.[13] In her account of antislavery fiction, Raimon positions her reading across racial boundaries, refusing a black versus white categorization that she perceives as a false representation of US national culture.

While some scholars such as Raimon seek to reinscribe the absent black presence at the founding of white American literature (in an approach encouraged by Toni Morrison in *Playing in the Dark*), others look to transnational and postcolonial contexts for the emergence of a national American literature. In their introduction to *Messy Beginnings: Postcoloniality and Early American Literature*, Malini Johar Schueller and Edward Watts suggest that whether accounts of American nationhood present a triumphal narrative of democracy and liberty or, instead, an apology for the hegemonic exercise of power that created a nation by genocide and enslavement, both approaches "unwittingly share a vision of the 'nation' as inalterably consolidated by the sheer fact of white settlement, ignoring the complex ways that 'Americanness' as a gendered, raced, and classed phenomenon was constantly negotiated through strategic identification and disidentification with Europeans, on the one hand, and American Indians, African-Americans, and other non-white populations, on the other hand."[14] Raimon's work can be located within this effort to shift the interpretation of US nationhood away from a dominant white paradigm.

A similar effort has been directed at representations of gender and the role of women in the early Republic, starting with the assumption that the Enlightenment thought which gave rise to the revolutionary concepts of liberty and democracy was emphatically masculinist. The concept of "Republican motherhood" was proposed by Linda Kerber in 1980 to describe the ideology of feminine patriotism that emerged during and in the years following the Revolution. This idea was based on the perception that women are well-placed to teach the values of republicanism to their children and to nurture civic-minded husbands and sons. Here again, the spectre of race returns to complicate the image: republican mothers were necessarily white bourgeois women because of the racial differentiation of femininity prescribed by slavery. Republican motherhood or domestic republicanism is seen by some as the precursor to what Barbara Welter (1966) has dubbed the "cult of True Womanhood."[15] This gender stereotype, influential through the nineteenth century, valorized piety, purity, submissiveness, and domesticity, and featured in feminine characterization particularly in sentimental novels. The value of purity was emphasized throughout the early republican period as the value most important to sustain the reproduction of white bourgeois citizens. Female purity, expressed as chastity, would ensure the purity of the national bloodstock and soothe anxieties about miscegenation. The racial identity of those coming into the new nation was policed by immigration and naturalization laws that controlled the racial nature of the national body politic, from the Naturalization Act of 1790, which set out the terms of citizenship for free white persons of good moral character, to the McCurran-Walters Act of 1952.

The best-known example of the domestic novel of sentiment remains Harriet Beecher Stowe's *Uncle Tom's Cabin* (1852) but the style has its roots in eighteenth-century reactions to Enlightenment rationality. Sentimentalism presented a new view of human nature which prized feeling over thinking, passion over reason, and personal instincts of pity, tenderness, and benevolence over social or civic duties. The sentimental heroine is typically sympathetic to others, to nature, and to social morality; her feelings and instincts are prioritized over thought, reason, and duty. The first American best-seller was Susanna Rowson's *Charlotte Temple* (1791), the story of a naive, impressionable, sentimental heroine who is persuaded to abandon her virtue by her teacher, the Frenchwoman Mademoiselle La Rue. Her seducer is Lieutenant Montraville: in their names American innocence is contrasted with European worldliness, corruption, and decadence. From a broadly republican perspective, the novel warns of the dangers of the sexual double-standard for women: Charlotte loses her social standing, is abandoned, succumbs to illness and poverty, and eventually dies in childbirth. This kind of sentimental fiction was criticized for obscuring the dangers of unrestrained imagination and for promoting subjective fantasy. Texts such as *Charlotte Temple* and the sequel *Lucy Temple* (1828) offer a contrast with the religious impulses that structure Susan Warner's later sentimental novel *The Wide, Wide World* (1851).

The effort to construct an American national literature has undergone close interrogation in terms of the racial, gendered, and class assumptions that prescribe the story of national formation told by literary history. The relationship between print culture and national formation itself has been the object of Trish Loughran's important work, especially *The Republic in Print: Print Culture in the Age of US Nation Building*. Loughran has challenged the assumption that literature—or printed texts more generally—is centrally important to the development of national identity. While literature in the wider sense of printed texts provided a means of national formation for "great men," the mass of people had more limited access to this print culture. Consequently, Loughran questions the extent to which narratives of American national identity have been based on texts that promote an image of the nation in terms of liberal rights and democratic freedoms. While foundational texts such as the Declaration of Independence and the Constitution were of paramount importance to the political and legislative construction of the United States, the degree to which all Americans were interested and able to participate in this creation of the nation is questioned. The story of US nationalism is a universalizing narrative, she suggests, that was not experienced in the same way by people of different regions within the new nation, of different classes, degrees of education, race, and gender. Loughran provides an essential corrective to prescriptive accounts of the emergence of an American national literature, and a valuable complement to recent scholarly work that highlights the differential nature of national experience.

Notes

1 S. Kalter, *Benjamin Franklin, Pennsylvania, and the First Nations: The Treaties of 1736–62*, Chicago: University of Illinois Press, 2006, p. x.

2 C. Womack, "The Integrity of American Indian Claims (Or, How I Learned to Stop Worrying and Love My Hybridity)," in J. Weaver, C. S. Womack, and R. Warrior, *American Indian Literary Nationalism*, Albuquerque: University of New Mexico Press, 2005, p. 163.

3 Kalter, *Benjamin Franklin*, pp. 23–29. See also J. Weaver, C. S. Womack, and R. Warrior, *American Indian Literary Nationalism*.

4 D. E. Stannard claims that 100 million indigenous people were subject to genocidal policies as the European conquest of the Americas unfolded; the number of casualties is disputed by critics such as R. J. Rummel who argues that between 2 and 15 million people died as a consequence of colonization, see D. E. Stannard, *American Holocaust: The Conquest of the New World*, Oxford: Oxford University Press, 1993; R. J. Rummel, *Death by Government*, New Brunswick, New Jersey: Transaction Publishers, 1994.

5 J. Winthrop, "A Modell of Christian Charity" (1630), *Collections of the Massachusetts Historical Society*, Boston, 1838, 3rd series, 7:31–48. Online Hanover Historical Texts Project. Available at: <http://history.hanover.edu/texts/winthmod.html> (accessed January 19, 2009).

6 The classic study is P. Miller, *Errand into the Wilderness*, Cambridge, MA: Harvard University Press, 1956.

7 E. Lazarus, 1876. "The New Colossus." Liberty State Park website. Online. Available at: <http://www.libertystatepark.com/emma.htm> (accessed November 21, 2007).

8 H. St. J. de Crèvecoeur, *Letters from an American Farmer* (1782), A. E. Stone (ed.), Harmondsworth: Penguin, 1986, p. 68.

9 Crèvecoeur, *Letters from an American Farmer*, p. 70.

10 See B. Anderson, *Imagined Communities: Reflections on the Origin and Spread of Nationalism*, London: Verso, 1983.

11 W. C. Spengemann, *A New World of Words: Redefining Early American Literature*, New Haven: Yale University Press, 1994, p. x.

12 C. Brockden Brown, *Edgar Huntley; or, Memoirs of a Sleep-Walker* (1799), Norman S. Grabo (ed.), Harmondsworth: Penguin, 1988, p. 3.

13 E. A. Raimon, *The "Tragic Mulatta" Revisited: Race and Nationalism in Nineteenth-Century Antislavery Fiction*, New Brunswick: Rutgers University Press, 2004, p. 1.

14 M. J. Schueller and E. Watts (eds), *Messy Beginnings: Postcoloniality and Early American Literature*, New Brunswick: Rutgers University Press, 2003, p. 2.

15 B. Welter, "The Cult of True Womanhood," *American Quarterly*, 18, 1966, pp. 151–74.

6

OCCUPATION, ASSIMILATION, PARTNERSHIP

Canadian Literature in English and French, 1769–1899

Andrea Cabajsky

In "What is a Nation?" (1888), Ernest Renan famously defines nations as "daily plebiscite[s]"—that is, as "perpetual affirmations [of a] common will" to sustain the "national idea."[1] Although Renan restricts the geographical boundaries of his inquiry to western and northern Europe, his definition presents a pertinent starting point from which to approach the complicated development of the "national idea" in Canada. For, according to Renan's model, some of the most successful European nations such as Switzerland—a nation, observes Renan, "so well made"—gained the spontaneous, unanimous consent of their different cultural constituents to converge, "in spite of diversity," into coherent national communities.[2] Yet Canadian nationhood did not develop according to the model held up by Renan, and Canadian cultural and political discourse from the eighteenth century to the end of the nineteenth bears witness to serious rhetorical problems that nation-builders writing in English and French encountered in their own attempts to generate consensus, if not enthusiasm, for a coherent "idea" of Canada.

What were some of the longstanding cultural, political, and rhetorical problems which nation-builders encountered in their attempts to forge a "national idea" of Canada? A colonial possession, first of France (1604–1763), then of Britain (1763–1867) and, from Confederation to the patriation of the Constitution (1867–1982), a Dominion of the British Empire and British Commonwealth, Canada occupied an anomalous, unstable position in the British, Anglo-colonial, and French-Canadian imaginations that shaped its early literature. Although Canada developed culturally and politically in reaction to times of testing endured with the War of 1812, the Rebellions of 1837, and the Act of Union (1841; the precursor to Confederation), Canadian literature arguably developed primarily in response to the Fall of New

France (1759–1760) which became a dominant theme of English- and French-Canadian fiction and poetry published in the eighteenth and nineteenth centuries, as one cultural group struggled to justify its conquest of a European colony and another to come to terms with its own defeat and near demise. As literature published from the mid-eighteenth century to the end of the nineteenth suggests, little consensus existed among the English and the French-Canadians about how they should understand themselves in relation to one another, and in relation to the fraught history of settlement, colonization, and conquest that formed the complicated basis of their shared nationality as "Canadians."

This chapter examines the ways in which this debate informs Canada's national literatures in English and French. It pays particular attention to the distinct yet overlapping ideologies of Anglo-Saxon supremacism, French-Canadian messianism, and biculturalism that shaped Canada's two national literatures, and whose thematic and ideological roots lie with the cultural and political legacy of the transfer of colonial power from France to Britain at the end of the Seven Years' War (1763). Hinging on the 1837 Rebellions and the Durham Report which attempted to transform Canada into an economically productive British possession (and which, in turn, stimulated a seismic wave of reactionary literary activity in French Canada), the chapter illuminates the cultural work that Canadian fiction, poetry, and literary commentary in English and French performed to negotiate, challenge, or naturalize the "idea" of Canada as a viable nation.

In 1838, British Prime Minister Lord Melbourne, alarmed by recent rebellions in the Canadian colonies, asked Britain's former ambassador to Russia to accept a new post in Canada. A known reformer, John George Lambton, First Earl of Durham, accepted the post of governor general and high commissioner to British North America in order to investigate colonial grievances that had come to light following the rebellions of 1837 in Upper and Lower Canada (the precursors to present-day Ontario and Quebec). Durham published the results of his investigation one year later in his *Report on the Affairs of British North America* (1839). A monumental text in Canada's early political history, the Durham Report proved also to be a pivotal text in its literary history, demonstrating the extent to which imperial politics and emergent colonial literatures were intimately tied.

In his report, Durham made two distinct recommendations for Upper and Lower Canada: political reform for the former; and political assimilation for the latter. Because he believed the roots of Upper Canada's rebellion to have lain in problems of colonial government, Durham advocated the creation of responsible government in order to encourage colonial expansion, to strengthen imperial ties with Britain, and to minimize American influences. Because he believed the roots of Lower Canada's rebellion to have lain in markedly different causes—in what he termed "racial" conflict,[3] rather than in problems of political system or colonial government—Durham recommended that the French-Canadians be assimilated to their English-Canadian neighbors, whom he judged superior in character and industry. The legislative Union of Upper and Lower Canada, which took place in 1841, secured the cultural and numerical majority of the English-Canadians. Historically a settler colony, French Canada effectively became an occupied colony; English Canada became, in turn, French Canada's "occupier," as well as its legislative "partner." Canada's early literature in English and French first anticipates and then reflects the fraught dynamic of occupation, assimilation, and partnership that the Durham Report and legislative Union encapsulate. The literature that gives foundational expression to this dynamic forms the focus of the remainder of this chapter, which begins with English Canada.

From its origins in the mid-eighteenth century in Frances Brooke's *The History of Emily Montague* (1769) and Thomas Cary's *Abram's Plains* (1789), to its formative development in the nineteenth, beginning with Julia Beckwith Hart (1796–1867) and John Richardson (1796–1852), Canada's early literature in English is rooted in a dual impulse: it situates the emergence of Anglo-colonial identity in the simultaneous growth of British imperial space and absorption of French Canada. The first Canadian novel to register, as Pam Perkins observes, the "anxieties of [British] colonial rule" in post-Conquest Quebec,[4] *The History of Emily Montague* was written by an English novelist and poet who resided in Quebec in the early 1760s, a handful of years following the fall of New France when the Treaty of Paris (1763) was ratified and New France ceded to Britain.[5] In *Emily Montague*, the character William Fermor is a mouthpiece for Brooke's views about the transformation of France's former colony into a profitable British possession. Like Cary, whose *Abram's Plains* celebrates the "mended state" and "better fate" of the French-Canadian peasantry under King George III,[6] *Emily Montague*'s Fermor, a colonial administrator, celebrates the material improvement that the "common people" of French Canada had acquired "by the change of [imperial] masters."[7] Anticipating Durham by seventy years, Fermor recommends that the French-Canadians be assimilated to the English, beginning with their language: "It were indeed . . . to be wished that we had here schools, at the expence of the public, to teach English to the rising generation [of French-Canadians]: nothing is a stronger tie of brotherhood and affection, a greater cement of union, than speaking one common language."[8] In *Emily Montague*, as in much subsequent English-Canadian literature by James de Mille (*The Lily and the Cross*, 1874), David Hickey (*William and Mary*, 1884), Charles G. D. Roberts (*The Raid from Beausejour*, 1894; *A Sister to Evangeline*, 1898), Blanche Lucile Macdonell (*Diana of Ville-Marie*, 1898), and many others, the development of the British Empire and the emergence of Anglo-colonial identity hinge on the repression of "Frenchness."[9]

In its assimilative treatment of French-Canadian culture, as well as in its encouragement of affective and economic ties between Anglo-colonial and

British societies, *Emily Montague* anticipates Durham's prescription for English Canada. The dual dynamic of internal absorption and transatlantic identification that shapes *Emily Montague* also informs subsequent colonial-era (1769–1860) novels by Douglas Huyghue (1847), William Charles McKinnon (1850; 1852), and Clotilda Jennings (1855),[10] which expand the earlier focus on French-Canadians in Quebec to include French-speaking Acadians as well as aboriginal peoples. As such, they bear witness to the extraordinary efforts of English-Canadian authors to transform historical wounds between the French, the Natives, and the English into suitable themes for literary treatment. Keenly aware of the phenomenal success of such products of Romantic literary nationalism as the poems of Ossian and the novels of Sir Walter Scott in gathering landscape, folklore, and history into the defining features of a national culture, early English-Canadian writers openly complained of the comparative absence of a usable past in the young colony. The anonymous author of an article entitled "The Literature of a New Country," published in 1841, succinctly captures literary nation-builders' concerns:

> The very nature and character of the land itself, its past history, its former inhabitants, all conspire against its literary success. . . . The inhabitant of this Continent has little, if any, early recollections to be entwined with the local characteristics of the land he inhabits; he has to cast his eyes beyond an ocean, should he ask for legends or memories of the past to awaken the inspiration of the present.[11]

Their goal to import literary models from Britain to a sparsely populated colony presented aesthetic and ideological challenges to early authors. The first two novels published in the Canadas at the beginning of the nineteenth century, Hart's *St. Ursula's Convent* (1824) and James Russell's *Matilda; or, The Indian's Captive* (1833), as well as those published in the end, including Agnes Maule Machar's *The Heir of Fairmount Grange* (1895) and R. L. Richardson's *Colin of the Ninth Concession* (1903),[12] register the effects of those challenges in their plots which close when their main characters move to England (even French-Canadians, in the case of *St. Ursula's Convent*) and leave Canada behind without regret. Despite—or perhaps because of—their "un-Canadian" resolutions, these novels remain important artifacts to students of literature interested in understanding such patterns of plot as the unintended effects of pressures to adapt European literary criteria to the complicated cultural context of a settler-colony and emergent nation.

That early- and mid-nineteenth-century writers experienced considerable difficulty adapting their literary preconceptions to Canadian settings is demonstrated by two recurring narrative patterns. The first, described above, features Canada as a place of hardship and adventure from which, as Carole Gerson observes, "deserving characters are ultimately permitted to escape in order to return to their estates in Europe."[13] This pattern appears in novels published in book form, as well as in fiction serialized in such early journals as the *Literary Miscellany* (Montreal, 1822–1823), the *Canadian Magazine and Literary Repository* (Montreal, 1823–1825), the *Acadian Recorder, or Literary Mirror* (Halifax, 1823–1825) and the *Literary Garland* (Montreal, 1838–1851). The second pattern features stories that begin and end in Canada, with the bulk of the action occurring elsewhere. As Gerson points out, this second pattern, though not as enduring as the first, was favoured by mid-century writers such as John Gibson (1838), Clarence Ormond (1846), and Mary Anne Sadlier (1861), whose fiction "cent[ers] on a character for whom Canada serves merely as a point of termination. These individuals either die here leaving behind manuscripts describing their pre-Canadian adventures, or else verbally relate their exploits in the Old World which resulted in their residence in the New."[14] Novels that attempt to break from this pattern include Thomas Chandler Haliburton's *The Clockmaker* (1836), a satirical novel set in Nova Scotia and a purported favourite of Mark Twain, and Major John Richardson's historical novel *Wacousta, or The Prophecy: A Tale of the Canadas* (1832),[15] which closes with a vision of intercultural harmony when soldiers from an English military garrison play a game of lacrosse with their former Iroquois enemies on the outskirts of the French-Canadian settlement at Fort Detroit. That it is written by Richardson—an expatriate who returned to Canada from Britain with the hope of obtaining a patronage appointment from Lord Durham—suggests *Wacousta*'s assimilationist approach to Canadian themes. Like its treatment of other cultural minorities, such as a black servant named "Sambo" whom it never once permits to speak and an Irish petty officer named Murphy whom it stereotypes (Murphy speaks little, apart from blasphemies), *Wacousta* anticipates a pattern found in many later novels, such as those by Rosanna Leprohon (1859–1860; 1864; 1868), William Kirby (1877), Graeme Mercer Adam and Ethelwyn Wetherald (1887), and Gilbert Parker (1895; 1896),[16] whose narratives express sympathy towards French-Canadians, Natives, and members of other marginal cultures, yet whose plots ultimately advocate the absorption of those minorities by the British majority.[17]

While the plot of *Wacousta* revolves largely around a series of massacres organized by the famed Iroquois chief Pontiac (1720–1769) in Upper Canada's western frontier (modern-day western Ontario), its opening chapter begins by examining French–English relations. It argues that social unrest and rebelliousness in Lower Canada in the 1830s represents anomalous behavior for the French-Canadians who were otherwise content with their treatment by the British crown. The French-Canadian view concerning these same matters, however, provides a remarkable contrast to the English-Canadian perspective that the author of *Wacousta* puts forward. In describing the French-Canadians as "a people with no literature and no history,"[18] Durham inadvertently provoked a nationalist recoil so extensive that it influenced the themes of French-Canadian writing for the remainder of the nineteenth century, and arguably well into the twentieth. The literary history of this nationalist recoil begins with the publication of the three-volume *Histoire du Canada depuis sa découverte jusqu'à nos jours* (1845–1848) (*The History of Canada from its Discovery to the Present Day*) by François-Xavier Garneau (1809–1866).[19] The phenomenal influence of Garneau's revisionist history resulted in French Canada's first wave of literary nationalism which lasted approximately three decades (1860–1890) and came to be known as the "Literary Movement of the 1860s."

Literary nationalism in nineteenth-century Quebec developed largely in the wake of controversy following the release of the Durham Report. Conceived in opposition to Durham's conclusions about the absence of French-Canadian culture, Garneau's *Histoire* transformed the history of the fall of New France into a Romantic national narrative celebrating the resilience of the French-Canadians in the face of various threats of assimilation by a hostile landscape, unfriendly Natives, and British imperialists. Given its phenomenal influence on more than a generation of French-Canadian poets, historians, essayists, and novelists, the *Histoire* can be said to have nearly singlehandedly made possible the exploration and definition of Quebec's emergent national consciousness through literature. As Maurice Lemire observes, Quebec's first wave of nationalism was largely political: it was inspired by John Locke, Edmund Burke, and Alexis de Tocqueville, among others; it was action-oriented; and it was extinguished after the failure of the 1837 rebellion.[20] The aftermath of that rebellion, including the repressive measures that Durham had approved while governor general, resulted in a split between official discourse—which, dominated by the clerical elite and other conservative ultramontanists, preached French-Canadian submission to the British crown throughout the nineteenth century—and popular nationalism, whose "aspirations for liberty," Lemire explains, sought their "clandestine" release in literature.[21] Garneau was inspired by the romantic historiographies of Jules Michelet (1798–1874), François Guizot (1787–1874), and Augustin Thierry (1795–1856), as well as by the actual example of the Irish political leader Daniel O'Connell (1775–1847), whom he joined in the 1830s as a member of the Society for the Friends of Poland while living in England, to portray the French-Canadians as a colonized people and nationalism as their just cause. He was inspired by Thierry's view, put forward in the *History of the Conquest of England by the Normans* (1838),[22] of the overwhelmingly atavistic nature of France's history with England. Concluding that such an antagonistic history could do little else but perpetuate itself in Canada, Garneau gave influential early expression to what would become known as French Canada's "messianic" nationalism. As Yves Dostaler explains, after Garneau, French-Canadian cultural discourse was dominated by

> the theme of a special vocation, of a mission that nourished itself with the idea that the Conquest by Britain in 1760 had been "providential"

> to the extent that it had prevented the horrors of 1789 and especially of 1793 from affecting the political and cultural development of Quebec.[23]

Motivated by the preservationist impulse to conserve the Catholic religion, the French language, and hence the defining features of French-Canadian culture, messianic nationalists like Garneau and Étienne Parent (1801–1874), editor of the newspaper *Le Canadien* (Quebec, 1817–1825), championed the idea that French Canada had a unique destiny to fulfill on the American continent.

Prior to the publication of Garneau's *Histoire*, Quebec's literary corpus largely comprised travel narratives and journals, such as the accounts of Jacques Cartier (1491–1557), the Jesuit *Relations* (1632–1672), and the spiritual writings of Marie de l'Incarnation (1599–1672). Few were literary in nature, with the exception of some poems and a play set in Acadia by the Parisian lawyer and traveller Marc Lescarbot (1570–1642).[24] The earliest French-Canadian novels by Philippe Aubert de Gaspé, Jr. (1837) and François-Réal Angers (1837) contain expressions of national consciousness, but are not openly nationalistic.[25] For example, Aubert de Gaspé's *L'influence d'un livre, ou Le chercheur de trésors* (1837) (translated into English as *The Influence of a Book*) claims to be a novel of manners inspired by Sir Walter Scott, yet lacks the evocation of place and history of Scott's Waverley novels. Nevertheless, in their recognizably French-Canadian settings, as well as in their appeals to local folklore and current events, early novels by Aubert de Gaspé, Jr., Angers, Joseph Doutre (1844), Patrice Lacombe (1848), Pierre-Joseph-Olivier Chauveau (1853),[26] and others, stand out from their English-Canadian contemporaries in their refusal to import characters, settings, and resolutions from Europe. Lacombe's only novel, for example, *La terre paternelle* (*The Father's Earth*, 1848), is historically significant for inaugurating what would become a common scene in subsequent French-Canadian fiction: that of an exiled patriarch who, upon his return, finds his home occupied by an English stranger.

The years that follow the publication of Garneau's *Histoire* reveal an abrupt shift in French-Canadians' collective self-understanding that led to a pronounced and intensive increase in literary activity. In poetry, Octave Crémazie (1827–1879) became known as Quebec's national poet with works such as *Drapeau de Carillon* (*Carillon's Flag*, 1858),[27] which celebrates Louis-Joseph de Montcalm's defence of Fort Carillon prior to his defeat on the Plains of Abraham. Other poets, such as Pamphile Lemay (1837–1918) and Louis-Honoré Fréchette (1839–1908) rose to prominence at this time. In history, Jean-Baptiste-Antoine Ferland (1805–1865) followed in Garneau's footsteps in publishing the *Cours d'histoire du Canada* (*A Course in Canadian History*, 1861).[28] Collections of local folklore appeared, including the influential *Légendes canadiennes* (*Canadian Legends*, 1876) by the "father of

Quebec literature" Henri-Raymond Casgrain (1831–1904), while the first literary history, James Huston's four-volume *Répertoire national* (1848–1850) gathered texts previously published in early French-Canadian newspapers, many of which were no longer in print.[29] The first literary journals were founded, most prominently among them the *Soirées canadiennes* (*Canadian Evenings*, 1861–1865), the *Foyer canadien* (*Canadian Homes*, 1863–1866) which boasted readers from northern Quebec to Detroit, and the long-lived *Revue canadienne* (1863–1922). By contrast to their English-Canadian counterparts, which competed with American and British journals and thus found it more profitable to publish imported materials over original Canadian texts, French-Canadian journals published local writers along with foreign (mostly French) authors. Many of these local writers have acquired canonical status with the passage of time.

French-Canadian literary nationalism remained fundamentally revisionary for the remainder of the nineteenth century. In doing so, it sustained a radical awareness of the alterity of French Canada's past in relation to dominant English-Canadian history. Nowhere was this notion of French-Canadian alterity more self-consciously expressed than in the novel which, in the nineteenth century, developed into two important forms: the "novel of the earth" (*le roman du terroir*), a utopian form that, as its name implies, advocates a proprietary relationship to the land and whose exemplary practitioners were Lacombe, Chauveau, and Antoine Guérin-Lajoie (1824–1882); and the historical novel, which Lemire has described as the "most important" contribution to the development of French-Canadian literary nationalism in the nineteenth century.[30] Inspired by the cultural nationalism of Scott and, to a lesser extent, of James Fenimore Cooper, French-Canadian writers used the historical novel as a didactic tool to educate French-Canadian readers about their past. They sought inspiration in history by revisiting pivotal events: Philippe Aubert de Gaspé, Sr., revisited the Battle of the Plains of Abraham and the fall of New France in 1759–1760 in *Les Anciens Canadiens* (1863) (trans. *Canadians of Old*); Georges Boucher de Boucherville looked to the 1837 rebellion for inspiration in *Une de perdue, deux de trouvées* (*One Lost, Two Found*, 1864); Napoléon Bourassa looked, in turn, to the Expulsion of the Acadians in 1755 in *Jacques et Marie* (1865); and Faucher de Saint-Maurice and John Talon Lesperance looked to the American invasion of Quebec in *Madeleine Bouvart* (1874) and *Les Bastonnais* (1877), respectively.[31] Joseph Marmette, Quebec's most prolific novelist, looked variously to the Battle of the Plains, to the first pioneers, and to the days of New France's governor general Louis de Buade Frontenac (1622–1698) in his novels, published between 1866 and 1875.[32] The historical novel arguably received its most innovative expression in the last decade of the nineteenth century with the publication of Jules-Paul Tardivel's futuristic *Pour la patrie* (1895), which imagines the founding of a French-Canadian religious state in 1945–1946.[33] Even foreigners, such as French writers, were inspired by

Quebec's past. The French historian François-Edme Rameau de Saint Père wrote a highly sympathetic history of New France in *La France aux colonies* (1859), while the author of *Twenty Thousand Leagues under the Sea* (1870), Jules Verne, wrote a historical novel about the 1837 rebellion in *Famille sans nom* (*Family without a Name*, 1889).[34] Even prior to the publication of Verne's novel, the literary historian Edmond Lareau had reviewed literary production in the nineteenth century and concluded that, despite its belated origins, French-Canadian literature had become recognizably "national" by the mid- to late nineteenth century, thanks to writers' widespread rejection of transatlantic literary models.[35]

It is difficult to overstate the impact of Garneau's *Histoire* on a generation of literary nationalists, not only in French Canada but also in English Canada, where cultural nationalists proved eager to produce a historian who could similarly inspire writers and readers to become enthusiasts for the "idea" of Canada. The Tory Robert Christie, for example, responded to Garneau by producing his six-volume *History of the Late Province of Lower Canada* (1848–1855). John Mercier McMullen, in turn, produced a counterpoint to Garneau in his *History of Canada from its First Discovery to the Present Time* (1855). A generation later, William Kingsford surpassed both his predecessors—at least in terms of quantity of output—with his ten-volume *History of Canada* (1887–1898), whose style Margaret Conrad has described as "eccentric."[36] While Christie aimed to offer readers a balanced, well-documented work of historiography, McMullen and Kingsford—along with other historians late in the century, such as Charles G. D. Roberts (1898)[37]—produced largely chauvinistic, imperialist narratives of Canada's past. By contrast to Garneau's *Histoire*, which aimed to revive the self-confidence of a vanquished culture, English-Canadian histories aimed either explicitly or implicitly to assuage contemporary readers, whose already fragile confidence in the viability of their bicultural nationality had been repeatedly shaken by such events as the Manitoba school crisis,[38] the apparent disloyalties of Louis Riel,[39] and, earlier in the century, the perceived disloyalties of Louis-Joseph Papineau (1786–1871), the leader of the group called the "Patriots," republicanists inspired by the model of the American Revolution who had been responsible for the 1837 Lower Canadian rebellion. As Elizabeth Waterston has noted, "confusion" about Canadian identity lay at the roots of English-Canadian historiographers' and literary nationalists' sustained difficulties to inspire patriotic sentiment in the nineteenth century. Rather than engendering popular nationalism, history and fiction produced in this period succeeded in registering English-Canadians' larger "doubt[s] about the future role of the French" in Canada.[40]

In the early 1860s, at the height of Britain's imperial power, intellectuals in England such as John Stuart Mill and Lord Acton debated the extent to which "the boundaries of governments should coincide . . . with those of nationalities"; during that same decade, intellectuals in Canada, such as the literary historian Henry J. Morgan, were considering how the "life of the New Dominion" created in 1867 could "develope [sic] itself unitedly."[41] As in Britain, in Canada literature was deemed as important as the sciences and law in drawing "the minds of men" together "in bonds of unanimity and social order."[42] In Canada, however, intellectuals were challenged, as was Morgan in his Introduction to *Bibliotheca Canadensis* (1867), a bicultural literary history of Canada that included over 100 French-Canadian works, to see "the two great branches, French and English" working together "to create for Canada" a literary identity "worthy" of its "British lineage and antecedents."[43] The equation of "Canadianness" with "Britishness" in Morgan's Introduction, as well as the subordination of French to English Canada in that equation, render the *Bibliotheca Canadensis* a pertinent example of trends whose roots go back, through Durham, to the eighteenth century in novels and poems by Brooke and Cary. Despite the efforts of Confederation-era cultural nationalists such as Morgan, Leprohon, Kirby, Lemay, and James Le Moine (1825–1912) in both English and French to create a viable bicultural identity for Canada by exploring positively the English–French theme in their original writings, as well as by translating one another's works, Canadian cultural nationalism remained fundamentally divided along English–French lines.

By the end of the nineteenth century, the impediments to the development of a national identity had come, in English and French Canada alike, from within and from without. In English Canada, Durham's earlier caution about the threat of American influence on the development of Anglo-colonial identity had proven prescient. The fact that English Canada had shared a national language with the United States, at the same time as the United States had come to rival Britain in cultural influence had raised a fundamental hurdle to the development of literary nationalism: when English Canada tried to create its own culture, Gerson observes, its "magnificent literary heritage reversed from an asset to a liability, depriving English-Canadians of the opportunity to develop their own literature, in their own language."[44] In English Canada, then, the expression of cultural nationalism aimed, in Gilbert Parker's apt words in the Preface to *The Trail of the Sword* (1895), to develop the idea of Canada as the North American extension of the "English character and the English . . . race."[45] In French Canada, threats to cultural nationalism over the course of the last century-and-a-half had come from British imperialists and American annexationists, but by the end of the nineteenth century they were coming largely from within. The clerical elite had succeeded in controlling cultural production and the plots and themes of much literature produced at this time, including the separatist *Pour la patrie* and the historical novels of French Canada's first woman novelist, Laure Conan (1845–1924; pseud. Félicité Angers), reflect the religious conservatism of the period.[46]

Despite these external and internal influences on the development of the national literatures of English and French Canada, the nineteenth century closes with similar laments by literary nationalists in both milieus that a new threat to local cultures—a lack of money—had emerged to stifle literary production. Echoing Lareau, who complained that "the man of letters [is] unable to live off the work of his pen" despite his best efforts to do so,[47] the humorist Robert Barr (1850–1912) looked with envy to Britain and America, where writers were relatively able to live professionally from their trade and had thus contributed materially to the perceived flourishing of their nations' literatures. A Glasgow-born, Canadian expatriate who had earned his living, along with his international reputation, in England, Barr famously complained, in the last year of the nineteenth century, about the "bald truth": "Canada has the money, but would rather spend it on whiskey than on books . . . The new Sir Walter [Scott] is probably tramping the streets of Toronto to-day, looking vainly for something to do."[48]

This chapter has examined, both telescopically and microscopically, the forces of cultural assimilation, nationalist recoil, and cultural reconciliation that have given foundational shape to Canada's early literatures in English and French. Although English- and French-Canadian cultures have been described as "two solitudes" in relation to one another (a description made popular in the mid-twentieth century with the publication of Hugh MacLennan's influential novel *Two Solitudes* [1945]), careful investigation reveals that, despite their belonging to "settler-invader" and "settler-invaded" societies, respectively, English- and French-Canadian literatures developed in reaction to international forces, and in constant relation to one another. The *Oxford English Dictionary* defines "solitude" as "the state of being or living alone . . . [in] seclusion." Instead of capturing various states of loneliness, Canada's early literatures in English and French register writers' self-awareness of Canada's bicultural nationality and of the unique theoretical and practical challenges that that nationality posed to nation-builders intent on employing literature in the complicated service of cultural self-definition, cultural self-preservation, and intercultural rapprochement.

Notes

1 E. Renan, "What is a Nation?" in H. K. Bhabha (ed.), *Nation and Narration*, London: Routledge, 1990, p. 19.
2 Renan, "What is a Nation?", p. 16.
3 Lord Durham, *Lord Durham's Report: An Abridgement of Report on the Affairs of British North America*, G. M. Craig (ed.), Toronto: McClelland, 1963, p. 23.
4 P. Perkins, "Imagining Eighteenth-Century Quebec: British Literature and Colonial Rhetoric," in L. Moss (ed.), *Is Canada Postcolonial? Unsettling Canadian Literature*, Waterloo, ON: Wilfrid Laurier University Press, 2003, p. 160.
5 With the Treaty of Paris, France formally relinquished to Britain its Canadian possessions, as well as its holdings east of the Mississippi River. In return, France retained Guadeloupe and the islands of Saint Pierre and Miquelon in the Gulf of St. Lawrence.
6 T. Cary, *Abram's Plains: A Poem*, ed. D. M. R. Bentley, London, ON: Canadian

Poetry Press, 1986, ll. 444–45. For an important examination of *Abram's Plains* as a poem that, despite imagining English Canada as a cultural and ideological extension of Britain, attempts to develop uniquely local poetic themes and conventions, see the Introduction by Bentley to this Canadian Poetry Press edition of *Abram's Plains*.

7 F. Brooke, *The History of Emily Montague*, L. Moss (ed.), Ottawa: Tecumseh, 2001, p. 215.

8 Brooke, *History of Emily Montague*, p. 214.

9 J. de Mille, *The Lily and the Cross: A Tale of Acadia*, Boston: Lee and Shepherd, 1874; D. Hickey, *William and Mary: A Tale of the Siege of Louisbourg, 1745*, Toronto: William Briggs, 1884; C. G. D. Roberts, *The Raid from Beauséjour*, Boston: Lamson Wolffe, 1894; C. G. D. Roberts, *A Sister to Evangeline. Being the Story of Yvonne de Lamourie*, Boston: Lamson Wolffe, 1898; and B. L. Macdonell, *Diane of Ville-Marie: A Romance of French Canada*, Toronto: Briggs, 1898. For more about the repression of "Frenchness" and the role of Canada in consolidating British identity in the eighteenth century, with specific reference to *The History of Emily Montague* and L. Colley's *Britons* (1992), see C. Devereux, "'One Firm Body': 'Britishness and Otherness' in *The History of Emily Montague*," in L. Moss (ed.), *The History of Emily Montague by F. Brooke*, Ottawa: Tecumseh, 2001, pp. 459–76.

10 D. Huyghue, *Argimou: A Legend of the Micmac*, reprinted Sackville, NB: Ralph Pickard Bell Library, 1977; W. C. McKinnon, *St. Castine, A Legend of Cape-Breton*, Sydney, NS: Cape Breton *Herald*, 1850; W. C. McKinnon, *St. George; or, The Canadian League. A Tale of the Outbreak of 1837*, Halifax: Fuller, 1852; and C. Jennings, *The White Rose in Acadia*, Halifax: Bowes, 1855.

11 Anon., "The Literature of a New Country," *The Monthly Review*, 1, 1841, pp. 59–60.

12 J. B. Hart, *St. Ursula's Convent: Or, the Nun of Canada. Containing Scenes from Real Life*, reprinted Sackville, NB: Ralph Pickard Bell Library, 1978; J. Russell, *Matilda; or, The Indian's Captive: A Canadian Tale Founded on Fact*, New York: Garland, 1977; A. M. Machar, *The Heir of Fairmount Grange*, London: Digby Long, 1895; and R. L. Richardson, *Colin of the Ninth Concession*, Toronto: Morang, 1903.

13 C. Gerson, *A Purer Taste: The Writing and Reading of Fiction in English in Nineteenth-Century Canada*, Toronto: University of Toronto Press, 1989, p. 43.

14 Gerson, *A Purer Taste*, p. 43; J. Gibson, "The Hermit of Saint Maurice," *Literary Garland*, 1, 1838, 5–15; C. Ormond, "Canadian Legends. 1. The Ruined Cottage," *Literary Garland*, 4, 1846, 177–79; and M. A. Sadlier, *Elinor Preston; or, Scenes at Home and Abroad*, New York: Sadlier, 1861.

15 T. C. Haliburton, *The Clockmaker: Series One, Two and Three*, Ottawa: Carleton University Press, 1995; and J. Richardson, *Wacousta, Or the Prophecy: A Tale of the Canadas*, Ottawa: Carleton University Press, 1983.

16 R. Leprohon, *Antoinette de Mirecourt, or, Secret Marrying and Secret Sorrowing: A Canadian Tale*, Ottawa: Carleton University Press, 1989; *Armand Durand; or, A Promise Fulfilled*, Montreal: Lovell, 1868; and *The Manor House of De Villerai*, reprinted *Journal of Canadian Fiction*, 34, 1985; W. Kirby, *The Golden Dog: A Tale of Louis Quinze in Quebec*, Montreal: Lovell, 1877; G. M. Adam and E. Wetherald, *An Algonquin Maiden: A Romance of the Early Days of Upper Canada*, Montreal: Lovell, 1887; G. Parker, *The Trail of the Sword*, New York: Scribner, 1895; and Parker, *The Seats of the Mighty*, New York: Scribner, 1896.

17 For her discussion of *Wacousta* at the roots of a Canadian literary consciousness which aimed to repress rebelliousness so that Canada appeared a peaceable colony, see K. Trumpener, *Bardic Nationalism: The Romantic Novel and the British*

Empire, Princeton: Princeton University Press, 1997, pp. 270–73. For more on *Wacousta* in the larger context of Canadian and Anglo-imperial novel-writing, see esp. chapter 6 of *Bardic Nationalism*, which focuses on Canadian literature written in English and French in the eighteenth and nineteenth centuries and pays particular attention to early Canadian literature's formal, thematic, and ideological ties to literary texts and movements in Britain's internal colonial peripheries in Scotland and Ireland. For an examination of literary and ideological connections between French-Canadian and Anglo-Irish cultural nationalisms in the nineteenth century, with particular emphasis on novel-writing as a form of nationalist recoil, see A. Cabajsky, "The National Tale from Ireland to French Canada: Putting Generic Incentive into a New Perspective," *Canadian Journal of Irish Studies*, 31, 2005, pp. 31–45. For his important and original examination of allegories of fraternity and fratricide in the novels of John Richardson, William Kirby, and Thomas Raddall, and the work they performed in promoting white British masculinity as the assumed norm for Canadian citizenship, see D. Coleman, "The National Allegory of Fraternity: Loyalist Literature and the Making of Canada's White British Origins," *Journal of Canadian Studies*, 36, 2001, pp. 131–56.

18 Durham, *Lord Durham's Report*, p. 262.

19 F. X. Garneau, *L'Histoire du Canada depuis la découverte jusqu'à nos jours*, Montreal: Bibliothèque québécoise, 1996.

20 M. Lemire, *Les grands thèmes nationalistes du roman historique canadien-français*, Quebec: Presses de l'Université Laval, 1970, p. 3.

21 Lemire, *Les grands thèmes*, pp. 3–4; my translation. Unless otherwise indicated, all translations in this chapter are my own.

22 A. Thierry, *History of the Conquest of England by the Normans: Its Causes, and Its Consequences in England, Scotland, Ireland, and On the Continent*, London: Bogue, 1847.

23 Y. Dostaler, *Les infortunes du roman dans le Québec du XIXe siècle*, Montreal: Hurtubise HMH, 1977, p. 47.

24 J. Cartier, *Relations*, Montreal: Presses de l'Université de Montréal, 1986; M. de l'Incarnation, *Textes choisis et presentés par Marie-Emmanuel Chabot*, Montreal: Fides, 1962; and M. Lescarbot, *The Theatre of Neptune in New France*, Boston: Mifflin, 1927. The Jesuit *Relations* comprise a series of annual narrative reports issued by the superior of the Jesuit missions in New France to his overseer in France from 1632 to 1673. Although early reports focus on conversion work in aboriginal communities, later reports aim to recruit settlers to North America, as well as to gather financial support for the missions, and are thus geared towards a general reading audience.

25 P.-I. Aubert de Gaspé, Jr., *L'Influence d'un livre, ou le chercheur des trésors*, Montreal: Boréal, 1996; and F. R. Angers, *Les révélations du crime, ou Cambray et ses complices: chroniques canadiennes de 1834*, Quebec: Nota Bene, 2003.

26 J. Doutre, *Les fiancés de 1812; essai de littérature canadienne*, Montreal: Réédition Québec, 1969; P. Lacombe, *La terre paternelle*, Montreal: Fides, 1981; and P.-J.-O. Chauveau, *Charles Guérin: Roman de mœurs canadiennes*, Montreal: Fides, 1978.

27 O. Crémazie, *Oeuvres*, Ottawa: University of Ottawa Press, 1972.

28 J.-B.-A. Ferland, *Cours d'histoire du Canada*, Quebec: Hardy, 1882.

29 H.-R. Casgrain, *Légendes canadiennes*, Quebec: A. Côté, 1876; and J. Huston, *Le Répertoire national, ou Recueil de littérature canadienne*, Montreal: Lovell, Gibson, 1848–1850.

30 A.-G. Lajoie, *Jean Rivard, le détricheur (récit de la vie réelle) suivi de Jean-Rivard économiste*, Montreal: Hurtubise HMH, 1977; Lemire, *Les grands thèmes*, pp. x–xi.

31 P. Aubert de Gaspé, Sr., *Les Anciens Canadiens*, Montreal: Fides, 1993; J. Brierley, *Canadians of Old*, translation of Philippe Aubert de Gaspé's *Les Anciens Canadiens*, Montreal: Véhicule, 1996; G. B. de Boucherville, *Une de perdue, deux de trouvées*, Montreal: Hurtubise HMH, 1973; N. Bourassa, *Jacques et Marie: Souvenirs d'un peuple dispersé*, Montreal: Fides, 1976; F. de Saint-Maurice, *Madeleine Bouvart*, *L'Opinion publique* 3.14 (April 4, 1872); and J. T. Lesperance, *The Bastonnais: A Tale of the American Invasion of Canada 1775, 1776*, Montreal: Lovell, 1877. For more on the conquest of New France and its traumatic repercussions in literature, with particular emphasis paid to French-Canadian adaptations of British gothic conventions in literary treatments of the Acadian Expulsion, see A. Cabajsky, "Catholic Gothic: Atavism, Orientalism, and Generic Change in Charles de Guise's *Le Cap au diable* (1863)," in C. Sugars (ed.), *Unsettled Remains: Canadian Literature and the Postcolonial Gothic*, Waterloo, ON: Wilfrid Laurier University Press, forthcoming 2009. For his important examination of the different uses to which history and pastoral romance were put in English- and French-Canadian novels of the conquest of New France, with particular emphasis on novels by Philippe Aubert de Gaspé and William Kirby, see R. D. Stacey, "Romance, Pastoral Romance, and the Nation in History," in J. Blair (ed.), *ReCalling Early Canada: Reading the Political in Literary and Cultural Production*, Edmonton: University of Alberta Press, 2005, pp. 91–116.

32 J. Marmette, *Charles et Eva*, Montreal: Éditions Lumen, 1954 (originally published in 1866); *François de Bienville, scènes de la vie canadienne au XVIIe siècle*, Quebec: Brousseau, 1870; *L'Intendant Bigot*, Montreal: Desbarats, 1872; *Le Chevalier de Mornac, chronique de la Nouvelle France, 1664*, Montreal: L'Opinion publique, 1873; and "La Fiancée du rebelle, épisode de la guerre des Bostonnais," in *la Revue canadienne*, 1875, vol. 12.

33 J.-P. Tardivel, *Pour la patrie: roman du XXe siècle*, Montreal: Bibliothèque québécoise, 1989.

34 E. Rameau de Saint-Père, *La France aux colonies*, Paris: A. Jouby, 1859; J. Verne, *Famille sans nom*, Montreal: Stanké, 1999.

35 E. Lareau, *Histoire de la littérature canadienne*, Montreal: Lovell, 1874, p. 274.

36 R. Christie, *A History of the Late Province of Lower Canada*, Quebec: Thomas Cary, 1848–1866; J. M. McMullen, *The History of Canada from Its First Discovery to the Present Time*, Brockville, ON: McMullen and Co., 1868; W. Kingsford, *The History of Canada*, Toronto: Rowsell and Hutchison, 1898; and M. Conrad, "Historiography," in W. H. New (ed.), *Encyclopedia of Literature in Canada*, Toronto: University of Toronto Press, 2002, p. 98.

37 C. G. D. Roberts, *A History of Canada*, Boston: Lamson Wolffe, 1898.

38 The Manitoba school crisis was a political crisis that involved French- and English-Canadians in the province of Manitoba in the late nineteenth century. It carried with it larger questions about the extent to which the French language and culture could (or should) survive in Western Canada.

39 Louis Riel (1844–1885) was a founder of the province of Manitoba and leader of the Métis people of mixed European French and aboriginal heritage. He was executed by hanging in 1885 for instigating a series of rebellions and came to be known as a traitor to English-Canadians and a martyr to French-Canadians. His execution was felt strongly in Quebec, where it influenced French–English relations for many years to come.

40 E. Waterston, "Gilbert Parker and the Rebellion of 1837," *Journal of Canadian Studies*, 20, 1985, p. 87.

41 J. S. Mill, *On Liberty; Representative Government; Subjection of Women: Three Essays by John Stuart Mill*, London: Oxford University Press, 1966, p. 298; Lord Acton, "Nationality," in Gopal Balakrishnan (ed.), *Mapping the Nation*, London:

Verso, 1996; and H. J. Morgan, *Bibliotheca Canadensis: or, A Manual of Canadian Literature*, Online, Available Early Canadiana Online Ebook Collection: <http://www.canadiana.org/ECO/mtq?doc=11068>, p. viii.

42 Morgan, *Bibliotheca Canadensis*, p. vii.

43 Morgan, *Bibliotheca Canadensis*, p. viii.

44 Gerson, *A Purer Taste*, p. 50. For an important, highly readable recent examination of the "expatriate" American origins of English-Canadian literature, with particular emphasis on the publishing industry in New York City and Canadian canon-formation (1890–1914), see N. Mount, *When Canadian Literature Moved to New York*, Toronto: University of Toronto Press, 2005.

45 Parker, *Trail of the Sword*, p. 191.

46 L. Conan, *À l'œuvre et à l'épreuve*, Montreal: Beauchemin, 1951.

47 Lareau, *Histoire de la littérature canadienne*, p. 135.

48 R. Barr, "Canadian literature," *The Canadian Magazine*, 14, 1899, pp. 3–4.

Part III

MODERN PERSPECTIVES

7

NO EARLY-MODERN NATIONS?

Revising Modern Theories of Nationalism

Andrew Escobedo

Most people have a casual impression that nations have been around a long time, since the Middle Ages if not earlier: France, England, and China have long been France, England, and China, common sense tells us. At first glance, then, there is nothing surprising about the historical scope of this volume, which reaches back to the mid-sixteenth century. Yet, as the editors suggest in their general introduction, this dating in fact cuts against the grain of many recent theories of nationalism, which locate its origin only in the nineteenth-century or later. This "modernist" school of thought, as it is often called, dominated the field of nation studies in the 1980s and remains influential, although alternative perspectives, emphasizing the varieties of national forms and differing paces of development, have played an increasingly significant role in the last two decades. This chapter sketches in broad strokes the theoretical debate about when nations began to appear, and suggests some reasons for why it is worthwhile to talk about "nationhood" in societies before the nineteenth century, especially in the case of Britain. After all, our sense of what a nation *is* will depend a good deal on what point in history we think national consciousness emerged.

If France, England, and China were not nations in the Middle Ages, what were they? The modernists answer that these societies were empires, or provinces, or kingdoms, but not nations. Societies before the late eighteenth century, so the argument goes, tended to be loosely combined collectivities in which differing social classes and segments had little in common. Such populations did not feel an attachment to a "homeland," although they might identify with a region, a religion, a monarch, a social class, or a city. A peasant in thirteenth-century England would have more in common with other *French* peasants than she would with English aristocrats. Furthermore, medieval and renaissance societies were often ruled, vis-à-vis dynastic circumstance, by rulers of alien ethnic origin. (England is a good example: between

1066 and the fourteenth century its rulers were Normans who spoke French and little or no English.) These early societies lacked the crucial elements that constitute a nation-state, elements that include, to summarize historian John Breuilly's influential formulation,

1 The belief that a nation exists and possesses an explicit and distinct national character.
2 The belief that national interests trump all other interests, be they religious, regional, or dynastic.
3 The belief that the nation has or ought to attain political sovereignty—the state should be congruent with the nation.[1]

The scholar Benedict Anderson has emphasized yet another element that has gained wide currency:

4 The sense that the members of a nation share a "horizontal comradeship," in which all citizens stand more or less on equal footing *as citizens*, despite actual disparities in wealth.[2]

There are important differences between the positions that modernists hold, but most of them basically subscribe to this list, arguing that before the late eighteenth century there were no societies possessing all these characteristics.

The modernists produced their work out of a desire to debunk the long-standing idea that nations are natural or organic ethnic collectivities that have existed since time immemorial. This idea, they argued, is in fact exactly what nationalist ideology wants you to believe. Elie Kedourie, one of the early contributors to the modernist interpretation, eloquently insisted that "[n]ationalists make use of the past in order to subvert the present": "when nationalist historiography applies itself to the European past, it produces a picture of nations slowly emerging and asserting themselves in territorial sovereign states."[3] In other words, the modern nation invents a bogus history that seems naturally to lead up to (and therefore to legitimize) the nation. On the contrary, the modernists argued, nations are recent political inventions created by the elite classes to keep the masses under control. This means that the feeling of national belonging *does not lead to* but rather *follows from* manipulative nationalist ideology, counter-intuitive as that may initially seem. As Eric J. Hobsbawm put it, "nationalism comes before nations. Nations do not make states and nationalisms but the other way round."[4]

The modernists placed the emergence of nationalism at various dates, ranging from the late-eighteenth century to the aftermath of World War I, but they always associated it with the changes that modernity had created in European society. Kedourie, writing only fifteen years after the horrors of World War II, traced nationalism back to late-eighteenth-century German intellectuals who used the philosophical separation between world and mind, which they derived from the famous thinker Immanuel Kant, to conceptualize a notion of an organic "folk" consciousness, one that could assure a distinct national character over disparate historical periods. The theorists who followed Kedourie in the 1980s agreed that nationhood was a modern fabrication, but were skeptical that an intellectual elite could have invented it all by themselves. Instead, they argued that multiple social factors contributed to the emergence of nationalism in the nineteenth century. Hobsbawm, an accomplished Marxist historian, believed that nationalism emerged when modern democratic movements began to dismantle traditional class structure, obliging the ruling classes of Europe to come up with a means of coopting the energy of mass participation in politics. Somewhat similarly, John Breuilly argued that social elites created nationalism to give the masses a sense of group identity in the nineteenth century, when the disappearance of the old guild labor structure deprived citizens of the social identity previously supplied by their institutions of work.[5]

Perhaps the most influential and nerviest of these "social function" views in the 1980s came from the polymath scholar Ernest Gellner, who located the nation in the massive transition from traditional society (characterized by strict class stratification, isolated local culture, and limited communication technologies) to modern society (social mobility, cultural uniformity, and widespread communication technologies). In the premodern world, longstanding social configurations controlled the population, and so power could ignore local cultural variations. In modernity, by contrast, power has to use culture to impose social control, since the modern world, according to Gellner, approximates an empiricist jumble in which, "in the very nature of things, nothing is inherently connected with anything else . . . Is the world like that? *Ours* is. This is the pre-condition, the price of a world of endless discovery."[6] With this striking statement, Gellner described the dissolution of traditional social givens that obliged state power, for the first time in history, to invent and become congruent with national culture. The old patterns of social organization were gone: the phantom of nationhood provided the new pattern.

Although scholars, like myself, who work on national identity in the early modern period can become frustrated by the narrowness of the modernist interpretation, we should not overlook its virtues. It attempts to define the nation as distinct kind of community, in terms more specific than the generic (and less useful) notion of "society." It guards against the naïve belief that nations are simply natural features of the world, and it reminds us how much ideology can shape the perceptions of whole communities. It also warns that, in premodern societies, the things written by an educated minority do not necessarily provide evidence for the beliefs of the illiterate majority. Indeed, it may be worth conceding Breuilly's claim (the third ingredient of nationalism on his list) that the strict congruence of state and nation is a modern phenomenon. There is relatively little sense through 1700 that

English national *character* demanded a specific kind of state, in the way that some nineteenth-century English writers appealed explicitly to this character to encourage the formation of the British welfare state, or that some German writers linked their national character to certain forms of militarism. In this sense, we might distinguish early-modern *nationhood* (the experience and expression of national belonging) from modern *nationalism* (the direct translation of national identity into political policy).

Yet political policy is not the only thing that *nationalism* can usefully mean. Despite the virtues of the modernist interpretation, scholars working on literary culture of the sixteenth through eighteenth centuries have found good reasons to doubt it. Some of these reasons they have derived from the work of historians and social scientists who provide alternative descriptions of the formation and nature of nationhood. One of these, Anthony D. Smith, has emphasized the role that ethnic identity plays in national identity, arguing that the character of a modern nation often owes something to the prior existing ethnic mix within that territory.[7] In other words, and *contra* Gellner, modern nationalists cannot invent *any* old nation: history partially constrains their fabrications. This suggests more continuity between early modern and modern than the modernist view allows.

Modernists have sought to downplay the role of early-modern ethnic identity in nation-formation, but it often remains unclear exactly to what degree a nation can ignore its ethnic past and invent itself out of whole cloth. Geoff Eley and Ronald Grigor Suny, for example, have conceded that common territory and culture provide *some* basis for shared identity, "but for that consciousness to become *nationalist* in any true sense . . . something else normally has to happen in the form of political intervention. In other words, creative political action is required to transform a segmented and disunited population into a coherent nationality."[8] But why assume that all populations are naturally segmented and disunited until the creative politics of modern nationalism unites them?[9] Ethnic identity itself assumes *some* degree of cultural unity, in the sense that it remains invisible and illegible until it is culturally elaborated. Eley and Suny do allow that prior to the nineteenth century Britain's enclosed territorial boundaries and history of successive invasions encouraged self-consciousness about its ethnic heritage, but still insist that its population lacked "national identifications . . . strong enough to override regional, religious, and even class loyalties for most of the population most of the time, at least in certain kinds of situations."[10] Undoubtedly, English national affiliation in the early-modern period rarely if ever superseded religious or class affiliation. But does that disqualify nationhood? How often in the modern era does national loyalty *really* override religious, racial, or class loyalty? Probably not "most of the time." Against John Breuilly's stated second ingredient for national identity—the belief that national interests always trump all other interests—it might be worth exploring the possibility that national consciousness can exist *alongside* the consciousness of other identities.[11]

In addition to Anthony Smith's work on ethnic identity, scholars of early-modern literature and culture have found an important resource, ironically, in the research of a modernist, Benedict Anderson. Although he dates the emergence of nationalism in the late-eighteenth century, he shares with Smith the conviction that nationhood is first and foremost an anthropological construct and cultural identity, not a political ideology. For Anderson, the nation is an "imagined community" because its members will never actually meet each other beyond a small circle of acquaintances. This means that the nation achieves its reality in our minds through the experience of imaginative cultural media, especially literature: the newspaper, whose daily appearance lends a national character to quotidian life, and the novel, which dramatizes the peculiarities of national character through interwoven storylines.[12] Anderson differs from Kedourie, Hobsbawm, and especially Gellner in his sense that the imagined quality of nationhood does not simply amount to a falsehood. If it did, then that would mean that *all* identities are false, since they all depend on some degree of creative rearrangement of empirical data. National identity is fictive (made, not found) but not necessarily fictitious (the false presented as true). These ideas have resonated with scholars working on early-modern literary forms, especially because Anderson locates the pre-history of modern nationalism in phenomena that occurred in the early-modern period: the Protestant reformation, the invention of print-capitalism, and the emergence of a modern sense of linear time.

Anderson's work has sometimes encouraged scholars to focus on early-modern cultural artifacts linked to nationhood, rather than on mass politics. Philip Schwyzer, in a study of the tension between English and British identity in Tudor literature, confines himself to a claim about national consciousness among the educated classes, but not generally among the English population: "To put it crudely, sixteenth-century nationalists talked the talk, but only after 1750 would whole nations walk the walk."[13] This witty sense of what we might call a "literary nationalism" might mark an important compromise between modernists and their opponents.[14] On the other hand, it might be worth keeping in mind how many vernacular literary forms were in fact beginning to reach a large portion of the population: domestic religious histories such as John Foxe's *Acts and Monuments*, communally-sung English metrical anthologies such as *The Whole Book of Psalms*,[15] English history plays performed weekly on the London stage for audiences of tens of thousands, and the exploding pamphlet market during the English Civil Wars. Several of these literary examples are London centered, and none can definitely be said to have reached a clear majority of English people, yet they certainly paint a picture different from the "segmented and disunited population" offered by the modernists. They also, by merit of their simultaneous civic and devotional functions, cast doubt on the idea that religion can only impede rather than cultivate nationhood.[16]

When thinking about early-modern nationhood, we ought also to consider that even modern citizens do not in fact experience their nations as simply homogeneous and unified communities. They regularly contest versions of nationhood they find unsatisfying, and they often doubt the sincerity and judgment of their fellow citizens. Assumptions of modern national unity have been usefully challenged by postcolonial and feminist theorists who consider, among other things, the symbolic function of borders in the national imaginary. Whereas ancient empires typically had a center (like Rome or Constantinople), nations have boundaries that separate and differentiate them from other nations. This places a higher premium on national purity than premodern societies did, but also creates a kind of forced cosmopolitanism or transnationalism that obliges nationalists to define themselves within a field of external, competing national identities. This arrangement crucially affects the manner in which colonized societies develop ethnic nationhoods in response to external aggression, as Partha Chatterjee has documented in the case of India.[17] It also affects the colonizers. The postcolonial theorist Homi K. Bhabha has influentially described this border ambiguity as a kind of "ambivalence," the impression that the very effort to keep nonnationals outside the border allows them a surreptitious presence within the nation. Ambivalence interferes with the effort to claim an innate national character derived internally from the "blood and soil," giving national identity an almost colonized quality.[18] Such an effect occurred, for example, when early-modern English writers tried to locate their national heritage with the ancient Britons, once the heroic people of King Arthur (whom the English idealized), but whose descendants were now found with the modern Welsh (whom the English wanted to subordinate). When the bishop of Bristol, John Thornborough, celebrating England's British lineage in 1605, reminds his readers that "[o]ur Countriemen, & neighbors of Wales, as Chronicles reporte, deriue themselues, from ancient true Brittaines,"[19] does that mean that English people like himself are *not* derived from the true Britain? Are the Welsh his *countrymen* (we're all British) or his *neighbors* (we're English and they're not)? Are the Welsh inside or outside the nation?[20]

Feminist scholars have likewise noted the crucial role that women have played in establishing figurative national borders, and they have criticized previous theorists for ignoring gender in investigations of national identity. For example, most scholars agree that nations idealize the past in order to make political claims about future progress, but Anne McClintock has argued that this temporal threshold between past and future often takes the form of a deeply gendered symbolic equation in which women represent "the atavistic and authentic body of national tradition," whereas men signify "the progressive agent of national modernity."[21] Thus, the nation does not imagine that its citizens simply live within a "horizontal community," as Anderson describes, but that they play disparate, even opposing, roles: women guard the old ways while men forge ahead toward the future. Nira Yuval-Davis has further suggested that nations use women as social "border guards," biologically as the reproducers of national consanguinity, and culturally as symbols of national chastity who (ideally) refuse to mix pure blood with ethnic aliens.[22] Again, early-modern literature abounds with examples of female characters who seem designed to protect national purity. The woman warrior Britomart, in Edmund Spenser's poem *The Faerie Queene*, is both the fictional British ancestor of Queen Elizabeth and the allegorical figure of chastity.[23] William Shakespeare's *Henry V* makes the point of insisting that the victorious King Henry woo Princess Katherine in English rather than in French, as if she might not be a suitable mate until linguistically conquered.

The postcolonial and feminist scholars I've discussed have no particular interest in the question of early-modern nationhood, but they do describe the nation and its effects in ways quite relevant to social forms prior to the nineteenth century. They also oblige us to qualify the assumptions of previous scholars that modern national identity is characterized by unanimity and uniformity. On the contrary, the nation must always maintain a sense of unity over against a consciousness of division and fissure. Whatever the earlier limitations of mass participation in national culture, early modern people articulated their sense of communal identity in ways that seem recognizably national. The debate between the modernists and their opponents is perhaps now old enough that no one is likely to change his mind. What will likely happen instead is that scholars of early-modern culture will continue to study the national meaning of literary forms, and they will use the terms *nationhood* and *nationalism*. Yet hopefully they will do so advisedly, with a critical awareness sharpened by the insights of the modernist interpretation. The modernists, after all, are perhaps the best opponents that early-modernists could hope to have.

Notes

1 J. Breuilly, *Nationalism and the State* (1982), reprinted Manchester: Manchester University Press, 1993, p. 2.
2 B. Anderson, *Imagined Communities: Reflections on the Origin and Spread of Nationalism*, London: Verso, 1983, pp. 15–16.
3 E. Kedourie, *Nationalism* (1960), reprinted Oxford: Blackwell, 1993, pp. 70, 71–72.
4 E. J. Hobsbawm, *Nations and Nationalism since 1780: Programme, Myth, Reality*, Cambridge: Cambridge University Press, 1990, p. 10.
5 Hobsbawm, *Nations and Nationalism;* Breuilly, *Nationalism and the State.*
6 E. Gellner, *Nations and Nationalism*, Ithaca: Cornell University Press, 1983, pp. 22–23.
7 A. D. Smith, *The Ethnic Origins of Nations*, Oxford: Blackwell, 1986, and *National Identity*, Oxford: Oxford University Press, 1986 reprinted London: Penguin, 1991.
8 G. Eley and R. C. Suny, "Introduction," in G. Eley and R. C. Suny (eds), *Becoming National: A Reader*, Oxford: Oxford University Press, 1996, p. 7.
9 On this question see A. D. Smith, "Nationalism in Early Modern Europe," *History and Theory*, 44, 2005, pp. 404–15, esp. p. 411.

10 G. Eley and R. C. Suny, *Becoming National*, p. 9. On debates about ethnic identity in early-modern Britain (Britons, Saxons, Normans), see C. Kidd, *British Identities before Nationalism: Ethnicity and Nationhood in the Atlantic World, 1600–1800*, Cambridge: Cambridge University Press, 1999.
11 P. Stevens makes this point forcefully in "How Milton's Nationalism Works: Globalization and the Possibilities of Positive Nationalism," in D. Loewenstein and P. Stevens (eds), *Early Modern Nationalism and Milton's England*, Toronto: University of Toronto Press, 2008, esp. pp. 274–77.
12 Anderson, *Imagined Communities*.
13 P. Schwyzer, *Literature, Nationalism, and Memory in Early Modern England and Wales*, Cambridge: Cambridge University Press, 2004, p. 9.
14 On the question of a specifically literary nationalism in early modern England, see also C. McEachern, *The Poetics of English Nationhood, 1590–1612*, Cambridge: Cambridge University Press, 1996, 2006.
15 B. Quitslund has estimated that by the end of the Elizabethan period at least 220,000 copies of this metrical psalter had been printed, or one copy for every eighteen inhabitants of England and Wales; see *The Reformation in Rhyme: Sternhold, Hopkins, and the English Metrical Psalter, 1547–1603*, Aldershot: Ashgate, 2008, p. 242.
16 For two studies examining religious nationhood in England, see L. Greenfeld, *Nationalism: Five Roads to Modernity*, Cambridge, MA: Harvard University Press, 1992, and A. Hastings, *The Construction of Nationhood: Ethnicity, Religion, and Nationalism*, Cambridge: Cambridge University Press, 1997, 1999.
17 P. Chatterjee, *The Nation and Its Fragments*, Princeton: Princeton University Press, 1993.
18 H. K. Bhabha, *The Location of Culture*, New York: Routledge, 1994, esp. pp. 85–92.
19 J. Thornborough, *The Joyful and Blessed Reuniting the Two Mighty and Famous Kingdoms, England and Scotland*, Oxford, 1605, pp. 44–45.
20 For more comments about the "British problem" within English nationalism, see W. Maley, *Nation, State, and Empire in English Renaissance Literature*, New York: Palgrave, 2003.
21 A. McClintock, "'No Longer in a Future Heaven': Nationalism, Gender, and Race," in Eley and Suny (eds), *Becoming National*, p. 263.
22 N. Yuval-Davis, *Gender and Nation*, London: Sage, 1997, esp. pp. 23, 39–51.
23 See also Andrew Hadfield's comments on Britomart and nationalism in his chapter in this volume.

8

NATIONALISM AND CANON-FORMATION

Sarah M. Corse

The great literary works of a nation form the national canon. The national canon contains that literature with which every educated person is assumed to be familiar. In the US the canon contains novels such as F. Scott Fitzgerald's *The Great Gatsby* and Herman Melville's *Moby Dick*; in Canada the national canon contains novels such as Frederick Philip Grove's *Fruits of the Earth* and Margaret Laurence's *The Stone Angel*; and the British canon includes novels such as Henry Fielding's *Tom Jones*, Jane Austen's *Pride and Prejudice*, and James Joyce's *Ulysses*. We valorize these novels as key symbols of the nation, requiring them to be read in schools, and teaching students to read them through a national lens, to understand the importance of the texts as due, in large part, to the role they play in symbolizing the nation that produces them.[1]

Such an idea seems obvious, indeed natural to us; of course each and every country has its own great books that we read to understand something about that country and of course each country's books are different from the books of other countries. When we think more carefully about the whole idea of how distinct national literatures arise, however, we encounter a number of questions. First and foremost, of course, we have the problem of where—and how—nations themselves originate. Many nation-states emerge slowly and with different borders at different times. Canada and the US both undergo a lengthy period of westward expansion that fundamentally changes the geographical form of the nation during the nineteenth and early twentieth centuries, making even the underlying specification of the nation problematic. The idea of the "nation" never quite matches the complicated histories and geographies of actual nations.

Despite these complexities, the underlying rationale for the idea of distinct literatures unique to each country is that those literatures are, in turn, assumed to embody the distinctive nature of the unique nation, its society, character, and experience (see on this point the chapters by both Du Ponceau and Hume in this volume). Because Canadians are different from the French, and the English different from Americans, they will produce different stories, different archetypes, different themes—in short, their literature will address the central concerns of their own unique character and experience. The idea of a distinctive national literature that embodies the character of the people is a recent one, however, dating only from the late eighteenth and early nineteenth centuries. In fact, if we look closely at historical ideas of and changes to literary canons, we can see how older ideas of literature's power and purpose become tied in the late eighteenth century to the rise of nationalism and to specific nation-building projects.

This "new" understanding of literary canons as an aspect of national identity is a process that excites a great deal of attention during the nationalizing projects that started at the end of the eighteenth century. Prior to the rise of the modern nation-state, literature was valued precisely for its ability to transcend locality and even history, to speak broadly to (what were assumed to be) universal human characteristics and situations. With the development of the modern nation-state, however, literature came to be seen as one embodiment of the uniqueness and distinctiveness of the nation-state. Literature became one way to symbolically represent the nation and its people. Because of this emphasis on the national role of literature, the criteria for the selection of texts into national canons became focused on difference, on themes and characteristics that distinguish one country's literature from another's, rather than on what were previously presumed to be universalistic criteria.[2] Rather than valuing a literature that speaks to all people across all times and places, we begin to see literature as valuable in its ability to represent a very particular people in a very specific place—the citizens of one particular nation-state.

Currently, we can see both underlying rationales for canons at work in different places. The older idea of a universalistic, transcendent value to literature persists alongside the more recent idea of canonical texts as key embodiments of national identity. In the United States, for example, students are taught that Shakespeare is a transcendent genius, one whose work is imbued with such universal characteristics that it can be read, produced, and appreciated by all despite the historical and geographic distance between today's audiences and those for whom *Romeo and Juliet* or *Hamlet* were written. Simultaneously, those same students are being taught that Mark Twain's *Adventures of Huckleberry Finn* is a uniquely American story and that its power and importance come from the way that it captures distinctively American themes—of freedom, of the rejection of "sivilizing" forces, and of the possible re-inventions of the self.[3] In Canada, we see a similar approach to teaching Shakespeare—a transcendent literary genius whose work is still timely and relevant as well as being an important part of the broad literary tradition within which Canadian literature falls—and a similar, simultaneous focus on a unique Canadian literature that helps "construct the place called Canada as a metaphor that's central to our daily lives" as one McGill University syllabus describes it.[4] In the remainder of this chapter I both discuss the complicated ideology underlying the idea of "the nation" and try to explicate the processes of canon-formation that are entwined with the processes that create and uphold the ideological construct of "the nation."

Let us first ask why and how literature came to be seen not as universal stories of man, but as stories of particular people in particular, specific places. Late eighteenth- and early nineteenth-century theorists of nationalism, particularly the German Romantic nationalists, first developed the now accepted idea that literature is defined by its national affiliation and should embody the unique characteristics of a nation.[5] The underlying premise of the literary nationalists was that humanity is naturally divided into homogeneous sub-groups marked by a unique set of values and concerns and by a distinctive "national character." This set of nationalist ideas created a vision both of the nation itself and of national literatures as naturally occurring, pre-existing entities that come into being and survive without any action by specifiable people. The nation is an organic community, "awoken" perhaps under pressure, but extant. In this view, the nations that underlie the new nation-states are understood as geographically bounded communities sharing a single language and a single culture; they are a "naturally" cohesive and coherent entity.

More recently, however, theorists of the nation have clearly demonstrated the constructed nature of nations; they are "imagined communities" constructed in the minds of people, not organic, natural bodies.[6] This newer and more analytic view of nations understands the modern nation-state as an abstract entity created through specifiable actions, rather than as a primordial and naturally occurring community. Because nations, and their attendant states, are not a manifestation of primordial identity, nor even necessarily of geographic and cultural singularity, their identity must be constructed and sustained in the minds of both the internal population and the international community.

Furthermore, despite Romantic nationalist imagery of the homogeneous culture that underlies the polity and unifies the population, most nation-states need be created from disparate groups. Nations, especially those formed in large part from immigration, such as Brazil and Australia, or those superimposed on a variety of groups or tribes such as many African or Eastern European nations, do not fit neatly into Romantic preconceptions of an existing cultural—or even linguistic –singularity. But even older nations presumed to be more homogeneous have internal divisions and competing ties. Geographic distinctions, traditional folkways, matters of dress, food, ritual, religion, and even language all separate regions of England, France, Germany, and Spain, for example. "National" attitudes, values, and characteristics are never representative of every member of a nation's population, even in relatively homogeneous nations.

Thus nation-states must work to create a unified and over-arching identity that unites people despite their differences. The modern history of nation-states bears eloquent witness to the number of competing allegiances that must be transcended by a strong national identity in order for the nation-state to prosper. Nation-states must construct a vision of "The Nation" that is powerful enough to subsume all other identities. A national identity must transcend commitments to ethnic identities, to religious communities, to familial, tribal, and kin networks, and other strong ties that may tear the nation apart. The number and intensity of civil wars and state partitionings offer compelling proof of the costs and consequences of the failure to build a sufficiently strong national identity.

In the face of these competing loyalties, nation-states mount explicitly nationalist campaigns to develop an identity and build a cohesive, committed national community. Many aspects of this are political—we are all familiar with propaganda such as military recruitment posters or exhortations to contribute to the glory of the mother- (or father-) land. Military parades celebrating independence and historic battles, and heroes, statues, monuments, grand capitol buildings, public education, especially civics classes—all of these are part of a process used to build a nation and a national identity that forges a citizenry from disparate populations. Cultural works, especially literature, play an important, though often more subtle, role in the nation-building process. Julia Wright, for example, demonstrates the role of poetry anthologies in helping to construct a "British, rather than an English, national identity" in the late eighteenth century.[7] National literatures help to create identities in new nations, to affirm identities in nations under attack, and to reinterpret and revise national identities in the face of conflict and change.[8]

Even after we understand that nations are active constructions in the hearts and minds of people as well as military and cartographic exercises, however, questions remain about how exactly the canon arises. Traditionally, the contents of the canon were assumed; the canon was simply an archive of "the best that has been thought and known."[9] To the extent that scholars thought about there being a *process* of canon-formation, they understood it to be a natural and automatic process in which "great books" transcend time and place to become classics. In the past thirty years, however, scholars have developed more sophisticated analytic models of canon-formation that focus on "the complex of circumstances that make texts visible initially and then maintain them in their preeminent position."[10] Scholars focusing on specific works and authors have attempted to "explode" the "myth of transcendently great literature"[11] by demonstrating how canons, like nations themselves are created by the cultural work of specific people engaged in an identifiable set of activities.

Jane Tompkins, for example, analyzed the development and trajectory of Nathaniel Hawthorne's canonical status in the US, demonstrating how political activity by interested factions first established his authorial reputation. In addition to arguing that his initial reputation was largely the conscious work of a small group of influential Boston literati, Tompkins argues that the aspects of Hawthorne's work that were admired by nineteenth-century critics are substantially different from those aspects of his work on which his current status rests. Thus Hawthorne's reputation rests on changing and indeed contradictory criteria and is the result of committed action by close friends and literary admirers.[12]

Once we recognize that nations must be constructed and that canons themselves are also constructed, then the cultural work of canon-building becomes visible. Understanding that the canon is a product of human choice and (often contested) authority, rather than a natural occurrence, allows us to think about the "why" and "how" of national canon-formation. National literatures help construct the not-so-primordial nation, the "transcendent realm of essential identity" that can overarch the subsidiary differences that divide the population.[13] Thus the first thing that national literatures need to do is to construct a unique identity. Because each nation must be unique, "difference from" other (historically relevant) nations begins to emerge as a key factor in the designation of a national canon. "Reading the nation" is more than a metaphor: it is a reference to the ways that national literatures may literally read a nation into being.

In addition to the substance national literatures provide to national identities (e.g., the American emphasis on individualism or the Canadian focus on communal solidarity), national literatures help build nations in another way. The *content* of specific texts may well be of less importance than the *form* of their existence as a national canon. When students read *Huck Finn* or *The Stone Angel* or *Pride and Prejudice* as students all across the US, Canada, or Great Britain are doing, and as their older siblings and maybe even parents did before them, they experience what Benedict Anderson calls "occasions for unisonality."[14] Although Anderson speaks of singing the national anthem as the archetypal occasion for unisonality, the common experience of reading national literature—whether read with passionate interest, dutifully skimmed in school, or only experienced through Cliff Notes or the illustrated comics version—is part of what sustains the image of national communion. By reading these texts as every other student in our country reads them, we experience participation in a national collectivity because it is explicitly acknowledged that the *national* context of the reading provides its significance.

Finally, in addition to aiding internal processes of nation-building and national identity formation, national literatures assist in these processes within the international community. National literatures have become identified within both national and international communities as an essential characteristic of nation-states. In order to lay claim to full nationhood, nascent nation-states need not only military and political independence, but also cultural independence. A viable national literature is one of the clearest signs of cultural independence. Once national literatures become understood as a basic requirement of a full-fledged nation-state, new nations have to have their own national literature or risk losing status in the international arena. Liah Greenfeld argues that in the nineteenth century, these ideals of cultural nationalism were so powerful that "the lack of a national culture raised the question as to the reality of the nation itself."[15] The equation of a unique, national culture and the reality of the nation itself may be no less important today. As the anthropologist Virginia Dominguez has noted regarding the current power of the value of national cultures:

> I am . . . struck by the apparent success European countries have had over the past 100 to 150 years convincing the rest of the world that culture is a "thing," that it has value, and that any self-respecting group of people must have it. People . . . are overwhelmingly buying into the elite European idea that there is such a thing as culture and that it is through one's culture that one's value is judged. We need only think about China's current "culture fever" or Japan's ongoing Nihonjinron or Papua New Guinea's panic about developing a national culture or the Quebequois insistence on Quebequois cultural identity.[16]

The world system evaluates the claims of nation-states and one of the measures is the vitality and uniqueness of a nation-state's culture.

Aldous Huxley wrote that "nations are to a very large extent invented by their poets and novelists."[17] This statement provides an excellent summary of the central task of a legitimated national literature: "to invent" a nation and a national identity that are capable of mobilizing loyalty and inspiring commitment from its citizens—the internal population—and of proclaiming full status to the international community—the external audience. National literatures are centrally bound up in the processes of national identity formation and maintenance. Nationalism is an "emotive identity" and national literatures are one method of fostering the emotions that forge a national community.[18]

We can see these processes particularly clearly if we look at the situation in the US in the late eighteenth and nineteenth centuries and in Canada in the twentieth century. In the US, public figures such as William Ellery Channing and authors including Walt Whitman and Herman Melville among others sent a loud, clear message about the necessity of a distinctive and powerful American cultural presence to challenge British cultural domination. James Russell Lowell summarized the prevailing attitude in the early part of the nineteenth century:

> It had been resolved unanimously that we must and would have a national literature. England, France, Spain, Italy, each already had one. Germany was getting one as fast as possible, and Ireland vowed

> that she once had one far surpassing them all. To be respectable, we must have one also.[19]

The search for and desire to find an "authentic" American literary voice preoccupied journalists, authors, poets, and the intellectual elite in the States throughout the late eighteenth and nineteenth centuries. The voices of the time are explicit in their understanding that the US needed to establish itself as a nation as well as a state: "political independence," it was argued, "only served to emphasize American cultural provincialism."[20]

Margaret Atwood has famously pointed out that a similar situation occurs in Canada over 100 years later as Canada moves away from its identity as part of the British Empire towards an independent nation-state. The strengthening waves of Canadian nationalism are accompanied by many calls for, and worries about, an "authentic" Canadian literature. Atwood writes about her graduate study at Harvard in the early 1960s and how her exposure to the history of American literature illuminated her understanding of the struggle for a viable national literature that was then occurring in Canada:

> I found myself reading my way through . . . anguished essays of the early nineteenth century, bemoaning the inferiority not only of American literary offerings but of American dress design, and wondering when the great American genius would come along. It sounded familiar.[21]

Atwood saw the then contemporary Canadian worry about national identity and the lack of a national canon in the 1960s as echoing American self-consciousness regarding the same fears and lacks in the early 1800s. Both the US and Canada needed a national canon when, and only when, they needed to establish themselves as independent nations.

The process of national canon-formation in the US and Canada occurred, however, within very different historical contexts. In the US, an "authentic" voice meant one thing—a non-British voice. In December 1818, the British critic Sydney Smith wrote: "Literature the Americans have none—no native literature, we mean. It is all imported. . . . But why should the Americans write books, when a six weeks' passage brings them . . . our sense, science, and genius, in bales and hogsheads?"[22] Smith contemptuously dismissed American claims to a "true," as opposed to merely political, independence from England. In January 1820, he again wrote on the American literary situation, asking his now infamous question in the *Edinburgh Review*: "In the four quarters of the globe, who reads an American book?"[23] These writings stimulated the creation of an American canon to such an extent that, thirty years later, Melville proudly responded "the day will come when you shall say who reads a book by an Englishman that is a modern?"[24] And indeed, by the middle of the nineteenth century Melville himself as well as Nathaniel

Hawthorne were publishing what would eventually come to be two cornerstones of the American canon, *The Scarlet Letter*, published in 1850, and *Moby Dick*, published in 1851.

Canada, however, faced a different situation. Establishing itself without revolution and understanding its identity as an essential piece of the British Empire for 200 years, Canada became a fully fledged nation, as well as a fully independent state, only in the twentieth century. By then it needed to distinguish itself not just from the colonial mother country, but also from its powerful neighbor to the south whose identity and power were no longer in question. Canadian canon-formation occurred within the doubly constrained territory of a reaction against both long-established British tradition and increasingly pervasive American cultural exportation.[25]

Thus the establishment of national literatures is fundamentally intertwined with the processes of nation-building, of national identity development, of the crucial distinctions new nations must make between themselves and other nations, and of the demands of the world system for national cultural coherence and uniqueness. Canon-formation is a political process driven by the work of specific cultural agents with identifiable interests and resources within particular historical contexts. The distinctiveness of national literatures is simultaneously and always both a source of national difference and a symbolic representation of it.

Notes

1 S. M. Corse, *Nationalism and Literature: The Politics of Culture in Canada and the United States*, Cambridge: Cambridge University Press, 1997; J. Guillory, *Cultural Capital: The Problem of Literary Canon Formation*, Chicago: University of Chicago Press, 1993.

2 See, for example, J. M. Wright's analysis of poetry anthologies in Britain in which she discusses the re-presentation of Chaucer as "the father of English poetry rather than a medieval poet with connections to a larger European tradition" (Wright, "The Order of Time: Nationalism and Literary Anthologies, 1774–1831," *Papers on Language and Literature*, 33, 1997, p. 341).

3 On this point see D. Lloyd, *Nationalism and Minor Literature: James Clarence Mangan and the Emergence of Irish Cultural Nationalism*, Berkeley: University of California Press, 1987, especially the "Introduction." See also L. Levine, *Highbrow/Lowbrow: The Emergence of Cultural Hierarchy in America*, Cambridge, MA: Harvard University Press, 1988, on the different receptions of Shakespeare in America over time.

4 R. Lecker, syllabus on McGill University website, Fall 2007, accessed September 28, 2007: www.arts.mcgill.ca/programs/english/courses/ENGL333.html.

5 T. D. Maclulich, "Thematic Criticism, Literary Nationalism, and the Critic's New Clothes," *Essays on Canadian Writing*, 35, 1987, pp. 17–36.

6 See B. Anderson, *Imagined Communities: Reflections on the Origin and Spread of Nationalism*, rev. edn., London: Verso Press, 1991; E. Gellner, *Encounters with Nationalism*, Oxford: Blackwell, 1994; E. Gellner, *Nations and Nationalism*, Ithaca: Cornell University Press, 1983; Oxford and Malden: Blackwell, 1983, 2nd edn. 2005; and E. Hobsbawm, *Nations and Nationalism since 1780:*

Programme, Myth, Reality, 2nd edn., Cambridge: Cambridge University Press, 1990/1997.

7 Wright, "The Order," p. 342.

8 See, for example, on this process in Nigeria, W. Griswold, "The Writing on the Mud Wall: Nigerian Novels and the Imaginary Village," *American Sociological Review*, 57, 1992, pp. 709–24.

9 M. Arnold, in *The Portable Matthew Arnold*, Lionel Trilling (ed.), New York: Viking, 1949, p. 499.

10 J. Tompkins, *Sensational Designs: The Cultural Work of American Fiction 1790–1860*, New York: Oxford University Press, 1985, p. xii; B. H. Smith, *Contingencies of Value: Alternative Perspectives for Critical Theory*, Cambridge, MA: Harvard University Press, 1988.

11 J. Wolff, "Excess and Inhibition: Interdisciplinarity in the Study of Art," in Lawrence Grossberg, Cary Nelson, and Paula A. Treichler (eds), *Cultural Studies*, New York: Routledge, 1992, p. 709.

12 See also S. M. Corse and S. D. Westervelt, "Gender and Literary Valorization: *The Awakening* of a Canonical Novel," *Sociological Perspectives*, 45, 2002, pp. 139–61 on the critical history of K. Chopin's *The Awakening*; S. M. Corse and M. Griffin, "Cultural Valorization and African-American Literary History: Re-Constructing the Canon," *Sociological Forum*, 12, 1997, pp. 173–203 on the critical re-evaluation of *Their Eyes Were Watching God*; and Tia DeNora, "Musical Patronage and Social Change in Beethoven's Vienna," *American Journal of Sociology*, 97, 1991, pp. 310–46 for a similar type of analysis focusing on Beethoven's reputation.

13 D. Lloyd, *Nationalism and Minor Literature: James Clarence Mangan and the Emergence of Irish Cultural Nationalism*, Berkeley: University of California Press, 1987, p. x.

14 Anderson, *Imagined Communities*, p. 145.

15 L. Greenfeld, *Nationalism: Five Roads to Modernity*, Cambridge, MA: Harvard University Press, 1992, p. 442.

16 V. R. Dominguez, "Invoking Culture: The Messy Side of 'Cultural Politics,'" *South Atlantic Quarterly*, 91, 1992, pp. 19–42, 36.

17 A. Huxley, *Texts and Pretexts*, London: Chatto & Windus, 1959, p. 50.

18 D. McCrone, *Understanding Scotland: The Sociology of a Stateless Nation*, London: Routledge, 1992, p. 6.

19 Quoted in J. B. Hubbell, *Who Are the Major American Writers? A Study of the Changing Literary Canon*, Durham, NC: Duke University Press, 1972, p. 5.

20 Richard Ruland (ed.), *The Native Muse: Theories of American Literature*, vol. I, New York: E. P. Dutton & Co., Inc., 1972, p. 48.

21 M. Atwood, *Second Words: Selected Critical Prose*, Boston: Beacon Press, 1982, p. 382.

22 Hubbell, *Major American Writers*, p. 5.

23 Ruland, *Native Muse*, p. 157.

24 B. Lease, *Anglo-American Encounters: England and the Rise of American Literature*, Cambridge: Cambridge University Press, 1981, p. xii.

25 For more on Canadian canon-formation, see R. Lecker, "The Canonization of Canadian Literature: An Inquiry into Value," *Critical Inquiry*, 16, 1990, pp. 656–71.

9

NATIONALISM AND GLOBALIZATION

Imre Szeman

If it has come to seem natural to talk about "nationalism" and "globalization" in relation to one another, this is because they are commonly seen as describing the same general phenomena, but at different times in human history. Both concepts name dominant, large-scale geo-political formations which are taken as materially structuring social and cultural life in inescapable ways; globalization is typically imagined as arising at the end of the historical period in which nations and nationalism were predominant. Correspondingly, the task for those engaged in literary theory and criticism would seem to be to consider the function of literature and criticism in the context of the historical circumstances named by both formations, paying careful attention to the specific structural realities mapped out by nationalism and globalization. The relationships between English literature, the nation and nationalism have been explored in some detail, especially in relation to the decolonizing struggles following World War II, when explicit expressions of cultural nationalism played a role in the process of national self-definition for these newly formed polities.[1] By contrast, while there has been an explosion of academic and public discourses related to globalization, there has been surprisingly little work on the specific relationship of literature and literary culture to it.[2] This is in part because scholarly work on globalization in relation to culture has focused on contemporary forms of electronic and visual culture, which are thought to have assumed key aspects of the social role once played by literature, and in part because the discourse of globalization has been greeted within literary studies by appropriate critical suspicion of the social and political imperatives the term contains and conceals.

The apparently clear temporal relationship between nationalism and globalization is the first of many issues that need to be challenged with respect to both concepts. There has been a tendency to concede too quickly the material and historical reality of each geopolitical formation and to overlook the fact that both are highly contested, discursive constructions that assemble diverse and discrete social, political, and cultural developments into dominant narratives that are then taken as defining the shape of the present and of the future to come.[3] The very idea that globalization has a temporal relationship to nationalism, coming *after* it, forms an essential part of the ideology of globalization, which has aggressively sought to mystify its fundamentally discursive origins in order to make the present and future it names inevitable—a property of reality as such, as opposed to a concept employed to try to make sense of that reality. Globalization names large-scale structural developments that are supposedly outside the ability not only of individuals but also of nation-states to challenge and change; it names a present in which capital is omnipresent, subjects are constituted as consumers rather than citizens, the individual is valued over any collective, and the future is one in which the primary function of the state is to guarantee the success of private enterprise.[4] The political use and abuse of the concept and discourses of globalization has been challenged not only within social and cultural theory, but also by political movements (from groups associated with the "anti-globalization" movement to populist nationalisms around the world), non-governmental organizations (NGOs), and extra-state actors such as the United Nations Educational, Scientific and Cultural Organization, which has recently reaffirmed the need to protect cultural diversity against the homogenizing tendencies of globalization.[5] The insistent presentism of globalization has also been critiqued by literary critics such as Balachandra Rajan and Ian Baucom, who insightfully point to the ongoing development of the global in and alongside the national, as opposed to seeing the former appearing only as a recent replacement for the latter.[6] Despite these challenges, however, globalization has become a near universal term used to describe the fundamental character of the world we collectively inhabit.

An exploration of the role of literature in and against nationalism has formed an important part of English literary studies over the past two decades. In both postcolonial literary studies (as exemplified canonically by the work of Edward Said, Gayatri Chakravorty Spivak, and Homi Bhabha) and in the highly influential work of the cultural historian Benedict Anderson, the long-assumed "natural" relationship between literature and nation has been exposed as one in need of critical examination. Historically, the concepts of nation and of literature have developed in lock-step. Indeed, the discourse or ideology of *nationalism* is unthinkable without the work carried out by both concepts: the nation as a defined geographic zone characterized by cultural and ethnic homogeneity, and literature as a body of imaginative texts distinct from other forms of writing which springs out of this cultural particularity and captures the intimate connection of space and ethnic identity. The origins of this connection between land and community expressed through and reinforced by literature are generally traced back to the late eighteenth century and to the literary movement of Romanticism. German critic Johann Gottfried von Herder claimed in the 1780s that "every nation is one people, having its own national form, as well as its own language."[7] The link between language, people, and political-spatial form which literature was thought to embody and express has shaped our understanding of literature and the activity of criticism in the two centuries that have followed.

Over the course of the nineteenth century, the nation became the primary form of political and social organization in Europe and North and South America, as reflected by the consolidation and production of national languages out of diverse dialects, and by the development of numerous social and cultural techniques, processes, and institutions (from mass educational systems to standing armies) whose function was to produce a homogeneous body of citizen-subjects loyal to the nation-state.[8] Just as the nation became a seemingly natural way of organizing groups of people, so too did the belief that literary and cultural products reflected the unique national soil from which they organically developed. The first professor of American literature, Fred Lewis Pattee, began his introductory text on the subject with a description of the relationship between literature and the nation that, by the end of the century, had become all but indisputable: "The literature of a nation is the entire body of literary productions that has emanated from the people of the nation during its history, preserved by the arts of writing and printing. It is the embodiment of the best thoughts and fancies of a people."[9] The system of national literatures which was developed during this period and which largely continues to define the institutional organization and division of literary studies—despite ongoing challenges to its conceptual problems and limits, as during the canon debates in the United States in the 1980s—provides evidence of the degree to which nation and literature have been tied together in ways that remain difficult to shake.

Given the nation's relatively long history as a political and cultural form, criticisms of the nation and of the links between the nation and literature arose surprisingly belatedly in the 1980s and 1990s from two directions: explorations of the nation-state within the social sciences and history,[10] and examinations of the limits of cultural nationalism and national identity within the newly emergent field of postcolonial studies. Of the former, it is Anderson's analysis of the formal relationship between "novel" and "nation" in *Imagined Communities* (1983) which has had the deepest and most prolonged impact on literary studies, opening up new ways of looking at nationalism and literature. In its attempt to make sense of the possible connections between novel and nation in the new geopolitical circumstances of the post-British Empire, it is postcolonial studies which has most directly addressed the complex intersection of national and *trans*national imperatives in literature—a "global" dimension to the literary that harkens back to Johann Wolfgang von Goethe's introduction of the term *Weltliteratur* (1827) and Karl Marx and Friedrich Engels' discussion of "world literature" in the *Communist Manifesto* (1848).

The shift from national to transnational or global is at the heart of the conceptual and political contexts addressed by postcolonial studies. Edward Said has argued that there are two moments of nationalist revival in the colonial world. The literature of the first moment, "the period of nationalist anti-imperialism," which extends from the 1930s to 1950s, is characterized above all by "the primacy of the geographical in it,"[11] that is, by the long-assumed linkages between literature and the production of defined and delineated spaces. One function of literature as a political tool in challenging imperialism and colonialism was to represent the fundamental uniqueness and difference of "native" or "local" cultures from European ones—a challenge that constituted an insistence, too, for an independent nation-state reflecting these cultural differences. The very real difficulties in creating postcolonial nations through literary expression—difficulties at once material (low literacy rates in some postcolonial nations, limited opportunities for publishing and circulating texts) and linguistic (multiple language communities creating challenges for widely-shared literary experiences except through English)—meant that even as the attempt was made to write new "imagined communities" into existence, a fundamental critique of the nation-state system began to emerge in postcolonial texts.[12] Suspicions of the nation-state system that enabled and supported colonialism were especially pronounced in postcolonial literature from the 1960s onwards. This second moment Said describes is that of a "liberationist anti-imperial resistance"[13] which goes beyond the limits of the discourse of nationalism to insist on a more profound transformation of imperial relations. In many parts of the decolonizing world, including so-called "settler countries" such as Canada and Australia, the 1960s and 1970s were characterized by anxious cultural nationalisms that saw attempts to belatedly generate national literary and artistic canons where none existed before, both in order to offer support to forms of nationalism already under threat by looming shifts in the geopolitical order and to legitimate new fields of national literary study.[14] However, as Said suggests, during this period contemporary postcolonial literatures, North American and British texts, and diasporic literatures of all kinds written in English were broadly suspicious of the remnants of both nationalist sentiment and the exclusions enacted by cultural nationalisms. It is in part for this reason that Fredric Jameson's claim that third-world texts were necessarily "national allegories" was greeted with such criticism[15]: postcolonial texts were seen to be "beyond" the nation in much the same way as literature in other parts of the world, and identifying them with the nation was seen to characterize them incorrectly as behind the times.

If globalization is the name for the period which follows nationalism—definitively so, with the end of the grand drama of the Cold War and its insistence on clear-cut political and cultural distinctions between the Communist and capitalist world-orders—then it might seem as if there is a natural link between postcolonial criticism and this new discourse about our contemporary political, social, and cultural circumstances: both describe a period in which nationalisms are (supposedly) on the wane and are being replaced by critical attention to processes occurring on a global scale (for instance, the world-wide movement of goods as well as people, the deep and unexpected interconnections of events and places geographically distant from one another, and so forth). However, with few exceptions, postcolonialism and globalization have remained distinct and separated—a situation characteristic of literary studies more generally with respect to the concept of globalization.[16] This might seem surprising given the ubiquity of the concept of globalization across a range of disciplines and, indeed, given the frequent evocation of "global" in conference and book titles. Even so, in the primary discursive form it has taken, globalization seems to have little to do with the shape and character of contemporary literature and literary criticism. For instance, while the categories "postcolonial" or "postmodern" name temporal moments as well as specific literary forms, contents, and histories, "global" or "world" is at best *only* a periodizing category that automatically (and uncritically) includes *all* literature produced since 1989 under its aegis, and at worst is an example of a bad universalism that takes texts translated into English from around the world as a new canon for a new age.

One of the potential difficulties in thinking about the significance of globalization for literary studies is the blizzard of topics, themes, and issues that have circulated around the concept since it began to be used with increasing regularity from the mid-1980s onward. At its core, globalization is intended to capture the absolute uniqueness of present-day experience which separates it definitively from even the immediate past. Fundamental to this difference is the sense of the globe as a single space (epistemologically, phenomenologically) and of the deep interconnections of human life across once geographically and socially distinct spaces; if the novel was key to the generation of the social simultaneity of the nation, the internet and satellite communications are central to the new spatio-temporal experience named globalization—one in which everyone lives in the same time, instead of temporally more advanced ("developed") and belated ("developing") political and cultural spaces. The newness and difference of key developments typically associated with globalization have been challenged by critics from a range of perspectives. For instance, Paul Hirst and Graeme Thompson have reminded us that the degree of international trade was greater at the end of the nineteenth century than at the end of the twentieth, and Stephen Greenblatt and others have echoed Goethe in pointing out that literary and cultural forms have always moved beyond the locales in which they were first produced.[17] While there are certainly reasons to resist the full extent of globalization's claims on naming a present that is heading towards the future in an unalterable way (globalization as another term for the "end of history" named by Francis Fukuyama that comes with the collapse of the Soviet bloc),[18] it does point to new historical circumstances with which literary criticism has to contend.

There are two main ways in which globalization can be seen as having implications for literature and literary criticism. The first and most direct involves the representation of processes, events, and practices associated with globalization *within* contemporary literary texts. This can range from literary treatments of anti-globalization movements (as in Robert Newman's *The Fountain at the Centre of the World*) to the dynamics of finance capital (Don DeLillo's *Cosmopolis*), from post-Cold War conspiracies of power (John Le Carré's *Absolute Friends*) to narratives of terrorism and fundamentalism (Mohsin Hamid's *The Reluctant Fundamentalist*), and also includes the huge number of novels currently dealing with the traumas and dislocations of diasporic movements and imaginings.[19] If all of this varied thematic content—and much more besides—has yet to be seen as being about "globalization," it is because while such fictions address a range of contemporary circumstances, they do so in a way that actively challenges the dominant narratives articulated about the shape of the global present and future. As with nationalism, there is a sense in which globalization is nowhere directly represented in literature in terms of content. Explorations of (for instance) the dynamics of cultural imperialism, or the complexity of living in more intensely hybridized spaces and places newly energized and traumatized by the energies of consumer culture, may well be examples of processes associated with globalization. However, literary treatments of these processes tend to work against their assimilation into an easy, dominant narrative of globalization as an inescapable, authorless process that "lifts all boats" by pulling everyone into capitalism. Literatures addressing contemporary political, social, and cultural circumstances engage with the complexity of the present and deal directly with the very real difficulties of making sense of a world made up of experiences both more intensive and extensive than in the past; in so doing, they interrupt the self-certainties of narratives of globalization that might be used to categorize certain literatures as fictions of globalization.

The second way in which globalization has had an impact on literary studies is through its influence on some of the directions taken by contemporary criticism. Within contemporary literary criticism, the developments and dynamics associated with globalization—including the theoretical contribution of sociological theories dealing with globalization and culture[20]—have found expression in a range of new forms of what might be described as postnationalist theory. Building on developments from within postcolonial theory and criticism, postnationalist theories insist on the need to see literature as transnational—as shaped by material circumstances and forces, ideas, genres, and forms that extend across national, ethnic, and linguistic boundaries. The focus of such theories is not only on a present that has been reshaped by forces such as international trade or the Internet, but on the past of literature as well. In this respect, the new experience of the globe as a single space has helped literary criticism and theory to push beyond the nation as a space within which to frame the production, consumption, and distribution of literature throughout its history. Postnational literary theories have taken various forms: explorations of the impact of the eclipse of the national and the emergence of the global on various national literatures; new attention to the meaning of "world literature" in the context of globalization; attempts to re-imagine and re-invigorate the field of comparative literature; theoretical attention to the concept of cosmopolitanism; interesting attempts to unsettle the certainties of postcolonial theory by reframing "world literature" as "world bank literature"; and investigations of the ways in which literary forms circulate around the globe, both in the longue durée and at present.[21]

The creation of a range of new approaches to literary study over the past decade promises to help us better understand the complex social drama of literature. While criticism of the national as a frame of reference may have been assisted by the transformative energies associated with globalization, the refusal to take up the most popular variants of this latter discourse has ensured that contemporary literature and theory remain crucial spaces for the critical imaginings of our past, present, and futures to come.

Notes

1 Studies of the role played by cultural nationalisms in relation to decolonization struggles include E. Boehmer, *Colonial and Postcolonial Literature: Migrant Metaphors*, New York: Oxford University Press, 1995; B. King, *New National Literatures: Cultural Nationalism in a Changing World*, New York: St. Martin's Press, 1980; N. Lazarus, *Nationalism and Cultural Practice in the Postcolonial World*, Cambridge: Cambridge University Press, 1999; and I. Szeman, *Zones of Instability: Literature, Postcolonialism and the Nation*, Baltimore: Johns Hopkins University Press, 2003.

2 Exceptions include S. Gupta's excellent *Globalization and Literature*, London: Polity, 2009, and S. O'Brien and I. Szeman, "Introduction: The Globalization of Fiction/The Fiction of Globalization," *South Atlantic Quarterly*, 100, 2001, pp. 601–24.

3 See Gupta, *Globalization and Literature*; O'Brien and Szeman, "Introduction"; I. Szeman, "Globalization," in J. Hawley (ed.), *Encyclopedia of Postcolonial Studies*, Westport, CT: Greenwood Press, 2001, pp. 209–17; and I. Szeman, "Globalization," in M. Groden, M. Kreiswirth, and I. Szeman (eds), *The Johns Hopkins Guide to Literary Theory and Criticism*, 2nd edn., Baltimore: Johns Hopkins University Press, 2005, pp. 458–65.

4 For descriptions of the politics of globalization, please see J. Comaroff and J. L. Comaroff, "Millennial Capitalism: First Thoughts on a Second Coming," *Public Culture* 12, 2000, pp. 291–343; N. G. Canclini, *Consumers and Citizens: Globalization and Multicultural Conflicts*, trans. G. Yudice et. al., Minneapolis: University of Minnesota Press, 2001; D. Harvey, *A Brief History of Neoliberalism*, New York: Oxford University Press, 2005; D. Harvey, *The New Imperialism*, New York: Oxford University Press, 2005; and N. Smith, *The Endgame of Globalization*, New York: Routledge, 2005.

5 UNESCO, "UNESCO Universal Declaration on Cultural Diversity," November 2, 2001. Available at: http://unesdoc.unesco.org/images/0012/001271/127160m.pdf. Last accessed February 1, 2008.

6 See B. Rajan, "Imperialism and the Other End of History," *University of Toronto Quarterly*, 73, 2004, pp. 707–24; and I. Baucom, "Globalit, Inc, or The Cultural Logic of Global Literary Studies," *PMLA*, 116, 2001, pp. 158–73.

7 J. G. von Herder, *Outlines of a Philosophy of the History of Man* (1784–1791), trans. T. Churchill, London: Johnson, 1800, p. 166.
8 See, for example, D. Lloyd and P. Thomas, *Culture and the State*, New York: Routledge, 1997, and the work of M. Foucault, including *Society Must Be Defended: Lectures at the Collège de France, 1975–76*, trans. D. Macey, New York: Picador, 2003.
9 Pattee quoted in C. Clausen, "'National Literatures' in English: Toward a New Paradigm," *New Literary History*, 25, 1994, p. 65.
10 See B. Anderson, *Imagined Communities: Reflections on the Origin and Spread of Nationalism*, New York: Verso, 1983; E. Gellner, *Nations and Nationalism*, Oxford: Blackwell, 1983; E. Hobsbawm, *Nations and Nationalism since 1780: Programme, Myth, Reality*, Cambridge: Cambridge University Press, 1990; and A. D. Smith, *The Ethnic Origin of Nations*, New York: Basil Blackwell, 1986.
11 E. Said, "Yeats and Decolonization," in T. Eagleton, F. Jameson, and E. Said (eds), *Nationalism, Colonialism, and Literature*, Minneapolis: University of Minnesota Press, 1990, p. 76.
12 See my exploration of this development in Szeman, *Zones of Instability*.
13 Said, "Yeats and Decolonization," p. 76.
14 See, for example, G. Johnston (ed.), *Australian Literary Criticism*, Melbourne: Oxford University Press, 1974; and R. Lecker, *Making It Real: The Canonization of English-Canadian Literature*, Concord, Ontario: Anansi, 1995.
15 F. Jameson, "Third-World Literature in the Era of Multinational Capitalism," *Social Text*, 15, 1986, pp. 65–88. The most significant criticism of Jameson's essay came from A. Ahmad in *In Theory: Nations, Classes, Literatures*, New York: Verso, 1992. For a reconsideration of Jameson's essay, see I. Szeman, "Who's Afraid of National Allegory? Jameson, Literary Criticism, Globalization," *South Atlantic Quarterly*, 100, 2001, pp. 801–25.
16 The exceptions include S. Gikandi, "Globalization and the Claims of Postcoloniality," *South Atlantic Quarterly* 100, 2001, pp. 627–58; R. Krishnaswamy, "The Criticism of Culture and the Culture of Criticism: At the Intersection of Postcolonialism and Globalization Theory," *Diacritics*, 32, 2002, pp. 106–28; R. Krishnaswamy and J. C. Hawley (eds), *The Postcolonial and the Global*, Minneapolis: University of Minnesota Press, 2007; and B. Rajan, "Imperialism and the Other End of History."
17 S. Greenblatt, "Racial Memory and Literary History," *PMLA*, 116, 2001, pp. 48–63; P. Hirst and G. Thompson, *Globalization in Question: The International Economy and the Possibilities of Governance*, London: Blackwell, 1999.
18 See F. Fukuyama, *The End of History and the Last Man*, Toronto: HarperCollins Canada, 1993.
19 D. DeLillo, *Cosmopolis*, New York: Scribner, 2004; M. Hamid, *The Reluctant Fundamentalist*, New York: Harcourt, 2007; J. Le Carré, *Absolute Friends*, New York: Little Brown and Company, 2005; and R. Newman, *The Fountain at the Centre of the World*, New York: Verso, 2003.
20 Of these, two that have had a particular impact are A. Appadurai, *Modernity at Large: Cultural Dimensions of Globalization*, Minneapolis: University of Minnesota Press, 1996; and J. Tomlinson, *Globalization and Culture*, Chicago: University of Chicago Press, 1999.
21 On the impact of the global on national literatures, see E. Apter, *Continental Drift: From National Characters to Virtual Subjects*, Chicago: University of Chicago Press, 1999; F. Buell, *National Culture and the New Global System*, Baltimore: Johns Hopkins University Press, 1994; and W. C. Dimock and L. Buell (eds), *Shades of the Planet: American Literature as World Literature*, Princeton: Princeton University Press, 2007. Explorations of world literature and

of new approaches to comparative literature include E. Apter, *The Translation Zone: A New Comparative Literature*, Princeton: Princeton University Press, 2005; D. Damrosch, *What Is World Literature?* Princeton: Princeton University Press, 2003; J. Pizer, *The Idea of World Literature: History and Pedagogical Practice*, Baton Rouge: Louisiana State University Press, 2006; C. Prendergast (ed.), *Debating World Literature*, London: Verso, 2004; and the provocative G. C. Spivak, *Death of a Discipline*, New York: Columbia University Press, 2003. On cosmopolitanism, see T. Brennan, "Cosmo-Theory," *South Atlantic Quarterly*, 100, 2001, pp. 659–91; and P. Cheah and B. Robbins (eds), *Cosmopolitics: Thinking and Feeling Beyond the Nation*, Minneapolis: University of Minnesota Press, 1998. The collection by A. Kumar (ed.), *World Bank Literature* (Minneapolis: University of Minnesota Press, 2003), offers an alternative take on the idea of world literature. New approaches to the global circulation of literary forms include P. Casanova, *The World Republic of Letters*, trans. M. B. DeBevoise, Cambridge, MA: Harvard University Press, 2005; and three recent books by F. Moretti: *Modern Epic: The World System from Goethe to García Márquez*, trans. Q. Hoare, London: Verso, 1996; *Atlas of the European Novel, 1800–1900*, New York: Verso, 1999; and *Graphs, Maps, Trees: Abstract Models for a Literary History*, New York: Verso, 2007.

Part IV

BIBLIOGRAPHY FOR PARTS II AND III

BIBLIOGRAPHY

Acton, Lord (1996) "Nationality," in G. Balakrishnan (ed.), *Mapping the Nation*, London: Verso, pp. 17–38.

Adam, G. M. and Wetherald, E. (1887) *An Algonquin Maiden: A Romance of the Early Days of Upper Canada*, Montreal: Lovell.

Adams, J. T. (1921) *The Founding of New England*, New York: Atlantic Monthly Press.

Ahmad, A. (1992) *In Theory: Nations, Classes, Literatures*, New York: Verso.

"American Memory" collection of the Library of Congress. Online. Available at: <http://memory.loc.gov/ammem/index.html>.

Anderson, B. (1983, 1991) *Imagined Communities: Reflections on the Origin and Spread of Nationalism*, London: Verso.

Angers, F.-R. (2003) *Les révélations du crime, ou Cambray et ses complices: chroniques canadiennes de 1834*, Quebec, QC: Nota Bene.

Anon. (1841) "The Literature of a New Country," *The Monthly Review*, 1, pp. 59–61.

Appadurai, A. (1996) *Modernity at Large: Cultural Dimensions of Globalization*, Minneapolis: University of Minnesota Press.

Apter, E. (1999) *Continental Drift: From National Characters to Virtual Subjects*, Chicago: University of Chicago Press.

—— (2005) *The Translation Zone: A New Comparative Literature*, Princeton: Princeton University Press.

Arnold, M. (1949) *The Portable Matthew Arnold*, L. Trilling (ed.), New York: Viking.

Atwood, M. (1982) *Second Words: Selected Critical Prose*, Boston: Beacon Press.

Aubert de Gaspé, P. (1993) *Les Anciens Canadiens*, Montreal: Fides.

—— (1996a) *Canadians of Old*, trans. J. Brierley, Montreal: Véhicule.

—— (1996b) *L'Influence d'un livre, ou Le chercheur des trésors*, Montreal: Boréal.

Axton, M. (1977) *The Queen's Two Bodies: Drama and the Elizabethan Succession*, London: Royal Historical Society.

Backscheider, P. (1989) *Daniel Defoe: His Life*, Baltimore: Johns Hopkins University Press.

Barbauld, A. L. (2002) *Anna Letitia Barbauld: Selected Poetry and Prose*, W. McCarthy and E. Kraft (eds), Peterborough, ON: Broadview Press.

Barker, E. (1971) *Oliver Cromwell and the English People*, Freeport, NY: Books for Libraries Press.

Barr, R. (1899) "Canadian literature," *The Canadian Magazine*, 14, pp. 3–7.
—— (1993) *The Influence of a Book*, trans. C. Rothman, Montreal: R. Davies.
Baucom, I. (2001) "Globalit, Inc., or The Cultural Logic of Global Literary Studies," *PMLA*, 116, pp. 158–73.
Baym, N. (1984) *Novels, Readers, and Reviewers: Responses to Fiction in Antebellum America*, Ithaca: Cornell University Press.
Behrendt, S. C. (1986) "'The Consequence of High Powers': Blake, Shelley, and Prophecy's Public Dimension," *Papers on Language and Literature*, 22, pp. 254–75.
Beik, W. (1985) *Absolutism and Society in Seventeenth-Century France: State Power and Provincial Aristocracy in Languedoc*, Cambridge: Cambridge University Press.
Bell, D. A. (2001) *The Cult of the Nation in France: Inventing Nationalism, 1680–1800*, Cambridge, MA: Harvard University Press.
Bentley, D. M. R. (1986) Introduction, *Abram's Plains: A Poem* by T. Cary, London, ON: Canadian Poetry Press, pp. xi–xlviii.
Bevington, D. (1968) *Tudor Drama and Politics: A Critical Approach to Topical Meaning*, Cambridge, MA: Harvard University Press.
Bhabha, H. K. (1994) *The Location of Culture*, New York: Routledge.
The Bible and Holy Scriptures Conteyned in the Olde and Newe Testament (1560), Geneva.
Blake, W. (1988) *Complete Poetry and Prose of William Blake*, D. V. Erdman (ed.), New York: Doubleday.
Blanning, T. C. W. (2003) *The Culture of Power and the Power of Culture: Old Regime Europe 1660–1789*, Oxford: Oxford University Press.
Boehmer, E. (1995) *Colonial and Postcolonial Literature: Migrant Metaphors*, New York: Oxford University Press.
Bolton, C. (2003) "*Thalaba the Destroyer*: Southey's Nationalist Romance," *Romanticism on the Net*, 32–33.
Boucherville, G. B. de (1973) *Une de perdue, deux de trouvées*, Montreal: Hurtubise HMH.
Bourassa, N. (1976) *Jacques et Marie: Souvenirs d'un peuple dispersé*, Montreal: Fides.
Bowers, T. N. (1997) "Reconstituting the National Body in Smollett's *Travels through France and Italy*," *Eighteenth-Century Life*, 21, pp. 1–25.
Bradford, W. (1952) *Of Plymouth Plantation, 1620–1647: The Complete Text*, S. E. Morison (ed. and intro.), New York: Alfred A. Knopf.
Brennan, T. (2001) "Cosmo-Theory," *South Atlantic Quarterly*, 100, pp. 659–91.
Breuilly, J. (1982, 1993) *Nationalism and the State*, Manchester: Manchester University Press.
Brewer, J. (1989) *The Sinews of Power: War, Money, and the English State, 1688–1783*, New York: Knopf.
Brierley, J. (trans.) (1996) *Canadians of Old*, Montreal: Véhicule.
Brockden Brown, C. (1799a) *Arthur Mervyn or, Memoirs of the Year 1793: With Related Texts*, P. Barnard and S. Shapiro (eds), Indianapolis: Hackett, 2008.
—— (1799b) *Edgar Huntley; or, Memoirs of a Sleep-Walker*, N. S. Grabo (ed.), Harmondsworth: Penguin, 1988.
Brooke, F. (2001) *The History of Emily Montague*, Ottawa: Tecumseh.
Buell, F. (1994) *National Culture and the New Global System*, Baltimore: Johns Hopkins University Press.

Buell, L. (1986) *New England Literary Culture: From Revolution through Renaissance*, Cambridge: Cambridge University Press.

Burgett, B. (1998) *Sentimental Bodies: Sex, Gender, and Citizenship in the Early Republic*, Princeton: Princeton University Press.

Burrough, E. (1661) *A Declaration of the Sad and Great Persecution of Martyrdom of the People of God, Called Quakers, in New-England*, London.

Cabajsky, A. (2005) "The National Tale from Ireland to French Canada: Putting Generic Incentive into a New Perspective," *Canadian Journal of Irish Studies*, 31, pp. 31–45.

—— (2009 forthcoming) "Catholic Gothic: Atavism, Orientalism, and Generic Change in Charles de Guise's *Le Cap au diable* (1863)," in C. Sugars (ed.), *Unsettled Remains: Canadian Literature and the Postcolonial Gothic*, Waterloo, ON: Wilfrid Laurier University Press.

Cain, T. H. (1978) *Praise in "The Faerie Queene,"* Lincoln: University of Nebraska Press.

Canclini, N. G. (2001) *Consumers and Citizens: Globalization and Multicultural Conflicts*, trans. G. Yudice et al., Minneapolis: University of Minnesota Press.

Carlyle, T. (1840) *Chartism*, London: James Fraser.

Cartier, J. (1986) *Relations*, Montreal: Presses de l'Université de Montréal.

Cary, T. (1789) *Abram's Plains: A Poem*, London, ON: Canadian Poetry Press, 1986.

Casanova, P. (2005) *The World Republic of Letters*, trans. M. B. DeBevoise, Cambridge, MA: Harvard University Press.

Casgrain, H.-R. (1876) *Légendes canadiennes*, Quebec: A. Côté.

Chatterjee, P. (1993) *The Nation and Its Fragments*, Princeton: Princeton University Press.

Chauveau, P.-J.-O. (1978) *Charles Guérin: Roman de mœurs canadiennes*, Montreal: Fides.

Cheah, P. and B. Robbins (eds) (1998) *Cosmopolitics: Thinking and Feeling beyond the Nation*, Minneapolis: University of Minnesota Press.

Christie, R. (1848–1866) *A History of the Late Province of Lower Canada*, Quebec: Thomas Cary.

Clark, S. (2006) "*Jerusalem* as Imperial Prophecy," in S. Clark and D. Worrall (eds), *Blake, Nation and Empire*, New York: Palgrave Macmillan, pp. 167–85.

Clarke, J. (1652) *Ill Newes from New-England, or, A Nar[r]ative of New-Englands Persecution Wherin Is Declared That While Old England Is Becoming New, New-England Is Become Old*, London.

Clausen, C. (1994) "'National Literatures' in English: Toward a New Paradigm," *New Literary History*, 25, pp. 61–72.

Coffey, J. (1998) "Puritanism and Liberty Revisited: The Case for Toleration in the English Revolution," *The Historical Journal*, 41.4, pp. 961–85.

Coleman, D. (2001) "The National Allegory of Fraternity: Loyalist Literature and the Making of Canada's White British Origins," *Journal of Canadian Studies*, 36, pp. 131–56.

Coleridge, S. T. (1997) *Coleridge: The Complete Poems*, W. Keach (ed.), New York: Penguin.

Colley, L. (1992) *Britons: Forging the Nation, 1707–1837*, New Haven: Yale University Press.

Collinson, P. (1997) "Biblical Rhetoric: The English Nation and National Sentiment in the Prophetic Mode," in C. McEachern and D. Shuger (eds), *Religion and Culture in Renaissance England*, Cambridge: Cambridge University Press, pp. 15–45.

Comaroff, J. and Comaroff, J. L. (2000) "Millennial Capitalism: First Thoughts on a Second Coming," *Public Culture*, 12, pp. 291–343.

Conan, L. (1951) *À l'œuvre et à l'épreuve*, Montreal: Beauchemin, 1951.

Conrad, M. (2002) "Historiography," in W. H. New (ed.), *Encyclopedia of Literature in Canada*, Toronto: University of Toronto Press, pp. 499–503.

Corse, S. M. (1997) *Nationalism and Literature: The Politics of Culture in Canada and the United States*, Chicago: University of Chicago Press.

Corse, S. M. and Griffin, M. (1997) "Cultural Valorization and African-American Literary History: Re-Constructing the Canon," *Sociological Forum*, 12, pp. 173–203.

Corse, S. M. and Westervelt, S. D. (2002) "Gender and Literary Valorization: The Awakening of a Canonical Novel," *Sociological Perspectives*, 45, pp. 139–61.

Crémazie, O. (1972) *Oeuvres*, Ottawa: University of Ottawa Press.

Cromwell, O. (1970) *The Writings and Speeches of Oliver Cromwell*, W. C. Abbott (ed.), 4 vols, New York: Russell & Russell.

Damrosch, D. (2003) *What Is World Literature?* Princeton: Princeton University Press.

Danforth, S. (1671) *A Brief Recognition of New-Englands Errand into the Wilderness; Made . . . at Boston in N. E.*, Cambridge, MA.

Darby, W. J. (2000) *Landscape and Identity: Geographies of Nation and Class in England*, New York: Berg.

Davidson, C. (2004) *Revolution and the Word: The Rise of the Novel in America*, rev. edn, New York: Oxford University Press.

Davis, T. (1846, 1998) *Literary and Historical Essays*, Washington: Woodstock Books.

Dean, J. (ed.) (1991) *Six Ecclesiastical Satires*, Kalamazoo: Medieval Institute Publications.

Deane, S. (1986) *A Short History of Irish Literature*, Notre Dame: University of Notre Dame Press.

de Crèvecoeur, H. St. J. (1782) *Letters from an American Farmer*, A. E. Stone (ed.), Harmondsworth: Penguin, 1986.

de Saint-Maurice, F. (1872), *Madeleine Bouvart*, *L'Opinion publique* 3.14 (April 4, 1872).

Defoe, D. (1843) *The Works of Daniel De Foe*, Vol. III, London: John Clements.

—— (1726) *The Complete English Tradesman* (Letter III), in J. T. Boulton (ed.), *Daniel Defoe*, New York: Schocken Books, 1965, pp. 227–38.

—— (1724–1726) *A Tour Thro' the Whole Island of Great Britain*, London: Frank Cass, 1968.

Dekker, G. (1987) *The American Historical Romance*, Cambridge: Cambridge University Press.

DeLillo, D. (2004) *Cosmopolis*, New York: Scribner.

de Mille, J. (1874) *The Lily and the Cross: A Tale of Acadia*, Boston: Lee and Shepherd.

DeNora, T. (1991) "Musical Patronage and Social Change in Beethoven's Vienna," *American Journal of Sociology*, 97, pp. 310–46.

De Quincey, T. (2009) *Confessions of an English Opium-Eater*, J. Faflak (ed.), Peterborough, ON: Broadview Press.

Devereux, C. (2001) "'One Firm Body': 'Britishness and Otherness' in *The History of Emily Montague*," in L. Moss (ed.), *The History of Emily Montague by F. Brooke*, Ottawa: Tecumseh, pp. 459–76.

Dimock, W. C. and Buell, L. (eds) (2007) *Shades of the Planet: American Literature as World Literature*, Princeton: Princeton University Press.

Dominguez, V. R. (1992) "Invoking Culture: The Messy Side of 'Cultural Politics,'" *South Atlantic Quarterly*, 91, pp. 19–42.

Doran, S. (1995) *Monarchy and Matrimony: Courtships of Elizabeth I*, London: Routledge.

Dostaler, Y. (1977) *Les infortunes du roman dans le Québec du XIXe siècle*, Montreal: Hurtubise HMH.

Doutre, J. (1969) *Les fiancés de 1812; essai de littérature canadienne*, Montreal: Réédition Québec.

Duncan-Jones, K. (1991) *Sir Philip Sidney: Courtier Poet*, London: Hamish Hamilton.

Durham, J. G. (1963) *Lord Durham's Report: An Abridgement of Report on the Affairs of British North America*, G. M. Craig (ed.), Toronto: McClelland.

Eley, G. and Suny, R. C. (1996) "Introduction," in G. Eley and R. C. Suny (eds), *Becoming National: A Reader*, Oxford: Oxford University Press, pp. 3–37.

Evans, J. M. (1996) *Milton's Imperial Epic: "Paradise Lost" and the Discourse of Colonialism*, Ithaca: Cornell University Press.

Ferland, J.-B.-A. (1882) *Cours d'histoire du Canada*, Quebec: Hardy.

Firth, K. R. (1979) *The Apocalyptic Tradition in Reformation Britain, 1530–1645*, Oxford: Oxford University Press.

Fliegelman, J. (1985) *Prodigals and Pilgrims: The American Revolution against Patriarchal Authority 1750–1800*, Cambridge: Cambridge University Press.

Foucault, M. (1979) *Discipline and Punish: The Birth of the Prison*, trans. Alan Sheridan, New York: Vintage, 1975.

—— (2003) *Society Must Be Defended: Lectures at the Collège de France, 1975–76*, trans. David Macey, New York: Picador.

Franklin, B. (1986) *The Autobiography and Other Writings*, K. Silverman (ed.), Harmondsworth: Penguin.

Fukuyama, F. (1993) *The End of History and the Last Man*, Toronto: HarperCollins Canada.

Garneau, F.-X. (1996) *L'Histoire du Canada depuis la découverte jusqu'à nos jours*, Montreal: Bibliothèque québécoise.

Gellner, E. (1983, 2005) *Nations and Nationalism*, Ithaca: Cornell University Press; Oxford and Malden: Blackwell; 2nd edn., Blackwell.

—— (1994) *Encounters with Nationalism*, Oxford: Blackwell.

Gerson, C. (1989) *A Purer Taste: The Writing and Reading of Fiction in English in Nineteenth-Century Canada*, Toronto: University of Toronto Press.

Gibson, J. (1838) "The Hermit of Saint Maurice," *Literary Garland*, 1, pp. 5–15.

Giddens, A. (1981, 1987a) *A Contemporary Critique of Historical Materialism: Vol. 1 Power, Property and State*, Berkeley: University of California Press.

—— (1987b) *The Nation-State and Violence: Volume Two of a Contemporary Critique of Historical Materialism*, Berkeley: University of California Press.

Gikandi, S. (2001) "Globalization and the Claims of Postcoloniality," *South Atlantic Quarterly*, 100, pp. 627–58.

Goddu, T. A. (1997) *Gothic America: Narrative, History, and Nation*, New York: Columbia University Press.

Greenblatt, S. (1980) *Renaissance Self-Fashioning from More to Shakespeare*, Chicago: Chicago University Press.

—— (2001) "Racial Memory and Literary History," *PMLA*, 116, pp. 48–63.

Greenfeld, L. (1992) *Nationalism: Five Roads to Modernity*, Cambridge, MA: Harvard University Press.

Gregerson, L. (1999) "Colonials Write the Nation," in B. Rajan and E. Sauer (eds), *Milton and Imperial Vision*, Pittsburgh: Duquesne University Press, pp. 169–90.

Griswold, W. (1992) "The Writing on the Mud Wall: Nigerian Novels and the Imaginary Village," *American Sociological Review*, 57, pp. 709–24.

Guibbory, A. (2008) "England, Israel, and the Jews in Milton's Prose, 1649–1660," in D. A. Brooks (ed.), *Milton and the Jews*, Cambridge: Cambridge University Press, pp. 1–34.

Guillory, J. (1993) *Cultural Capital: The Problem of Literary Canon Formation*, Chicago: Chicago University Press.

Gupta, S. (2009) *Globalization and Literature*, London: Polity.

Habermas, J. (1989) *The Structural Transformation of the Public Sphere: An Inquiry into a Category of Bourgeois Society*, trans. T. Burger with F. Lawrence, Cambridge, MA: MIT Press.

Hadfield, A. (1994) *Literature, Politics and National Identity: Reformation to Renaissance*, Cambridge: Cambridge University Press.

—— (1997) *Spenser's Irish Experience: Wilde Fruyt and Salvage Soyl*, Oxford: Clarendon Press.

—— (2005) *Shakespeare and Republicanism*, Cambridge: Cambridge University Press.

Hale, J. (1996) "England as Israel in Milton's Writings," *Early Modern Library Studies*, 2:2, 3:1–54.

Haliburton, T. C. (1995) *The Clockmaker: Series One, Two and Three*, Ottawa: Carleton University Press.

Haller, W. (1963) *Foxe's Book of Martyrs and the Elect Nation*, London: Jonathan Cape.

Halpenny, F. G. (1966) *Dictionary of Canadian Biography*, vol. 6, Toronto: University of Toronto Press

Hamid, M. (2007) *The Reluctant Fundamentalist*, New York: Harcourt.

Harley, J. B. (1983) "Meaning and Ambiguity in Tudor Cartography," in S. Tyacke (ed.), *English Map-Making 1500–1650*, London: British Library, pp. 22–45.

Harrington, J. (1659) *Aphorisms Political*, in D. M. Wolfe (ed.) (1953–1982), *Complete Prose Works of John Milton*, 8 vols, New Haven: Yale University Press, vol. 7, pp. 518–21.

Hart, J. B. (1978) *St. Ursula's Convent: or, The Nun of Canada. Containing Scenes from Real Life*, Sackville, NB: Ralph Pickard Bell Library.

Harvey, D. (2005a) *A Brief History of Neoliberalism*, New York: Oxford University Press.

—— (2005b) *The New Imperialism*, New York: Oxford University Press.

Hastings, A. (1997, 1999) *The Construction of Nationhood: Ethnicity, Religion and Nationalism*, Cambridge: Cambridge University Press.

Helgerson, R. (1992) *Forms of Nationhood: The Elizabethan Writing of England*, Chicago: Chicago University Press.

Hemans, F. (2002) *Felicia Hemans: Selected Poems, Prose and Letters*, G. Kelly (ed.), Peterborough, ON: Broadview Press.
Herder, J. G.[von] (1800) *Outlines of a Philosophy of the History of Man* (1784–1791), trans. T. Churchill, London: J. Johnson.
Hickey, D. (1884) *William and Mary: A Tale of the Siege of Louisbourg, 1745*, Toronto: William Briggs.
Hill, C. (1986) "The Protestant Nation," in *The Collected Essays of Christopher Hill, Volume II: Religion and Politics in Seventeenth Century England*, Brighton: Harvester Press, pp. 21–36.
—— (1993) *The English Bible and the Seventeenth-Century Revolution*, London: Penguin.
Hirst, P. and Thompson, G. (1999) *Globalization in Question: The International Economy and the Possibilities of Governance*, London: Blackwell.
Hobsbawm, E. J. (1990, 1997) *Nations and Nationalism since 1780: Programme, Myth, Reality*, New York and Cambridge: Cambridge University Press.
Hubbell, J. B. (1972) *Who Are the Major American Writers? A Study of the Changing Literary Canon*, Durham, NC: Duke University Press.
Hughes, E. (1856) *Select Specimens of English Poetry*, London: Longman, Brown, Green, and Longmans.
Huston, J. (1848–1850) *Le Répertoire national, ou Recueil de littérature canadienne*, Montreal: Lovell, Gibson.
Huxley, A. (1959) *Texts and Pretexts*, London: Chatto & Windus.
Huyghue, D. (1977) *Argimou: A Legend of the Micmac*, Sackville, NB: Ralph Pickard Bell Library.
Jameson, F. (1986) "Third-World Literature in the Era of Multinational Capitalism," *Social Text*, 15, pp. 65–88.
Jennings, C. (1855) *The White Rose in Acadia*, Halifax: Bowes.
Johnston, G. (ed.) (1974) *Australian Literary Criticism*, Melbourne: Oxford University Press.
Kalter, S. (2006) *Benjamin Franklin, Pennsylvania, and the First Nations: The Treaties of 1736–62*, Chicago: University of Illinois Press.
Kantorowicz, E. H. (1957, 1970) *The King's Two Bodies: A Study in Mediaeval Political Theory*, Princeton: Princeton University Press.
Kedourie, E. (1960, 1993) *Nationalism*, Oxford: Blackwell.
Keeble, N. H. (1987) *Literary Culture of Nonconformity in Later Seventeenth-Century England*, Leicester: Leicester University Press.
Kelly, J. (1998) Introduction, *Literary and Historical Essays by T. Davis*, Washington: Woodstock Books.
Kerber, L. K. (1980, 1997) *Women of the Republic: Intellect and Ideology in Revolutionary America*, Chapel Hill: University of North Carolina Press.
Kidd, C. (1999) *British Identities before Nationalism: Ethnicity and Nationhood in the Atlantic World, 1600–1800*, Cambridge: Cambridge University Press.
King, B. (1980) *New National Literatures: Cultural Nationalism in a Changing World*, New York: St. Martin's Press.
Kingsford, W. (1898) *The History of Canada*, Toronto: Rowsell and Hutchison.
Kirby, W. (1877) *The Golden Dog: A Romance of the Days of Louis Quinze in Quebec*, Montreal: The Montreal News Co.

Kohn, H. (1967, 2005) *The Idea of Nationalism: A Study in its Origins*, New York: Transaction Books.

Krishnaswamy, R. (2002) "The Criticism of Culture and the Culture of Criticism: At the Intersection of Postcolonialism and Globalization Theory," *Diacritics*, 32, pp. 106–28.

Krishnaswamy, R. and Hawley, J. C. (eds) (2007) *The Postcolonial and the Global*, Minneapolis: University of Minnesota Press.

Kumar, A. (ed.) (2003) *World Bank Literature*, Minneapolis: University of Minnesota Press.

Lacombe, P. (1981) *La terre paternelle*, Montreal: Fides.

Lajoie, A.-G. (1977) *Jean Rivard, le détricheur (récit de la vie réelle) suivi de Jean-Rivard économiste*, Montreal: Hurtubise HMH.

Lander, J. (1997) "Foxe's *Book of Martyrs*: Printing and Popularizing the *Acts and Monuments*," in C. McEachern and D. Shuger (eds), *Religion and Culture in Renaissance England*, Cambridge: Cambridge University Press, pp. 69–92.

Langford, P. (1989) *A Polite and Commercial People: England 1727–1783*, Oxford: Oxford University Press.

Lareau, E. (1874) *Histoire de la littérature canadienne*, Montreal: Lovell.

Larkin, J. F. (ed.) (1991) *The Trial of William Drennan*, Dublin: Irish Academic Press.

Lazarus, E. (1876) "The New Colossus," Liberty State Park website, Statue of Liberty National Monument. Accessed November 21, 2007. http://www.libertystatepark.com/emma.htm.

Lazarus, N. (1999) *Nationalism and Cultural Practice in the Postcolonial World*, Cambridge: Cambridge University Press.

Lease, B. (1981) *Anglo-American Encounters: England and the Rise of American Literature*, Cambridge: Cambridge University Press.

Le Carré, J. (2005) *Absolute Friends*, New York: Little Brown and Company.

Lecker, R. (1990) "The Canonization of Canadian Literature: An Inquiry into Value," *Critical Inquiry*, 16, pp. 656–71.

—— (1995) *Making It Real: The Canonization of English-Canadian Literature*, Concord, ON: Anansi.

—— (2007) syllabus on McGill University website, September 27, 2008. Available at: <http://www.arts.mcgill.ca/programs/english/courses/ENGL333.html.>

Lemire, M. (1970) *Les grands thèmes nationalistes du roman historique canadien-français*, Quebec: Presses de l'Université Laval.

Leprohon, R. (1868) *Armand Durand; or, A Promise Fulfilled*, Montreal: Lovell.

—— (1985) *The Manor House of De Villerai*, rpt. *Journal of Canadian Fiction*, no. 34.

—— (1989) *Antoinette de Mirecourt, or, Secret Marrying and Secret Sorrowing: A Canadian Tale*, Ottawa: Carleton University Press.

Lescarbot, M. (1927) *The Theatre of Neptune in New France*, Boston: Mifflin.

Lesperance, J. T. (1877) *The Bastonnais: A Tale of the American Invasion of Canada 1775, 1776*, Montreal: Lovell.

Levine, L. (1988) *Highbrow/Lowbrow: The Emergence of Cultural Hierarchy in America*, Cambridge, MA: Harvard University Press.

L'Incarnation, M. de. (1962) *Textes choisis et presentés par Marie-Emmanuel Chabot*, Montreal: Fides.

Lloyd, D. (1987) *Nationalism and Minor Literature: James Clarence Mangan and the Emergence of Irish Cultural Nationalism*, Berkeley: University of California Press.

Lloyd, D. and Thomas, P. (1997) *Culture and the State*, New York: Routledge.

Loewenstein, D. and Stevens, P. (eds) (2008) *Early Modern Nationalism and Milton's England*, Toronto: University of Toronto Press.

Loughran, T. (2007) *The Republic in Print: Print Culture in the Age of US Nation Building*, New York: Columbia University Press.

Lowance, M. I. (1981) *The Language of Canaan: Metaphor and Symbol in New England from the Puritans to the Transcendentalists*, Cambridge, MA: Harvard University Press.

Lyly, J. (1580) *Euphues*, in R. W. Bond (ed.), *The Complete Works of John Lyly*, 3 vols, Oxford: Clarendon Press, 1967, vol. 2, pp. 1–228.

MacCarthy, D. F. (2008) "A Walk by the Bay of Dublin," in J. M. Wright (ed.), *Irish Literature, 1750–1900: An Anthology*, Oxford: Blackwell, pp. 433–35.

Macdonell, B. (1898) *Diane of Ville-Marie: A Romance of French Canada*, Toronto: William Briggs.

Machar, A. M. (1895) *The Heir of Fairmount Grange*, London: Digby Long.

Mack, P. (2002) *Elizabethan Rhetoric: Theory and Practice*, Cambridge: Cambridge University Press.

MacLennan, H. (2003) *Two Solitudes*, Toronto: MacClelland and Stewart.

Maclulich, T. D. (1987) "Thematic Criticism, Literary Nationalism, and the Critic's New Clothes," *Essays on Canadian Writing*, 35, pp. 16–36.

Maley, W. (1994) *A Spenser Chronology*, Basingstoke: Macmillan.

—— (2003) *Nation, State, and Empire in English Renaissance Literature: Shakespeare to Milton*, New York: Palgrave.

Mann, Charles C. (2005) *1491: New Revelations of the Americas before Columbus*, New York: Knopf.

Marmette, J. (1870) *François de Bienville, scènes de la vie canadienne au XVIIe siècle*, Quebec: Brousseau.

—— (1872) *L'Intendant Bigot*, Montreal: Desbarats.

—— (1873) *Le Chevalier de Mornac, chronique de la Nouvelle France, 1664*, Montreal: L'Opinion publique.

—— (1875) "La Fiancée du rebelle, épisode de la guerre des Bostonnais," *Revue canadienne*, 12.

—— (1954) *Charles et Eva*, Montreal: Éditions Lumen.

Matthews, S. (1998) "Jerusalem and Nationalism," in J. Lucas (ed.), *William Blake*, New York: Longman, pp. 80–100.

McClintock, A. (1996) "'No Longer in a Future Heaven': Nationalism, Gender, and Race," in G. Eley and R. C. Suny (eds), *Becoming National: A Reader*, Oxford: Oxford University Press, pp. 260–84.

McCrone, D. (1992) *Understanding Scotland: The Sociology of a Stateless Nation*, London: Routledge.

McDiarmid, J. F. (ed.) (2007) *The Monarchical Republic of Early Modern England: Essays in Response to Patrick Collinson*, Aldershot: Ashgate.

McEachern, C. (1996, 2006) *The Poetics of English Nationhood, 1590–1612*, Cambridge: Cambridge University Press.

—— (2002) "Literature and National Identity," in D. Loewenstein and J. Mueller (eds), *The Cambridge History of Early Modern English Literature*, Cambridge: Cambridge University Press, pp. 313–42.

McGee, T. D. (1845) *Historical Sketches of O'Connell and his Friends, with a Glance at the Future Destiny of Ireland*, 3rd edn., Boston: Donahoe and Rohan.

McKenna, J. W. (1982) "How God Became an Englishman," in D. J. Guth and J. W. McKenna (eds), *Tudor Rule and Revolution: Essays for G. R. Elton from His American Friends*, Cambridge: Cambridge University Press, pp. 25–43.

McKinnon, W. C. (1850) *St. Castine. A Legend of Cape-Breton*, Sydney, NS: Cape Breton Herald.

—— (1852) *St. George; or, The Canadian League. A Tale of the Outbreak of 1837*, Halifax: Fuller.

McLane, P. E. (1961) *Spenser's Shepheardes Calender: A Study in Elizabethan Allegory*, Notre Dame: Notre Dame University Press.

McMullen, J. M. (1868) *The History of Canada from Its First Discovery to the Present Time*, Brockville, ON: McMullen and Co.

Mill, J. S. (1966) *On Liberty; Representative Government; Subjection of Women: Three Essays by John Stuart Mill*, London: Oxford University Press.

Miller, P. (1956) *Errand into the Wilderness*, Cambridge, MA: Harvard University Press.

Milton, J. (1953–1982) *Complete Prose Works of John Milton*, D. M. Wolfe (ed.), 8 vols, New Haven: Yale University Press.

—— (1957) *Paradise Lost*, in *John Milton: Complete Poems and Major Prose*, M. Y. Hughes (ed.), New York: Macmillan, pp. 207–469.

Moretti, F. (1996) *Modern Epic: The World System from Goethe to García Márquez*, trans. Q. Hoare, London: Verso.

—— (1999) *Atlas of the European Novel, 1800–1900*, New York: Verso.

—— (2007) *Graphs, Maps, Trees: Abstract Models for a Literary History*, New York: Verso.

Morgan, H. J. (1867) *Bibliotheca Canadensis: or, A Manual of Canadian Literature.* Online. Available Early Canadiana Online Ebook Collection: <http://www.canadiana.org/ ECO/mtq?doc=11068>.

Morrison, T. (1992) *Playing in the Dark: Whiteness and the Literary Imagination*, Cambridge, MA: Harvard University Press.

Mount, N. (2005) *When Canadian Literature Moved to New York*, Toronto: University of Toronto Press.

Newman, G. (1997) *The Rise of English Nationalism: A Cultural History 1740–1830*, rev. ed., New York: St. Martin's Press.

Newman, R. (2003) *The Fountain at the Centre of the World*, New York: Verso.

O'Brien, S. and Szeman, I. (2001) "Introduction: The Globalization of Fiction/The Fiction of Globalization," *South Atlantic Quarterly*, 100, pp. 601–24.

O'Callaghan, M. (2000) *The "Shepheardes Nation": Jacobean Spenserians and Early Stuart Political Culture, 1612–1625*, Oxford: Clarendon Press.

"Ode to Glendwr" (1784) in E. Jones, *Musical and Poetical Relicks of the Welsh Bards*, London: printed for the author, pp. 21–24.

O'Neil, D. J. (1989) "The Cult of Self-Sacrifice: The Irish Experience," *Éire-Ireland*, 24, pp. 89–105.

Ong, W. J. (1958) *Ramus, Method, and the Decay of Dialogue: From the Art of Discourse to the Art of Reason*, Cambridge, MA: Harvard University Press.

Ormond, C. (1846) "Canadian Legends. 1. The Ruined Cottage," *Literary Garland*, 4, pp. 177–79.

Owenson, S. (1807) *Lay of an Irish Harp*, Philadelphia: T. S. Manning.

Parker, G. (1895) *The Trail of the Sword*, New York: Scribner.

—— (1896) *The Seats of the Mighty*, New York: Scribner.

Pawson, E. (1977) *Transport and Economy: The Turnpike Roads of Eighteenth-Century Britain*, London: Academic Press.

Perkins, P. (2003) "Imagining Eighteenth-Century Quebec: British Literature and Colonial Rhetoric," in L. Moss (ed.), *Is Canada Postcolonial? Unsettling Canadian Literature*, Waterloo, ON: Wilfrid Laurier University Press, pp. 151–61.

Pizer, J. (2006) *The Idea of World Literature: History and Pedagogical Practice*, Baton Rouge: Louisiana State University Press.

Porter, R. (1982) *English Society in the Eighteenth Century*, Harmondsworth: Penguin.

Pratt, L. (2001) "Patriot Poetics and the Romantic National Epic: Placing and Displacing Southey's *Joan of Arc*," in P. J. Kitson (ed.), *Placing and Displacing Romanticism*, Aldershot: Ashgate, pp. 88–105.

Prendergast, C. (ed.) (2004) *Debating World Literature*, London: Verso.

Quinn, D. B., Quinn, A., and Hillier, S. (eds) (1979) *New American World: A Documentary History of North America to 1612*, 5 vols, London: Macmillan.

Quint, D. (1993) *Epic and Empire: Politics and Generic Form from Virgil to Milton*, Princeton: Princeton University Press.

Quitslund, B. (2008) *The Reformation in Rhyme: Sternhold, Hopkins, and the English Metrical Psalter, 1547–1603*, Aldershot: Ashgate.

Ragussis, M. (2000) "Jews and Other 'Outlandish Englishmen': Ethnic Performance and the Invention of British Identity under the Georges," *Critical Inquiry*, 26, pp. 773–97.

Raimon, E. A. (2004) *The "Tragic Mulatta" Revisited: Race and Nationalism in Nineteenth-Century Antislavery Fiction*, New Brunswick, NJ: Rutgers University Press.

Rajan, B. (2004) "Imperialism and the Other End of History," *University of Toronto Quarterly*, 73, pp. 707–24.

Raymond, J. (1996) *The Invention of the Newspaper: English Newsbooks, 1641–1649*, Oxford: Clarendon Press.

Renan, E. (1888) "What is a Nation?" trans. M. Thom, in H. K. Bhabha (ed.), *Nation and Narration*, London: Routledge, 1990, pp. 8–22.

Richards, J. (2003) *Rhetoric and Courtliness in Early Modern Literature*, Cambridge: Cambridge University Press.

Richardson, J. (1983) *Wacousta, or The Prophecy: A Tale of the Canadas*, Ottawa: Carleton University Press.

Richardson, R. L. (1903) *Colin of the Ninth Concession*, Toronto: Morang.

Roberts, C. G. D. (1894) *The Raid from Beauséjour*, Boston: Lamson Wolffe.

—— (1897) *A History of Canada*, Boston: Lamson Wolffe.

—— (1898) *A Sister to Evangeline. Being the Story of Yvonne de Lamourie*, Boston: Lamson Wolffe.

Rogers, B. (2003) *Beef and Liberty: Roast Beef, John Bull, and English Liberty*, London: Chatto & Windus.

Rosenblatt, J. (1990) "Eden, Israel, England: Milton's Spiritual Geography," in

J. McVeagh (ed.), *All before Them: Attitudes to Abroad in English Literature 1660–1780*, London: Ashfield, pp. 49–63.

Ross, M. B. (1991) "Romancing the Nation-State: The Poetics of Romantic Nationalism," in J. Arac and H. Ritvo (eds), *Macropolitics of Nineteenth-Century Literature: Nationalism, Exoticism, Imperialism*, Philadelphia: University of Pennsylvania Press, pp. 56–85.

Ruland, R. (ed.) (1972) *The Native Muse: Theories of American Literature*, vol. I, New York: E. P. Dutton & Co.

Rummel, R. J. (1994) *Death by Government.* New Brunswick, NJ: Transaction Publishers.

Russell, J. (1977) *Matilda; or, The Indian's Captive: A Canadian Tale Founded on Fact*, New York: Garland.

Sadlier, M. A. (1861) *Elinor Preston; or, Scenes at Home and Abroad*, New York: Sadlier.

Said, E. (1990) "Yeats and Decolonization," in T. Eagleton, F. Jameson, and E. Said (eds), *Nationalism, Colonialism, and Literature*, Minneapolis: University of Minnesota Press, pp. 69–95.

Schiller, F. (1795) *On the Naive and Sentimental in Literature*, trans. H. Watanabe-O'Kelly, Manchester: Carcanet New Press, 1981.

Schueller, M. J. and Watts, E. (eds) (2003) *Messy Beginnings: Postcoloniality and Early American Literature*, New Brunswick, NJ: Rutgers University Press.

Schwyzer, P. (2004) *Literature, Nationalism, and Memory in Early Modern England and Wales*, Cambridge: Cambridge University Press.

Sensabaugh, G. (1964) *Milton in Early America*, Princeton: Princeton University Press.

Shepard, T. (1645) *New Englands Lamentation for Old Englands Present Errours and Divisions*, London.

Shoulson, J. S. (2001) *Milton and the Rabbis: Hebraism, Hellenism and Christianity*, New York: Columbia University Press.

Shrank, C. (2004) *Writing the Nation in Reformation England, 1530–1580*, Oxford: Oxford University Press.

Shuger, D. (1990) *Habits of Thought in the English Renaissance: Religion, Politics, and the Dominant Culture*, Berkeley: University of California Press.

Sidney, P. (2002) *An Apology for Poetry (or The Defense of Poesy)*, G. Shepherd (ed.), rev. and exp. by R. Maslen, Manchester: Manchester University Press.

Skelton, J. (1983) *The Complete Poems*, J. Scattergood (ed.), Harmondsworth: Penguin.

Smith, A. D. (1976) "Neo-Classicist and Romantic Elements in the Emergence of Nationalist Conceptions," in A. D. Smith (ed.), *Nationalist Movements*, London: Macmillan Press, pp. 74–87.

—— (1986a) *National Identity*, Oxford: Oxford University Press, reprinted London: Penguin, 1991.

—— (1986b) *The Ethnic Origins of Nations*, Oxford: Blackwell.

—— (2000) *The Nation in History: Historiographical Debates about Ethnicity and Nationalism*, Hanover: University Press of New England.

—— (2003) *Chosen Peoples: Sacred Sources of National Identity*, Oxford: Oxford University Press, 2003, reprinted 2008.

—— (2005) "Nationalism in Early Modern Europe," *History and Theory*, 44, pp. 404–15.

Smith, B. H. (1988) *Contingencies of Value: Alternative Perspectives for Critical Theory*, Cambridge, MA: Harvard University Press.

Smith, G. (ed.) (1904) *Elizabethan Critical Essays*, 2 vols, Oxford: Clarendon Press.

Smith, J. A. (1970) "Some Eighteenth-Century Ideas of Scotland," in N. T. Phillipson and R. Mitchison (eds), *Scotland in the Age of Improvement*, Edinburgh: Edinburgh University Press, pp. 107–24.

Smith, L. B. (1996) "This Realm of England Is an Empire," in *This Realm of England 1399 to 1688*, 7th edn., Lexington, MA: D. C. Heath and Co., pp. 112–30.

Smith, N. (2005) *The Endgame of Globalization*, New York: Routledge.

Smith, T. (1972, 1906) *De Republica Anglorum: A Discourse on the Commonwealth of England*, L. Alston (ed.), Shannon: Irish Academic Press.

—— (1963) *Certaigne Psalmes or Songues of David Translated into Englishe Meter, Literary and Linguistic Works*, vol. I, in B. Danielsson (ed.), *Stockholm Studies in English*, 12, Stockholm: Almqvist and Wiksell.

Spengemann, W. C. (1994) *A New World of Words: Redefining Early American Literature*, New Haven, CT: Yale University Press.

Spenser, E. (1999) *The Shorter Poems*, R. A. McCabe (ed.), Harmondsworth: Penguin.

—— (2001) *The Faerie Queene*, A. C. Hamilton (ed.), Harlow: Longman.

Spittlehouse, J. (1653) *A Warning-Piece Discharged*, London.

Spivak, G. C. (2003) *Death of a Discipline*, New York: Columbia University Press.

Stacey, R. D. (2005) "Romance, Pastoral Romance, and the Nation in History," in J. Blair (ed.), *Recalling Early Canada: Reading the Political in Literary and Cultural Production*, Edmonton: University of Alberta Press, pp. 91–116.

Stannard, D. E. (1993) *American Holocaust: The Conquest of the New World*, Oxford: Oxford University Press.

Stevens, P. (2008) "How Milton's Nationalism Works: Globalization and the Possibilities of Positive Nationalism," in D. Loewenstein and P. Stevens (eds), *Early Modern Nationalism and Milton's England*, Toronto: University of Toronto Press, pp. 274–77.

Szeman, I. (2001a) "Globalization," in J. Hawley (ed.), *Encyclopedia of Postcolonial Studies*, Westport, CT: Greenwood Press, pp. 209–17.

—— (2001b) "Who's Afraid of National Allegory? Jameson, Literary Criticism, Globalization," *South Atlantic Quarterly*, 100, pp. 801–25.

—— (2003) *Zones of Instability: Literature, Postcolonialism and the Nation*, Baltimore: Johns Hopkins University Press.

—— (2005) "Globalization," in M. Groden, M. Kreiswirth, and I. Szeman (eds), *The Johns Hopkins Guide to Literary Theory and Criticism*, 2nd edn., Baltimore: Johns Hopkins University Press, pp. 458–65.

Tardivel, J.-P. (1989) *Pour la patrie: roman du XXe siècle*, Montreal: Bibliothèque québécoise.

Thierry, A. (1847) *History of the Conquest of England by the Normans: Its Causes, and Its Consequences in England, Scotland, Ireland, and on the Continent*, London: Bogue.

Thornborough, J. (1605) *The Joyful and Blessed Reuniting the Two Mighty and Famous Kingdoms, England and Scotland*, Oxford.

Tomlinson, J. (1999) *Globalization and Culture*, Chicago: University of Chicago Press.

Tompkins, J. (1985) *Sensational Designs: The Cultural Work of American Fiction 1790–1860*, New York: Oxford University Press.

Trumpener, K. (1997) *Bardic Nationalism: The Romantic Novel and the British Empire*, Princeton: Princeton University Press.

Tyler, R. (2006) *The Contrast: A Comedy in Five Acts*, in P. Lauter et al. (eds), *The Heath Anthology of American Literature*, vol. A: Colonial Period to 1800, 5th edn., Boston: Houghton Mifflin, pp. 1293–333.

UNESCO (2001) "UNESCO Universal Declaration on Cultural Diversity," November 2, 2001. Available at: http://unesdoc.unesco.org/images/0012/001271/127160m.pdf

Vickers, B. (ed.) (1999) *English Renaissance Literary Criticism*, Oxford: Oxford University Press.

Walker, G. (1988) *John Skelton and the Politics of the 1520s*, Cambridge: Cambridge University Press.

Warner, S. (1993) *The Wide, Wide World* (1851), reprinted New York: The Feminist Press at CUNY.

Warton, T. (1774–1781) *The History of English Poetry*, 4 vols, London: J. Dodsley.

Waterston, E. (1985) "Gilbert Parker and the Rebellion of 1837," *Journal of Canadian Studies*, 20, pp. 80–89.

Weaver, J., Womack, C. S., and Warrior, R. (2005) *American Indian Literary Nationalism*, Albuquerque: University of New Mexico Press.

Weber, M. (1919) *Politics as a Vocation*, in H. H. Gerth and C. Wright Mills (eds), *From Max Weber: Essays in Sociology*, New York: Oxford University Press, 1946, pp. 77–128.

Welter, B. (1966) "The Cult of True Womanhood," *American Quarterly*, 18, pp. 151–74.

Williams, R. (1963) "Christenings Make Not Christians," in P. Miller (ed.), *The Complete Writings of Roger Williams*, 3rd edn., 7 vols, New York: Russell & Russell, 7, pp. 29–41.

Winthrop, J. (1630) "'A Modell of Christian Charity,'" *Collections of the Massachusetts Historical Society* (Boston, 1838), 3rd series, vol. 7, pp. 31–48. Online Hanover Historical Texts Project. Available at: <http://history.hanover.edu/texts/winthmod.html> (accessed January 19, 2009).

Wolfe, D. M. (ed.) (1953–1982) *Complete Prose Works of John Milton*, 8 vols, New Haven: Yale University Press.

—— (ed.) (1967) *Leveller Manifestoes of the Puritan Revolution*, New York: Humanities Press.

Wolff, J. (1992) "Excess and Inhibition: Interdisciplinarity in the Study of Art," in L. Grossberg, C. Nelson, and P. A. Treichler (eds), *Cultural Studies*, New York: Routledge, pp. 706–18.

Wright, J. M. (1997) "'The Order of Time': Nationalism and Literary Anthologies, 1774–1831," *Papers on Language and Literature*, 33, pp. 339–65.

—— (2004) *Blake, Nationalism, and the Politics of Alienation*, Athens: Ohio University Press.

Yuval-Davis, N. (1997) *Gender and Nation*, London: Sage.

INDEX

Acadian Recorder 190
Act of Supremacy (1534) 144
Acts of Union: (1707) 7, 158, 165; (1800) 7, 104–5, 122, 165; (1841) 186, 188
Actaeon, myth of 142
Acton, Lord 3, 194
Adam, Graeme Mercer 190
Adams, James Truslow 150
Agreement of the Free People of England, An 8, 52–62
Aikin, John 103
almanacs 158
America/American nation *see* United States
"American Dream" 178
American Gothic 180, 181, 182
American historical romance 182
American War of Independence 118, 120–21, 169
Americans, Native 115–16, 175
Ancillon, Friedrich 130
Anderson, Benedict 2, 215, 221; *Imagined Communities* 3, 7, 157–58, 180, 204, 207, 213, 222; *Spectre of Comparisons* 11
Angers, François-Réal 192
Anglo-Mysore wars (India) 169
anthologies 5, 12, 14, 167, 171–72, 207, 214
anti-globalization movements 221, 225
Aristides 95, 98
aristocracy 91, 127, 130, 136, 161, 162, 179, 203
Aristogiton 106
Arthur, King 208
Askew, Anne 26–29
Atheneus 93
Atwood, Margaret 217
Aubert de Gaspé, Jr, Philippe: *L'influence d'un livre* 192
Aubert de Gaspé, Sr, Philippe 193
Austen, Jane: *Pride and Prejudice* 211
Aylmer, John 145

Bacon, Francis 85
Baillie, Joanna 168
Bale, Johan 26
Barbauld, Anna Letitia 103; "Eighteen Hundred and Eleven" 167–68, 170; "To a Great Nation" 103–4
Barker, Ernest 144
Barlow, Joel: *The Hasty Pudding* 180
Barr, Robert 196
Baucom, Ian 221
Baym, Nina 180
Behn, Aphra: *Oroonoko* 9
Behrendt, Stephen 167
Bell, David Avrom 2
Bhabha, Homi K. 208, 221
Bible 44, 144; King James 6, 44–52; New Testament 151, 152, 177
biblical typology 148, 177
Blackwood's Edinburgh Magazine 14, 108
Blake, William: *Jerusalem* 167
body geographic 158–59
body politic 8, 159, 183

Book of Common Prayer 7
borders 208
Boucher de Boucherville, Georges 193
Boulter, Hugh 85
Bourassa, Napoléon 193
Bowers, Terence N. 10, 155–62
Bradford, William: *Of Plymouth Plantation* 149
Bradstreet, Anne 62–63, 148; "A Dialogue between Old *England* and New" 13, 62–71
Breuilly, John 204, 205, 206
Brewer, John 156
Britain/England: analogies with Israel 144, 147–48, 152; and "British problem" 6–7, 164–65; as empire 6, 165, 169, 170–72, 177, 186, 188, 217, 218, 222; as John Bull 160, 162; national canon 14–15, 211; national identity, 15, 145, 146, 149, 151–52, 160; Roman conquest of 165
Brockden Brown, Charles: *Arthur Mervyn* 181–82; *Edgar Huntley* 181
Brooke, Charlotte: *Reliques of Irish Poetry* 14
Brooke, Frances 195: *The History of Emily Montague* 188–89
Brutus 7, 89n
Buchanan, George 36n
Buell, Lawrence 180
Burgett, Bruce 180, 181
Burke, Edmund 3, 191
Burnet, Gilbert (Bishop of Salisbury) 72
Burrough, Edward 150
Byron, Lord 115

Cabajsky, Andrea 9, 13, 186–96
Cabot, John 40, 176
Callimachus 34
Camden, William: *Britannia* 6
Campbell, Thomas 13, 14
Campbell, Thomas: "To the Rainbow" 123n
Canada 9, 13, 43, 99, 114, 115–16, 175, 186, 212; and canon-formation 211, 217, 218; and Durham Report 187–88, 191; national identity 186–87, 195; Rebellion (1837) 186, 187, 191, 193, 194; Union of Upper and Lower (1841) 186, 188; *see also* English-Canadian histories; English-Canadian literature
Canadian literature 186–96; English 188–91, 194, 195, 196; French 187, 188, 191–94, 195, 196; French-Canadian journals 193; French-Canadian literary nationalism 193–94
Canadian Magazine and Literary Repository 190
canon/canon-formation 12, 14–15, 167, 211–18
Canute, King 64n
capitalism 13, 156, 207, 225
Carlyle, Thomas: *Chartism* 170–71
Cartier, Jacques 192
Cary, Thomas 13, 99, 195; *Abram's Plains: A Poem* 99–102, 188
Casgrain, Henri-Raymond: *Légendes canadiennes* 192–93
Catholicism: resistance to *see* Protestantism
Celtic Periphery 14, 165, 167
"Celtic Revival" 167; *see also* Gaelic Literary Revival
Celts 122, 123–24, 164
Cervantes, Miguel de 87, 119
Channing, William Ellery 14, 216
Charles I, King 8, 52, 71, 72; *Eikon Basilike* 71
Chatterjee, Partha 208
Chauveau, Pierre-Joseph-Olivier 192, 193
China/Chinese 89, 123, 124, 203
Christie, Robert 194
Cicero: *De Officiis* 25n, 93n
citizenship 7–8, 156, 170, 172, 180, 183, 198n, 204
"City upon a Hill" 9, 177
Clarke, John 150
class 8, 130, 136–38, 161, 162, 180, 184, 203, 205, 206
Coffey, John 151
Coleridge, S. T.: "Fears in Solitude" 167, 168, 170

Colley, Linda 158
colonial captivity narratives 177
colonialism/imperialism 8–9, 30, 37–38, 120, 121, 140, 170–71, 223; and Canada 187, 188–89, 218; and United States 175–77
Columbus, Christopher 41, 176
Communist Manifesto 222
Complaynt of Scotland, The 6, 7, 23–25
Conan, Laure 195
Congress of Vienna (1814–1815) 125, 129n
Constitution, United States 5, 177, 184
Cooper, James Fenimore 182, 193
Corse, Sarah M. 1, 15, 211–18
Crémazie, Octave: *Drapeau de Carillon* 192
Crèvecoeur, Hector St. John 179–80, 182
Croesus, King of Lydia 98
Cromwell, Oliver 8, 124n, 145–46, 151, 178
Crown of Ireland Act (1542) 86n
cultural imperialism 225
cultural nationalism 122, 193, 194, 195, 198n, 216, 220, 222, 223

Danforth, Samuel 148, 152
Darby, Wendy Joy 172
Davidson, Cathy 180
Davis, Thomas Osborne: "The West's Asleep" 4; "Influences of Education" 167
Day, John 26
De Quincey, Thomas 169
DeCastro, Juan E. 2
Declaration of Independence 177–78, 184
decolonization 220, 223, 226n
Defoe, Daniel 78, 159–60; *The Complete English Tradesman* 159–60; *The Original Power of the Collective Body of the People of England* 7, 11, 78–83, 160; *A Plan of the English Commerce* 160; *A Tour Thro' the Whole Island of Great Britain* 159
Dekker, George 182
DeLillo, Don: *Cosmopolis* 225
democracy 4, 5, 12, 91, 95n, 136, 145, 166, 175, 179, 181, 182, 183, 184, 205
Dermody, Thomas 112
Desmond, Earl of 140
Dominguez, Virginia 216
Dostaler, Yves 191–92
Doutre, Joseph 192
Drayton, Michael: *Poly-Olbion* 7
Drennan, William 104–5; *Letter to the Right Honorable William Pitt* 7, 104–8, 167
Du Ponceau, Peter 12, 118; *Discourse* 1, 6, 7, 12, 13, 118–22, 211
Duffy, Charles Gavan 122
Durham, Earl of (John George Lambton) 187, 188, 189, 190, 191, 195
Durham Report 187–88, 191

East India Company 99, 165
economics 12–13, 37, 83, 159–60, 178, 182, 188–89
Edgeworth, Maria 12
education 2, 7, 9, 10–11, 12, 14, 15, 97, 113, 129, 130, 166, 167, 193, 214, 222
Edward II, King 64n
Edward III, King 65n
Edward VI, King 149
Eley, Geoff 206
Elizabeth I, Queen 7, 64n, 85, 135, 138–42, 145, 150; Spenser on 4, 138–42, 209
empire, definition of 5, 6
Engels, Friedrich 222
England *see* Britain/England
English-Canadian histories 194
English-Canadian literature *see* Canadian Literature, English
English Civil War(s) 8, 52, 54n, 63, 68n, 207
English studies: institutionalization of 15
Enlightenment 3, 9–11, 13, 14, 87, 155–62; emergence of national symbols 160; making nation legible 155–60; on national identity 10–11,

159, 160–62; and reading public 156–57
epic genre 167
Escobedo, Andrew 2, 203–9
ethnicity 4–5, 30, 37, 161, 203, 204, 206–7, 208, 209, 214, 221, 225
European Revolutions (1848) 126, 130

Fall of New France 186–87, 191
feminism 208–9
Ferland, Jean-Baptiste-Antoine 192
Fielding, Henry: *Tom Jones* 211
Fitzgerald, F. Scott: *The Great Gatsby* 211
Fitzgibbon, John (Earl of Clare) 114
Fliegelman, Jay 180
Foreign Library Company 118–19
Foster, Hannah 181
Fouli (Africa) 98–9
Founding Fathers 175, 180
Four Articles of Prague (1420) 128n
Foxe, John 26, 145; *Actes and Monuments* (also known as *Book of Martyrs*) 5, 7, 26–29, 158, 207
France 6, 64, 65, 103–4, 121, 125, 126, 128, 129, 144, 157, 159, 162, 176, 186, 191; and national character 90, 96n, 162
François, Duc of Alençon 138
Franklin, Benjamin 114n, 120, 180; *Autobiography* 178–79
Fréchette, Louis-Honoré 192
Freeport, Sir Andrew 161
French-Canadian literature *see* Canadian literature, French
French Revolution 103, 162
French Revolutionary Wars 169
Fukuyama, Francis 224

Gadsden Purchase (1853) 176
Gaelic Literary Revival 12; *see also* "Celtic Revival"
Garneau, François-Xavier 192; *History of Canada* 191, 192, 194
Gellner, Ernest 2, 3, 7, 10, 11, 158, 161, 205, 206, 207
gender 23, 63, 160, 162, 165, 180, 182, 183, 184, 198n, 208
General Shop Book, The 160
Geneva 177
Genghis Khan 125
Geoffrey of Monmouth: *Historia regum Britanniae* 4
George III, King 99, 188
Gerson, Carole 189, 190, 195
Gibson, John 190
Giddens, Anthony 155
Gilbert, Sir Humphrey 37–38, 39, 42, 43
globalization: and nationalism 13, 15, 220–26
"God Save the King" 160
Goddu, Teresa 180, 181
Goethe, Johann Wolfgang von 119, 222, 224
Goldsmith, Oliver: "The Deserted Village" 100
Goldsmith, Oliver: *The Rising Village* 100n
Goodwin, Dr. Thomas 146
Gothic 170, 181, 199n; American 180, 181, 182
Greco-Persian wars 93–95, 98
Greek War of Independence (1821–1832) 126n
Greenblatt, Stephen 143n, 224
Greenfeld, Liah 149, 216
Grey, Lord 30
Grimm, Jacob and Wilhelm 167
Grove, Frederick Philip: *Fruits of the Earth* 211
Guadalupe Hidalgo, Treaty of (1848) 176
Guillory, John 15
Guizot, François 191
Guy, Josephine M. 15

Habermas, Jürgen 11, 157
Hadfield, Andrew 2, 6, 135–42
Hadrian, Emperor 97
Hakluyt, Richard 37–38, 44, 177; *The Principal Navigations* 5, 6, 8–9, 37, 38–39; *The Third and Last Volume* 5, 37–38, 39–43
Hale, John 153n
Hale, J. R. 159

Haliburton, Thomas Chandler: *The Clockmaker* 190
Hallam, Arthur Henry: "On Some of the Characteristics of Modern Poetry" 14
Hamid, Mohsin 225
Hamilton, Thomas: *Men and Manners in America* 120n
Harmodius 106n
Harrington, James 151
Hart, Julia Beckwith 188; *St. Ursula's Convent* 189
Hastings, Adrian: *The Construction of Nationhood* 6, 145, 158
Hawthorne, Nathaniel 214–15, 217–18
Hayes, Edward 38
Hebel, Udo J. 2
Helgerson, Richard 2, 17n, 152n
Hemans, Felicia: "England's Dead" 170, 171–72
Hengist the Saxon 7, 64n, 170, 171
Henry III, King 138
Henry VII, King 64n, 176
Henry VIII, King 26, 144, 149
Herder, Johann Gottfried von 3, 10, 11, 12, 164, 166, 167, 221
Herodotus 34, 36
Hickey, David 188
Hirst, Paul 224
historians: Spenser on 139–40
historical novel: French-Canadian 193–94, 195
historical romance: American 182
historiography 194, 204
Hobbes, Thomas: *Leviathan* 8
Hobsbawm, Eric J.: *Nations and Nationalism* 2, 3, 6, 158, 204, 205, 207
Hogarth, William 160
Holinshed, Raphael: *Chronicles of England, Scotland and Ireland* 6, 36n
Home, Henry 92; *Sketches of the History of Man* 6, 25n, 92–99
Homer 168
Hooker, Richard: *Laws of Ecclesiastical Polity* 7
Horsa 170, 171
Hughes, Edward: *Select Specimens of English Poetry* 170, 171–72
Hume, David 87, 160, 161; *Essays, Moral and Political* 87; "Of National Characters" 10, 11, 87–92, 211
Hussites 128
Huston, James: *Répertoire national* 193
Huxley, Aldous 216
Huyghue, Douglas 189

"imagined communities" *see* Anderson, Benedict
imperialism *see* colonialism
Incarnation, Marie de l' 192
Industrial Revolution 3, 11
Ireland 6, 7, 12, 67, 83, 87, 104, 140, 165; and Act of Union (1800) 7, 104–5, 122, 165; coinage issue 83–86; Drennan on 105–8; Morgan (Owenson) on 112–14; Spenser on 30–35, 140; Swift on 84–86
Irenaeus 30
Irish Uprising (1798) 169
Iroquois Confederation 175, 190
Islam 124
Israel, ancient 44, 63, 144, 146–51
Italy 125–26, 166

Jacobs, Harriet 181
James VI and I, King 7, 8
Jameson, Fredric 223
Jamestown colony (Virginia) 176
Jennings, Clotilda 189
Jerusalem 177
Johnson, Edward 148
Jones, Edward: *Musical and Poetical Relicks of the Welsh Bards* 14, 165–66
Joyce, James: *Ulysses* 211

Kalter, Susan 175
Kant, Immanuel 205
Kedourie, Elie 204
Keimer, Samuel 179
Kerber, Linda 183
Kerrigan, John 2
Kidd, Adam 114–15; *The Huron Chief, and Other Poems* 13, 114–18
King James Bible 6, 44–52

Kingsford, William: *History of Canada* 194
Kirby, William 190, 195
Kohn, Hans 144, 149

Lacombe, Patrice 192, 193
Lamartine, Alphonse de: "Manifesto to Europe" 129
Lambton, John George *see* Durham, Earl of
Lareau, Edmond 194, 196
Larkin, Philip: "Church Going" 13
Laud, William 68n
Laurence, Margaret: *The Stone Angel* 211
law 27, 67, 104; divine/religious 71, 127, 150; establishment of 60, 150; lawfulness 31, 33, 35, 68, 104; of nations 108; of nature 25n, 71, 85; uniformity of 165, 166, 175, 195
Lazarus, Emma: "The New Colossus" 178
Le Carré, John 225
Leerssen, Joep 3, 4
Lefanu, Alicia Sheridan 112
Lemay, Pamphile 192, 195
Lemire, Maurice 191, 193
Leprohon, Rosanna 190, 195
Lescarbot, Marc 192
Lesperance, John Talon 193
Levellers: 52–53; *Agreement of the Free People of England* 8, 53–62; *see also* Lilburne, John
Lewis, Matthew: "The Anaconda" 170
liberty: ancient 91–97; Christian 8, 71, 146–47; civil 74, 93, 150; conscience 9, 149–52; and democracy 182–83; enfranchisement 61; feature of English nationhood 8, 91, 130, 145–47, 149, 153n; Irish 114; and patriotism 94; and republicanism 180; Scottish 4; Statue of 178
Lilburne, John 5, 52–53
literacy 8, 9, 12, 135, 156–57, 158, 161, 223
Literary Garland 190
Literary Miscellany 190
"Literature of a New Country, The" (article) 189
Locke, John 5, 10, 107, 156, 170, 172, 191; *Second Treatise of Government* 159
Loewenstein, David 2
Loughran, Trish 184
Louis VIII, King of France 65n
Louis XIV, King of France 155, 156
Louisiana Purchase (1803) 176
Lowell, James Russell 216–17
Lycurgus 122
Lyly, John 144

MacCarthy, Denis Florence: "A Walk by the Bay of Dublin" 172
McClintock, Anne 208
McCurran-Walters Act (1952) 183
Macdonell, Blanche Lucile 188
McEachern, Claire 2, 17n, 147
McGee, Thomas D'Arcy 115, 167
Machar, Agnes Maule: *The Heir of Fairmount Grange* 189
McKinnon, William Charles 189
Mackworth, Sir Humphrey: *A Vindication of the Rights of the Commons of England* 78, 79
MacLennan, Hugh: *Two Solitudes* 196
McMullen, John Mercier 194
Macpherson, James 116n; *see also* Ossian
Madsen, Deborah L. 12, 13, 175–84
Maley, Willy 2, 18n, 30n, 210n
Mangan, James Clarence 122
Maria Theresa, Queen 125n
Marmette, Joseph 193
Marx, Karl 222
Mary I, Queen 149
Massachusetts 176, 177, 178
Massacre of Saint Bartholomew's Day 138
Mather, Cotton 148
Maud (daughter of Henry I) 64
Mayflower Compact 177
Mazzini, Giuseppe 3, 125–26; "Europe: Its Condition and Prospects" 125–31
Melbourne, Lord 187
Melville, Herman 216, 217–18; *Moby Dick* 211
Mexican-American War 176
Michelet, Jules 191

migration 13, 177, 178
Mill, John Stuart 194
Mille, James de 188
Miltiades 95, 98
Milton, John 12, 71–72, 145, 146–52, 168, 170; *Areopagitica* 150–51; *A Defence of the People of England* 5, 8, 72–78 (*Pro Populo Anglicano Defensio* 8, 71); *Eikonoklastes* 71; *The History of Britain* 1, 4; *Paradise Lost* 71, 113n, 147–49, 150, 151, 152; *The Reason of Church-Government* 146–47
monarchy: support of 68, 71, 136; opposition to 103, 136, 147, 149–50; and nation 5, 7, 8, 159, 203
Monmouth's Rebellion (1685) 78
Montesquieu 10, 160
Moore, Thomas 114–15; *Lalla Rookh* 114, 117n
Morgan, Henry J. 195; *Bibliotheca Canadensis* 195
Morgan, Lady Sydney 12, 112, 164, 168; *Absenteeism* 13, 112–14; *see also* Owenson, Sydney
Morrison, Toni: *Playing in the Dark* 182
Moses 77, 146, 178
mutinies 169

Napoleon I 124, 125n
Napoleonic Wars 169
nation: definitions 3–13, 157, 186; and geography 3, 5, 8, 13, 107, 130, 131, 158–60, 170, 211, 213, 221, 223, 224; and government 4, 5, 8, 31, 44, 93, 107, 114, 119, 121, 144, 155, 165, 168, 179, 187, 194; and land/landscape 5, 109, 115, 157, 159, 164–65, 166, 170–72, 189, 221; and language 3, 4, 5, 6, 15, 44, 89, 90, 91, 92, 110, 111, 119, 121, 130, 131, 144, 164, 165, 166, 167, 180, 181, 188, 192, 195, 213, 221–22; as natural/organic 1, 11, 12–13, 158, 164, 166, 168–69, 170, 172, 204, 205, 206, 213, 222; populist 3, 4, 5, 8, 9, 12, 157, 164, 166, 169, 180, 191, 192, 194, 204, 215, 221; and rights 5, 8, 12, 53, 78–83, 108, 114, 166, 180, 182, 184; *see also* liberty
Nation, The 122, 164, 167, 169–70
nation-state 4, 5, 7, 8, 11, 15, 155–56, 157–58, 166, 168–69, 170, 172, 176, 180, 204, 213–14, 215–17, 221, 222, 223
national character(s) 10, 13, 14, 160–62, 164, 179–80, 204, 205, 206, 207, 208, 213; Home on 95; Hume on 87–92; in literature 14, 108–11
"National Character" (article) 122–25
national literature(s) 1–3, 10, 13–16, 44, 108–11, 118–22, 180, 184, 212, 215–16, 217, 222; *see also* canon/canon-formation
nationalism 1, 135, 204, 221; and canon-formation 211–18; civic 5; cultural 122, 193, 194, 195, 216, 220, 222, 223; definitions 3–5; diasporic 3, 5; and globalization 220–26; history of 7–13, 15–16, 135, 144, 145, 147, 155, 157, 158, 161–62, 172, 181, 184, 191, 193, 203–9, 212, 220–21, 223; modernist view of 1, 2, 3, 5–6, 10, 161, 203–9; popular 191; Protestant 145, 158; and Reformation 7; Romantic 5, 164–66, 169; *see also* nation
nationalism studies 2–3, 4, 6, 203–9, 213
Naturalization Act (1790) 183
New England 63, 148–52, 177
Newfoundland 37, 40, 42–43
Newman, Robert 225
newspapers 135, 157, 193, 207
Newton, Isaac 95, 120
Norman Conquest (1066) 165, 191
Norse sagas 176

O'Connell, Daniel 191
"Of a National Character in Literature" (anon.) 14, 108–11
O'Neil, Daniel J. 169
Ormond, Clarence 190
Ossian 116, 189
Overton, Richard 52–53

Owen, John: *Indulgence and Toleration Considered* 8
Owenson, Sydney 112, 164, 168; *see also* Morgan, Lady Sydney

Paine, Thomas 156; *Common Sense* 181
Papineau, Louis-Joseph 194
Parent, Étienne 192
pariahs 122–23
Paris, Treaty of (1763) 99, 176, 179, 188
Parker, Gilbert 190; *The Trail of the Sword* 195
pastoral 137, 138, 172, 199n
patriotism 4, 113, 183, 194; Home on 92–99
Patriots (group) 194
Pattee, Fred Lewis 222
Peninsular War 124n
Percy, Bishop: *Reliques of Ancient English Poetry* 14
Pericles 95
Perkins, Pam 188
Philadelphia 119
Philip II, King of Spain 94
Pisistratus 94
Pitt, William: 104, 170; Drennan's letter to (1799) 104–8
Pius IX, Pope 127
Plains of Abraham, Battle of the (1759) 99, 192, 193
Pliny the Elder 115n
Plutarch 90
Plymouth (Massachusetts) 177
Pocock, J. G. A. 6, 18n
Pope, Alexander 100; *The Rape of the Lock* 180
popular culture 11, 12
postcolonialism 2, 181, 182, 208, 209, 221, 222–24, 225
postnationalist theory 13, 225–26
Prince, Thomas 52–53
print capitalism 207
print culture 10, 11, 13, 156–57, 158, 184
Prometheus 128
prophecy genre 167
Protestantism 6, 11, 26, 30, 44, 63, 140, 158; as internationalism 145, 146; Reformation 7, 128n, 144, 149, 207; vs Roman Catholicism 9, 26, 37n, 106, 138, 144, 146, 158
public sphere 5, 157
Puritans 148, 149, 151, 152, 177, 178
Putney Debates (1647) 8, 52
Puttenham, George: *Arte of Poesie* 136–38, 139

Quakers 119, 178
Quebec 99, 187, 188, 189, 191, 192–94
Quebec Mercury 99

race 10, 87, 171, 182, 183, 184; and scientific racism 10
Ragussis, Michael 161
Raimon, Eve Allegra 180, 183; *The "Tragic Mulatta" Revisited* 182
Rajan, Balachandra xi, 221
Ramus, Peter 137
Readings, Bill 15
Renaissance and early modernism 3, 6, 7–9, 135–42, 144–52, 155, 205
Renan, Ernest: "What is a Nation?" 186
"Republican motherhood" 183
republicanism 8, 91, 96, 107, 119, 135, 136, 142, 178, 179, 180–81, 182, 183; commercial 181–82
Restoration (1660) 151, 178
Restraint of Appeals Act (1533) 6
Review (journal) 159
Richard II, King 64n
Richard III, King 64n
Richardson, Major John 188; *Wacousta* 190–91
Richardson, R. L.: *Colin of the Ninth Concession* 189
Roberts, Charles G. D. 188, 194
Romanticism 3, 10, 11–13, 14, 168, 171, 172, 221; German 166–67, 213
Ross, Marlon B. 170
Rowlandson, Mary: *Sovereignty and Goodness of God* 177
Rowson, Susanna: *Charlotte Temple* 183–84; *Lucy Temple* 184
"Rule Britannia" 160
Russell, James: *Matilda* 189

Sadlier, Mary Anne 190
Saga of Eric the Red 176
Saga of the Greenlanders 176
Said, Edward 221, 222–23
Saint Père, François-Edme Rameau de 194
Saint-Maurice, Faucher de 193
Salmasius: *Defensio Regia* 71, 72
Sauer, Elizabeth 1–16, 144–52
Schiller, Friedrich 12, 119, 166
Schueller, Malini Johar 180–81, 182
Schwyzer, Patrick 2
Schwyzer, Philip 207
Scotland 1, 6, 10, 12, 36–37, 65, 165; and Act of Union (1707) 7, 158, 165; *Complaynt of Scotland* (1549?) 23–25; Declaration of Arbroath (1320) 4; and France 6
Scott, Sir Walter 165, 172n, 182, 189, 193; *Minstrelsy of the Scottish Border* 14; *Waverley* novels 12, 182, 192
Sensabaugh, George: *Milton in Early America* 149, 150
Seven Years' War 99, 187; *see also* Paris, Treaty of; Plains of Abraham, Battle of the
Sewall, Samuel 148
Shakespeare, William 12, 142, 170, 212; *Henry V* 6, 18n, 65n, 209; *The Tempest* 176
Shepard, Thomas 148, 149
Sheridan, Richard Brinsley: *The Critic* 11; *A School for Scandal* 180
Sidney, Sir Philip 138, 139
Skelton, John 136
slavery 103, 179, 181, 182, 183
Small, Ian 15
Smith, Adam 12
Smith, Anthony D. 2, 3, 6, 10, 11, 13, 158, 166, 206, 207
Smith, Captain John 176–77
Smith, Sir Thomas: *Certaigne Psalmes* 144–45; *De Republica Anglorum* 135–37
Smith, Sydney 217
Society of United Irishmen *see* United Irishmen
Southey, Robert 167
sovereignty: of monarch 4, 5, 6, 8, 159; of people 4, 5, 12, 108, 164, 166, 180; of state 5, 6, 204
Spain 9, 64, 65, 146, 176
Spectator 161
Speed, John: *Theatre of the Empire of Great Britaine* 7–8
Spengemann, William 181
Spenser, Edmund 2, 30, 138, 142; *Epithalamion* 141–42; *The Faerie Queene* 4, 13, 30, 138–41, 142, 176, 209; *The Shepheardes Calender* 138; "Two Cantos of Mutabilitie" 141; *A View of the Present State of Ireland* 6, 7, 30–37, 140
Spittlehouse, John: *A Warning-Piece Discharged* 146
Spivak, Gayatri Chakravorty 221
Stanhope, Philip Dormer 112n
Stanyhurst, Richard 36n
Starke, Mariana 11
Stephen, King of England 39, 64n
Stevens, Paul xi, 2, 210n
Stowe, Harriet Beecher: *Uncle Tom's Cabin* 183
Strafford, Earl of (Sir Thomas Wentworth) 68n
Suny, Ronald Grigor 206
Swift, Jonathan 15, 83, 113; *The Drapier's Letters* 83, 121, 161; *A Letter to the Whole People of Ireland* 5, 11, 83–86
Switzerland 186
Szeman, Imre 13, 220–26

Tardivel, Jules-Paul: *Pour la partrie* 193
theater 11, 161
Themistocles 95, 98
Thierry, Augustin 191
Thompson, Graeme 224
Thomson, James 100, 168
Thornborough, John 208
Tocqueville, Alexis de 191
Tompkins, Jane 214–15
Townshend, George 112n, 113n
Twain, Mark 190; *Adventures of Huckleberry Finn* 212

Tyler, Royall: *The Contrast* 180
typology, biblical 148, 177, 178
tyranny 8, 41, 71, 74, 80, 97, 124, 129, 167

Union of Utrecht (1579) 94n
United Irishmen 104, 166
United Nations Educational, Scientific and Cultural Organization 221
United States 12, 175–84, 212; canon-formation 211, 216–17; and commercial republicanism 181–82; Constitution 5, 184; European colonization 175–77; exceptionalism 149, 178; as haven 178; and Iroquois Confederation 175; national character 179–80; national literature 12, 118–22, 180–84, 211, 216–17; and race 182, 183; and republicanism 180–81; and slavery 179, 181, 182; and territorial expansion 175–77; and women 183

Vellore Mutiny (1806) 169
Verne, Jules: *Famille sans nom* 194
Virgil 34, 138, 168
Voltaire 161

Wales 1, 4, 6, 7, 12; union with England (1536) 165, 208; with Ireland (1800) 165; with Scotland (1707) 165
Walwyn, William 52–53
Warner, Susan: *The Wide, Wide World* 184
Warton, Thomas: *History of English Poetry* 13, 14, 167
Washington, George 170, 181
Waterloo, Battle of 169
Waterston, Elizabeth 194
Watts, Edward 182
Weber, Max 155
Wedderburn, Robert 23
Welter, Barbara 183
Wetherald, Ethelwyn 190
Whitman, Walt 216
Whole Book of Psalms, The 207
Wigglesworth, Michael 148
Wilde, Lady (Speranza) 122
William the Conqueror 7, 64n
Williams, Raymond 13
Williams, Roger 149–50
Wilson, John 108
Winthrop, John 148, 177–78; *A Modell of Christian Charity* 9, 44, 177
Wollstonecraft, Mary 156
Wolsey, Cardinal 136
Womack, Craig 175
Wood, William 83–86
Woodbridge, John 62
Wordsworth, William 12, 172; Preface to *Lyrical Ballads* 11–12
Wright, Julia M. 1–16, 164–72, 214, 218n

Young Italy 126
Yuval-Davis, Nira 208–9